W9-COF-949

POWERS OF THE PRESS

also by Martin Walker

non-fiction
The National Front
Daily Sketches : Cartoon History of Twentieth Century Britain

poetry
The Happy Unicorns (anthology)
Poems on the Glass of Windows (editor and co-translator)

fiction
The Infiltrator
A Mercenary Calling

Powers of the Press

The World's Great Newspapers

Martin Walker

QUARTET BOOKS
LONDON MELBOURNE NEW YORK

First published by Quartet Books Limited 1982
A member of the Namara Group
27/29 Goodge Street, London W1P 1FD

Copyright © 1982 by Martin Walker

British Library Cataloguing in Publication Data

Walker, Martin
Powers of the press.
1. Journalism – Objectivity
2. Newspapers
I. Title
070.4'12   PN4778

ISBN 0-7043-2271-4

Phototypeset by MC Typeset, Rochester, Kent
Printed and bound in Great Britain by
Mackays of Chatham, Kent

Contents

Author's note

The twelve newspapers studied in this book are part of an elite, a collection of multilingual household names in the global communications business. But the twelve do not form an exclusive list. One could undertake the same exercise, and probably get broadly similar results, with an identical book that dealt with the *Guardian*, the *Los Angeles Times*, the *Frankfurter Allgemeine Zeitung*, the *Neue Zürcher Zeitung*, *El Pais*, *La Prensa*, *Jornal do Brasil*, *Izvestia*, *La Stampa*, the *People's Daily*, *Yomiuri* and *Le Figaro*. But books must end somewhere and choices must be made. Had I not spent the bulk of my working life as a *Guardian* journalist, my own newspaper would have been the first to select itself. And certainly, tested against this book's analysis of the way each paper covered Iran during the 1970s, the *Guardian* would emerge triumphant. It was the first newspaper to realize that the public poetry readings of 1976 and 1977 represented an internal and intellectual challenge to the Shah's rule which was spreading ripples of cultural dissent and pride throughout the country. Its readers were never allowed to forget that, for all its apparent strategic and economic value to the West, the Shah's Iran was a ruthless and autocratic dictatorship. And so when I dedicate this book to Alastair Hetherington and Peter Preston, my past and present editors, and my colleagues on the finest newspaper in the world, other journalists will recognize that I give them no more than their due.

It is a matter of considerable personal regret that some of the best newspapers in the business are not described in this book. Papers as good as Austria's *Die Presse*, Yugoslavia's *Borba* and Sweden's *Dagbladet* have the disadvantage of coming from small countries which are not international news centres in themselves. The *Neue Zürcher Zeitung*, the *Wall Street Journal* and the *Financial Times* are magnificent papers in their primarily economic field. The latter's international and cultural coverage, and *Neue Zürcher Zeitung*'s political columns establish further credentials, but sadly there is no room to praise them here. The *Frankfurter Allgemeine Zeitung* is, by any standard, one of the world's outstanding dailies; but in choosing between writing about that paper or *Die Welt*, the overwhelming impact of Axel Springer on post-war German publishing swung the balance. In South America, *La Prensa* of Argentina, whose editors fought so heroically for their freedom against Peron, *Jornal do Brasil* and, fortunately to a lesser extent, Mexico's *Excelsior* are papers that have suffered from governmental constraints upon their freedom. They may yet outlive the governments that dominate them; indeed, in the case of the *Jornal do Brasil*, they very nearly have.

This book has taken three years to research and to write. While the final revisions were being made, *Al-Ahram*'s Mohammed Heykal was imprisoned, *Die Welt*'s editor was fired, *The Times* of London was once again threatened with closure and the *Washington Post*'s Watergate-proud features could barely be discerned from the egg that spattered it with the Pulitzer Prize débâcle. Events and reputations move fast in the newspaper business. That grandest of the old China newspaper hounds, Richard Hughes, entertained me in the Hong Kong Press Club and impressed upon me the distilled wisdom of a lifetime's reporting. 'We're only as good as tomorrow's edition,' he said, looking at me to make sure I hadn't really believed him. Because in the end, none of us in journalism would dare to swallow such a heresy. Newspapers are greater than the sum of their parts. They go on longer than individual editors or journalists, longer than governments, longer than recessions. And for all the cynicism which is an occupational hazard for journalists, I suspect that deep down we are a sentimental, even a maudlin lot, very much more attached to our trade and our papers than we would ever care publicly to admit. The twelve newspaper biographies in this book perhaps go some way to explaining why.

I owe a great deal to the kindness and courtesy of newspaper colleagues around the world. Most of the individuals who helped me with advice or documents or insights and interviews will find themselves named in the relevant chapter notes. In some obvious cases, particularly regarding *Pravda*, the *Rand Daily Mail* and *Al-Ahram*, my mentors must remain anonymous. The library staffs of the various newspapers, and the librarians of the International Press Institute in London, of the City University, of London University's School of Oriental and African Studies, of the BBC Monitoring Department, the British Museum, the Colindale Newspaper Library, the Tokyo Press Club and the Press Association all have my heartfelt gratitude. Acknowledgements are due also to the help and support of Hugh Sandeman in Tokyo, Ella Hensell in Melbourne and Stan McNeill in Sydney, Anthony and Amanda Holden in Washington, Connie Bessie in New York and Robert and Heather Bothwell in Toronto, and to Tom Walker and Graham Watson in Britain.

My wife Julia, herself a journalist, shared the research with me, translated for me, typed manuscripts and sustained me when I was threatened with drowning in a sea of multilingual photocopies, interview transcripts, statistics and newsprint. It is, in a very profound way, the first joint product of our marriage. So the personal dedication of this book must be to her, and to that marriage's second joint production, our daughter Kate.

M.W.

POWERS OF THE PRESS

1

Introduction

The world of 1945, of the Grand Alliance that defeated Hitler's Germany and Japan, has almost disappeared. The four-power diplomatic system on which it was based lasted barely ten years, and died with the Suez invasion. The international economic order it established, at Bretton Woods, was transformed by the devaluation of the pound sterling in the 1960s and the collapse of the dollar in the 1970s. The United Nations, which that Grand Alliance founded as the symbol of its hopes for a new kind of world, has changed beyond recognition. Some of the victors of that Grand Alliance, for instance Britain, have lurched downwards in wealth and influence; the defeated powers of Germany and Japan have more than recovered.

But one remnant of that world of 1945 still dominates much of the earth's intellectual, political and cultural life. The newspapers of the Grand Alliance have survived, and even expanded their influence. With the conquering armies of the Allies of 1945 travelled reporters from the *New York Times*, the *Washington Post*, the Toronto *Globe and Mail*, the Melbourne *Age*, the *Rand Daily Mail*, *Pravda* and *The Times* of London. By act of conquest, those armies founded other newspapers. In Paris, *Le Monde* was born with General de Gaulle's liberation. In Hamburg, the British Military Government founded *Die Welt*. In Milan, it was British and American officers who re-founded *Corriere della Sera*. In Tokyo, the American Military Government re-established *Asahi Shimbun*. One could even stretch a point and argue that Egypt's *Al-Ahram*, representing an associated power of the British Empire's war effort, fits the pattern.

These twelve newspapers are devoured in embassies, in government offices, in TV newsrooms and in other newspapers the world over. They are read partly for their traditional function of providing news (in spite of the faster reaction times of the electronic media), partly for their commitment to providing a large proportion of international news that radio and TV have no time to cover, partly for their views and editorials, and partly because these papers are perceived, in some fundamentally important way, to be reflecting the concerns and the ideas of the Establishments, if not the governments, in the societies where they are based. And partly because everyone else in public life is reading them; they are the house magazines, the daily shared experience, of their nations' ruling classes. Pierre Salinger, President Kennedy's Press Secretary, described the process precisely: 'No top policy-maker in Washington starts his day without reading the *New York Times* . . . The *Washington Post* derives its importance from being read every morning by Washington officialdom from the President on down.'

These are loose concepts, impossible to define. In the course of researching this book, I have interviewed over 100 journalists in a dozen countries, and I have asked each one if he or she could define the nature of a newspaper's 'influence'. The *Washington Post* could point to Watergate and argue that in an extreme case it held the power of life or death over a presidency, through the devotion of massive resources of time and manpower, and a total deployment of whatever credit and trust the newspaper had built up in its lifetime. At another level, and in a harsher environment for the press, the *Rand Daily Mail* could argue that by strict devotion to the law, it could fend off a hostile government's attempts at control and that by simply existing, day after day, it could rally and re-affirm the existence of a liberal, non-racist tradition – and thus a constituency – in an almost authoritarian State. The Melbourne *Age* defined its own influence as the power to set the agenda for public debate, to identify issues of concern and, by regular reporting, force them on to the attention of the public. It was in this sense that *Le Monde*, by focusing on the use of torture by the French Army in Algeria in 1957, persuaded enough French voters that a colonial war was a moral, as well as a political, issue. The *New York Times* rammed home a similar message, and risked prison terms for its editors, on the principle of the public's right to know the secret machinations of their masters, when it published the Pentagon Papers. In this sense, press influence is the power, by right of publication, to impose a newspaper's values and concerns upon society's attention – at the risk of commercial failure, imprisonment, or even suppression.

There have been sad times when newspapers have paid that price. In the years from 1922 to 1925, when Mussolini's fascist government moved steadily from constitutional legitimacy to dictatorship, *Corriere della Sera* remained one of the last bastions of opposition, and certainly the last national institution with the resources to expose, and the courage and means to publish, evidence of Mussolini's own responsibility for political murders. It was very brave, and it doomed *Corriere*'s independence. *Corriere*'s very courage might even have provoked a tightening of fascist authoritarianism.

The fact is that in the last resort, newspapers are fragile bodies. Their presses and their typefaces are at the mercy of the kind of rampaging military mob that wrecked *Asahi Shimbun*'s offices in 1934. Their journalists can be tied to a tree and stoned, as *Asahi*'s were in 1919, or shot dead on the newspaper steps, as *Corriere*'s Walter Tobagi was murdered in Milan in 1980. Or imprisoned for saying that a journalist's ethical duty to his sources must override a court's insistence on disclosure, as was the *New York Times*'s Myron Farber in 1977, or as two British journalists were in 1962. Or papers and their staff can be fined, as Lawrence Gandar and Ben Pogrund of the *Rand Daily Mail* were for printing entirely true statements on South African prison conditions. Or have their homes exploded by terrorist bombs, as the French OAS did to *Le Monde* journalists in 1961 and 1962. The newspaper delivery vans can be blocked by hostile demonstrators, as happened to Axel Springer's *Die Welt* in 1968.

It is society as a whole which gives newspapers their credibility and their importance, but governments hold the final sanction. In a perverse way, suppression is the ultimate act of flattery to a newspaper. But governments can build up newspapers more subtly, as President Nasser built up the *Al-Ahram* of Mohammed Heykal as the quasi-official voice of Cairo, as the privileged ear to the deliberations of the Arab leaders. And President Sadat took that brief and borrowed power away, and tumbled Heykal from his pinnacle. Newspapers can be suffocated by an advertising boycott, as was the radical *Age* of Melbourne in the 1850s, or the *Manchester Guardian* of 1956, after its opposition to the Suez invasion. A readers' boycott, of the kind organized by German students against *Die Welt*, can be almost as damaging. Newspapers depend on a number of spindly supports, each of them a hostage to fortune. To live in the commercial marketplace, a paper must appeal to readers and to advertisers. To gather its raw material, it needs a degree of trust from those official and governmental bodies who generate the bulk of public information. It is vulnerable to the angers and frustrations of its own workforce, and to the incompetence of its own management, as *The Times* proved in its sad implosion of 1978–81.

Each of these examples, of newspapers as victims, or of journalists as targets, has been drawn from that handful of newspapers which are household names around the world, most of then synonymous with that sonorous phrase 'the freedom of the press'. Significantly, so far I have not mentioned one of the newspapers which is examined in this book – *Pravda*, the official journal of the Communist Party of the Soviet Union. In many significant ways, it does not fit here. It is not a 'free' newspaper in the Western sense. Its editors follow the lines laid down by its political masters. Russian journalists question whether this is very different from the Western practice, in which editors are told to follow the line laid down by their proprietors. But proprietors in the West tend not to be the national government; the West's tradition of pluralism means that a proprietor is, as often as not, likely to be at loggerheads with government, and it also means that large swathes of his newspaper tend to remain outside a particular proprietor's knowledge and control – particularly when, in the West, commercial success imposes its own freedoms. But *Pravda* differs in other ways. It does not exist in the commercial marketplace. It does not need to attract advertising. Its readers do not have to be seduced into buying it; *Pravda* comes with their party membership card, or with the job they do. *Pravda*'s choice of news stories does not react to events in the world, but to political orders and priorities. *Pravda* does not have to compete in the provision of news.

These twelve newspapers, with the exception of *Pravda* and, to a lesser extent, of *Al-Ahram*, have to compete not only in their domestic markets but among one another. They are all newspapers with a commitment to covering international affairs, to devoting at least two pages a day, and usually more, to the world outside their national frontiers. They are read by one another, and judge one another in a kind of daily international marketplace of news and ideas. *Pravda* and *Al-Ahram* re-enter the group at this point. What *Pravda* says is news; what *Al-Ahram* has to say about the Arab world is recognized to be uniquely informed, therefore valuable, and therefore news.

One of the highly subjective ways in which I chose these twelve newspapers stemmed from own experience reporting in Europe, in

America, in Asia and Africa for the *Guardian* – a famous and historic paper that would merit inclusion in this book were it not for the invidious fact that a *Guardian* journalist is writing it. Whether covering a revolution in Portugal, the assassination of a president in Korea, a drought in Africa or a war in the Sahara, it has been plain to me that only a handful of the world's newspapers feel the sense of obligation to and interest in international affairs to go to the considerable expense of sending its own journalists to cover them. With a few regional exceptions, the colleagues that one tends to see come from these twelve papers.

There are dangers in this. The recent UNESCO attack upon the dominance of the world's news supply by Western agencies, with the West's interests at heart and based on preconceptions that distort the image of the Third World that they report, not only flies in the face of many hard-won lessons about the nature of and the need for press freedom, the UNESCO argument is also profoundly irrelevant. It has been focused largely upon the dominance of the four main wire services, the press agencies who supply the world's raw news data: AP, UPI, Reuters and Agence France Presse. On the whole, their product is read by other newspapers, rather than by general readers or opinion-makers. And although all sorts of bias can emerge in the selection of which bits of news data to cover and to send down the wires, the influence of the raw material of news is very much less than the influence of the major newspapers who put that raw news into context, who assess and analyse, who make and form judgements from it. But the newspapers covered in this book have their own newsgathering resources, their own foreign correspondents and political journalists and different subject specialists who function independently of the wire services. Significantly, the wire services, as a matter of course, report the major articles and the editorials of a handful of internationally renowned newspapers as raw news data. In fact, much of the fame of the newspapers in this book stems from the fact that the wire services regularly quote them. What a great paper says can itself be news, whether it be *Pravda*'s comment on Russian foreign policy, the *Washington Post*'s latest revelation about presidential wrongdoings, *The Times*'s judgement on the state of the British nation, or the *Rand Daily Mail*'s assessment of the gravity of a new wave of riots in Soweto.

Of course, the bulk of the world's governments, and their embassies and their officials, receive their impressions of the world filtered through the judgements of the major newspapers. And apart from fast-breaking news stories like wars and disasters, the electronic media too depend upon the judgement of the great papers to delineate those stories which are significant enough to be worth the considerable expense of sending a TV crew to cover them. In most countries, the 8 a.m. radio news is defined by the front pages of that day's newspapers. An event is made significant by the endorsement given it in a major newspaper.

To take an example from the *Guardian* in 1976; the operations of the South African armed forces in Namibia had been causing concern among church and human-rights groups for some years. It was the publication in the *Guardian*, taking up the whole of the front page, of eye-witness descriptions of the systematic torture of civilians, based on the sworn testimony of individual South African soldiers, which led to a world scandal and a debate on the issue by the UN Security Council – and the subsequent attention of the world's radio and TV. A great newspaper has the unique power of insisting that the world share its own priorities about the news. Radio and TV tend to follow, rather than lead the press.

It takes about a minute to speak 100 words – the length of an average newspaper paragraph. An entire thirty-minute news programme on radio or TV will contain as many individual words – as much raw information – as the lead news story and one feature article in a serious newspaper. So newspapers can consider and report matters in considerably greater depth. Moreover, newspaper reporters are more flexible. In covering the great Sahel drought in 1973–4 for the *Guardian* and the *New York Times*, I was able to hitch rides on military and aid-ferrying aircraft around the remote desert landing strips of the Sahara – often enough leaving a frustrated TV crew of three or four men with their equipment at main airports. Newspaper reporters are less visible. Most foreign correspondents describe themselves on their passports as 'representative' or even as 'writer' (a little doctoring makes the occupation read 'waiter' to suspicious immigration men), and most of us have boldly declared our purpose on entering a country to be 'tourism'; a TV crew can rarely slip in unnoticed. TV journalists in particular depend heavily upon reporting occasions: a press conference; a riot or demonstration; the aftermath of a natural disaster; a televised interview with somebody who is prepared to be seen to be making a public statement. But not all events take place in such formal settings; the newspaper journalist can live and work in the interstices of these public events. TV cannot film somebody speaking off the record. For the electronic media, the world is theatre; it takes place on stage. The newspaper journalist can work backstage, where the props and structure of the performance are more easily seen.

But these technicalities do not explain the special status of the press, least of all of the great papers. A part of that special status lies in tradition. One of the finest newspapers in the world, and one that I would like to have examined, is the Spanish daily, *El Pais*. It has built up an impressive record of editorial courage and competence, of cultural significance and commercial success. But it has only had five years. It is building a tradition, creating that sense of institution and of obligation upon which all established papers depend. But five years is not enough; not set against the 200 years of *The Times*, or even the thirty-six years of *Le Monde*. Newspapers have to build traditions and then live up to them. The weight of longevity and tradition imposes a kind of press responsibility, in much the same way as Dr Johnson's man who was to be hanged in the morning felt that the prospect concentrated his mind wonderfully. After all, newspapers stand to be hanged every morning they appear; you might as well be hanged for living up to a tradition of which you are proud. Longevity in a newspaper suggests a number of important merits: a capacity to survive in a series of different social and economic environments; a capacity to adapt; a capacity to reflect the changing society it serves; a capacity to withstand the various kinds of crisis that succeeding decades tend to bring; and, above all, a sense of historical perspective, of proportion. In much the same way that the British monarchy, when planning a coronation, is able to check back on what the royal ancestors did for their coronations in previous centuries, so a newspaper of tradition is able to look to its own precedents. For both *Corriere della Sera* and *Asahi Shimbun*, the re-publication after the Allied victories of 1945 was made the easier because there were traditions to uphold, that dated back long before the grim hand of Italian fascism or Japanese militarism. There were men, too, who remembered how an independent paper should be run. It is a remarkable and heartening historical fact that great newspapers can outlive the regimes that would suppress them.

For any newspaperman who has made his living and developed his friendships in the profession, there is always a danger of sentimentality when writing about the more ponderous aspects of the press tradition. It can be swiftly cured by looking at the actual record of the daily press with the advantage of hindsight. It was Adolph Ochs, founder of the modern *New York Times*, who observed: 'No reader of my newspaper should ever be surprised.' I take this to mean that political events of global significance do not come upon the world overnight; that there are social, economic and cultural precursors which a diligent journalist should be able to observe and assess. The age of the lightning military coup makes this less easy, but a swelling popular revolution of the kind that toppled the Shah of Iran ought to catch the attention of the world's press. It is for this reason that an important section of this book compares and assesses the skills of these twelve newspapers in reporting Iran during the decade before the Shah fell. It would be fair to say, *pace* Mr Adolph Ochs, that even an acute reader of the *New York Times* would have been somewhat astonished at the feebleness of the Shah's grip on power. Some papers come out of the exercise moderately well; the Melbourne *Age* for one; *Le Monde* (with considerable reservations about the decline in its reports of internal Iranian repression at the time when the Shah was seducing the West with promises of fat industrial contracts) for another. By contrast, the reader of *The Times* (had its managers and workforce let it appear at the relevant time) would have been stunned by his fall. Just as *The Times* supported the Vietnam war longer than Richard Nixon, and supported Richard Nixon longer even than his wretched White House aides, it found almost everything in the Shah's Persian Garden to be excellently ordered. The example of *The Times* serves to show how a newspaper can maintain, largely on the strength of its tradition, a global reputation even when it persistently gets matters wrong. Be it the advisability of appeasing Hitler before 1939, the Suez invasions, or what successive British governments should do about the miners, *The Times* has endeavoured to be wrong. However, tradition saves it every time; its merits cannot be attributed simply to its letters columns, its crosswords and its Court Circular.

But then newspapers are fallible organizations, producing, in great haste and against imperious deadlines, a daily account of the world and trying simultaneously to analyse it. Historians with the aid of documents and hindsight argue among themselves often enough to excuse daily journalism for its mistakes and failures. To call a newspaper a daily miracle is a cliché, but an illuminating one. A story breaks, somewhere in the world. A journalist flies in to the trouble-spot, argues his way past the immigration officials (and possibly the soldiers too), finds a hotel with a telex or an efficient phone switchboard, talks to people in embassies and ministries and in trade unions, or the opposition, or makes contact among dissidents who are living underground, and has to file his story back to his newspaper in time for it to be sub-edited, slotted on to the page, composed into type . . . and all in time to catch the printing presses and the trains that distribute the paper.

Most journalists know the kind of chaos and panic that underlie this brief account. Putting your story on to a telex machine that is being guarded by a suspicious soldier with a loaded machine gun . . . trying to find the phone numbers of people when the directories are in impenetrable Korean . . . writing a story by hand in block letters and giving it to a pilot or to some traveller who will smuggle it out or pass it to the Reuters office in the capital city . . . poring over the local newspapers with pocket dictionaries and finding someone who can translate the local radio bulletins . . . trying to become an instant expert on the local political scene with the aid of a sheaf of photo-copies of clippings from your newspaper library and whatever inter-views can be scrambled before deadline . . . bribing telex operators in obscure post offices, and pressing flowers on unfriendly switchboard operators in the only hotel.

In these circumstances, it is probably inevitable that the various journalists should tend to stick together. On the whole, when all assemble in a country for a particular story, we tend to stay at the same hotel, a propinquity imposed by telexes and phones and con-venience. Press conferences tend to be held in the hotels where the press gather; therefore more journalists try to stay there. People with stories to tell, arguments to put forward, axes to grind, frequent the hotel which then becomes a kind of informal press centre. The journalists, having interviewed the same people (leader of opposi-tion, government spokesman, trade union boss, army spokesman, church leader, ambassadors, etc.), then tend to drink together, to eat together, to socialize and to discuss 'the situation'. A kind of con-sensus press view emerges. Within hours of the shooting of President Park in his South Korean capital of Seoul in 1979, the key press question had been formulated – did the Americans know in advance? The follow-up question was whether Park's death would mean more human rights and greater liberalization. Accordingly, the US Embassy briefings (off the record) concentrated on denying the first and expressing pious hopes for the second. It took the Western press some days to realize that the great Korean concern was whether this made an invasion from the north more likely, and which particular year's graduates from the Korean Military Academy were going to come out on top this time.

Consensus or 'herd' journalism is something that worries the profession even while we accept that it is largely inevitable. A major media event like a US presidential convention will attract 6,000 media people; an Iraq–Iran war will attract about 700; a Portuguese revolution is good for 300; a severe drought in Africa draws about eighty, and a presidential assassination in Korea about thirty. Journalists in these numbers are both an opportunity and a threat to the host government. On the one hand, few countries want to be seen hindering the press (knowing the sort of illiberal reputation that follows); on the other, they want the press to see things their way. Coach tours are laid on, hotels set aside, guided tours arranged to reasonably safe sectors of the front line, press conferences scheduled, exclusive interviews promised on a stick-and-carrot basis. We see the same things, talk to the same people, and discuss matters among ourselves. The consensus follows.

The consensus can be badly adrift. In 1968, when the shoestring primary campaign of Senator Eugene McCarthy, with his cohorts of anti-war student volunteers, shook the hold of the incumbent President Lyndon Johnson in New Hampshire, the consensus was that the American voter was turning against the Vietnam war, that he wanted peace and an end to the draft. That media consensus was an essential factor in persuading President Johnson not to seek re-election, in persuading Senator Robert Kennedy to stand, and in candidate Nixon's promise to bring 'peace with honour'. But in the course of 1969, the University of Michigan conducted a series of polls, interviews and surveys among New Hampshire voters, which showed that almost 60% of McCarthy's votes had come from 'Hawks' who were dissatisfied with President Johnson's limited prosecution of the war, and that the single most vehement anti-war group in the State, the black population, had voted most loyally for LBJ. None the less, the media consensus of 1968 created a reality of its own, that there was indeed a powerful anti-war current; the more the media looked for it, the more of that current it found. The media consensus became, in the course of the 1968 campaign, a self-fulfilling prophecy.

Thumbing back through the yellowed files of the world's press, one comes across endless examples of a consensus that was to be proved wrong. In 1914, there was a consensus among the neutrals that Germany would win the First World War; in 1917, that the Bolshevik Revolution would not last a year; in 1929, (with the honourable exception of the *New York Times*) that there would be no Wall Street crash; in 1940, that Hitler would speedily defeat Britain (except in the British press); and in 1941, that he would speedily defeat the Soviet

Union (except in *Pravda*). Between the analysis and assessment of news that serious papers must attempt, and actual prophecy, there is a very slim line. And, inevitably, the press will often be wrong, even in its collective wisdom.

That wisdom is made the more collective because, certainly among Western journalists, they share a broad consensus of moral viewpoints and values. The Western media depends upon, and believes in, 'freedom of the press'. Inevitably, this means that other freedoms, of religion, of speech, of opinion, and human rights in general, find favour with journalists. The press as a whole dislikes dictators, is suspicious of military regimes, approves of countries with civilian rule, a vocal opposition, free trade unions and the rule of law. In Portugal in 1975, *Le Monde* was bitterly criticized because it chose not to condemn the takeover of a centre-right newspaper, *La Republica*, by its Communist-backed workforce. *Le Monde* asked whether, in a society which had just emerged from forty years of fascist rule, there should be freedom of the press for political groups which had previously denied that freedom to others. *Le Monde* did this clumsily, and without sufficient inquiry into the political antecedents of the groups involved. It was, however, a legitimate question to ask, and one which the press generally accepted in 1946, when the British Military Government in Germany vetoed the appointment of Hans Zehrer to the editorship of *Die Welt*. Zehrer had not been a Nazi; but before Hitler came to power in 1933, he could have been described as an ideological fellow-traveller.

The press in general, and journalists in particular, are human enough to carry around in their heads and hearts a vaguely organized baggage of moral values that can become biases and even prejudices. They stem partly from the nature of the profession, partly from the prevailing values of the countries where their papers are based. The Japanese press, for example, only began to take much interest in Britain's great spy scandal of 1979 when a friend of the unmasked spy, Anthony Blunt, performed the honourable act of hurling himself from a high window. Harikiri had been attempted; the story was now news. (In putting it that way, I am exerting my own national prejudices.) More seriously, the perhaps admirable bias of *Le Monde* towards the interests of the Third World exposed it to heavy criticism in 1975, when it chose not to accept the swelling evidence that an act of calculated genocide was taking place in Kampuchea. On the other hand, the conservative bias of Germany's *Die Welt* had it hunting for Bolshevik bloodbaths in the streets of Saigon as soon as the North

Vietnamese army took it. Where *Le Monde* looks for fascists under the bed, *Die Welt* looks for Communists, which says something for the available spread of opinion in the West's press. And the dramatic turnaround in the American newspapers' coverage of China between the 1960s, when the US government still refused to recognize the existence of Red China, and the 1970s when Nixon and Kissinger 'normalized' relations with Peking, says something rather less creditable about the ways in which opinions change.

It may be a mistake to write about 'the West's press'; the differences between national experience are crucial. A number of senior and respected Italian journalists hold the view that press criticism of an elected government should be restrained in a country where democracy is young and threatened. Hubert Beuve-Méry, the first editor of *Le Monde* and one of the great journalists of the century, felt that in the desperate crisis of France in 1958, a kind of dictator, in the form of de Gaulle, was needed to save some kind of democracy. In Japan, proud and democratic newspapers felt no qualms at an agreement with the Chinese government to base correspondents there, on the understanding that there would be no hostile comment about China in the papers. It takes a great and powerful newspaper to overcome the weight of national custom – and national propaganda. When the *New York Times* sent Harrison Salisbury to Hanoi to report on the effect of American bombing, he and his paper were widely accused of being unpatriotic, of giving aid and comfort to the enemy. In Britain, the *Guardian* suffered similar attacks when it interviewed leading members of the IRA in an effort to comprehend the forces convulsing Northern Ireland. And acts of press courage, even when they arouse the admiration of the media, do not always succeed with the reading public. Scoops do not necessarily bring circulation; sales of the *Washington Post* declined slightly during their historic Watergate campaign, the circulation of the *Rand Daily Mail* suffered during and after its heroic series on South African prison abuses, and in the wake of its courageous decision to publish the Pentagon Papers and fight the Nixon government's attempt to stop them, the *New York Times* slid into its deepest financial crisis of the century.

The different national cultures in which the various papers are based impose their own constraints. Different laws governing the press, different traditions concerning the role of the press, different economic environments and methods of distribution and different proportions of advertising – each of these factors imposes a specifically national character for a newspaper. None the less, the bulk of these newspapers have more in common with each other than with other newspapers in their own countries. From the list of the characteristics they do have in common we can approach some kind of definition as to what makes for the world's elite press.

Each of them devotes a large proportion, at least 10%, of editorial space to foreign affairs. Each paper has, and prominently presents, its editorial column as the paper's own institutional voice. Each paper is known and read outside its own national boundaries, and each paper can be characterized as the house magazine of the elite groups and classes in its own country. Senator Moynihan explained a part of the process: 'Journalism has become, if not an elite profession, a profession attractive to elites.' Journalists around the world are well paid. In Egypt, Nasser followed the nationalization of the press with a financial provision which put journalists into the same privileged economic class as army officers and professional people. In Russia, *Pravda* journalists are paid about three times the average wage, and have other privileges in housing, in car ownership, in bonuses for each article printed.

The elite press seeks to recruit from the elite universities, of Moscow, Tokyo, Oxford and Cambridge, Harvard and Yale, and the *Ecoles Normales*. Their classmates go into government, diplomacy, the academic life, the professions; the graduate journalists remain a part of that intellectual, power-broking, economic and administrative magic circle which runs the country. They spend their professional lives as journalists in explaining the decisions and options of the various segments of that magic circle to the others. They socialize, investigate, report and comment within that dominant layer of public life. There is an old Fleet Street joke which explains the process. The Duke of Someshire has been sued for divorce. The press arrive at the stately home, ring the bell, and inform the butler that they would like to talk to the duke. The butler enters the duke's study: 'There are some reporters and a gentleman from *The Times* to see you, your Grace.' And the British class system is not solely to blame. *Pravda* receives some 400,000 readers' letters a year, many of them written in the belief that *Pravda* is the nearest thing the USSR has to an Ombudsman, the kindly institution that can investigate and right official misdeeds and mistakes. *Pravda* runs a regular feature, under the title 'They reply to *Pravda* – Measures Taken', of reports from officials explaining how they have put right the mistake of which *Pravda* had complained. When *Pravda* makes such an inquiry, things happen. Correspondents for small regional papers pull less weight:

they have been known to lose their jobs or their apartments—or both—
for emulating *Pravda*.

When the US government takes the *New York Times* to court over
the publication of the Pentagon Papers, or when the French government indicts the editor of *Le Monde* for contempt of the judicial
system, it is news around the world. Not only is it unusual, it points to
a major argument within the nation's Establishment. The press is
more than just the arena within which a national debate can take
place; a major newspaper is enough of an institution of itself to
become spokesman and protagonist in that debate. Nor is this a
phenomenon restricted to Western countries. In Russia in 1928, when
Stalin's grip upon the Communist Party was almost complete, the
only outlet for the right-wing opposition within the Party to the
collectivization and anti-kulak campaigns came from the columns of
Pravda. In April 1917, when the Bolsheviks were working out their
response to the first revolution, the debate took place in *Pravda*'s
pages, with Lenin's views coming under sharp criticism. Similarly, in
Nasser's Egypt after the 1967 war, the only outlet for public criticism
of the regime was Heykal's *Al-Ahram*.

From the histories of these twelve papers, there is one distinct
pattern that emerges. Newspapers originally achieve elite status by
supporting a radical opposition at a time when the old order is
crumbling. Whether one looks at the growth of the Melbourne *Age*
from a bankrupt radical sheet of the 1850s to the dominant voice of
Australian life in 1900; or at the Toronto *Globe* developing from a
religious weekly in the 1840s to the thundering voice of Canadian
liberalism in the 1870s, we are watching a political outsider becoming
a part of the governing elite at just the time when the State itself was
taking its modern form. This is not a process unique to the former
British colonies. Exactly the same process was at work with *Corriere
della Sera*, which between 1880 and 1920 developed from a minor
broadsheet to become the voice of northern Italian liberalism, the last
institution with the courage and status to condemn Mussolini's
fascism. In Italy, as in Canada and Australia, the nations remained
embryonic enough for the ruling elites to be tiny. Prime Ministers
were groomed in the Melbourne *Age*'s newsroom; some of Italy's
leading writers were dependent on *Corriere*'s stipends. As forum, as
paymaster, as platform – the press played a vital role in nation
building that virtually guaranteed it a place of privilege once that
nation was built. And when the young radicals grew and aged into a
political Establishment of their own, they found that precedents had

been established, licensing the press which had nurtured and supported them in opposition, to criticize them now they were in power. The process could falter, as it did in Australia where 'King David' Syme of the *Age* allowed his paper's arteries to harden with his own advancing and powerful years. But enough momentum of prestige had been attained for the *Age* to live on its reputation, until its influence was recovered by its own merits.

When we talk of a newspaper's tradition, we should not simply talk of institutions, but of men growing up together, young reporters and ambitious young politicians, maintaining their friendships as they become editors and ministers. The process is acknowledged in Russia, where the official history of the Communist Party waxes almost lyrical: 'A whole generation of revolutionary proletariat, which later carried out the October Revolution, grew up with *Pravda*.' A lot of them grew up on it. Lenin, Stalin, Trotsky, Kamenev, Molotov, Bukharin – they all sat in the editor's chair.

The then future president of the USA, John Kennedy, and the future editor of the *Washington Post*, Ben Bradlee, took with them a youthful friendship as Washington neighbours into the White House. *Le Monde* was able to survive its desperate crisis of 1951 because of journalists who had served de Gaulle during the war. De Gaulle saved *Le Monde*, and *Le Monde* was able to return the favour when the General deigned to seize power in 1958. Mohammed Heykal's friendship with Nasser began in 1948 when a young war reporter covering the attempted invasion of the infant Israel met and liked a young officer. Six years later, the youthful Colonel Nasser mounted his coup and Heykal climbed with him. At this personal level, elites are tiny groups. In a war, a revolution, a young country, these small and personal elites can wield enormous power. But once the emergency is over and the country is stable and growing again, and enough time has lapsed for the personal friends to die and be replaced by strangers, the role of the press becomes critical. In a country which observes the rule of law, which accepts a pluralist system, the press will usually have won enough ground to establish its independence as a principle. In other countries, under totalitarian forms, the press is a threat which must be conscripted into service – just as Stalin did when he fired Bukharin as editor of *Pravda* and brought in his creature, Mekhlis. Or just as Sadat found it as easy to topple Heykal as Nasser had found it to raise him.

It is in the stable societies, Britain or America or Canada or Australia, where the press, or at least one key paper, can grow over generations into that curiously atypical role that we call the 'fourth estate'. It is a rare and privileged position to hold, even though it now has behind it the force of precedent and the force of Anglo-American cultural domination. We tend to think that because the role of the press is privileged in the Anglo-American culture, buttressed by law and by precedent, that is how it should be. Before we give the usual reflex agreement to that, there are (at least) three fundamental questions to ask: first, does that privilege really exist?; second, is it not the atypical outcome of two nations lucky enough to have known wealth without revolution and war without invasion for the last few centuries?; and third, why is so much of the world following another model?

The questions almost answer themselves. Does the privilege really exist in the West? Certainly not in Britain, where stringent libel laws, an all-embracing Official Secrets Act and the D-notice system led *Sunday Times* editor Harold Evans to describe the British condition as 'the half-free press'. In the USA, the First Amendment to the Constitution states bluntly that Congress shall make no law abridging the freedom of the press. The government's Solicitor-General, Erwin Griswold, former dean of the Harvard Law School, told the Supreme Court during the Pentagon Papers case, 'It is to me obvious that "no law" does not mean "no law" and I would seek to persuade the court that that is true.' Mr Griswold failed. The First Amendment was upheld. But government and judicial encroachments on the press have continued. The courts sent to prison a *New York Times* reporter who refused to make his notes and confidential sources available to the court. And in an admittedly extreme case, when a tiny radical magazine called *The Progressive* tried to publish an article on the danger of nuclear proliferation which included a step-by-step blueprint on how to build a nuclear bomb, the courts granted the government the right of prior restraint, the right to censor a publication in advance, which was the very issue the government had lost in the Pentagon Papers case.

Is the Anglo-American concept of press freedom, limited as it is, the result of economic privilege and political stability in those countries? Almost certainly it is, and rooted moreover in the pluralist nature of those two countries, and in the Anglo-American concept of the Law as an historic constitutional entity in its own right, independent of government. In any state where the balance of powers is maintained between the executive, the legislature and the judiciary, the press will develop a tradition of freedom in the tensions and the cracks between them, just as grass grows between paving stones. A pluralist nation that does not have such a concept of law or of the separation of powers, such as France, is a less fertile field for press freedom. The case of *Le Monde*, censored by official fiat in 1958 and persecuted by the government and the judiciary in 1980, illustrates the difference. The tangled history of *Corriere della Sera* in the 1970s, moving to the Left and back again at the behest of the owner, the editor he chose to appoint, and the financial constraints upon him, shows the vulnerability of press freedom within the capitalist marketplace.

The case of Japan is unique. Its newspapers were free enough and powerful enough to topple Prime Minister Tanaka after the press probings of the Lockheed bribery scandals. Yet *Asahi Shimbun* is dependent on the government for a disguised subsidy through the land on which its headquarters are built. Exclusive stories which touch on state security and secrets have to be published, not in the pages of the press, but in speeches in the Diet, given by politicians who have been briefed by the journalists. The doctrine of the separation of powers is to be found in the Japanese constitution, but Japanese society does not really work that way – in part because the Japanese concept of the law is different, and the role of the judiciary (and the number and importance of lawyers) is minuscule by Western standards. The Japanese are a practical, pragmatic people, and the journalists of *Asahi Shimbun* have an honourable record. Against the warlords, against attempted military coups, against political thugs and hostile governments, *Asahi Shimbun* fought for its freedoms, even while its owner and his journalists were being beaten, and while the soldiers were occupying the paper and wrecking the presses. *Asahi* fought until the struggle was hopeless, and then co-operated.

Asahi was lucky. The military regime which crushed its freedom was itself crushed, and *Asahi* was reborn after its defeat. But in Lee Kuan Yew's Singapore, in India during Mrs Gandhi's emergency, in West Africa and in South America, newspapers which were born under that Anglo-American tradition of press freedom have seen their reporters and editors imprisoned, their columns censored, their freedoms stubbed out. And at the time of writing, not only is there little prospect of those freedoms being restored, but there are concerted efforts being made by Third World governments, with the support of UNESCO, to 'export their kind of censorship into what's left of the world's free press'. This is the view, expressed with characteristic flamboyance and lack of compromise, of Abe

Rosenthal, editor of the *New York Times*. 'There are complaints about the way the West has handled Third World stories, but the motives of our critics are suspect. They want a kind of licensing, a kind of inspection of the press. They want us to operate by their standards, and I see little reason to respect those standards, or to trust them.'

The sharpest opposing view was expressed in a *Pravda* editorial (24 November 1978): 'The bourgeois press in the West mounted a campaign of attacks on UNESCO, distorting the contents of the document [The Declaration on the Mass Media], trying to keep a free hand to conduct militarist propaganda, to interfere in the affairs of others and to maintain the untrammelled domination of the Western organs of information in the spiritual life of Asia, Africa and Latin America.'

Between those two viewpoints the other great papers take their various positions. *Le Monde*, long sympathetic to the problems of the Third World, has for years followed a policy that solves some of the problems. They post intelligent and sympathetic journalists to Third World areas and keep them there for years, until they become part-journalist, part-academic expert on the region. And then *Le Monde* publishes articles in dense and endless series, explaining the issues and problems in often tedious depth, an intensity of coverage that few other editors who work in the commercial marketplace would dare impose on their readers. And even then, *Le Monde*'s policy can lead it into difficulties; it is one thing to write and edit with sympathy and even bias for underdeveloped countries, but it is disturbing that *Le Monde*'s sympathies should lead it for so long to disbelieve, and even suppress, the mounting evidence of genocide in Kampuchea.

The Melbourne *Age* and *Washington Post* are jointly working on a project which seems more promising. It begins from the premise that the Western press must resist any attempt by the Third World to export their press controls. The answer therefore is to export Western concepts of press freedom to the Third World, by training and hiring and publishing and protecting, as far as possible, Third World journalists. Men like Tarzie Vittachi and Mohammed Heykal and Cameron Duodu and Yusuf Ibrahim and Peter Enaharo and Godwin Mtasa have proved that the West has no monopoly of able and courageous journalists, and a Third World covered by men such as these would be well and fairly reported. The *Age–Post* plan calls for a regular page of reports and columns from Third World journalists, earning them enough money and prestige to enable them to be independent of the controlled press of their own countries, while trying to provide them with the kind of international press protection which could let them report freely. It is on this kind of openness to good journalists, wherever they come from, that much of the merit of the great papers has traditionally depended. Canadians like Beaverbrook and Australians like Bruce Page and Murray Sayle have in their time injected new life into Fleet Street; Scotty Reston, probably the finest journalist to work on the *New York Times*, came from Scotland. Heykal of Egypt and Vittachi from Sri Lanka are journalists whose by-lines are now international, and the press is the healthier for it.

But neither the cause of the Third World nor the cause of a free press was helped by the crass intervention of the United Nations in 1981. Some £630,000 had been given to the UN by a wealthy Japanese businessman, Ryoichi Sasakaya, to promote the UN's views on helping the Third World. Two-thirds of this sum was spent on bureaucratic expenses; the remainder was given, as subsidy or as fee, to the fifteen Western and Third World newspapers which agreed to publicize the UN's arguments – and, in some cases, print articles written by the UN's own staff.[1] *Asahi Shimbun* of Tokyo and *Le Monde* accepted the money, although *Asahi* did so only on condition that it retained editorial control over whatever was published. *Le Monde* and *Asahi* each received a maximum grant of £23,000. The project was co-ordinated by *Le Monde*'s former diplomatic correspondent, Jean Schwoebel, who had become a highly paid (£33,700 a year) UN official. Among the articles presented for publication in the UN package was one by Mr Bhaskar Menon of the UN's Social and Economic Information division which called for 'the decolonization of the world economy'.[2] The consequent and predictable scandal centred rather more on the remarkable generosity of the UN to its own officials in the distribution of the funds than on the questionable precedent that had been established of newspapers selling their editorial space – however 'noble' the object. This was unfortunate. But the row did at least serve to undermine the plausibility of what had become an orthodox definition of the difference between the press of East and West.

One recent survey argued that: 'Through the elite press is disseminated either the thoughtful, pluralistic and sophisticated dialogue of a free society, or the necessary social and political guidance of a closed society.'[3] But if that dictum is applied to the particular case of *Le Monde, Asahi Shimbun* and the UN, it is very hard to tell the difference between 'free dialogue' and 'closed guidance'. Corruption was not the issue – £23,000 is a little enough sum to *Le Monde* or to *Asahi*. But the degree of concern voiced by other newspapers pointed to the importance of the principle that the UN had so crudely put at risk.

But this does not go to the core of the problem. The bulk of the world's governments neither recognize nor accept the traditional Anglo-American concept of a free press. And British and American governments in recent years have shown an increasing hostility to the idea in their own countries. A government, by definition, is sovereign in its country. An independent and often critical voice, with direct and daily access to the public, must be a limitation on that sovereignty. Nor can the press itself claim much of a special status. Papers like *Le Monde* or the *Guardian* are owned by trusts, which frees them from the whims of proprietors, but the histories of *Die Welt* and *Corriere della Sera* show that even powerful and respected papers run by honest and honourable journalists are still, in the last resort, under the thumb of owners whose wealth enables them to deploy the papers as if they were a personal political weapon. But there are no firm rules; the *New York Times* and the *Washington Post* and the Melbourne *Age* are owned by powerful and opinionated proprietors; yet they have built up an independence, based on tradition, upon commercial success and profit, and upon excellence, which counters the perils of private ownership.

We tend to forget just how recent is the new concept of the free and independent Western press. Throughout the Cold War, through the 1950s and well into the 1960s, the relevant chapters in this book document the intimacy between US government policy in general (the CIA in particular) and the *New York Times* and *Washington Post*. Vietnam, the Pentagon Papers and Watergate combined to end that process. But throughout the Cold War years, the off-the-record letters sent back through the US embassies' diplomatic pouches to Arthur Sulzberger, the *New York Times*'s publisher, by his correspondents abroad were being shown to the CIA – without the journalists' knowledge. As Harrison Salisbury observed, in recounting the story: 'that, in the definition of Soviet law, would be espionage, and the penalty for that was death'. Salisbury was the *New York Times*'s Moscow correspondent at the time.

Incidents such as these were commonplace during the Cold War. Endless efforts were made by Western intelligence agencies to use journalism and journalists for their own purposes. One British-based international press agency, Forum World Features, was run as a CIA operation. Kim Philby, the master-spy of the post-war generation, was an accredited journalist for the British *Economist* and *Observer* when he skipped to Russia from the Lebanon. And even when the press-intelligence relationship was less blatant, it was insistent and insidious – and the environment in which it bred persists to this day. To quote Harrison Salisbury again: 'The world of foreign correspondents, diplomats and intelligence agents is parochial. They trade in the same kind of goods, move from one capital to another, frequent the same bars, go to the same cocktail parties, have the same interests. They know each other. They talk shop together. We all feed at the same trough.'

As a working journalist, I do not know how this can be avoided. As a matter of course, when on a foreign story, I will call at the British Embassy and ask for an off-the-record briefing on the local situation. Given time, I will call on the American and French Embassies, and others too. When back in London, I meet British and foreign diplomats socially; I go to their parties and receptions. Some become close personal friends and naturally we pick each other's brains. These are essential tools of the journalist's trade. How does one persuade a suspicious Third World official that a Western journalist can then try to be independent, honest and objective? How does one refute the kind of allegations about the sinister role of the West's press that the *Pravda* editorial made? And true though it be, it is not good enough simply to retort that Soviet journalists have been used by, and have on occasion been members of, the KGB. The Soviet press makes no secret of its duty to serve the Soviet State and the Communist Party. They do not even attempt to be judged by the standards of the press in the West.

We in the West tend to pride ourselves upon our democracies, our open governments, our freedoms – including the freedom of the press – without really comprehending the secretive, conspiratorial and self-serving ways in which our systems have been made to function. To the general public, the very word 'secret' implies spies, treachery, patriotism and betrayal. That is not the way matters work at all. In 1976, two American citizens living in Britain, Mark Hosenball (a journalist) and Philip Agee (a former CIA agent who had resigned and written an angry, critical account of his work for the CIA) were informed that they were to be deported for reasons of national security. No court hearing was needed – it was an administrative decision. But to show that Britain still had some sense of justice, the two men were allowed a hearing before 'three wise men', appointed by the government, who could make a confidential recommendation to the Home Secretary. (This is the homely British title for the Minister of the Interior; the functions are indistinguishable.) One of the grounds on which they were being deported was that they had had 'contact with foreign agents'. A number of British journalists were called to make statements on their behalf. I told the 'three wise men' that any decent journalist was in contact with foreign agents as a matter of course. I specified four, a Russian, a Frenchman and two Arabs, whose brains I regularly picked. They had information; and I, as a journalist, was in the information business. I lunched with them, drank with them, went to parties with them. To condemn a journalist for having 'contact with foreign agents' was tantamount to condemning a priest for having contact with sinners. I know not what impact my statement had. The three wise men deliberated, and made their report in secret. The two Americans were deported. The four 'foreign agents' stayed.

Secrecy, as a tool of government, has very little to do with foreign affairs, and even less to do with national security. Secrecy is a system of self-protection that governments and bureaucracies wear like a skin. Journalists cover the British parliament under a code of secrecy that makes them into the Trappist monks of Fleet Street. When they are called together for their regular meetings with the Prime Minister's spokesman, they write down what is said, but the code of the lobby does not permit them to let their readers know who said it. Hence the absurd fictions of 'Cabinet sources' and 'senior Ministers believe . . .' and so on. When a Fleet Street reporter telephones the Foreign Office for the British view on some international matter, he or she will be given, on the record, the text of the last ministerial answer in Parliament, or a formal statement. One then asks, 'Is there any background?', and off the record, not for attribution, comes the formal view. Exactly the same process takes place when one telephones Scotland Yard. And in the meantime, ministers, politicians, diplomats, officials and senior policemen are happy to meet for a drink or a lunch and talk 'off the record', knowing full well that they are not answerable for what they say, that nothing can be attributed to them; they can mislead or distort as much as they wish; their 'secrets' are favours to be traded at table while the public, the voter, the taxpayer is left with the crumbs.

This is not simply a British hypocrisy. The classic statement of the currency in secrets between state and journalism was made by a *New York Times* journalist, Max Frankel, in an affidavit presented to the court during the Pentagon Papers hearings. Frankel was a veteran of the Washington bureau. He recounted how he had stood waist-deep in a swimming-pool with Lyndon Johnson while the President told him, off the record, the 'secrets' of his conversations the day before with Premier Kosygin of the Soviet Union. He recounted Dean Rusk, the US Secretary of State, telling him that Laos was 'not worth the life of a single Kansas farm boy', shortly before 600,000 American troops were committed to South-East Asia. He recounted the State Department leaking the 'top-secret' discussions between President Kennedy and Soviet Foreign Minister Gromyko during the Cuban missile crisis, to illustrate Russian perfidy.

Frankel's affidavit began thus: 'Without the use of "secrets" there could be no adequate diplomatic, military and political reporting of the kind our people take for granted, either abroad or in Washington and there could be no mature spirit of communication between the government and the people . . . The governmental, political and personal interests of the participants are inseparable in this process. Presidents make "secret" decisions only to reveal them for the purposes of frightening an adversary nation, wooing a friendly electorate, protecting their reputations. The military services conduct "secret" research in weaponry only to reveal it for the purposes of enhancing their budgets, appearing superior or inferior to a foreign army, gaining the vote of a congressman or the favour of a contractor. High officials of the government reveal secrets in the search for support of their policies, or to help sabotage the plans or policies of rival departments. Middle-rank officials reveal secrets so as to attract the attention of their superiors or to lobby against the orders of those superiors.'

Within this kind of framework, with secrets and foreign agents flying around the journalists like so much confetti, one has to try and construct some kind of defence against the criticisms of UNESCO, against the sneers of *Pravda*, against the doubts of our own condition. In the end, the press is judged by its works, by its articles, by its honesty and by its readiness to examine its faults and its problems and its records with the same honesty that it tries to bring to its reports. This book is one such effort, to examine a round dozen of the world's great papers, to see how they work, how they survive, how they are financed, to tell their histories.

It has been a monumental task. The history of a newspaper is, almost by definition, the history of the country in which it is published. Newspapers range far beyond the politics of their nations. The literary and artistic life, the way ordinary people live; the goods that advertisers are trying to sell; the way a nation's children are to be educated; the way its believers worship; the way its businesses and its banks function; the style of its criminals and the behaviour of its police; the justice of its courts – they are all there. A newspaper is a daily diary of the culture of a nation.

But this does not imply any kind of determinism. If the studies in this book make any overwhelming point, it is that societies do not get the newspapers they deserve. Newspapers are the products of men, fallible enough and marvellous enough to sink below or rise above the societies that gave them birth. The *Rand Daily Mail* is a far, far better newspaper than apartheid-ridden South Africa deserves, and the *New York Times* and *Washington Post* were far better publications than Nixon's America deserved. One of the reasons why these twelve newspapers are in this book, why they chose themselves for inclusion, is that each of them, even *Pravda*, has at key times imposed its own decency, its own conviction, its own morality upon its readers and its nation: *Le Monde* during the Algerian war, *Corriere* fighting Mussolini, *Asahi Shimbun* defying the soldiers and the militarism of a Japan gone mad, the Melbourne *Age* publishing the proof of corruption which brought down a government it had supported, *Pravda* publishing the great debates between Bolshevism's confused leaders at the very moment of revolution in 1917, and again on the eve of Stalin's dictatorship. They were tasks, or duties, that only newspapers could perform.

This book has been written at the end of an era. While the research was under way, the technology and the craft which had created a mass daily press was itself dying. The computers, the cold type, the laser beams were being introduced, and the noise and heat of the linotypes, the bustle of the printer's stone, and even the clatter of a newsroom's typewriters were being stilled. And the plans were under way for new kinds of newspapers, a thin *Washington Post* that had surrendered its massed columns of classified ads to the data banks, for a Toronto *Globe and Mail* and a *New York Times* that are beamed across their countries by satellites, printed not in the big city headquarters but across a continent, with editions and advertising that can be changed and channelled with the humming of computers. Within my lifetime as a journalist, I expect to see grass growing in Fleet Street, as the giant printing presses are removed, and the midnight newspaper trains cancelled. Britain's daily newspapers will be printed at small, regional plants around the country, with later deadlines, cheaper distribution costs, and advertisements that can be tailored to local markets. That old financial albatross of Fleet Street, the need to attract national advertisers with products that sell, like the papers do, from Land's End to John O'Groats, will finally flap away.

There will still be reporters, finding and writing the stories that will be set by computers and electronically transmitted to as many regional printing presses as are needed. There will always be reporters. There will still be editors, imposing their own personalities and priorities upon whatever package of information is spewing from the data terminal. There will still be advertisements to defray the costs. There will still be circulation managers and copy tasters and cartoonists. But the rumbling, inky heart of the business will die with the passing of the great rotary press machines. An industrial mystique, a craftsmanship and a tradition will die with them, that deep emotional bond between the printer and the tools of his skill that goes far towards explaining the bitterness of the strikes and sabotage and lock-outs that have marked and marred the coming of the new newspaper technology around the world.

It is a truism to say that Gutenberg and Caxton could, within minutes of entering any newspaper composing room up to the 1970s, have fully comprehended the technology that was employed. But that continuity of printing processes tends to obscure a most important truth: the concept of press freedom has changed almost fundamentally since the early decades of printing. The freedom of the press, as a moral imperative, is usually dated from Milton's remarkable essay *Areopagitica*. But Milton's claim was a relatively modest one. He simply demanded freedom to publicize an opinion, the right to publish a book or a pamphlet and offer it in the intellectual marketplace of public opinion. Today, freedom of the press implies a great deal more than this. It involves the right to probe and investigate, to pester witnesses and recruit sources. It can mean using the concept of press freedom to suborn a witness from loyalty to an employer, in the name of alternative loyalties, be it the public's right to know, the newspaper's right to expose, or the employee's right to get his own back. It also involves the right of a newspaper to campaign tirelessly for a particular idea, to use the rest of its pages as a sugar-coating over some particular pill the editors want the public to swallow. No doubt ex-President Nixon would describe the *Washington Post*'s coverage of Watergate in these terms, but that should not deter us from admitting that the *Washington Post*'s definition of press freedom in the 1970s is a very great deal wider than that of John Milton in the 1660s.

Newspapers can claim that they embody democratic choice; that they are in a sense 'elected' every time a member of the public pays for his paper, and that commercial failure is the price of offending the readers. This argument would be stronger were it not for those papers, such as *The Times, Die Welt*, on occasion *Corriere della Sera* and the *Washington Post*, who have depended for their financial survival upon outside resources. And the current trend towards monopoly newspapers in the USA, with the *Washington Post*, for example, facing no rival paper in its market, weakens the press argument still further. High-minded appeals to the public's right to know (or to know what the press chooses to tell them) must confront other high-minded appeals to the government's right to govern, an individual's right to privacy, a commercial right to confidentiality, and so on. Our broad new definition of press freedom should stand on firmer ground than this.

There is a very strong pragmatic case for it. On occasions, and in some countries, individual newspapers have enacted that civic role that the ancient Romans defined: *Quis custodiet ipsos custodes?* – Who shall guard against the guardians themselves? When governments themselves become corrupt, and deploy the tools of office to disguise that corruption from the citizens, then how is the public to find out? In South Africa, the *Rand Daily Mail* found out and provoked a scandal that toppled the head of state and the chief of the secret police. In the US, the *Washington Post* found out and helped to destroy the Nixon administration. In Australia, the *Age* unearthed the scandal of improper commission payments on foreign loans and helped to topple the Whitlam government. In France, *Le Monde*'s exposure of torture during the Algerian war helped to kill off the Fourth Republic. In Japan, it was several arms of the press, the foreign correspondents, the weekly magazines and finally the heavy daily papers, which combined to drive the corrupt government of Premier Tanaka from office.

But in all those cases it was a very close-run thing, accomplished while the governments in question were making threats and drafting plans to curb the press and ensure it would never wield such power again. If we are to accept that events have justified the wider new press freedom, then the newspapers need stronger support than precedent and pragmatism. Ironically, this is not an issue on which the press around the world is accustomed to campaign. There are obvious exceptions: the *Rand Daily Mail* since the early 1960s, the *New York Times* and *Washington Post* during the Pentagon Papers and Watergate years, *Le Monde* while the Giscardian Establishment and the French judiciary sought to victimize it during 1980 – but, almost without exception, the need for judicial support for the rights of a free press is something newspapers only seriously address themselves to when events force the issue upon them. Nor is it easy to argue that judicial protection is the answer. The threats to the *New York Times* and *Washington Post* took place in the one country in the world where press freedom has a full constitutional guarantee: the First Amendment which bluntly states that 'Congress shall make no law to curtail the freedom of the press'.

Once again, pragmatism comes to the aid of the press. Few governments are monolithic: if one section of government hates the press, another is likely to find it a useful ally. The Supreme Court came to the rescue of the *New York Times* during the Pentagon Papers case, and Congress backed the *Washington Post* during Watergate. Moreover, a serious and sober national newspaper is almost inevitably a part of the nation's Establishment. The *Rand Daily Mail* is perhaps the one exception to that rule in this book. But even the *Rand Daily Mail* would not challenge the legitimacy of the South African Republic, nor of its government. The *Rand Daily Mail* would generally support the national legal system, and agree that change should come by peaceful and constitutional means. In short, these newspapers do not seek to challenge the basic ground rules of the societies they serve. Economic systems, legal processes and governmental forms are broadly seen to be legitimate and acceptable. These are all newspapers with at least one foot in the camp of the Establishment. The most successful seem to be those, like the *New York Times, Washington Post*, the *Rand Daily Mail* and *Le Monde*, which firmly keep the other foot in opposition, in touch with (and prepared to publicize) those parts of society which question the state's legitimacy.

Looking at these twelve newspapers, and in this context I do not wholly exclude either *Pravda* or *Al-Ahram*, it would seem that the standard position is to be *of* the national Establishment, without necessarily always being *for* it. In suggesting this, I am echoing from a different standpoint an argument of a pioneer scholar of the world's press, Wilbur Schramm, who observed: 'Prestige papers are shaped, to an important degree, by what the leadership in the country wants to know and wants known. The leadership in the country is also shaped, to an important degree, by what the papers tell them.' We are talking of a process of complex and endless feedback, with today's paper provoking a response which will become news in tomorrow's edition, with politicians reacting to a newspaper's editorial comment and so on. A newspaper is not something that can be seen and defined from a single edition; it is a process, a moving film rather than a still photograph. It was for this reason that the performance of these twelve newspapers on a particular story is judged over a decade. And if the history of each newspaper shows how bravely or how well most of them did in the difficult task of preserving their independence from governments, then the way they covered Iran during the 1970s shows how badly they did at the simple and customary task of gathering and presenting the news.

Notes

1. *Sunday Telegraph*, London, 12.vi.81.
2. *Daily Telegraph*, London, 29.v.81.
3. *The World's Great Dailies*. Merril & Fisher (Communications Arts Books, NY, 1980) p.9.

2

The Times

The Times was founded in 1785, under the title of *The Daily Universal Register*, in order to help restore the fortunes of John Walter, an insurance underwriter who had been ruined by the loss of ships to privateers during the American War of Independence. The news-paper was but a sideline, a vehicle to show off the merits of a new printing process to which Walter held the patent, and to promote his campaign to become the government's chief printer. Selling at 2½d, when most of its rivals cost 3d, it contained more shipping and commercial news and less politics and culture than most. Its priorities were plain; rather than delay publication beyond 6 a.m., parliamentary debates that went on too long could expect to be summarized rather than quoted. The businessmen of the City wanted their information to be prompt. Sadly, the first issue was delayed until late morning by delays with the printing process. It contained ten columns of advertisements, three of news and three of the new paper's prospectus: it described itself as: 'The Register of the times, the faithful recorder of every species of Intelligence; it ought not to be engrossed by any particular object, but like a well-covered table it should contain something suited to every palate.'[1]

But newspapers of the day were rarely founded for profit; the government kept far too tight a control to permit the press the independence that would come with commercial success. The method of control preferred was the Stamp Duty, a tax levied on the raw newsprint, on each advertisement, and on each copy sold. The Stamp looked like a revenue-raising tax; in fact, it acted as a government licence to print. Stamps accounted for about two-thirds of publishing costs. In 1797, John Walter's weekly outgoings were £25.4.0 for paper, £35.2.10 for wages, and £96 for stamp duties.[2] But while collecting that money with one hand, governments passed it back with the other. The secret-service accounts of Pitt's government annually recorded £300 to the owner of *The Times*. 'Though £300 a year was to be my reward for the politics of the paper, when it is considered that I lost all the advertisements and the civilities of the Opposition, I doubt any real profit arose from it,' John Walter wrote to Lord Hawkesbury.[3] But there were limits to the government's favours; Walter was in prison when he wrote it, convicted of libelling the Prince of Wales and Duke of York. Loyalty to the government meant loyalty to the King; *The Times* had accused the King's ambitious sons of 'insincerity in their joy' when the King recovered from an illness which had looked serious enough to put the Prince on the throne.[4] Walter was released after a year, with £250 in compensation from the secret-service funds, his printing company had been given the lucrative Customs contract and throughout the early 1790s, *The Times* was carefully fed with official scoops by the government.

This political involvement was to define the character of the paper. It had begun as a commercial sheet, aimed at the City, and had briefly dallied with the fashionable world of the West End and the theatre (where an excellent income was to be gained from suppression fees, for not printing certain paragraphs), before casting in its lot with William Pitt's government. In return for government cash, *The Times* gave political support, filled its pages with political and foreign news, roundly attacked the French Revolution and any signs of radicalism in England, and saw its circulation rise to a healthy 2,900. But that political commitment had to be total. When circulation fell to 1,700 during the unpopular peace of 1801, *The Times* had no choice but to continue to support the government. And when the government briefly transferred its patronage to other papers, *The Times* was left pathetically loyal, reminding Pitt of John Walter's sufferings in the King's cause.[5]

In 1803, this traditional dependence began to change. John Walter II, the able son, took over the paper. The printing side of the business was sound, jobbing business alone earning over £1,000 profit in 1805. He decided that the Napoleonic wars had created a new market, independent of the government, for swift and reliable news from abroad. He began by paying the clerks of the Post Office sixty guineas a year to give *The Times* copies of the latest dispatches. Then he fought the Post Office for the right to gather his own news.[6] He hired smugglers to bring the latest issues of the French and European papers directly to *The Times*. By 1813, Lord Castlereagh, the Foreign Secretary, was asking Walter for the latest information from Europe. Walter also believed that people wanted an independent paper. In 1807, he insisted that critics for *The Times* pay for their theatre seats and be honestly critical. Nobody was allowed to interfere with Walter; when his printers struck for better wages in 1810, Walter had nineteen of them tried and sentenced to prison for illegal combination. Four years later, he developed and introduced the first steam printing machine – and did it in secret, to stop his printers striking again.[7]

When governments discreetly offered subsidies in return for editorial support, Walter bluntly refused and published the first leader to lay out the basic rules of press independence: 'The paper continued that support of the men in power, but without suffering them to repay its partiality by contributions, because the editor was conscious he should have sacrificed the right of condemning any act which he might esteem detrimental to the public welfare.' (10 February 1810).

And equally importantly, Walter refused to continue the tradition of hiring scribblers who wrote at a penny a line; he wanted good writing, and there was no shortage. Men like Leigh Hunt and Barron Field were campaigning for a new journalism, of style and literary merit, and practising what they preached in the new weekly magazines. Walter hired each of them as theatre critics for *The Times*, and began hiring from their set. Henry Robinson, a friend of Wordsworth and Lamb, became European correspondent, based in Hamburg. The Reverend Peter Fraser, a fellow of a Cambridge college, was hired to write leaders. The great essayist William Hazlitt wrote for *The Times*, and the poet Samuel Taylor Coleridge applied for a job; his friend Thomas Barnes, destined to be one of the great editors, was hired as parliamentary writer. Circulation had risen to 7,000 under John Walter's new policy, and the paper was profitable enough to pay Dr John Stoddart, its editor elect, £1,400 a year in 1814, an astonishing sum.[8]

Walter's determined independence meant that the pre-eminent political journal was the pro-government *Morning Chronicle*. *The Times* steadily became identified with the middle classes, the commercial interests, the stock exchange and the manufacturers, and increasingly hostile to a government that was based on the traditional landowning aristocracy. In a sense, *The Times* was placing itself on the side of the future, and the pro-government press regularly accused it of 'championing sedition' as the government reacted to popular unrest and economic recession with a wave of arrests and repressive laws. When political demonstrators were killed by the Yeomanry at Peterloo, *The Times* condemned the government for 'putting down by force every culpable, however pitiable, expression of popular suffering'.[9] When the government threatened to curb *The Times*, the paper responded stoutly: 'The question is, if the freedom of the press be destroyed, or its actual freedom sensibly curtailed, we may not exchange occasional turbulence and conflict for the calm of despotism and the repose of death.' (25 September 1819).

The Times was the voice of cautious reform, not revolution. William Hazlitt, writing in the *Edinburgh Review*, acknowledged that it was 'the leading journal of Europe and perhaps the greatest engine of temporary opinion in the world', but added, 'it takes up no falling cause, fights no uphill battle, advocates no great principle'.[10] And it was less the politics than the salacious details of the court case through which King George IV tried to divorce Queen Caroline that accounted for its circulation rising from 7,000 to 15,000. But the effect of the political unrest and Peterloo, the wave of criticism of the government, led by *The Times*, and the quite unprecedented public interest in the Queen Caroline trial had all combined to create public opinion as a real, if shadowy, political force. *The Times* was a key part of that process, a responsible and legitimate voice, acting as both channel and symbol of criticism. Until this period, governments had responded to opposition by arresting it or by calling out the troops. While *The Times*'s editorials were slowly defining that alarming new concept, freedom of the press, they were also questioning the traditional nature of government itself.

It was only just in time. The agitation which led to the Great Reform Bill of 1832, the first faltering step on the road to universal suffrage, was beginning to build, led by those commercial classes who bought *The Times* and wanted some political influence to go with their rising economic power. There was nothing inevitable about *The Times*'s part in this; it rested on the reformist convictions of its editor, Thomas Barnes. John Walter may have been clear in his own mind about the independence of his paper; he was less concerned with its politics. Barnes was only given the job in 1818 after the arch-Tory and poet laureate, Robert Southey, had turned it down.[11] But having placed the paper firmly on the side of reform and of the commercial middle classes, Barnes found that those policies were rewarded in increased circulation, which in turn increased the paper's political influence. In 1830, *The Times* was paying for 10,900 stamps a day; in 1831 for 13,827. And increasingly those papers were selling outside London. Speeches for the Reform Bill were made in Birmingham on a Monday evening and printed in *The Times* of Wednesday, which went on sale in Manchester on a Thursday.[12]

Part of Barnes's genius as an editor rested on the network of correspondents and reporters that he established in the major provincial cities, the growing centres of industrial revolution. Barnes understood communications; *The Times* had teams of fast horses based on the turnpikes up and down the country. By 1834, Barnes was able to print in Wednesday's paper a speech made in Edinburgh on a Monday night – 400 miles in less than thirty-six hours. By the end of the decade, *The Times* was on sale in Liverpool, 200 miles away, by mid-afternoon of publication day, and in 1840 *The Times* printed the French king's speech to the National Assembly in Paris, just twenty-two hours after it was delivered. Home news or foreign, Barnes realized that success lay in *The Times* being first to print it, and to present it with conviction and panache. 'The Bill, the whole Bill, and nothing but the Bill',[13] was the paper's motto for reform; *The Times* became almost apocalyptic in its fervour: 'Unless the people, the people everywhere, come forward and petition – aye, thunder for reform, then reform, Minister and people too are lost.' (26 January 1831).

The Times was becoming celebrated not only for the intensity of its convictions, but for the increasingly characteristic language in which they were expressed. Barnes was deliberate about this: 'John Bull dozes composedly over his prejudices, which his conceit calls opinions, and you must fire ten-pounders at his densely compacted intellect before you can make it comprehend your meaning,' he observed.[14] So when George IV died, the paper was blunt: 'There was never an individual less regretted by his fellow creatures than this deceased King.' (16 July 1830). When *The Times* felt that some radicals were going too far, it spoke with the voice that earned it the title of 'The Thunderer': 'The vile propensities professed by those execrable monsters who style themselves Socialists'.[15] Or when the government of the Great Reform Bill seemed less reforming than Barnes had expected: 'Our fear was that old clothes would be turned, old holes darned, rags new turned and all this nicknamed a reformed or even amended Cabinet.' (31 May 1834).

The Times's waxing influence alarmed the politicians – even those reformers whose political careers had rested on the paper's support. Lord Chancellor Brougham, in an incautious note to a friend which was later delivered to *The Times*, declared secret war. £16,500 was raised to revive the rival *Chronicle*, and the Stamp Duties were amended to support the thin *Chronicle* and penalize the increasingly thick *Times*.[16] In 1806, *The Times* had begun including extra four-page sheets for news of important events. By 1825, extra four-page advertising supplements were common. By 1836, they were appearing four days a week, and the paper was becoming profitable enough to ignore government hostility. In 1841, it made a profit of £17,100, and four years later profits had risen to £29,600. It was the overwhelming and dominant press voice. For events of national importance, everyone bought *The Times*; 30,000 copies were sold on the day of Queen Victoria's betrothal. In 1841, *The Times* sold twice as many copies as its rivals, the *Post*, *Herald* and *Chronicle*, put together; by 1850, it sold four times as many. With its own foreign correspondents in New York, Paris, Madrid, Lisbon, Brussels, The Hague, Hamburg and Constantinople; with correspondents of the calibre of Disraeli in London and Thackeray in Paris, its dominance was assured.

Its influence was unique. There had been nothing like this before in the history of the press, or of governments. When Lord Brougham dared to mobilize the Whig government against *The Times*, he paid for it. He had published a book, a translation of Demosthenes; *The Times* tore it to shreds – over six pages. When Sir Robert Peel was planning the revival of the Conservative Party by forcing it to accept the principles of the Reform Bill, he felt it wise to submit his draft proposals to *The Times* for approval.[17] When the first multinational, frontier-crossing financial frauds began, the only institution wealthy enough and determined enough to investigate and expose them was *The Times* – and it was awarded a monument in Lloyd's insurance buildings in gratitude.[18] When governments tried to threaten *The Times*, or to outflank it by supporting rival papers, the rebukes thundered to the attack: 'A committee regularly organised, an inquisition, a secret tribunal used to hold daily sittings in a government office and contrive things for the reward of the servile and the damage of the intractable . . . our power enabled us to defy such arts.' (22 December 1834).

In 1841, Barnes died. Having insisted on anonymity in the paper's columns, the first time his name was published was in the notice of his death. He was replaced by John Thaddeus Delane, whose father was already treasurer. Nepotism flourished under Delane. His deputy editor, Dasent, was also his brother-in-law. He hired his old Oxford tutor, Robert Lowe, to be leader writer, and Lowe felt no qualms writing his anonymous editorials even after he became a member of the government, just as Delane felt it proper to lobby the Prime Minister to promote his younger brother, a clerk in HM Customs.[19] Delane was a man who believed in favours; the reputation of *The Times* rested on getting reliable news first. Most news stemmed from governments, and it was Delane's pride to publish advance texts of the Queen's Speech, or of government treaties, with the connivance of a friendly Minister if possible, and despite Ministers if necessary. Delane's closest political contact was Lord Aberdeen, the Foreign Secretary. And when *The Times* leader of 28 October 1845 said firmly: 'The fact is that British influence was never more cordially admitted, or more established at Constantinople than at the present moment', it took historians of a later generation to discover that *The Times* was simply repeating, word for word, a letter Aberdeen had written to Delane.[20] John Walter had tried in vain to persuade the government to announce its news to all newspapers simultaneously and avoid what he saw as an undignified and potentially damaging race for scoops and favours. His efforts were in vain; news management was and remains too useful a tool of government.

Delane was firm in resisting other pressures. The 1840s saw the great railway boom and the enormous temptation of bountiful railway advertising. The *Morning Herald* supported every railway venture that was announced, ran twenty-page advertising supplements and used the profits to challenge *The Times*'s monopoly of foreign news. More creditably, *The Times* was cautious and, in November 1845 in one of the first carefully researched examples of investigative reporting, announced that the railway companies were now seeking more loan capital than there was money in Britain – that the bubble was about to burst.[21] But again, one of the few railway companies *The Times* did support was the London–Exeter, in which William Delane, the editor's father, was a shareholder. And the collapse of the railway boom led to a financial crisis for *The Times*, although William Delane, the treasurer, and Alsager, the business manager, disguised it by improperly carrying forward contingency funds to show a profit where there was none. Alsager, who had been a brilliant pioneer in financial journalism, later committed suicide, and the elder Delane finally resigned after almost costing his son the editorship.[22] One result of this unsavoury affair was that Delane was never editor in the solitary, all-powerful sense that Thomas Barnes had been. John

Walter III, grandson of the founder, came in as manager. Moreover, Delane did little writing, although he once observed that 'not a column has been published in *The Times* which has not had some of my handwriting in the margin'.[23] The most cost-sensitive part of the paper, the foreign news, was run by Mowbray Morris, whose budget was over £10,000 a year. There were agents at Marseilles, Malta and Alexandria to speed the dispatches from India. The couriers overland through France were paid £1 bonus for each hour saved if they could travel from Marseilles to Paris in less than sixty hours.[24]

Foreign news was seen as a means of lightening the paper, and relieving the dense coverage of parliamentary debates, which normally occupied two of the paper's eight pages. Mowbray Morris once wrote to his Austrian correspondent, a man who always sent long, learned but dull articles on the minutiae of politics and diplomacy, a heartfelt plea for more liveliness: 'Do the Viennese never commit murder or rape?'[25] Ethical standards were higher for foreign correspondents; *The Times*'s man in Greece, O'Brien, was dismissed for accepting a decoration and a holiday cruise in a Greek naval vessel.[26] This served to make *The Times* even more tempting for a certain kind of statesman. The French Emperor, Napoleon III, never tired of trying to bribe and influence *The Times* – which remained one of his sternest critics. Ironically, it was Napoleon's effort to bring pressure on *The Times* through the British government that gave rise to the series of definitive statements on the nature, the prerogatives, the rights and the pomposities of a free press. Perceived as a response to British Ministers who had accused *The Times* of irresponsibly publishing information which statesmanship would keep secret, the paper replied: 'The press lives by disclosures – it is daily and forever appealing to the enlightened force of public opinion, anticipating if possible the march of events, standing upon the breach between the present and the future.' The paper's duty was clear: 'To investigate truth and apply it on fixed principles to the affairs of the world.' Journalism was international: 'We assert that the opinion of this country, against which all else is powerless, claims and demands to be freely exercised not merely on the conduct of our own Government, but on that of every power on the face of the earth . . . We aspire indeed to participate in the government of the world . . . but the power we seek is exercised solely and freely by sway of language and reason over the minds of men.' (6 and 7 February 1852, and 4 March 1854).

The Times was reaching the very pinnacle of this power. Having opposed war with Russia in defence of Turkey, *The Times* changed its mind, advocated war, and the Tsar of Russia duly learned that war was declared from *The Times*'s columns. The war in the Balkans having stalled, *The Times* suggested that it might continue in the Crimea; it did so. The war was appallingly mismanaged by the British government and war ministry. Denounced by *The Times*, the government fell. When one of its executives was sent out with £12,000 raised by its readers to help the wounded, it was *The Times* which provided winter clothing to the shivering troops the government had sent direct from the tropics. On behalf of *The Times*, W.H. Russell invented the art of being a war correspondent and in its pages, Florence Nightingale became the first media superstar. When the Russians finally accepted the peace terms *The Times* had suggested, the new British government learned of this through its pages.

'This tyranny of *The Times* must be cut off,' vowed Lord Johnny Russell, whose government *The Times* had helped to bring down.[27] He had no shortage of allies: the Radical politicians like Cobden and Bright had never forgiven its centrist politics, its sneers at the Radicals, and its metropolitan dominance of the press throughout the country. Reactionaries had never forgiven *The Times* its support for reform. In 1855, in a deliberate step to clip the paper's wings, the Stamp Duties, Cobden's 'taxes on knowledge', were repealed, and the monopoly of *The Times* drew towards its close. The Stamps had helped to subsidize the paper's national distribution, and the high cost of *The Times* had made it harder for any new competitor to grow. Almost overnight, provincial papers like the *Manchester Guardian* and *Liverpool Post* and *The Scotsman* began to flourish. A new tax on the weight of newspapers was designed to penalize the thick *Times*. Circulation fell from 58,000 in 1855 to 50,000 three years later, as a new cheap London press began to give the paper effective competition for the first time in a generation. *The Times* cost 4d against 2d for an eight-page *Standard*, and 1d for a four-page *Telegraph*.

At the same time, costs began to rise drastically. During the Indian Mutiny, *The Times*'s bill for telegraphs alone came to over £5,000. And in 1858, the telegraph cable to America was laid, and the City was clamouring for American commercial news, which cost *The Times* £2 a word. By dropping its price to 3d, by investing in new and efficient printing machines, by increasing its discounts to wholesalers to keep the price down, *The Times* increased its circulation to 70,405 in 1870. But in the same year, the *Daily News* sold 150,000 and the *Daily Telegraph* attained 250,000 at 1d a copy. *The Times* now

dominated by merit and by reputation, not by numbers. An era
had ended.[28]

That change had been heralded in a number of ways. *The Times* of
Barnes's day had been the product of a literary generation, the friends
of Byron and Coleridge, worldly and cultivated men. *The Times* of
young Delane's day had been shaped by the preciously evangelical
attitudes of the Oxford Movement – of which John Walter III had
been a passionate adherent.[29] But just as the 1860s saw a new intensity
in political journalism, with new publications like the *Pall Mall
Gazette*, it saw the emergence of a new intellectual fashion.
Darwinism, agnosticism, a new passion for science; the moment was
signalled when *The Times* commissioned Thomas Huxley to review
Darwin's *Origin of the Species* in 1859. But there was a new scientific
mind at *The Times* itself – Walter's own workshops developed the
Walter printing machine, an automatic-feed rotary press. And having
become an institution, the paper's politics were steadily more sympathetic to conservatism. Liberals had been disheartened by the
paper's support for Austrian absolutism in the revolutions of 1848–9;
during the American Civil War they were to be dismayed by *The
Times*'s support for the South: 'The cause of the South gallantly
defending itself against the cruel and desolating invasion of the North
is the cause of freedom,' ran its leader for 19 January 1863. The
emancipation of the slaves was dismissed as a cheap political device
on Lincoln's part – although Lincoln himself had been keen to flatter
The Times's correspondent Russell, observing that he knew of
nothing so powerful as *The Times* 'unless it be the Mississippi'.[30]

The Times chose to blame its US correspondent, one Mackay, and
sacked him for 'presenting a distorted picture'. But during the
Franco-Prussian war of 1870, the rival *Daily News* regularly beat *The
Times*'s coverage. Forbes, the enterprising reporter for the *News*,
cabled reports of battles in advance, based upon the plans of the
Prussian general staff, and then sent instructions whether or not to
print them when the battle was joined.

By contrast, *The Times* was complacent and running to fat, employ-
ing over 100 journalists to produce twenty-four pages of editorial
copy in a week. There were eighteen reporters in parliament, another
fourteen to cover the police courts, another six leader writers. The
paper was becoming locked into its own ritual and reputation. Delane
spent three hours a day personally reading the 200 or so letters to the
editor, and stayed up to produce the paper all night. Russell once
commented that his editor had 'seen more dawns than any other man

in London'.[31] No longer protected by its privileges of the Stamp Duties, *The Times* was losing its grip. The owners, mainly various branches of the Walter family, voted in 1867 to share out the reserve fund of £190,000 among themselves, rather than invest it in the newspaper. John Walter's decision in 1861 to reduce the price to 3d, to compete against the new cheap press, had already reduced revenue by £70,000 a year, and only £15,000 could be clawed back from higher advertising charges. The easy pickings of the previous generation, when every thousand readers meant a steady profit of a thousand pounds a year, were still good for a profit of £90,000 in 1870. But it was ending. In 1877, when Delane retired, he was replaced by Thomas Chenery, a pillar of his serious and scientifically minded generation; he had learned several Eastern languages while correspondent for *The Times* in Turkey, and was Professor of Arabic at Oxford while its editor. He filled its pages with learned articles on Persian literature, philology, the Hittites and Arabic antiquities, and the circulation declined to below 50,000 in the seven years of his editorship.[32]

Under George Buckle, his successor, *The Times* was almost to sink. Buckle came in as a new broom, introducing separate articles on politics, rather than incorporating them in the editorials, and moving the paper further into the Conservative camp. Buckle wanted scoops, to make his own name and to show that *The Times* still led the press even as W.T. Stead was transforming the *Pall Mall Gazette* and the new mass journalism of *Titbits* and the *Daily Mail* began to flourish. Buckle's policy was not without success; the editor himself secured the exclusive news that Lord Randolph Churchill was resigning from the government; and one of the three Englishmen besieged in Khartoum with General Gordon was *The Times*'s correspondent. But the hunger for scoops led to disaster when, as part of its campaign against Home Rule for Ireland, the paper printed letters which purported to implicate the Irish leader Parnell in political assassinations. For the first time, *The Times* ran a headline bigger than a single column. Buckle paid £1,780 for the letters, which turned out to be forgeries. Only perfunctory checks were made, from inadequate sources. Buckle was almost criminally negligent. The costs of the libel case, of the special commission which the government established to investigate the affair, and of printing the transcripts of the commission's inquiry in full, amounted to some £200,000. *The Times* was crippled, and discredited, for years to come.[33] And the Parnell affair exacerbated the financial problems of a paper that had become hide-bound, antiquated and set in its ways. As late as 1908, there was no typewriter in the editorial department, and no linotype machines in the printing works. There were no sub-editors or layout men, no one to design the pages but the printers who simply laid out the stories, column after dense column. The Walter family's organization divided paper from print works, so the executives of *The Times* were simply not empowered to demand improvements from the printers. The paper's design had not changed for a century. The inner sheets contained the leaders and the late news, laid out in the order in which the printer had set them. The outer sheets were printed earlier and contained the advertisements and articles which had been held over, some of them a week and more old. That hallmark of the paper until 1966, advertisements on the front page, had begun (and lasted) as a printers' convenience.

The Times was also taking itself too seriously. When its legendary diplomatic correspondent, Henri de Blowitz, secured Queen Victoria's telegram to the Paris Embassy deploring the verdict in the Dreyfus case, the paper refused to risk its standing at Court by printing it.[34] When Wallace, the man brought in to streamline foreign coverage, wanted to hire a colonial correspondent, he asked the senior civil servant at the Colonial Office to recommend someone. Flora Shaw was accordingly hired, who was to conspire with Cecil Rhodes in the planning of the Jameson Raid and the abortive Uitlander rebellion against the Boer Republics. *The Times* was not alone in seeing its function as ambassadorial; when Wallace sailed to the USA to cover the Russo-Japanese peace negotiations, King Edward VII gave him a series of formal messages to be passed on to President Roosevelt. Colonel Repington, the military correspondent, initiated the military discussions with the French General Staff that slowly transformed the *entente cordiale* into a military alliance. Valentine Chirol, the foreign editor, saw himself as the guarantor of European peace, and regularly censored and altered his correspondents' articles. Bourchier in the Balkans and the famous Morrison in Peking regularly and vainly complained. The German Kaiser firmly believed that his most dangerous enemy in Britain was Moberley Bell, the manager of *The Times*.

Bell had his own problems. By 1905, circulation had sunk to 37,400, and with 55% of revenues already coming from advertising, Bell was under increasing pressure from the shareholders to increase their dividends.[37] Since the newspaper could not generate profits, Bell turned to a dubious publishing alliance with two American businessmen. They reprinted the old *Encyclopaedia Britannica* under *The Times*'s prestigious imprint and launched book clubs and book discounts (which led to all British publishers withdrawing their advertising in fury). This venture made £151,000, but it was not enough. The owner of the *Standard*, Sir Arthur Pearson, and Baron Rothschild, who wanted to fire Bell and make *The Times* pro-German, formed a consortium to bid for *The Times*. Buckle, the editor, first learned of this from the *Observer*'s columns, but Bell had already launched his own secret negotiations with a man he would only name as Mr X. Bell wrote to Mr X promising 'to carry out your absolute instructions'. Mr X promised (verbally) to avoid sensationalism, to keep the paper at twenty-four pages and 3d a copy, and to modernize the print machinery.[38]

Mr X was Alfred Harmsworth, the prince of sensationalism, the man who had taken the *Daily Mail* to a circulation of 800,000 and profits of £140,000. He paid £320,000 for *The Times* (although in 1900 he had offered £1,000,000). '*The Times* is in my life what a yacht or a racing stable is to others – it is merely a hobby,' Harmsworth commented.[39] In fact, he brought a professional business and news sense to the moribund paper. Typewriters, Monotype composers, and the latest Goss presses were installed, a fleet of canvassers hired to sell advertising, and the design and layout of the paper was taken out of the hands of the printers and transformed. Special issues began to appear, like the seventy-two-page Empire Day supplement, thirty-six of whose pages were lucrative display advertising. Within three years, *The Times* was selling an extra 10,000 copies a day – not enough for the new proprietor. Buckle, the editor, and Chirol, the foreign editor, were fired, and the price was cut to 2d in 1913, a price that included a free literary and an engineering supplement each week, and a free education supplement each month. In March of 1914, he cut the price to a penny, sold 150,000 copies on the first day, and 140,000 copies thereafter. *The Times*'s presses could not handle the demand, and extra copies had to be printed by Harmsworth's *Daily Mail*.

Harmsworth, elevated to the peerage as Lord Northcliffe, exacted a stiff price for restoring the paper's fortunes. The leader writers were peremptorily told not to argue in favour of the Treaty of London, and editorials on the Marconi scandals were banned and then re-written by Northcliffe himself. He felt endlessly frustrated by the leader writers, the custodians of the paper's tradition, whom he called 'The Black Friars' and accused of running *The Times* 'for their own comfort or dignity, or knighthoods, or War Office blackmail or Canonries'.[40] Northcliffe wanted shorter articles with more punch and less elegance, more controversy and less gravity. His requests could be graciously put: 'Humbly beg for a light leading article daily till I return – Chief' ran one typical telegram.[41] But they were orders just the same. A books page was introduced, and something very close to a gossip column masqueraded under the title of second Court page. The Black Friars remained as opinionated as ever on the great themes of the day. 'The exercise of the vote by women would be a danger to the country,' (18 January 1913) was their reaction to the suffragette movement.

The First World War saw *The Times* at its worst. It co-operated almost eagerly with the new and clumsy censorship arrangement. Its readers were never told of the shattering French losses of 250,000 men in the Battle of the Frontiers, and six months were to pass before it was deemed safe to tell them of the catastrophic defeat of the Russian allies at Tanneberg. The official censor, F.E. Smith, approved (and also wrote) a very much franker account of the defeat of Mons than *The Times* had intended to print. The foreign editor, Wickham Steed, was informed by letter from his Russian correspondent of the manner of Rasputin's death, of the Russian food crisis, of the lack of support for the Tsar and the desperate vulnerability of his regime. The letters were not printed, and no hint of their implications reached *The Times*'s readers. Lord Lansdowne's celebrated letter calling for a negotiated peace in 1917 was not printed by *The Times* (the *Telegraph* later obliged), and the paper was deployed as one more weapon in Northcliffe's vendetta against the Asquith government. Dawson's leader of 1 December 1916, 'Weak Methods and Weak Men', signalled Asquith's fall – and inspired the *Daily News* to accuse Northcliffe of attempting a dictatorship. In January 1918, when Northcliffe had himself appointed Director of Propaganda, the charge was very nearly true. Northcliffe knew well why he had been given the job; as he wrote to his editor: 'I do not wonder that *The Times* is regarded as a government organ . . . it has been very non-critical for months.'[42] But the paper had inflicted real damage elsewhere. Its attacks throughout 1917 on the fledgling provisional government of Kerensky, who had replaced the Tsar after the February Revolution, were seen by the liberal *Manchester Guardian* as a major cause of Kerensky's downfall. Certainly he never got the kind of British support that he had relied upon. Once the Bolsheviks took power, *The Times* called for British troops to be sent against

these 'adventurers of German-Jewish blood in German pay whose
sole object is to incite the ignorant masses in the interests of their own
employers in Berlin' (23 November 1917).[43]

By late 1918, Dawson was writing to Lloyd George, warning the
Prime Minister of Northcliffe's 'restless vanity, almost a disease',
which helped to justify Lloyd George's resistance to Northcliffe's
demand that he be appointed British plenipotentiary for the peace,
and that Lloyd George submit his proposed Cabinet appointments for
Northcliffe's approval.[44] Dawson himself was forced to resign the
following year for failing to co-ordinate editorial policy with the *Daily
Mail*, and he was replaced by Wickham Steed.

Steed ran immediately into a financial crisis. War inflation meant
that a week's supply of paper and ink cost £5,663 more than in 1914,
that home editorial costs had increased by £857 a week, and foreign
costs by £847. The post-war recession meant that circulation fell from
126,296 in December 1919 to 110,818 in March 1922. In the same
period, advertising revenue fell by 9%. The crisis led the last of the
Walter family to sell his last 215,000 shares to Northcliffe, severing a
family connection that had lasted 140 years. Part of the circulation fall
was explained by *The Times*'s 'moderate' stand on the Irish question,
advocating that the hunger strikers be freed as an act of grace, and
that Ireland be given effective independence with dominion status.
Irish Protestant hostility led to the editor and Northcliffe being given
armed police guards. Northcliffe's characteristic response, even as
the final phase of his mental illness was upon him, was to cut the price
to 1½d in March 1922, half of the 3d to which it had crept during the
war. In the long term, it worked, circulation leaping to 187,323 in
June. But the paper was losing £5,000 a week. Lord Rothermere was
trying to buy it and install Lloyd George as editor. Northcliffe's final
illness, marked by his being banned from *The Times* building by his
own staff, ended in death on 14 August 1922. He left a chaotic will,
and various consortia competed to buy *The Times*. John Walter, still
company chairman although he had sold his shares, mobilized the
American fortune of John J. Astor, and secured the key shares for
£1,580,000.[45]

The first action of the new owners was to dismiss Wickham Steed,
and bring back Geoffrey Dawson, on his own very strict and written
terms of editorial independence.[46] Astor and Walter saw themselves
as buying an international institution, rather than just a newspaper,
and they established a group of trustees who embodied the British
Establishment: the Lord Chief Justice; the Governor of the Bank of

England; the Master of All Souls College; the President of the Royal Society; and the President of the Institute of Chartered Accountants. Their duty was 'to ensure that the ownership of *The Times* shall never be regarded as a mere matter of commerce, or fall into unworthy hands'.[47]

The cover price was raised to 2d, and Northcliffe's free insurance scheme for subscribers was dropped, saving £500 a week. Dawson resolved to reverse Northcliffe's lightening of the paper, and wrote that he intended 'a year or two of steadiness, even stodginess'. Dawson identified the paper very firmly with the Conservative Party, bitterly opposing the attempt of the first Labour Government of 1923–4 to re-open diplomatic relations with the infant Soviet Union. During the general strike of 1926, *The Times* was the only newspaper to maintain publication, in the form of amateurish and attenuated broadsheets brought out by a volunteer squad of strike-breakers. The political crisis of 1931 was marked by a whiff of class war in the editorials: 'This general election is being fought primarily to secure a definite and unqualified result – namely, the resounding repudiation of Socialist irresponsibility.'[48] Dawson was deeply, almost besottedly involved in domestic and dominion politics. This would have been less significant had he not insisted on being his own foreign editor. His predecessor, Wickham Steed, had been a good European, fluent in several languages, a familiar in most European cities and, as a result, he edited a newspaper with an international perspective. Dawson was much more the little Englander, wary of foreign entanglements, and deeply suspicious of the Versailles peace treaty, which rested on an Anglo-French condominium to maintain some kind of equilibrium in Europe. It was this suspicion, and his fear of England taking on responsibilities that the Empire might refuse to accept, that led to Dawson's desperately controversial support for the policies of appeasement. He was also deeply embarrassed by the spate of books by American historians citing the editorials of *The Times* up to 1914 as significant causes of the Great War. Dawson believed in the British Empire, and bitterly attacked General Dyer's massacre of Indian demonstrators at Amritsar on the grounds that his troops had 'monstrously perverted a great system of government'. Gandhi, by contrast, was dismissed as 'a mischievous crank with a talent for fomenting disorder'.[49]

The attacks upon Dawson's appeasement of Hitler have focused too often upon one letter to his Berlin correspondent, commenting on an anti-*Times* campaign in the Nazi press: 'I did my utmost, night after night, to keep out of the paper anything that might hurt their susceptibilities.'[50] Dawson's excellent dominion contacts persuaded him that the loyal colonials of the trenches would not readily shed their blood in another European quarrel unless vital British interests were at stake. Certainly Dawson's editorials show a *Times* rather more concerned to look on the bright side of diplomacy, to take the long view. Austria, Dawson opined, 'was destined sooner or later to find herself in close association with the German Reich . . . there would have been no British protest if the process of attraction had developed naturally through growing confidence and mutual good-will'.[51] In June of 1938, three months before the Munich agreement, an editorial raised the possibility that the Czechs might cede the Sudetenland to Germany. Even John Walter protested that Dawson was 'advocating the cause of the wolf against the lamb. No wonder there is rejoicing in Berlin.'[52] On the eve of the Munich meetings, the Foreign Office had to distance themselves publicly from a Dawson editorial which again rehearsed the advantages of dismembering Czechoslovakia. Even when Hitler had absorbed the Austrians and Sudeten Czechs, *The Times* pleaded: 'Must there be resistance to demands which ought to have been granted when Germany was weak, merely because she is no longer weak?' (7 November 1938). *The Times* spoke from the best of motives: Germany had been un-justly treated by the Versailles peace treaty, and her grievances should be resolved. The sentiment would have been the more admirable had not other nations been in Germany's way, and when Dawson spoke of meeting German grievances what he really meant was abandoning Austrians, Czechs and Poles to Nazism.

What was most remarkable about Dawson and appeasement was the way he resolutely insisted that *The Times* nail its colours to the mast. On most issues of controversy, an editorial in *The Times* would even-handedly present both (or all) points of view in a particular argument, without feeling bound to any one of them. The politics of the Great Depression provide an admirable example. While backing the orthodox deflationary economic policies of the National Government, in March 1934 the paper published a series of deeply sympathetic articles on the plight of County Durham, savaged by unemployment and poverty that those government policies had aggravated. Similarly, during the Abdication crisis, *The Times* loyally refrained from informing its readers of the affair (along with the rest of the British press) and did not take a firm editorial view until Baldwin and his Cabinet had already decided the crown's fate. King

Edward pressed Baldwin very hard to discover what *The Times* would say but, in the event, when it finally broke silence it said very little. Mention was made of 'a marriage incompatible with the throne'. Mrs Simpson was not named, and the self-censorship of the national press was ascribed to 'a common self-restraint'. In domestic as in foreign affairs, Dawson presided over a newspaper that was uncompromisingly, and without any apology, elitist in the news it chose to publish and that which it chose to suppress. And when its influence could be deployed, *The Times* imposed its values on the rest of the press. The editors of the *Yorkshire Post* and of the *Nineteenth Century* were personally dissuaded from writing of the King's marriage plans by Geoffrey Dawson.[53] However controversial, the prestige of *The Times* stood high, enhanced further by the invention and adoption of the loveliest and most dignified of typefaces, Times Roman.[54]

As Europe moved towards war, *The Times*'s military correspondent was insisting that Britain must under no circumstances repeat the horrors of the First War. There must be no large British Army sent to fight in Europe; there should be no conscription.[55] The Air Force and the Navy would suffice. When war came, *The Times* itself became a victim, with two floors blown out by a bomb during the London blitz. The presses were stopped for only eighteen minutes. Restrictions on newsprint did more damage than the enemy, with the paper reduced to four pages, and appeals to readers to share, and then send on their used copies to RAF welfare officers who would transmit them to troops in the Far East.[56] The paper even became junior partner in its own premises, which were used to publish the US soldiers' paper, the *Stars and Stripes*, which reached a circulation of 700,000 by 1944.

On 1 October 1941, Dawson retired, still under the shadow of the appeasement he had advocated, and was replaced by Barrington-Ward, a devoutly Christian Tory who flung himself and his paper wholeheartedly behind the war effort, and the Socialist government which followed it. Partly because of the widespread feeling that the war had been fought to build a better, fairer Britain, and partly because *The Times* believed in supporting the government of the day, Barrington-Ward supported the Welfare State with such zeal that *The Times* became known in some circles as 'The Threepenny *Daily Worker*'. Much as Thomas Barnes in the late 1830s had helped to reconcile the Tories to parliamentary reform and Catholic emancipation, so Barrington-Ward felt it his duty to convince the thinking Conservatives of his day to accept the fundamental social reforms of the Labour government. When that government's policy of austerity tightened the rationing of newsprint and dashed the editor's hopes of returning to a ten-page paper, he decided to reduce the number of copies printed, rather than the number of pages.[57]

In 1952, with the Conservatives in office again, a new reign and the economic growth of the 1950s beginning, *The Times* had a new editor, Sir William Haley. A self-made man who became a classic figure of an outdated Establishment, he had worked for the *Manchester Guardian*, for *The Times*, had re-organized Reuters news agency and been director general of the BBC from 1944. The sense of promise that marked the early 1950s was symbolized by the Coronation and, with marvellous timing, Haley's support for the expedition to climb Mount Everest, and the presence of *Times* journalist James Morris on the expedition, led to the Coronation scoop of Everest's conquest. But it was no longer *The Times* it had been. In 1950, the paper regularly ran fifty-six columns of news a day – barely half what it had published in 1930. Even as late as 1960, it was still a thin paper, with an average eighty-four editorial columns a day – against the 135 columns of 1970.[58] The paper was solvent, with its cover price covering half of its costs, but wage inflation and commercial television's inroads into advertising budgets meant profits that were too small to re-invest in new plant, or more news coverage. In 1957, profits were barely £42,000, and in the good year of 1958, but £114,000. With circulation almost static at 240,000, mainly among the upper-middle classes, Haley reversed the centre-left drive of Barrington-Ward and took the paper back to a safe and increasingly dull conservatism. The doomed decision to invade Suez in 1956, which split the country and high-lighted Britain's steadily diminishing role in the world, found *The Times* uncertain but nostalgic of imperial days. The *Observer* and the *Manchester Guardian* were clear, forthright and courageous in their opposition to the whole disastrous venture, and suffered an advertising boycott as a result. If *The Times* had retained any pretension of speaking for the nation or for international justice, it temporized them away over Suez. And when the paper did attempt to don once more the mantle of 'The Thunderer', it was in the tragi-comic and salacious context of the Profumo scandal, when a Minister of War lied to his Cabinet and to Parliament about his dalliance with a whore. Out of date, out of step, and in the querulous tones of a faded morality, *The Times* editorial proclaimed: 'It *is* a moral issue'. Few noticed, and fewer still paid much attention.[59]

While remaining a national institution, *The Times* had gained the image of a rather eccentric and aged aunt, celebrated for its letters on hearing the year's first cuckoo, and its unique personal column which ran astonishing notices, such as 'Fire eaters, sword swallowers, preferably with ecclesiastical experience, required May–June'. The advertisement was for actors in a performance in the thirteenth-century 'Play of Daniel'. Some £200,000 was spent on a national campaign which advertised *The Times* as the paper for 'The Top People'; this did little for a circulation which remained obstinately at about 250,000, but explained much of how the paper perceived its function. In 1963, it proudly announced that 70% of the names in *Who's Who* read *The Times*, but the financial position was becoming difficult.[60] In 1960, profits were almost £300,000, a healthy 10.7% of revenues. Five years later, profits were below £200,000 – a mere 3.4% of income. The market share of advertising had fallen and circulation was down to 228,000. The £2 million spent on a new building at Blackfriars was an expensive investment.[61]

In 1965, Gavin Astor had his first negotiations with the Canadian press magnate Roy Thomson. 1966 was looking to be a disastrous year, in which the paper was to lose £327,000. It saw an almost desperate attempt to rejuvenate the paper's image, with news replacing the traditional advertising on the front page – and a lead story which boldly, but falsely, predicted that NATO HQ was being shifted to Britain. In September, amid considerable national debate, *The Times* was sold to the quickly ennobled Lord Thomson, a man whose interest in newspapers was said to be centred upon their advertising profits. He promised to keep the paper running for twenty-one years, to maintain its editorial independence and to keep Astor as President and Haley as chairman of the board. The alternatives were a merger with the equally straitened *Guardian*, a syndicate of the Berry family (who owned the profitable *Daily Telegraph*) and a South Wales publisher, Claud Morris, and even possible immolation as a national trust, on the lines of, and perhaps run with, the BBC.[62]

The Thomson family were to spend some £70 million in the next fifteen years on their new investment. From 1967, money was poured into *The Times*. A new advertising campaign cost £300,000; the addition of four extra pages cost £600,000 a year; editorial staff were increased by 40%, five new overseas posts were established and, by June of 1967, circulation was up to 340,000. Advertising volume had risen by 9.2% (while that of the *Guardian* and *Telegraph* had fallen sharply), there was a new editor in William Rees-Mogg, a new Business section and lively and popular women's page. Every kind of

advertising was sought. The number of special advertising supplements leapt fourfold from twenty-six in 1965 to 106 in 1968, earning
£750,000. By the end of that year, with circulation above 400,000,
Lord Thomson had spent £4 million on his investment – or about £30
to attract each new reader. He gave them value for money – thirty-one
pages a day on average in 1968, against twenty-two only two years
earlier.[63] But the paper was losing authority. It was not just that some
days saw three pages on male fashions and only three for news; it was
the alarmist way it predicted that demonstrators against the Vietnam
war in 1968 were planning to storm Scotland Yard, Whitehall and the
BBC. It was the folly of hiring Cecil King, the sacked chairman of the
Daily Mirror, who tried to recruit Lord Mountbatten to lead a vague
coup against the government of Harold Wilson. Having hired King,
The Times upheld his bizarre ideas of the need for a government of
national unity, of the nation being engulfed by crisis. It was a monumental misjudgement of the politics and mood of the day.[64] Even
where the new stridency of *The Times* succeeded, it was in most
un-Timesian ways, sending its reporters equipped with secret micro-
phones to expose a corrupt policeman. Nor was it much good. It still
cost a total of 30d to produce each copy of a paper (7d each on newsgathering and newsprint, and 16d to administer, print and distribute
it) which sold for only 8d. The *Telegraph*, with a circulation of 1.3
million, three times that of *The Times*, had more than twice as many
classified ads. With a staff swollen to 2,400, and an expensive 140
editorial columns a day being published, Lord Thomson's expensive
gamble was failing. He decided to draw in his horns, take the paper
into his family company to ease the burden on his shareholders,
sharply to increase the cover price, and lose readers.

There is an apocryphal story told in Fleet Street about the way
Rees-Mogg conveyed the news to his staff. 'You will have to be very
much more boring,' he is supposed to have said, 'even more boring
than usual.' *The Times* decided to lose readers as fast as it had won
them. The new readership were not the affluent, A–B social groups
that advertisers wanted to reach. As the paper's own advertisements
to the marketing trade put it: 'trimming the wastage off our profile to
give you one certain medium for reaching the true top end of the
market'.[65] The paper was given a face-lift, going back to its classical,
modular traditions. By 1973, with circulation down to 353,000, the
paper was almost breaking even.

It was a brief respite. As the 1970s wore on into a general recession,
the financial straits of *The Times* became a news story, at times

shouldering aside from other front pages the events of international significance which *The Times* had once dominantly covered. It could still rise to an occasion, getting every head of government in the EEC to write an article for its issue to commemorate Britain's entry into Europe in 1973. *The Times* itself joined in a Euro-consortium with *Le Monde*, *Stampa* and *Die Welt* to publish a regular supplement. For the royal wedding in 1981, the whole front page could be devoted to a colour picture.

Much of its coverage, from Northern Ireland in the mid '70s to the Middle East and Africa in the late '70s, was first rate. Its reputation for amiable eccentricity was maintained by a judicious use of columnists; Philip Howard on the oddities of language, Michael Leapman on the oddities of New York, Bernard Levin on the oddities of himself. Its crosswords remained excellent, its law reports made it essential reading for the legal profession, and the Court Circular continued to announce the social engagements of the Royal Family. But its editorial judgements were erratic. During the Watergate affair, it supported President Nixon almost to the end. Rees-Mogg's growing conviction that international disaster could be averted only by a restoration of the gold standard made for some curious economic stands. Circulation ebbed steadily away, down to 335,000 in the half-year to March 1975, and to 310,000 on the eve of its closure in 1978.[66]

There had been other martyrs to the cruel economics and cruder labour relations of Fleet Street. The *News Chronicle*, the *Daily Sketch* and the old *Sun* had all died. The *Guardian* had depended for a generation upon the profits of its partner, the *Manchester Evening News*. The *Evening Standard* and *Evening News* spent the late 1970s in a death struggle until, locked into each other's arms, they plunged over the Reichenbach Falls of Fleet Street together . . . Only one returned. But *The Times* was suffering less from competition than from internal warfare. In the last six weeks of 1975, through a combination of high newsprint costs, inflation and industrial stoppages, it lost £500,000. In the course of 1978, industrial action interrupted printing seventy-four times, with a loss of 4 million copies – over two weeks of production. In the first ten years of owning *The Times*, the Thomson family lost £20 million. The unions grumbled that this meant little, beside the company's North Sea holdings in the Piper and Claymore oilfields – the Thomson share of production was £150 million in 1978. Losing copies, readers and morale, *The Times* management gambled on the savings that investment in new technology and computer-setting might bring, and marched with their eyes open into battle with the unions.[67]

Faced with the extinction of their ancient craft and modern privileges, the National Graphical Association insisted that their members should control the computers. Matters were made worse by the interlinking difficulties of *The Times* and the *Sunday Times*, whose Saturday-night print-run of 1.5 million copies of a seventy-two-page paper was the longest in the world. Working conditions in the machine-room were like something from a medieval engraving of Hell. At 3.55a.m. on the last day of November 1978, the presses stopped and the management fulfilled its threat. The editor began his leader: 'It is the first duty of an editor of *The Times* not to be the last one.' But with this precise prospect staring him in the face, Rees-Mogg condemned the unions for the 'slide into anarchy' which had engulfed the 4,300 employees of Times Newspapers. Nonetheless, thanks to its separate supplements and the *Sunday Times*, the company made a small profit in those first ten months of 1978.[68]

The closure lasted almost exactly a year. On 13 November 1979, *The Times* returned. The stoppage had cost Thomson between £35 million and £46 million, depending on the accounting. The unions agreed to a steady reduction of manning levels by a total of 16%, and the NGA kept their grip on typesetting. There were vague agreements on the introduction of new technology, which were still not ratified when the company announced in October 1980 that it would get rid of the papers at any cost, either by sale or closure. The circulation of *The Times* remained obstinately depressed, while sales of the rival *Guardian* and *Telegraph* bounded upwards, the *Guardian* to 400,000 and beyond. With a strike of its own journalists in August, after management rejected an arbitrated pay agreement, the humiliation of *The Times* was almost complete.

Among the interested buyers were Associated Newspapers, whose losses on the *Evening News* and *Daily Mail* were made up by oil and property interests; Lonrho, the African mining company which Tiny Rowland had built into a multinational; a consortium of *Times* journalists with a cautious interest by the *Guardian*; and Rupert Murdoch, whose use of bare-bosomed models and bare-faced sensation at the lowest end of Fleet Street had brought wealth to the *Sun* and *News of the World*. Accumulating press and TV and airline companies in Australia, and the *Daily News* and *Village Voice* in New York, Murdoch was a publisher of genius and few scruples. In February 1981, he bought *The Times* for a song. For a £12 million cheque, he secured freehold property worth £8 million, with assets and machinery valued at £17.9 million. As he informed the unions when briskly re-negotiating on jobs and the use of new technology, he could close down and sell up . . . and still be in profit. *The Times* published a barbed farewell to the Thomson family, which suggested that 'the most successful aspect of the Thomson association with Times Newspapers after fourteen years of disappointment and disruption was the way they ended it'.[69]

For the second time, the sensational end of Fleet Street had come to the rescue of *The Times*. The wary mistrust which greeted Murdoch was similar to the fears which Northcliffe had inspired. Murdoch gave guarantees of editorial independence, to be backed up by a board of independent directors which included Lord Astor of the former owning family, Lord Drogheda of the *Financial Times*, Sir Denis Hamilton of Times Newspapers, and Sir Edward Pickering, a former editor of the *Daily Express* and chairman of IPC. They were the Establishment of Fleet Street, but there was no more talk of that earlier and grander band of trustees, including the Lord Chief Justice and the Governor of the Bank of England. The empire of *The Times* had shrunk. It was another London quality paper – and not necessarily the most respected. It had the problem of sustaining an international news service and national distribution on a very limited amount of national advertising. The opportunity of saving on the mounting costs of foreign reporting, co-ordinating his various papers' international coverage through a common pool of journalists, suggested that a multinational publisher such as Murdoch could ease the burden on *The Times*.

Rees-Mogg resigned, and Murdoch appointed Harold Evans as editor. His success with the *Northern Echo* and the *Sunday Times* and his lucid books on newspaper design had made Evans the most acclaimed British editor of his time. He hired much new blood, brought news to the back page, bought middle-brow books to serialize daily, and a crisper and sharper newspaper quickly emerged. But the savage equation which had haunted *The Times* throughout the century was still unchanged: increase the circulation, and the result was a diluted readership which advertisers had refused to pay to reach; keep the circulation limited to the traditional upper-middle and professional classes, and insufficient revenue could be generated to support the expense of producing an international and authoritative newspaper in a medium-sized, and not very rich, European country. It was this fundamental dilemma which led Murdoch in

March 1982 to dismiss Harold Evans, much to the relief of *The Times*'s more traditional journalists. Its very survival, as the 200th birthday approached, was something of a triumph against the odds. In its day, *The Times* had been the model, the trail-blazer for the press throughout the world. More than most newspapers, *The Times* had mirrored the country which had bred it. As Britain prospered, so did *The Times*. As the nation subsided, the newspaper followed. In the respective rises of the *New York Times* and *Washington Post* we can see a similar process, editorial success as the handmaiden of raw political power. But then, had it not been for the example of *The Times*, raw political power might never have been tamed at all.

Notes

1. *History of The Times (HOTT)*, vol. 1.
2. *ibid.*, p. 40.
3. *ibid.*, pp. 58–9
4. *The Times*, 21.ii.1789.
5. *HOTT, op. cit.*, p. 121.
6. *ibid.*, p. 108. See also 'The Times', Report of the Monopolies Commission.
7. *HOTT, op. cit.*, p. 109.
8. *ibid.*, pp. 135ff.
9. *ibid.*, p. 234.
10. *Edinburgh Review*, May 1823.
11. *HOTT, op. cit.*, p. 216.
12. *The Times*, 17.ix.1834. Also *HOTT, op. cit.*, p. 430.
13. *ibid.*, p. 274.
14. *ibid.*, p. 211.
15. *ibid.*, p. 410. Ironically, Barnes had been a great friend of the socialist idealist, Robert Owen.
16. *ibid.*, p. 305.
17. *ibid.*, pp. 382–3.
18. The celebrated Bogle affair led to a libel suit being brought against *The Times*, which paid in the end a derisory one farthing in damages. The case is reported throughout the May issues of *The Times* for 1840.
19. *The Rise and Fall of the British Political Press*, S. Koss, p. 63.
20. *The Times*, 28.x.1845.
21. *The Times*, 4.xii.1845.
22. *HOTT*, vol. 2 (London, 1938) pp. 23–5.
23. *ibid.*, p. 60.
24. *ibid.*, p. 73.
25. *ibid.*, p. 135.
26. *ibid.*

27. For the flavour of contemporary venom against *The Times*, see 'Revelations from Printing House Square', W. Hargreaves (London, 1855), for a diatribe against the patronage bestowed on the paper's managers. Delane had an annual sinecure of £800 as treasurer of Kent County Council, and Knox £1,200 as a police magistrate.

28. 'Editorial Sovereignty', by Jeremy Tunstall, in Working Paper 3, part c, section 2. Royal Commission on the Press.

29. *HOTT, ibid.*, p. 310.

30. *ibid.*, pp. 363–4.

31. Tunstall, *op. cit.*, p. 268.

32. *HOTT, op cit.*, pp. 520ff.

33. *HOTT*, vol. 3 (London, 1947), p. 89. As late as 1947, the explanation in *The Times*'s own official history was a shameful travesty of the truth, which a future volume had to correct.

34. *ibid.*, p. 134.

35. *ibid.*, p. 424.

36. *ibid.*, pp. 460–61, 472.

37. *ibid.*, p. 447.

38. *ibid.*, p. 560.

39. *ibid.*, p. 640.

40. *ibid.*, p. 763.

41. *HOTT, The 150th anniversary and beyond.* Part One. Plate facing p. 142.

42. *ibid.*, p. 354.

43. 'The Times and the Bolshevik Revolution', *Journalism Quarterly*, vol. 56, 1979, pp. 69ff.

44. *HOTT, op. cit.*, p. 448.

45. *ibid.*, pp. 691–790.

46. Tunstall, *op. cit.*

47. *Anatomy of Britain*, A. Sampson, p. 152.

48. *The Times*, 9.ix.1931.

49. *The Times*, 8.vii.1920 and 22.xi.1921 respectively.

50. *HOTT, The 150th anniversary and beyond.* Part Two. p. 907.

51. *The Times*, 9.iii.1938.

52. *HOTT, op. cit.*, p. 921.

53. *ibid.*, p. 1033.

54. *The Times*, 3.x.1932.

55. *The Times*, 7,8.ii.1939.

56. *The Times*, 12.xii.1945.

57. *The Times*, 15.vii.1947. See also *In the chair: Barrington-Ward of The Times.* Donald McLachlan.

58. *The Times*, 9.x.1970, report of a spech by Denis Hamilton.

59. *The Times*, 11.vi.1963.

60. Sampson., *op. cit.*, p. 152.

61. *Observer*, 1.i.1967.

62. Monopolies Commission Report, *op. cit.* See also *The Times*, 1.ix.1965.

63. *Commonwealth Press Union Quarterly*, December 1969. Article by Lord Thomson.

64. As Rees-Mogg later admitted, author's interview.

65. *Campaign*, week of 21 September 1970.
66. ABC. Audit Bureau for Circulation.
67. See *Stop Press*. Eric Jacobs.
68. *The Times*, 30.xi.1978.
69. *The Times*, 13.ii.1981.

AN INTRODUCTORY NOTE: EDITORIALS

The editorial is the formal, corporate voice of a newspaper. Usually written by the editor or by a specialist team, it is distinguished from the main body of the newspaper in such a way that the layout, or the positioning, suggests that this is official opinion, rather than just plain news. Editorials have a curious and almost accidental history. For the first century of its life, the editorials of *The Times* were not solemn statements of the editor's opinion. They were the paper's political columns, in which *The Times*'s comments were interspersed with reports of Cabinet shuffles, rumours of elections, and so on. The bulk of *The Times*'s political reporting was provided by the verbatim accounts of parliamentary debates, and so the leader columns (so named because they led the paper's editorial contents) had to do the job of commentary, of placing in context, and analysis – the kind of function that Features desks and the diary column and the parliamentary sketch provide in our own day.

The editorial as we know it today is very much an Anglo-Saxon phenomenon. Indeed, all the English-language newspapers in this book, and Japan's *Asahi Shimbun*, run a daily editorial of a conventional kind. Simply by doing so, they reinforce one of the traditional myths about journalism – that facts are different from opinions, and a paper should show very clearly where it draws the line. This is a specious distinction. Just as much bias can go into which facts a newspaper chooses to publish, or to emphasize, or the words it chooses to clothe those 'facts' in, as in the most partisan statement of the editor's opinion. European newspapers have a rather different tradition. They do publish formal editorial columns, such as *Le*

Monde's *Bulletin de l'Etranger*, which is used for formal greetings to visiting heads of state, as well as for the paper's dignified commentary of world events. But signed articles by the editor (sometimes using a pen-name, as Beuve-Méry signed himself 'Sirius') or by senior journalists are also used as formal vehicles of the paper's opinion. In a similar way, *Al-Ahram* has a formal editorial column, but during Mohammed Heykal's editorship, the real voice of the paper was to be found in Heykal's personal column, 'Frankly Speaking' each Friday.

Corriere follows a similar pattern to *Le Monde*, and *Die Welt* has effectively abolished the formal editorial in favour of several short, signed notes from senior editors. *Pravda* publishes editorial statements, but also prints long verbatim tracts from the Politburo, or other sectors of the Party hierarchy which are presented more as editorials than as news stories.

This variety of editorial styles means that some of the quotations which follow do not come from those parts of a newspaper which an Anglo-Saxon reader would usually regard as being the editorial section. In the case of *Al-Ahram*, when it came to choosing between Heykal's commentary and the bland, formal statements of the main body of the paper, common sense dictated using Heykal.

It is significant that the editorial-page editors of the *New York Times*, the *Washington Post* and the *Age* of Melbourne each said in interview that were such editorials not already an established part of newspapers, they doubted whether they would now be adopted. Max Frankel of the *New York Times* had some thoughtful comments to make: 'The concept of a newspaper's voice, other than the way it handles the news, is an artificial posture left over from the old days when papers were run by a publisher or owner with ambitions. It is now a custom, and readers are used to it, and it can be useful, even though the very presence of an editorial perpetuates the myth that the rest of the paper is objective. There have been occasions, with the "End to Neutrality" leader of 1938, or the way we put our entire credit behind a controversial view of the Vietnam war, when the *New York Times* editorial has significantly affected the thinking of the nation.'

Ms Meg Greenfield of the *Washington Post* (where the distinction between the news pages and the editorial and opinion section is very strictly maintained) described her editorials as 'the Vatican City inside the Italian Republic – surrounded, but sovereign and independent'. Mr Ben Bradlee, the editor, was not allowed to her editorial meetings; she was not invited to his news meetings. Eight journalists worked in her department; at *Asahi Shimbun,* more than twenty journalists work in the editorial section.

There is little doubt that editorials do have considerable influence. It was President Lyndon Johnson, at the height of the controversies over the Vietnam war, who said that the support of the *Washington Post*'s editorials was 'worth two divisions'. General de Gaulle viewed the support of *Le Monde* in similar terms in 1958, during the prolonged constitutional crisis which saw his return to power. But there is a further sense in which editorials are important. Newspapers are very loosely organized bodies. They have journalists who spend their lives covering football, or politics, or arcane diplomatic manoeuvres, or wars, or banks, or crossword puzzles. Individual journalists have dramatically different political opinions. And in a very profound way the formal voice of a newspaper, as expressed in its editorials, defines its identity, and gives these differing journalists and their varied skills a vital coherence. During the New York newspaper strike of 1963, Scotty Reston commented: 'How do I know what I think if I can't read what I write?' Without editorials, how would readers, and the journalists themselves, know what kind of newspaper they read and write?

Because of the importance of editorials, the following survey was undertaken as a key part of this book. I believe it is the first such international comparison to have been made. I have chosen twenty topics, seventeen of them international crises since 1945, and quoted from each newspaper's relevant editorials. The three non-crises that have been chosen as topics – the questions of sport and politics, man's venture into space, and each newspaper's view on the fundamental issue of freedom of information – were chosen to try and discern how each newspaper saw and approached issues that went beyond immediate diplomacy, politics and crisis. In the end, an editorial is a value judgement, even a moral judgement, in which a newspaper is forced to grapple with the interplay of national self-interest, the prejudices of its readers and the dictates of its own institutional conscience – insofar as it has one.

Some patterns emerge quite clearly from this survey. There was a broad consensus in favour of America's position at the beginning of her military involvement in the Vietnam war, during the Gulf of Tonkin incident of 1964. (It should be remembered that the Pentagon Papers suggest that the American government deliberately provoked that naval battle in order to justify further military intervention.) By 1975, when Saigon fell to the tank armies of North Vietnam, the consensus of editorial opinion had shifted. Well after the time of the Suez invasions of 1956, and up to Rhodesia's declaration of independence of 1965, one can discern a kind of Commonwealth consciousness, with the newspapers of Australia, Canada and Britain and South Africa taking a broadly parallel line. Most of the international crises saw a broad unanimity of opinion at least among the Western newspapers, with obvious objections from *Pravda, Al-Ahram* and, to a lesser extent, *Asahi Shimbun* and *Le Monde*. There is a considerable degree of discord between the newspapers on the question of China's admission to the UN, on the Cuba missile crisis, the Bay of Pigs invasion, and the OPEC price rise. But, on the whole, these editorials speak for themselves, and the reader should make his own judgements on their joint significance. The concept of 'public opinion' is a cloudy one; but if there is such a thing as the world's opinion (and the American Declaration of Independence was specifically written with 'a decent respect to the opinions of Mankind') then some timbre of its voice should be heard here.

THE TIMES: EDITORIALS

The independence of India: 5 July 1947

'The creation of the Asiatic Dominions in the manner set out by the Bill is an event without parallel in the history of the Commonwealth. It is another remarkable illustration – the USA was the first – of the power of those political ideas fashioned in this island of which, as Burke argued so eloquently when American independence was at stake, freedom is the first.'

The independence of Israel: 15 May 1948

'Today's tragedy springs from the refusal of Jews and Arabs to learn that, unless they can live together amicably in the land common to them both, they cannot hope to regain the peace and prosperity conferred upon them with British rule for a generation. This they now choose to learn in the hard school of war, and the British people share deeply in the sorrow and regret at this failure – for a grim time at least – of a great mission.'

The Berlin blockade and airlift: 22 July 1948

'When first they imposed the blockade in the Western sectors, the Russians sought to gain mastery over those sectors (and therefore over the whole of Berlin) by starving the population. They seem to have expected that the Germans in those sectors, deprived of all food from the West, would themselves turn against the Western powers that stood out against capitulation to the Soviet terms. The supreme effort of the British and American air forces destroyed any such plan, and that effort, as the Russians know, can be made still greater.'

The Communists win power in China: 22 October 1949

'A great revolution has been accomplished in China, which has changed the balance of power throughout Asia and the Far East. Like all revolutions it is likely to release hidden energies in the Chinese people and to stimulate that nationalism and xenophobia which have always been part of the Chinese character. The new China will not be easy to deal with.'

The Korean war: 29 September 1950

'Until now, it can be argued, the Western powers and the United Nations have made it their business, in all the many crises since the war, to withstand Communist aggression. But they have not them-selves gone into any area that had conceivably become a Soviet field of interest. Their aim has been deliberately defensive and unpro-vocative. Yet it would be wrong to apply such an argument too far in the case of Korea.'

The Suez invasion: 1 November 1956

'There was much to be said for intervention in the Suez crisis. Yet many who were most firmly convinced of that must ask whether the move now, in what is being pictured as collusion with Israel and after Arab feelings had been inflamed afresh against the French, is not likely to make Arab unity almost certain . . . Was the need for speed really so great that President Eisenhower had to hear about the Anglo-French ultimatum from Press reports?'

The Russian invasion of Hungary: 5 November 1956

'Probably all the Soviet leaders, as Marxists, refused to allow any threat to the one-party system; and all of them, as leaders of the Russian empire, decided on force to retain a satellite that had risen for elementary freedom and neutrality. It was a confession that ten years of Communist rule might bring a popular response that could sweep away even the basis of Marxist Socialism. The tanks opened fire in Budapest.'

The Bay of Pigs assault on Cuba: 21 April 1961

'The fact remains that President Kennedy endorsed the invasion of Cuba by exiles . . . he seems to have been the victim of bad intelligence advice. One immediate consequence of the whole unfortunate affair should be a severely critical look at the powers and organisation of the CIA.'

The Cuban missile crisis: 24 October 1962

'While each side holds the supreme deterrent it is just possible, if the Cuban affair settles down to a kind of long stalemate – admittedly a big if – that they may consider a bargain whereby each does away with a forward base or two. With a ban on nuclear testing added, the world's nerves could become steadier.'

The Gulf of Tonkin incident: 6 August 1964

'On both occasions when attacked, the American destroyers were moving on the High Seas in the Gulf of Tonkin, where they had every right to be. They were showing the flag rather than trailing their coat.'

China's nuclear weapon: 17 October 1964

'The most populated and most introverted state on earth, the one with the greatest pride and ambition, is joining the ranks of the nuclear powers. It is an accomplishment which will make all states look at their own policies again and ask how the nuclear race can be ended – a task trebly difficult so long as China is not in the comity of nations.'

Rhodesia's UDI: 12 November 1965

'Ian Smith's action in declaring Rhodesia's independence is stupid, reckless and bad. The party most concerned, the British Government, have one over-riding interest – to return Rhodesia to the path of ordered, Constitutional development that has been abandoned. This is essential; punishing Mr Smith and his colleagues is secondary to this chief aim . . . Getting this rogue elephant back under control is the most intricate, and it could be the most dangerous, challenge Africa and the Commonwealth have had to face.'

The Russian invasion of Czechoslovakia: 22 August 1968

'What Russia feared was the infection of liberal, humane ideas spreading from Czechoslovakia to Poland and Hungary first of all and then to Russia itself. To many Westerners – even to many Western Communists – the Czechoslovak movement seemed to hold out the last hope for the future of Marxist Communism itself. It offered a way forward out of the familiar bureaucratic dictatorial kind of regime which, besides being unworthy of human beings, is grossly inefficient.'

Israel's occupation of the West Bank: 19 October 1973

'There would remain the problem of Palestine, or rather, of those parts of it which were not incorporated into Israel in 1948 – i.e. the West Bank, East Jerusalem and the Gaza Strip – and of the Palestinians who fled from Israel in 1948 and became refugees. This problem can probably only be solved by the creation of some small Palestinian state, either fully independent or in federation with Jordan. Its territorial limits would not have to coincide precisely with the Armistice lines of 1949, but could be negotiated directly between Israelis and Palestinians (the latter being represented partly but not exclusively by the Jordanian government).'

The OPEC price rise: 24 November 1973

'At this stage in history it is not in the interest of the Arab countries to handle their control of oil supplies so as to force a massive and enormous international investment in shale oil or in tar sand. That will come sooner or later in any case. The Shah of Persia is quite right and King Faisal is unfortunately quite mistaken in thinking that it can be in the interests of the Middle Eastern countries to explore their advantage to the point at which the world mobilizes to counteract it.'

Watergate: 31 July 1974

'The argument against resignation is that in the long run the American system will benefit from allowing the majestic process [i.e. impeachment] to run its full course. Justice must not only be done but be seen to be done. Only in this way can the evidence be fully examined and the President allowed a proper opportunity to refute in detail the charges against him. Only in this way can Mr Nixon or his friends, or his political heirs, be prevented from fostering the legend that he was hounded out of office by his political enemies . . . Impeachment is – and is intended to be – a slow and elaborate process, hedged around with safeguards. To short-circuit it would be to diminish it and leave unresolved a number of vital points in the case against Mr Nixon.'

The fall of Saigon: 1 May 1975

'The American armed forces were not militarily defeated in Vietnam any more than the French armed forces were militarily defeated in Algeria. But America has undoubtedly suffered a political defeat, as France did: both countries were obliged to accept a political result which they had been trying to prevent because they found the military cost of preventing it was higher than they were prepared to pay.'

Sport and politics: 23 July 1976

In effect, the African walk-out is a demonstration against the individual liberties enjoyed by a happier land with better laws than theirs . . . Governments are going to have to decide whether international sport is simply a continuation of diplomacy and the ideological struggles they promote, or whether the Olympic Games are an athletic contest during which politics are temporarily and locally put in abeyance. If they admit they subscribe to the former, they need some new rules.'

The space venture: 17 October 1957

'Admiration there must be, and also gratitude at such a milestone in scientific progress. But in most people's minds those feelings will not be unmixed with fear. An earth satellite has little military significance in itself, but the significance of Russia's ability to launch an object of such a size into space, with at least the critical accuracy to get it correctly on to the predicted orbit, is clear enough.'

Freedom of information: 5 August 1976

'Wherever the West ruled in Asia or Africa a free press usually existed. It was thought to be part of the political tradition of democracy that was introduced into those countries. Backed by an active and free press in the Western world and with a general confidence in representative government, the end of empire found free newspapers functioning all over the world. In the last two decades, country after country in the Third World has not merely thrown over representative government but has gone a long way to abolishing any press freedom . . . To take the simple standard of news freely printed and of articles critical of the government freely written and printed, where does the standard of freedom still fly without question? In Asia, Japan; in the Middle East, Israel and Lebanon; in Africa only South Africa would pass the test and even there with limitations; in Latin America, none; and in the Caribbean, Jamaica and one or two others. The list is much smaller than might have been drawn up twenty years ago. It remains shameful that the vaue of a free press has not been better appreciated and more stoutly defended so that no voice is to be found in so many countries that can be raised in criticism of government.'

3

Le Monde

Le Monde was founded, as an act of France's liberation, by the authority of General de Gaulle in December 1944. Its duty was to replace *Le Temps*, the traditional semi-official paper of the Third Republic, whose editorials had always been known to reflect the views of the French government, and which was owned, and its editorials dominated, by the great financial and industrial interests of France.[1] De Gaulle was dedicated to a fundamental reform of those French institutions which had so clearly failed in 1940, and he led a government composed in part of those Communists who had played such a leading and heroic part in the Resistance. The reformist, liberal-left current of the liberation meant equally that *Le Monde* was to be guaranteed its freedom from direct official control. The paper was fated, then, to be a curious hybrid, part official journal of France, part free and independent voice.

Much would depend upon the calibre of the men chosen to edit the new paper. They were appointed by Pierre-Henri Teitgen, de Gaulle's Minister of Information, and his secretary-general, Joannes Dupraz.[2] They decided upon a triumvirate, made up of Christian Funck-Brentano, a senior administrator at the Bibliothèque National and a loyal Gaullist; René Courtin, a well-connected law professor and leading member of the internal Resistance and Hubert Beuve-Méry, self-made man, an anti-fascist journalist and Resistance intellectual. Beuve-Méry was to dominate the paper for its next twenty-five years, and his background is worth examination.

Born into a poor family in 1902, raised by an aunt who was house-keeper for a Paris priest, Beuve-Méry's education came late in life (after some time as a porter) when he was taken up by a friendly priest, who supported him while he took a degree in law, and encouraged him to work on *Les Nouvelles Religieuses*, a Catholic intellectual magazine. From this liberal Catholic background, Beuve-Méry went to Czechoslovakia, where his Professor had secured him a teaching post at the Institut Français in Prague. He stayed there for ten years, until 1938, exposed to the democratic genius of Thomas Masaryk, to the rising threat of Hitler's Germany, and to regular journalism. By tradition, the teachers at the Institute were the corres-pondents of the Paris papers. Beginning as correspondent for *Le Matin* and *Le Journal*, by 1935 Beuve-Méry had become *Le Temps*'s man in Prague, and he used the official French newspaper to warn of the menace of Hitler, to demand support for the Czechs and to oppose the Munich agreement of 1938 by which Britain and France agreed to appease Hitler by dismembering Czechoslovakia. He had tried to go beyond journalism, travelling back to Paris to urge senior French officials to back the Czechs, and sadly reporting to Masaryk his fears of a French betrayal. Characteristically, Masaryk was furious, refusing to believe that France could do such a thing.[3] With the Munich agreement, he returned to Paris to resign from *Le Temps*, to publish a book on the German expansionist menace, to work briefly at the Ministry of Information, and finally to join the army and go to war in August 1939.[4] After the defeat of 1940, with his family safe in the countryside, Beuve-Méry went to Lyons, where he began by publishing his own duplicated daily news-sheet, hand-delivered by him locally, and then joined the intellectual magazine *Esprit* and a team of dissident intellectuals who were anti-Hitler, critical of the Vichy regime, but equally critical of the failed Third Republic which had brought France so low. They were looking for new directions for France, boldly enough for *Esprit* to be banned by 1942 but, at this stage, they were not ready to join what little Resistance existed. Beuve-Méry's concern for France's future led him to the curious, uniquely French group of men at the château of Uriage, a self-appointed training school for the future leaders of France. At first alarmingly close to the more liberal spirits of the Vichy regime, it was later to be a cell of the Resistance, once Vichy France itself was occupied by the Germans late in 1942. Uriage was an almost monastic institution, high-minded, patriotic, Christian-democrat and ideal-istic, dreaming of a united Europe and a restored, reborn, reformed

France. Uriage was against fascism and Communism, against the materialism of the American way of life, and against the 'golden capitalism' of the City of London.

Beuve-Méry went from Uriage into the Resistance, fighting at first secretly and then in open war in southern France, taking part in forcing the surrender of 5,000 German troops at the town of Castres. It was an old colleague of Uriage, Paul Reuter, joint director of de Gaulle's new Ministry of Information, who recommended Beuve-Méry for the post at *Le Monde*.[5]

It was a less than glorious beginning. The paper appeared on two sides of a sheet of paper, with a handful of advertisements (including one for the reborn Folies Bergère), clumsily printed on the antique machinery of *Le Temps*, whose presses, premises and staff (sanitized of open collaborators) had been requisitioned for the purpose. 'I feel like a naked man sitting on the front of a huge tank advancing into open combat,' Beuve-Méry wrote to a friend that day. 'I have 999 chances in a 1000 of being sacrificed.'[6] His alarm stemmed, in part, from government intervention. The independence of *Le Monde* was to be established by setting up a holding company with 200 shares, forty for each member of the triumvirate, and the remainder divided among independent leading citizens. René Courtin understood that the triumvirate could nominate their own friends, but the Minister of Information insisted on his own appointees, all of them loyalists of the MRP Party.[7] Because of the need to get the paper published, and the constant presence of the war – the paper's earliest front pages were dominated by news of the German counter-attack at the Battle of the Bulge – the precise nature of Beuve-Méry's editorial authority, compared to that of Courtin and Funck-Brentano, was never formally established, and this was to lead to the constant crises of the next six years. The first began within weeks, with René Courtin's submission of a lengthy article which criticized the government's 'socialist' planning policies, and called for more of a free market in economic affairs. Beuve-Méry refused at first to publish it, choosing not to embark on a course of fundamental criticism of the government, at a time when the infant paper was already under fire from the Communist Left, as a new mouthpiece for big business, and from big business itself, who claimed that *Le Temps* had been stolen from them.[8]

'*Le Monde*'s first ambition is to assure the reader of information that is clear, true and, as far as possible, rapid and complete,' read the first editorial on 18 December, 1944. (As always with *Le Monde*, the paper was dated 19 December, but it appeared in the afternoon of the previous day.) 'But our epoch is not one in which men can be content to observe and describe,' it went on. *Le Monde* announced from the beginning its right to judge and to advise.[9] In its fifth issue, it hailed the re-establishment of the Radical Party, the dominant force of the Third Republic, while warning it that the old chiefs would have to be replaced by men of the Resistance.[10]

The first issue sold 140,000 copies of broadsheet size, but the wartime shortages of paper forced it within a month to reduce to its current tabloid form. A 50% cut in paper allocations meant that for a week it published 140,000 copies of a two-page tabloid sheet, but in mid-January 1945, the triumvirate decided that it would rather print a fuller paper, and used its paper allocation to print only 70,000 copies of a four-page paper. There was no shortage of demand, and its finances were healthy enough to allow it, the only paper to do so, to repay the 1 million franc government loan (available to all new papers after the liberation) by April 1945. In that year it printed an average of 108,000 copies, and 160,000 the following year.[11] In 1947, with a similar average daily printing, it was healthy enough to put over 6 million francs into its reserves. Its success led to angry protests from other Parisian papers that *Le Monde* was being favourably treated by the government, subsidized by generous allocations of paper and official advertising.[12]

The crises of French governments immediately after the war, with de Gaulle angrily leaving the government early in 1946, the establishment of the Fourth Republic (to de Gaulle's implacable hostility) and the subsequent departure of the Communists from government in 1947, meant that a paper as serious and informative as *Le Monde* could expect to sell well. More than a dozen of its rivals, born in a flush of liberation enthusiasm, had folded by 1949.[13] But those who had expected, from its formation, that *Le Monde* would follow the MRP party line were to be confounded. The opening of the Cold War, the Atlantic Alliance and the political implications of American economic aid through the Marshall Plan, and the worsening colonial war in Indochina, were to make of Beuve-Méry's *Le Monde* the most potent institutional critic of the enfeebled Fourth Republic. The debates led to something like open war within the triumvirate. Beuve-Méry argued for neutralism, for France (and Europe as whole) to evade having to join one or other of the great power blocs. Courtin and Funck-Brentano were for the Atlantic Alliance. The battle was fought at first by proxy, over the articles of the leading French historian Etienne Gilson, who from the beginning of 1948 until late 1950 wrote a total of twenty-five major articles for *Le Monde*, whose essential theme was this: 'That which America is disposed to buy from us with her dollars is our blood, once again, in a third invasion of Western Europe which will make the earlier two of 1914 and 1940 look like pleasure parties. It is too much to pay. We have a right to refuse to sacrifice ourselves for the USA. European neutrality is not inconceivable, so long as it is well armed.'[14]

Beuve-Méry, at least in the early years of the debate, wrote his increasingly parallel views in the ill-fated weekly *Une Semaine dans le Monde*, or in *Temps Présent*. But against the increasingly strident opposition of Courtin (and some sections of the government), Beuve-Méry insisted on running Gilson's articles. A spate of letters from French Ambassadors flowed into the Quai d'Orsay, saying that governments around the world were taking *Le Monde*'s view as the private sentiments of the French government, and that this must stop.[15]

The arguments over the Atlantic Alliance were made the more bitter as Beuve-Méry began to oppose the colonial war in Indochina, with a celebrated article which ended with a comment on France's role there: 'There are some generosities which pay well, and some acts of egoism, said to be sacred, which cost outrageously dear.' Decoded from the sybilline French, this was widely, and rightly, taken to mean that France should abandon what Beuve-Méry was beginning to call 'the dirty war'.[16]

After endless arguments, Courtin and Funck-Brentano resigned from the executive committee of *Le Monde* in December 1949, with Courtin writing to his former editor: 'If the USA, disheartened by the way in which we thank them for their aid, abandon Europe and France to misery, despair and Bolshevism, *Le Monde*, Gilson and you will bear some of the responsibility.'[17] But Beuve-Méry had the support of the bulk of the staff, and particularly of the influential Pierre Emmanuel, who noted the ugly developments of McCarthyism in the US and wrote gloomily of 'the FBI one day becoming a kind of Gestapo . . . through fear of themselves, are the Americans erecting an iron curtain around themselves, a kind of American fascism?'[18]

Whether it was the hope of a last compromise, or the better to renew their attacks, Courtin and Funck-Brentano returned to *Le Monde*'s executive committee, after a meeting of the SARL holding company in April 1951. The three men, with Joannes Dupraz (now an MRP deputy) as a fourth, reviewed the week's copies of *Le Monde* each Thursday, with Courtin in the role of prosecutor, alleging that 'the same neutralist and demoralizing policies continued, the more dangerous because the more discreet'.[19] Within three months, Courtin and Funck-Brentano had again resigned, but this time knowing that they retained a tenuous majority of the voting shares on the SARL board. A fortnight later, partly in disgust and partly in recognition of the direction of the votes, Beuve-Méry announced his own resignation, to take effect from 1 November. The SARL board had nominated a loyal Gaullist, André Catrice, who ran the Gaullist paper L'Aube, to replace him.[20]

It was at this point that Le Monde began to demonstrate why it was different from the rest of the French press, to prove the special relationship Beuve-Méry had developed with his own staff, and with the readers themselves. The initiative came from Le Monde's own journalists, who established an editorial committee and demanded that they should be given some say in the newspaper's administration and a right of veto on the choice of editor-in-chief. In effect, they were voting to keep Beuve-Méry. In a furious joint letter, three of the paper's leading writers, Jacques Fauvet the political editor, Robert Gauthier the news editor and André Fontaine the foreign editor, led the way by denouncing the formal statement Courtin had given to the news agencies on Beuve-Méry's resignation. Courtin had announced that 'Le Monde had been established to serve a strictly national policy; it had ceased to be faithful to this vocation.'[21] Added to the three journalists' criticism was a note from Gauthier, pointing out that the exceedingly rare appearances of Funck-Brentano at the paper had become something of a scandal. 'He could not even recognize the journalists,' Gauthier said.[22]

Then Maurice Duverger, a professor at the University of Bordeaux and an occasional contributor to the paper, organized a series of petitions at universities across France, asking for Beuve-Méry to return as editor. At Lyons, where Beuve-Méry's journalism in the days of Vichy was respectfully remembered, the reponse was brisk. From the universities of Strasbourg, Bordeaux, Lyons, Caen and the Sorbonne was formed a Federation of Committees for the support of Le Monde. There was a mass-meeting in Paris, a spate of letters to the press, broadcasts – and, more to the point, an impressive lobby of intellectuals putting pressure on the MRP, the very political group which had hoped to benefit from a new editor.

Finally, the last word was spoken by Charles de Gaulle himself. Two of his loyal supporters from the Resistance, Edouard Sablier, a foreign affairs reporter on *Le Monde*, and Maurice Ferro, *Le Monde*'s Washington correspondent, lobbied the General at his Paris office on the rue de Solferino. De Gaulle finally agreed that Beuve-Méry's policy of French nationalism and neutrality from the two great powers was not too distant from his own, and asked Funck-Brentano to change his vote at the SARL board meetings.[23] Briefly, the Gaullist pondered the prospect of becoming editor himself, but the combined pressure of readers, journalists and the General was too much. At a new SARL board meeting on 12 December, it was decided to create eighty new shares, to be held in trust by the editorial committee or by the journalists themselves. This gave them the right of veto. Beuve-Méry was thereupon re-appointed. All in all, it represented a unique rallying of support to Beuve-Méry.

For all its publicity and political importance, *Le Monde* had yet to make a breakthrough as a newspaper, gaining new readers. The print order did not go above 160,000 (apart from one year of 1948 with 163,000) until 1956 when it suddenly leapt to 183,000. The paper was prosperous enough; in 1951 alone, some 13 million francs were placed in the reserves, whence they would be used to pay off its 'debts' to the old owners of *Le Temps*.[24] Advertising income, depressed by the endless French economic crises (themselves largely caused by the ruinous costs of colonial wars in Indochina and then in Algeria), rose steadily throughout the 1950s, but advertisements never occupied more than 34% of the paper – to the point that a myth arose that *Le Monde* had taken a vow to limit advertising to less than one-third of its pages. But then *Le Monde* had chosen, in the style of *Le Temps* before it, to function almost regardless of profit. Its independent structure of ownership allowed it to plough income back into the newspaper, always spending 30% and more of the editorial budget on foreign reporting.[25] Journalists' salaries were kept deliberately low to reflect 'the honour of writing for *Le Monde*'. And the paper made a virtue of what had been an austere liberation necessity, of publishing only news and comment, and banishing pictures and frivolities. Readers too were implicitly supposed to feel honoured at having this utterly serious journal available.

The breakthrough came with the collapse of the Fourth Republic and the bitter intensification of the Algerian war. The Republic began to die with the disasters of the Indochinese war, the humiliation of Dien-Bien-Phu and French prisoners-of-war in Viet-Minh camps. The old Socialist, Pierre Mendès-France, was voted into office to save the name of the Republic. He was to form the only French government which could ever claim *Le Monde*'s full support.'It has been constantly written in this newspaper that the war of Indochina was a madness; that the Atlantic Alliance could only be strong and healthy if we knew how to speak to the Americans in the frank language of friendship, and not in the tongue of servants; that Germany should be progressively re-integrated into Europe with all the rights of a free people, but without becoming the steel tip of a lance aimed at Eastern Europe; that the application of the same methods, the obstinate renewal of the same errors would lead us fatally in Algeria and Africa to the same tragic results we knew in Asia; and in the end that it is vain to desire or to try to achieve anything at all as long as the same old interest groups in Parliament make sure that their own ends prevail over the interests of the nation.'[26] This classic Beuve-Méry editorial, signed with his old Resistance nom-de-plume of Sirius, greeted what he saw as the new dawn of Mendès-France. But within seven months the Mendès-France government was to fail in its turn, having achieved a not dishonourable peace in Indochina and muddled its way to accepting German re-armament. But the attempts at administrative and parliamentary reform were stillborn. And Algeria grew more ugly.

It was in December 1957, after sitting on it for six months, that *Le Monde* decided to publish the secret 'Béteille Report', the more stunning because it officially admitted that systematic torture was part of the French security system in Algeria.[27] But in the years before 1957, *Le Monde*'s constant criticism of the Algerian war had brought two challenges to its very existence. The first came from the large industrial groups who had never forgiven the paper for not being their public voice, in the way that *Le Temps* had been. With over $2 million of capital, most of it raised from industrial and oil companies, from the Banque Worms and, significantly, from Moroccan and Algerian colonist groups, *Le Temps de Paris* was launched, not only to compete with *Le Monde*, but to overwhelm it. Philippe Boegner, the editor of the reborn *Temps*, defined his task as 'taking enough readers to put *Le Monde* into a difficult financial situation, in such a way as to bring about its capitulation'.[28] In the event, the challenge failed miserably, unsupported by the major distributing groups, with a confused editorial package that was not able to survive beyond sixty-six issues. Significantly, the one place where it outsold *Le Monde* was in Algeria.

The second threat was the more insidious, coming from the government itself. It refused permission for *Le Monde* to raise its selling price from eighteen to twenty francs, after a period of sharp inflation, and threatening Beuve-Méry with fines and imprisonment if he went ahead. At the same time, although *Le Monde* was subject to censorship in France itself only during the time of the army's *coup d'état* in 1958, it began regularly to be seized and confiscated in Algeria. It was as much an act of financial penalty as of censorship, forcing *Le Monde* to go to the expense of printing and delivering copies to North Africa, without knowing whether there would be any sales income from them. Whereas public and political pressure persuaded the government of Guy Mollet to let the price be raised to twenty francs after a year of delays, the Algerian seizures continued throughout the decade.[29] There were other harassments, such as an attempted defamation suit brought on behalf of the army's notorious parachutists, which brought sympathetic editorials from foreign papers who suspected, not without reason, a deliberate campaign to silence the paper.[30]

The Fourth Republic was fighting for its life, and with the army coup in Algeria in May of 1958, it was visibly losing. *Le Monde*'s leading role in the national debate was reflected in its steadily climbing sales, up by 12% in 1956, 18% in 1957, 7% in 1958.[31] But after the critical role *Le Monde* had played, came the surprise, with *Le Monde* grudgingly supporting the appeal of the army in Algeria, that de Gaulle should return to power, to save France from herself. At first, there was more grudge than support: 'As head of the Government before [in 1944–6] he did not achieve much success – with errors that disturb one, although with scruples that reassure. It is not by chance that after fifteen years, there is no man, no team close to him whose competence and prestige match their undoubted loyalty. He is alone, too alone,' wrote Beuve-Méry, when matters were still in the balance.[32] With de Gaulle's vital referendum in September 1958, which buried the Fouth Republic and began his personal rule, *Le Monde* recorded 'a conditional and provisional "Yes", while we deplore the fact that it cannot be enthusiastic and definitive'.[33]

Thus began the curious love-hate relationship between the paper and the General. The more de Gaulle began putting into practice that independent foreign policy, based upon freedom of action and French interests which *Le Monde* had once advocated, the more *Le Monde* (and Beuve-Méry in particular) began to criticize. The more de Gaulle moved towards ending the Algerian war by a French withdrawal and Algerian independence, the more *Le Monde* floated the vague idea of some kind of North African Federation, with close links to France.[34] The more de Gaulle drove forward the programme to give France its own nuclear weapon (which had been the logical conclusion of the Gilson programme for well-armed neutrality), the more *Le Monde* condemned it.[35] It became a classic feature of French political life in the 1960s, that de Gaulle would give one of his rare press conferences, and the next day *Le Monde* would print Beuve-Méry's critical analysis of the General's course. In one sense, it was a theatre review of a great actor; in another, it was Beuve-Méry taking upon himself the role of official Opposition, now that de Gaulle's new Constitution had emasculated parliament. Ironically, the de Gaulle years saw the great spurt in the fortunes of *Le Monde*, its circulation leaping from 164,000 in the year de Gaulle took power to 354,000 in 1969, the year he left it. The paper grew fatter, from an average of twelve pages in 1958, to an average of almost thirty by 1969. It grew sleeker, too, with advertising taking up 35% of its pages in 1958 to just over 50% in 1969.[36] Freed at last of the burden of colonial wars, the French economy began to expand, and *Le Monde* with it. And with expansion came a new generation of journalists, as the editorial team was doubled in size. Throughout the 1960s, with profits rising by more than 10% a year to 15 million francs in 1969, the money was ploughed back into new printing works at St Denis, to double the capacity of the presses in the rue des Italiens, where the old machines of *Le Temps* had themselves been replaced in 1962. And the internal mood of the paper had changed, thanks largely to Algeria. There had been no coherent sense of Algerian policy at *Le Monde*. Jean Lacouture spoke for half the staff when he admitted, 'I took part in the campaigns against the methods of war, rather than for the idea of pulling out altogether.'[37] But a process of internal, almost collegiate democracy was at work. Beuve-Méry's lone decision to swing the support of his paper behind de Gaulle in 1958 had led to resignations; the steady unfolding of the Algerian tragedy was to initiate a process of staff consultation which culminated, under another editor in the 1970s, in a virtual internal referendum on whether or not to support the Communist–Socialist coalition against the presidency of Giscard d'Estaing.[38]

Le Monde reflected the long post-war agony of France. The paper was formed in a series of crucibles; the joy of liberation, the tumults of Indochina, of Algeria, of the military coups of 1958 and 1961, the quasi-dictatorship of de Gaulle, the domestic terror of the OAS and the wave of plastic bombs. *Le Monde* was part of this fray, suffering bombs at its offices in the rue des Italiens. Its staff were bombed at their homes. Beuve-Méry's home was bombed twice, leading to a characteristically defiant, ironic editorial.[39] In the bloody confusion of terror and principle that was France's civil war, *Le Monde* stayed honourably exposed in the front line. And like all veterans, it was changed in the process.

The expression of that change came early in 1968, when the structure of the SARL holding company, which had remained in force since the crisis of 1951, was dramatically revised. There had been six years of discussions between the founders and the staff, and the new structure reduced the founders' share in SARL from 72% to 40%, while the share of the employees rose from 28% to 49%. The new arrangements gave the journalists themselves a 40% share, and a further 9% to the other employees.[40] Within two months of that reform, France reaped the harvest of the years of political stagnation and economic growth under de Gaulle with the student revolts of May 1968. What began as student unrest at Nanterre University led to barricades and riots in the Latin Quarter, to brutal police and paramilitary repression, and to a wave of strikes in the factories. The student passions ebbed away, the strikes were bought off by a deal with the Communist Party and a 10% pay raise, but de Gaulle's regime had trembled. So had *Le Monde*. The young journalists who had been hired in the prosperous years of the 1960s sympathized with the student revolt. The old guard of *Le Monde* were acute enough to have been writing, in the months before the barricades, penetrating analyses of the apathetic, prosperous tranquillity of de Gaulle's rule. 'France is bored' was the title of a celebrated article by Pierre Viansson-Ponté in March 1968, contrasting the passion and political activism of students in the rest of the world with the apparent quiescence in France.[41] Jacques Fauvet, soon to replace Beuve-Méry, went to Nanterre University and wrote of 'a kernel of students, more nihilist than revolutionary'.[42] *Le Monde* was also responding to the steady change in its readership that the 1960s had brought. In 1958, only 17% of its readers had been under the age of twenty-four. By 1968, that figure had grown to 30.5%. The proportion of 'workers' in the readership had tripled, to 9%, in the same period.[43]

Perhaps more significantly, Beuve-Méry was out of France (as was de Gaulle) at the critical period. *Le Monde* entered, almost joyfully, into the days of the barricades, reporting almost uncritically the ludicrously exaggerated reports of seventy dead from police brutality, performing heroics of reporting and production to continue publishing while strikes paralysed telephones, transport and distribution. *Le Monde*'s circulation leapt to unprecedented peaks: 640,000 on

15 May, to 740,000 on 30 May, to 770,000 on 6 June, to 820,000 on 25 June. The journalists themselves, in a mass-meeting effectively dominated by the young writers, 'the May generation', declared that if there were any censorship of their work, from within the paper or without, they would close it down.[44] It was a heady period, and it is to *Le Monde* that future historians will look for much of the flavour of the endless teach-ins at the Sorbonne, the sense of excitement that ruled Paris in the days when the Stock Exchange was burned and the CRS riot-police defied. But Beuve-Méry's return was the signal for re-appraisal. He himself went to the Sorbonne, did his own reporting and, as so often, waited for de Gaulle to speak before he made his own editorial comment. While calling for reforms in the universities, in the unions and in the factories, he echoed de Gaulle's speech: 'There is need to re-establish public order and the basic necessities of national life – a policy of any government worthy of the name.'[45] He summoned outside contributors, mainly academics, to describe the 'drunken ship that the Sorbonne has become', to point to the sinister presence of the 'Katangais', a group of ex-mercenaries who had taken over part of the university.[46] More to the point, Beuve-Méry pointed to the potential dangers of the right-wing backlash that was mobilizing, in the name of support for de Gaulle.The symbiosis between Beuve-Méry and de Gaulle continued. The two men re-established order, one at *Le Monde*, the other in France. The next year, defeated in his last referendum, de Gaulle retired. Beuve-Méry, choosing the twenty-fifth anniversary of the paper's foundation, retired in his turn, and chose the old political editor, Jacques Fauvet, to replace him. Beuve-Méry had represented one wing of wartime France, the liberation. Fauvet, like his colleague Robert Gauthier, represented another, that generation of French soldiers who spent their war in German PoW camps. He took over a paper that was dramatically successful, with a profit margin of 14% of its record income of 11.7 million francs. It had gone way beyond the original readership of *Le Temps*, of the European chancelleries and the French bourgeoisie. In the 1950s, it had attracted the French intelligentsia and the professional classes; in the 1960s it had attracted the workers and students. And it had become a significant exporter, 12% of its sales going abroad.[47]

Le Monde's success continued to burgeon, while the rest of the Parisian press was in crisis. From 1965, the circulation of *France-Soir* has shrunk from over 1 million to below 500,000; that of *Le Figaro* from 420,000 to below 300,000. *Le Monde* now outsells them both.

Part of the problem is an archaic and inefficient system of distribution for French newspapers which means that *Le Monde* (and other papers) receives only about 33% of the cover price for each paper sold. Worse than that, the distribution system means that an alarmingly high proportion of the papers printed are returned unsold. With *Le Monde*, that proportion has never fallen below 20% since 1950. For the French press as a whole, the average of unsold returns has been static at 30%.[48] Over the same period, the press's share of advertising has been reduced by radio and TV competition. Even *Le Monde*'s success, with a steadily climbing circulation and a steadily swelling proportion of the paper allocated to advertising, has not succeeded in solving the paper's basic financial problem – a lack of resources for further investment. The rest of *Le Monde*'s empire, its diplomatic, philatelic, educational, documentary and weekly supplements, constitute about 25% of its net profits.[49] The high costs of the new printing plant at St Denis were an embarrassment, not fully resolved by the acceptance of contract printing. In the 1970s, the rising cost of newsprint, and the stagnation of economic growth (and thus advertising) has meant that *Le Monde*'s profit margin has been less than 8% every year since 1970, and less than 3% since 1976. In 1977, *Le Monde* made a loss of 200,000 francs. And in 1980, it began to gather money commercially to finance its technological development, to introduce photo-composition and computer-setting, unable to finance it internally.[50]

The years of Jacques Fauvet, without a de Gaulle, have seen a revival of French domestic politics, a new electoral battle between the Left coalition of the Socialist and Communist parties, and the new government majority of Gaullists, radicals and centrists behind Giscard d'Estaing. *Le Monde* has been editorially on the side of the Left. And as in its early years, it has faced criticism for its alleged complaisance to the USSR, its waspish attitude towards Solzhenitsyn and the more flamboyant of the Russian dissidents. One major area of change has been in *Le Monde*'s always fulsome economic coverage. From its first issues, it has always reported the Stock Exchange results, and in the days of René Courtin and of Michel Tardy who ran the business section until 1961 it was broadly in favour of investment, profit and capitalism. But recently under Gilbert Mathieu, it has become known for its critical attitude towards finance and its insistence that industry must recognize, and redeem, the social costs of its profits.[51] It has faced a bitter attack from one of its own former journalists, Michel Legris, who accused it of manipulating the news and becoming a propaganda sheet of the Left.[52] Legris made three basic charges. He attacked *Le Monde*'s coverage of the Pol Pot regime in Cambodia, saying that, at best it excused its excesses and, at worst, covered up the fact of a Khmer genocide. Legris went on to accuse *Le Monde* of being almost criminal in its uncritical reports of China. He accused its Peking staff of Maoist tendencies, and quoted an admiring piece from Henri Fosquet, the religious correspondent, who returned from China to write; 'It is not repressive. It is exact to compare it to a sort of monastery where each individual only exists in function of the [religious] rule.'[53] Most tellingly, Legris attacked *Le Monde*'s coverage of the Portuguese revolution of 1974–6, specifically on its apparent acceptance of the denial of press freedom. He quoted, as had other critics like Raymond Aron before him, from *Le Monde*'s editorial of 21 June 1975, on the takeover of the Portuguese paper *Republica*. *Le Monde* suggested that there was some justice in closing the newspaper if it was to be a spokesman for counter-revolution. 'Is not the real question, whether in permitting freedom of expression to all, one might not be thus allowing some to abuse it?' was the editorial's front-page conclusion.[54] The shock came, not from the Portuguese situation itself, confused enough in the aftermath of a generation of fascist rule, with the army still in effective power, the Communists testing their strength, and democratic groups still finding their frail feet, but from *Le Monde*'s apparent betrayal of the principle of press freedom. This was a criticism that Fauvet, in the course of a public debate, managed to deflect, partly by quoting André Malraux's classic justification 'No liberty to the enemies of liberty'. But more to the root of the matter was Legris' conclusion, that *Le Monde* had become a victim of the confluence of its own Christian-Democrat, liberal and anti-colonial tradition, and the new spirit of revolt that stemmed from 1968. Nevertheless, it was a bold, provocative decision (and one which led to a flurry of diplomatic protests) which persuaded *Le Monde* to publish Jean Genet's defiant defence of the Baader-Meinhof terrorists in West Germany. But it was a decision within a *Le Monde* tradition that dated back to the days of Etienne Gilson's unpopular articles on neutralism: if the French dissident intelligentsia has something startling to say, it should be said in *Le Monde*.[55]

Significantly, these criticisms were formulated at the same time that *Le Monde* was coming under fire from the Left. Another former journalist, Philippe Simmonot, was fired in 1976 for having 'wrongfully obtained and published' a confidential state document on the role of the multinational petrol corporations.[56] The *New York Times* observed at the time 'if this occurred in Washington he would have got a Pulitzer Prize'.[57] Simmonot's subsequent book on the affair suggested that Le Monde had bowed to government pressure. He also analysed Le Monde's coverage of a major domestic event, the Barre government's anti-inflation plan, and showed that of the twenty-five showcase commentaries published from prestigious outside contributors, twelve stemmed from the government's own majority group, and only three from the Opposition. Two key groups of French society, the Communist Party and the CGT trade union, were not asked to contribute. (Both the CP and the CGT had their own journals in which to promote their views; but then, so did the government.)[58]

There were other indications that Le Monde was becoming more conscious of the prevailing winds of power. Having led the world's journalism in exposing and criticizing the police state of the Shah's Iran, with thirty-nine articles on SAVAK in 1972 and twenty-six in 1973, during 1974 and 1975 when Le Monde and the rest of the world's press was celebrating the post-OPEC majesty of the oil-rich Shah and his welcome purchases in Europe, Le Monde's coverage of SAVAK dwindled to less than one token article a month.[59] Le Monde's dependence on its advertisers was increasing. In 1974, Le Monde had prided itself on giving only 38.4% of its pages to advertising, compared to Le Figaro's 48.6%. By 1980, Le Monde was 45% advertising, and depended on advertising for over 70% of its total income.[60] On 5 October 1978, Le Monde commented acidly on the failure of the French President to make any comment on human rights in the course of his official visit to Brazil, pointing out that the US President Jimmy Carter had done rather better. The next day, Le Monde ran a sixteen-page supplement, packed with official advertisements, on Brazil. The supplement too was silent on human rights.[61] Le Monde could properly reply that Brazil's savage record in the field had been well reported, just as it could say that it was its duty as a paper of record, and not any servile echo of Le Temps, that led it to report presidential press conferences in full, and to reprint the complete texts of treaties.[62] But there was a sense in which Le Monde tried to have it all ways; as the official paper of France; as the successful participant in the press marketplace; as the loyal Opposition to government in France; as the custodian of French liberties; as the conscience of the Third World, and as the Galahad of the world's press, disdaining pictures, crosswords, puzzles and the trivia which attract readers.[63] There has been a modification of the paper's content in recent years,

mainly because of a growth in advertising. *Le Monde*'s own content
survey in 1974, and my own analysis in 1980, breaks down as follows:

	week 1974 %	week 1980 %
Internal/Economic Affairs	20.0	19.8
Foreign Affairs	13.3	16.5
Leisure/Arts, Radio, TV, Lit.	16.0	11.7
General News	5.9	2.7
Science, Medicine	2.8	2.6
Sports	1.8	1.2
Education	1.8	1.0
Advertisements	38.4	44.5

In 1977, on the occasion of the 10,000th issue, Jacques Fauvet
wrote a long editorial on the complexity of views that encompassed *Le
Monde*'s journalists and concluded 'the editors and journalists of this
paper have held a minimum of ideas in common – above all, a passion
for justice'.[64]

It is this passion which explains *Le Monde*'s long support and
sympathy for the anti-colonial struggle and for the subsequent trials of
the Third World, still a victim of the rich white world's economic
power, and of the social demoralization that colonialism imposed. It
explains also *Le Monde*'s long and sometimes solitary struggle for
liberty and reform in France itself, and its defence of the spirit of a
vaguely-deprived but independent Europe in a bi-polar world. It
explains, after agonized and even bitter internal debates, the choice
made by its journalists, in July of 1980, of Claude Julien, the leftist
editor of *Le Monde Diplomatique*, to replace Fauvet as editor-in-
chief after 1981.[65] 'Julien was elected, with the required 60% of the
votes, in spite of his opinions, not because of them,' Fauvet insists.[66]
But the current of sympathy for the Third World which Julien
encouraged at *Le Monde Diplo* has been as constant a feature of the
paper as Fauvet's 'passion for justice'.

Le Monde's determination to give a fair, and perhaps more than
fair hearing to the Third World was emphasized by the revelation that
it, along with other prestigious newspapers such as *Asahi Shimbun*,
had accepted money from the UN to publish UN-commissioned
articles on the need for a new international economic order.[67] In fact,
Le Monde's journalists had been writing precisely this argument for

the last decade, without subsidies from any quarter. But *Le Monde*'s embarrassment at receiving some £23,000 of UN money was reinforced when an internal letter from two senior editors, André Fontaine and Jacques Amalric, was leaked to other French newspapers. The letter said that the election of M. Claude Julien to the editorship 'has not succeeded in bringing about the reconciliation of a divided editorial staff', and that M. Julien's assurances that a 'pluralism of political opinions would be maintained' was insufficient.[68] At the same time, *Le Monde* was subjected to an unprecedented attack by the judicial machinery of the French state. One of the last acts of the government of President Giscard d'Estaing was to prosecute the paper and one of its journalists under a little-used law that prohibits attacks upon the judiciary – which *Le Monde* had suggested was too much under the government's thumb.[69] Even the temporary closure of *Libération*, the youth-cult and leftist daily which had reached a circulation of 60,000, did not help a troubled *Le Monde* to break even in 1981. Circulation began to fall in 1980, and the costs of new technology imposed losses which *Le Monde* was ill equipped to cover. And ironically, *Le Monde*'s campaign for the Socialist candidate, François Mitterrand, in the 1981 presidential elections saw the defeat of Giscard, but began a new kind of difficulty. The available evidence from Britain, Italy and Spain suggests that a left-liberal newspaper gains most circulation when a conservative government is in power.[70] Once a left-liberal paper becomes pro-government it tends to lose circulation to other newspapers which have become, thanks to the turns of political fortune, journals of the Opposition. Perhaps with this thought in mind, *Le Monde* startled its readers in October 1981 with a front-page article by Baron Rothschild bewailing the Socialist government's scheme to nationalize the French banks – including his own. (His foreign interests, including an American bank, were spared.)[71]

There is little new in *Le Monde* being attacked from the Left and from the Right. But what is new in the paper's surprisingly brief history is the way that, while it has gained in prestige and in the respect of its readers, it seems to have lost that vast affection which sustained it, through those readers' committees, during the crisis of 1951. There is a deliberate aloofness about the paper, in its bleakly serious (but aesthetically pleasing) layout, as well as in the classicism of its prose, the detached intellectualism of its editorials. It has started to make compromises, in its new Sunday section, as in its evident hunger for advertisements. It is often criticized in France as 'the finest

Anglo-Saxon newspaper of Europe',[72] but Anglo-Saxon journalists judge it 'the best something in the world, but it sure as hell ain't a newspaper'.[73] It is to journalism what de Gaulle was to international politics, something proud, mysterious, aloof and grand, dedicated to its own sense of greatness and of mission, and uniquely French; a magnificent illusion which is also a daily fact.

Notes

1. See *Le Monde de Beuve-Méry*, Jeanneny & Julliard, pp. 47–54. See also the monumental *Histoire générale de la Presse française* by Bellanger *et al.* vol. 4.
2. *ibid.*, Jeanneny & Julliard, *op cit*, pp. 54–6.
3. *ibid.*, p. 25. See also *Vers La Plus Grande Allemagne*, by H. Beuve-Méry. Centre de politique étrangère, Paris, 1939.
4. Jeanneny & Julliard, *op cit.*, pp. 27–32.
5. *ibid.*, pp. 32–44.
6. Letter from H. B.-M. to Paul Thisse (Beuve-Méry archives).
7. See Jeanneny & Julliard, *op. cit.*, pp. 61–5.
8. See *Histoire de la spoliation de la presse française*, Claude Hisard. La Librairie Française, Paris, 1955.
9. *Le Monde*, 19.xii.1944.
10. *Le Monde*, 24.xii.1944.
11. Sauvageot documents, international accounts from SARL Le Monde, made available to the author by M. Jacques Fauvet.
12. See the official 'Débats de l'Assemblée consultative', 7 March 1945, p. 352. Speech of Georges Cogniot.
13. *Le Monde*, 8.xi.1974.
14. *Le Monde*, 2.iii.1949.
15. See, for example, letter to H. B.-M., from Robert Schumann, then Foreign Minister, 29 November 1949 (H. B.-M. archives).
16. *Une Semaine dans Le Monde*, 17.i.1948.
17. Quoted in Jeanneny & Julliard, *op. cit.*, p. 110.
18. *Le Monde*, 28.x.1949.
19. *Note sur la direction du journal Le Monde communiquée par MM. René Courtin et Christian Funck-Brentano*, 18 July 1951. Archives of René Courtin, quoted in Jeanneny & Julliard, *op. cit.*, p. 123.
20. *ibid.*, pp. 142–3.
21. *ibid.*, p. 124.
22. Letter from Robert Gauthier to René Courtin, 24 July 1951.
23. Jeanneny & Julliard, *op. cit.*, pp. 151–7.
24. *ibid.*, p. 79.
25. Author's interviews, Jacques Fauvet, Bernard Feron.
26. *Le Monde*, 19.vi.1954.
27. *Le Monde*, 14.xii.1957.

28. Memorandum Boegner. Quoted in Jeanneny & Julliard, *op. cit.*, p. 181.
29. *ibid.*, pp. 198–205. See also *Le Monde* for 8.i.1957, 7.v.1958, 18.xii.1960 and 18.ii.1961.
30. See, for example, the *Washington Post*, 1.viii.1957, or the *Economist*, 11.xi.1956.
31. SARL Le Monde, reports of the directors to the General Assembly, 6 June 1980. Prepared by M. Jacques Sauvageot and M. Jacques Fauvet, made available to the author by M. Fauvet. Hereafter referred to as Sauvageot–Fauvet.
32. *Le Monde*, 31.v.1958.
33. *ibid.*, 26.ix.1958.
34. *ibid.*, 6.ii.1965.
35. *ibid.*, 27.viii.1959.
36. Sauvageot–Fauvet report, however, contradicts this, saying that in 1969 there were 33.6% of advertisements in the pages. But, for the figures quoted in the text, see *Le Monde*, 25.ix.1970, a series on the French press by Jacques Sauvageot.
37. *Un sang d'encre*, Jean Lacouture (Stock, Paris, 1974) p. 180.
38. Author's interview, Jacques Fauvet.
39. See *Le Monde*, 18.ii.1961, 26.i.1962 and 17.ii.1962.
40. See *Le Monde, supplément aux dossiers et documents du Monde*, December 1977 (published by *Le Monde*) p. 4. Also see Jeanneny & Julliard, *op. cit.*, pp. 273–8. Also author's interview, Jacques Fauvet.
41. *Le Monde*, 15.iii.1968.
42. *ibid.*
43. Jeanneny & Julliard, *op. cit.*, p. 364. See also *Le Monde supplément, op. cit.*, p. 5.
44. Jeanneny & Julliard, *op. cit.*, p. 251.
45. *Le Monde*, 26.v.1968.
46. *ibid.*, 11.vi.1968, article by Bertrand Girod de l'Ain.
47. Sauvageot–Fauvet report.
48. Author's interview, Jacques Fauvet. Also article by Sauvageot, *Le Monde*, 8.xi.1974. Also Sauvageot–Fauvet report, p. 4.
49. *Le Monde supplément, op. cit.*, p. 27. Sauvageot–Fauvet report, *op. cit.*, p. 14.
50. Author's interview, Jacques Fauvet.
51. Jeanneny & Julliard, *op. cit.*, p. 283. Also author's interview, Jean-François Fogel.
52. *Le Monde tel qu'il est*, Michel Legris.
53. *Le Monde*, 16.xi.1975.
54. *ibid.*, 21.vi.1975.
55. *Le Monde*, 2.ix.1977.
56. *Le Monde et le pouvoir*, Philippe Simmonot.
57. *ibid.*, and *NYT*, 16.v.1976.
58. Simmonot, *op. cit.*, p. 178.
59. Author's research.
60. Sauvageot–Fauvet report, *op. cit.*, p. 4.
61. Jeanneny & Julliard, *op. cit.*, p. 285 n,
62. Author's interview, Jacques Fauvet.
63. From *Le Monde*, 9.xi.1974, and author's research for week of 11–18 October 1980.

64. *Le Monde supplément, op. cit.*, p. 2. Also *Le Monde*, 25.iii.1977.
65. See *Daily Telegraph*, 5.vii.1980.
66. Author's interview, Jacques Fauvet.
67. *Daily Telegraph*, 12.vi.1981.
68. *The Times*, 15.iv.1981.
69. *Sunday Times*, 14.iv.1981.
70. Author's interview, P. Preston, editor, the *Guardian*, London.
71. *Le Monde*, 29.x.1981.
72. Jean Lacouture, *op. cit.*, p. 107.
73. Author's interview with Abe Rosenthal, editor,*NYT*.

LE MONDE: EDITORIALS

The independence of India: 15 August 1947

'By a decision as practical as it was bold, it is Britain herself, of her own free will, who has sealed this independence and should by these means succeed in safeguarding what is essential in the British presence . . .But it now would be foolish to ignore for long the implications of India's independence for the rest of Asia.'

The independence of Israel: 16 May 1948

'Whatever the outcome of the Israeli conflict, the Arab states are now confronted with their responsibilities. . .Instead of searching in Palestine or in North Africa as an outlet for the discontent of the Arab masses, their leaders will find themselves constrained by the developments in Palestine to conceive internal reforms and an improvement of living standards through the Near East.'

The Berlin blockade and airlift: 25 June 1948

'The Western allies should quit Berlin; nothing can justify their continued presence once the four-power government of Germany no longer functions.'

The Communists win power in China: 30 October 1949

'The Communist victory in China clearly gives the Indochinese problem an importance far beyond the relations between France and Vietnam. It is no longer simply a question of whether Vietnam will enjoy independence under a Bao-Dai government, or under Viet-Minh authority, or if the three Indochinese countries remain inside the French Union, or leave it. The question now is whether Vietnam can exist as a buffer-state of the anti-Communist world on the Asian continent? . . .Will the Americans make of Vietnam a new Greece, and give the French the supplies and backing which they need so much?'

The Korean war: 19 October 1950

'In spite of their agreement to the UN intervention in Korea, Asian members of the UN regard it with mixed feelings. One cannot but see in it a colonial expedition undertaken by whites against the coloured people of the continent.'

The Suez invasion: 1 November 1956

'The intervention of Britain and France has stunned and provoked disquiet and even indignation round the world. The relations between the USA and its European allies will undergo a grave crisis, the gravest perhaps since NATO was founded. One could indeed wish that this intervention had taken place in circumstances where the legal right was better established, but Britain and France are not the only ones to blame.'

The Russian invasion of Hungary: 4 November 1956

'So long as the group of "moderates" remain in powerful positions in Moscow, it hardly seems probable that the USSR will try to drown the Hungarian revolution in its own blood. This would, in effect, be an act with incalculable consequences and which would affront the greater part of world opinion.'

The Bay of Pigs assault on Cuba: 19 April 1961

'If the regime of Havana succeeds, the popularity of Fidel will be proved, and Soviet propaganda will find it easy to convince world opinion, starting with the peoples of Latin America, Africa and Asia, that the vaunted anti-colonialism of the USA is no more than a façade behind which shelters a hypocritical imperialism. Essentially, it is up to the people of Cuba to determine, by their attitude, the victor of this resort to force.'

The Cuban missile crisis: 24 October 1962

'It is curious to note that the Americans, who find it perfectly normal that a state like Turkey, on the borders of the USSR, should have missile launchers which menace the whole Donetz basin, contest the right of the USSR to conclude a similar agreement with Cuba.'

The Gulf of Tonkin incident: 6 August 1964

'The forces in the field being so ill-balanced, one cannot see why Hanoi should take an initiative which makes it worth their while to submit to President Johnson's "limited riposte" upon their own territory. . .One must wish that President Johnson, in his firmness, may also give some evidence of that prudence of his predecessor.'

China's nuclear weapon: 18 October 1964

'The news of the first Chinese atomic explosion has aroused many comments, whose almost unanimous conclusion is that it is high time to give China a seat at the UN, where one at least can discuss with her problems as decisive for humanity as an end to nuclear tests.'

Rhodesia's UDI: 13 November 1965

'The real objective of the Rhodesian colonists is to preserve indefinitely those privileges which assure them of the racial segregation which prevails there. By political realism, as much as by principled conviction, the British government oppose these pretensions. . .But however rigorous the envisaged sanctions, months if not years may roll by before the Europeans in Rhodesia judge their position untenable.'

The Russian invasion of Czechoslovakia: 22 August 1968

'With an entirely Stalinist logic, the idea finally prevailed that it was better to entrust to armies of occupation the task of putting a brutal end to the Prague Spring. . . But sooner or later, as Thomas Masaryk taught his people, Truth will prevail.'

Israel's occupation of the West Bank: 3 November 1973

'In view of the concerted moves of Moscow and Washington, the isolation of Israel on the international scene, and because it is not possible to impose peace through a policy of *"faits accomplis"*, Jerusalem should in the end accept compromises so that co-existence can be established between the states of the whole region.'

The OPEC price rise: 6 November 1973

'Until now, one always said that European union would progress only by being tested. But today the question is whether the ordeal by oil that the Arabs are imposing on Europe is not too stern a test, and that European unity will actually go into reverse . . .France is going to continue to evade having to choose between the two axes, Arab and European, of her foreign policy.'

Watergate: 7 November 1973

'Instead of one Watergate affair, twenty others are now surging from the shadows, implicating not only those complicities covered up by the White House, but also the current practices of the Executive and therefore, above all, the credit and the democratic rectitude of the President. There was already the Watergate scandal, revealing enough in itself. Now there is the Nixon case.'

The fall of Saigon: 2 May 1975

'For this people of rice farmers, the word peace will have an immediate meaning – a return to the land, to the sensuality of a new planting season which neither the Americans nor their local protégés ever understood and, without which, the Communist victory over the greatest power on earth would remain a mystery.'

Sport and politics: 20 July 1980

'One may accord to each side the judgement of sincerity. The arguments of those who seek to separate as far as possible sport and politics, to maintain the privilege of the Olympic ideal and the brotherhood of sport behind the great politico-commercial manoeuvres of the modern Games, are perfectly honourable. Nor should the motives of the boycott partisans be contested. In this matter, the choice is supported only by intimate conviction and visceral reaction. It seeks to be a purely moral condemnation.'

The space venture: 14 April 1961

'Humanity would prefer it if the two giants, instead of indulging in a rivalry which becomes daily more demanding of those resources which are needed for simple existence, found in the exploration of space the opportunity to join their efforts and at last overcome a cold war that is more and more anachronistic.'

Freedom of information: 27 May 1958

'The peril to the unity of France to which the revolutionary course is leading has persuaded the government to submit radio, TV and the press to "preventive control". This is a grave measure, which can only be justified by circumstances of extreme gravity. From today, the responsibility for the information they publish has passed from the papers more or less directly into the hands of representatives of the State. Their best justification is to stop extremists of all sorts from promoting and exploiting, for their own ends, disquiet and fear among the public. One may assume that this is the essential part.

In return, two kinds of inconvenience seem inevitable. Reduced to official information alone, the French show themselves sceptical and ready to lend an ear to any rumour. Moreover, men very deeply attached to republican legality may be tempted to maintain a certain reserve, for fear that a profession of honest faith might appear sullied by some complaisance in regard to the powers that be.

May the return to civil peace soon permit the press to recover its free role in the normal pursuit of its obligations and its rights.'

(Translations by the author)

4

Die Welt

Die Welt was founded, as an act of enlightened conquest, by the British military authorities in April 1946. Colonel H. B. Garland, later a professor of German at the University of Exeter, conceived the idea of *Die Welt* while driving in a staff car in December 1945 through the war-shattered, half-demolished streets of Hamburg. Were Germany to become a democracy, and recover from the disasters of Nazism he argued, then it would need a free and reliable press.[1]

Garland won official approval for his idea, but his first proposal as editor, Hans Zehrer, proved too controversial. Although Zehrer had spent the years of Hitler in self-imposed exile on the island of Sylt, his conservative, nationalist record as editor of *Die Tat* in the early 1930s led to protests from British Labour politicians and from the left-leaning Hamburg City Council.[2] Rudolf Küstermeier, a Social Democrat whose anti-Nazi credentials had been cruelly established when British troops rescued him from Belsen concentration camp in April 1945, took over Zehrer's chair.

But the editorial team that Küstermeier led had been recruited by Zehrer, and it was Zehrer's dream, 'to establish a German version of the London *Times*', that Küstermeier began to fulfil.[3] He did so in impossible conditions. 'The first office had been two telephone stalls, and someone had torn down the dividing walls. There was just enough room to put down a camp-bed,' recalled Kurt Marek, one of the first journalists.[4] The first salaries were paid with borrowed money, the next by the British military organization which hired German labourers. The building itself had been requisitioned by the British authorities, and the Hamburg City Council managed to find a subsidy for the paper through the convenient fiction of saying the money came from the non-existent 'German Reich'.[5]

The first issue appeared on 2 April 1946, with six pages, and a half-page of advertisements – mainly from people looking for somewhere to live. It contained two pages of news, two on the economy and two pages of *feuilletons*, or cultural affairs. Küstermeier's first editorial announced that the paper would be 'a bridge to other people, to other ways of life and of thought that have been denied to us for twelve years'.[6] Veterans of those days still dispute how far it was a British, how far an independent German publication.[7] But there is little doubt that its early issues were rooted in a sense of German guilt. The war, and its bitter aftermath, stalked the pages. In the fifth issue, the anniversary of his freedom from Belsen, Küstermeier wrote a front-page editorial on Belsen – 'The word will be a reminder of what barbarity was possible for a people who thought themselves the most civilized on earth.'[8] There were special editions for lists of German PoWs still in Poland, still in Russian camps. Even when the Russians unreasonably stalled in the four-power negotiations for Germany's future, Küstermeier wrote: 'Russia can point to the enormous damage Germany has already caused, and could do again if rebuilt.'[9]

In Britain, there were protests even at the limited independence of thought that Steel McRitchie, the British Controller, allowed. At first it was published twice a week, but the enormous success of the paper, selling 160,000 in its first week, led quickly to three editions a week, and to a constant stream of applications from German printers and journalists who knew that a job guaranteed food, some pay, and some kind of future. Under Küstermeier, it had a centre-left bias, welcomed by Hamburg's Social-Democrat City Council. Konrad Adenauer, the chairman of the fledgling Christian-Democrat centre-right party, sniffed: 'For a so-called non-party publication, it marched in the front rank of the Social-Democrat interest.'[10]

The British influence was pervasive. In 1947, *Die Welt* began to receive *The Times* international news service. In the same year, it serialized Winston Churchill's memoirs. There were constant bickerings for more independence from the British supervisors. 'They used to read and approve every word we wrote,' remembers Bernt Conrad, a young Berlin journalist who was flown out of the blockade to join *Die Welt*.[11] But the British officers themselves usually took the side of the German journalists in the arguments with London.[12] The steady realization in London, as in Washington, that a rebuilt Germany was the best bulwark against the seeming menace of Soviet Russia helped to resolve the arguments. In 1948, *Die Welt* was banned in the Soviet Zone of occupied Germany. In the same year, the Berlin blockade drew up the battle-lines of the Cold War. It did not stop Hans Zehrer attacking *Die Welt* as 'the British daily in the German language'.[13] Nor did it explain the dramatic tactlessness of the British General Robertson, who ordered the paper to describe itself on its front page as 'non-party German newspaper – German–English editorship'. This was not even true. It was stopped only by the determined lobbying of Bernhard Menne, an ex-Communist refugee from Hitler who had lived in Britain during the war, and used his personal contacts with British Labour MPs to get the General's order rescinded.[14] But there was little doubt that *Die Welt* was a success. Menne himself was editor of a sign of that success, the Sunday edition of *Welt am Sonntag*, founded in August 1948. By the end of 1947, *Die Welt* was selling 600,000 copies a day; by the end of 1948, 950,000. In 1949, it peaked at 1,050,000. Advertising income grew from 445,000 Reichsmarks in 1946, to RM 994,000 in 1947, to over a million Deutsche Marks in 1948, the year of the currency reform which financially certified the split with the Eastern Zone and launched the German economic revival.[15] In 1949, advertising income totalled DM 5.8 million, and *Die Welt* was self-confident enough to launch editorial attacks on 'the Communist danger of Soviet expansion'. Heinrich Schulte, a key figure for the future, had joined the paper as publishing manager.[16]

'King Heinrich' had been an executive in Max Amman's EherVerlag, the state-controlled press monopoly of the Hitler years. But he knew how to run newspapers, and he realized that the imminent end of British licensing controls on German publications meant that *Die Welt*'s profitable monopoly was about to collapse in the face of dozens of new competitors. He gambled on establishing a new sales system, with *Die Welt* subsidizing its distributors and launching a determined campaign to win advertising. Heinrich Krebs later recalled the difficulty of selling ads in a 'British paper' to German businessmen in the Ruhr, while they and Krebs listened to the demolition teams blowing up the Krupp factories outside.[17] Schulte also built up the printing capacity of *Die Welt*'s presses, and began to lease them out to other publishers, like the *Westdeutsche Allgemeine Zeitung*, and to the *Hamburger Abendblatt* and *Hör Zu!*, owned by a rising young publisher from Altona called Axel Springer.

Schulte's diversification scheme came only just in time. In the five months after the British eased the licensing system, the number of German papers leapt from 178 to 568. From over 1 million in February 1949, *Die Welt*'s circulation sank to just 300,000 in February 1950.[18] 'Several journalists were fired, the rest of us had our salaries cut,' remembers Bernt Conrad. 'We did not starve, but they were hard times.'[19]

Schulte had also negotiated a new management structure with the British Controller, Steel McRitchie, which allowed the British to retain a veto, but put most of the day-to-day responsibility into German hands. Küstermeier presented an ultimatum for further changes, including an end to the British veto, and resigned when he was turned down. Editorial confusion followed. Bernhard Menne took over as editor for five months, followed by Adenauer's former press adviser, Paul Bourdin, and then by a triumvirate led by Dr Adalbert Worliczek, a man so dedicated to the Adenauer cause that Schulte replaced him with a liberal refugee from the *Frankfurter Allgemeine Zeitung*, Albert Komma.

The circulation continued to decline. By the end of 1952, the balance sheet showed a loss of DM 1,080,000. The trade unions were demanding more money, the cost of newsprint had risen and, worst of all, Axel Springer had withdrawn his vital printing contracts. The British authorities wanted to be rid of *Die Welt* and there was no shortage of potential buyers. The revived old publishing house of Ullstein was interested, but worried about *Die Welt*'s financial losses. The German government itself, recalling that polite fiction of Reich money being used to found the paper, made discreet inquiries until Hamburg Social-Democrats and trade unionists jointly protested to London. Axel Springer's bid, low as it was, was eventually accepted, in spite of the fears of Steel McRitchie that this would put too great a concentration of press power into a single pair of hands.[20] For the deal involved not only *Die Welt* and *Welt am Sonntag*, but also the buildings and site in Essen, a thriving travel-bureau, the sales network, the printing capacity and the successful magazine *Das Neue Blatt*. British sources hinted that Springer had paid only DM 2 million for the consortium; the German press estimated he had paid DM 3.5 million, and the well-informed *Times* announced that Springer had paid altogether DM 6 million. Springer himself never confirmed any figure. Since he never had to subsidize the *Welt* empire until 1970, and by 1956 was earning a regular DM 8 to 11 million annual profit from it, he had reason to be discreet.[21]

Other questions remain. Steel McRitchie's initial opposition to

Springer was overcome in part by Springer's promise to establish a Trust structure to share ownership with him. In fact the Trust never had more than 25% of the shares, leaving Springer in full control. It was used as a convenient bank, never drawing its full profit share, and by 1970 it had been formally wound up. But until his death in 1963, Heinrich Schulte had used the Trust's veto on senior editorial appointments to keep Springer's influence from dominating the paper.

Although it has never been confirmed, there is some evidence to suggest that political influence played a part in Springer's success. When the prospect of a sale first arose, a meeting between Springer and the conservative German Chancellor, Dr Adenauer, was arranged. It took place between 19 and 22 April at the CDU conference in Hamburg, arranged by the Hamburg CDU leader, Erik Blumenfeld, who was to remain Springer's key ally in the governing party, later leading the political fight for commercial TV in Germany – another Springer ambition. Three weeks after that meeting with Springer, Adenauer went to Britain where, among other matters, he discussed the future of *Die Welt* with the British Foreign Office. The day after Adenauer's discussions, *Die Welt*'s advisory council in Hamburg agreed in principle to sell *Die Welt* to Axel Springer. Certainly, once Springer had formally purchased the paper, it took him only two weeks to appoint Hans Zehrer as editor, and to begin the process of turning *Die Welt* from a 'non-party paper' to a conservative, deeply political paper that almost invariably supported Adenauer's CDU.[22] Steel McRitchie had shrewdly guessed that this might happen. When Springer had insisted that he had no political ambitions, McRitchie had been blunt. 'If you have *Die Welt*, you will become a politician yourself,' he told him.[23]

Springer did so, but in a classically British, rather than German, way. He became a press baron, a Northcliffe or Beaverbrook or even a Randolph Hearst figure, with enormous apparent influence at his disposal. By 1964, he owned over 40% of German daily papers sold, over 80% of Sunday papers, 45% of youth magazines, and 48% of its radio and TV magazines.[24] In Germany, this concentration of press power inevitably reminded his critics of the monopolistic Eher Verlag combine that had ruled the German press in Hitler's day. But Axel Springer was to learn, as Beaverbrook and the other press barons had learnt before him, that the power to sell papers is a very different thing from the power to mould opinions. Just as Beaverbrook's attempts at Empire-propaganda in Britain were doomed to watch that Empire disappear, so Springer's conservative, nationalist and anti-Communist campaigns took place as Germany's voters approved *Ostpolitik*, retreated from nationalism, and elected left-liberal coalitions to govern them. Springer's admiration for the British press lords such as Cecil King was echoed in the way that his most popular paper, *Bild-Zeitung*, was deliberately modelled on King's *Daily Mirror*, with big bold headlines, dramatic pictures, a sense of tumultuous, lively action in the very design of the pages. Started in June 1952, by the time Springer bought *Die Welt*, the strident *Bild* was selling over 1 million copies a day. By 1956, it was selling 3 million.[25]

While concentrating on *Bild-Zeitung*, Springer was content to let Hans Zehrer, the grand old man of German journalism, re-shape *Die Welt* as a platform for his curious blend of mystic, progressive and nationalistically conservative beliefs that had, in the early 1930s, unwittingly helped to pave the ideological way for Adolf Hitler. We cannot understand Zehrer's politics without examining the German concept of *'die Volk'*. It translates into English as 'people', but it means a very great deal more than that. The word *Volk* carries overtones of moral purpose; of national destiny; of simple, peasant-rooted wisdom; of enormous sentimentality – and justified ruthlessness when the interests of the *Volk* require it. It suggests a chosen people, a rustic innocence, and a historical mission, all at once. Zehrer hardly ever wrote an article (just as Hitler never made a speech) without using the word. Zehrer's great dream was of a re-united Germany, with its capital in Berlin. He transmitted this dream to Springer. Even through the Cold War, the evidence of Soviet determination to crush any dissidence in its Eastern European empire, even after the brutal invasion of Hungary in 1956, Zehrer clung not only to this dream but to the view that somehow an agreement could be reached with Moscow that could permit German reunification to take place. In the week after Soviet tanks rolled into Budapest, Zehrer wrote a front-page editorial in *Die Welt*: 'In two years at the latest, we shall again have Berlin as the metropolis of an all-German state.'[26]

In witness to that belief, in January 1955 *Die Welt* began printing a special Berlin edition, at first flying it in from the Western Zone, and in 1956 became the first European paper to use the latest teletype systems print in Hamburg, Essen and in Berlin itself.[27] In 1955, Zehrer and Springer travelled together to Moscow to promote their dream of one Germany. At a time when Adenauer's CDU government was almost proudly joining the Western alliance as a re-armed, democratic and anti-Communist state, Zehrer was spelling out in *Die Welt* the price he would pay for reunification: 'only one way is open; to co-exist with the Russians by moving towards a non-aligned, independent state'.[28] Given the realities of the Cold War of the 1950s, Zehrer's scenario was probably doomed from the start. But such was his reputation, and so great the influence of *Die Welt*, that Zehrer's argument loomed over German domestic politics throughout the 1950s. Circulation recovered from its low point of 165,000 in 1954 to 191,000 by the end of 1955, to 217,000 in 1959.[29]

In 1958, a second, less successful visit to Khrushchev seems to have dampened the ardour of the two men. Certainly the prospect of a reunited Germany, not linked to either NATO or the Warsaw Pact, steadily ebbs from *Die Welt*'s pages. And Zehrer's orotund, rhetorical style, set in the longwinded, pompous prose that had been fashionable a generation earlier, was ever less in tune with the new Germany of the economic miracle. A private poll of its readers commissioned by *Die Welt* found Zehrer slipping badly down the league of 'most respected commentators'.[30] Zehrer's news values sometimes fell victim to his politics. When Franz-Josef Strauß began the Spiegel Affair by having the Spanish police arrest a Spiegel journalist who had criticized him, Zehrer originally wanted to dismiss it in twenty lines, on the grounds that the row would blow over. But he was persuaded otherwise by his staff, and *Die Welt*'s political commentator, Bernt Conrad, ran a powerful editorial that thundered 'Strauß has become an oppressive burden upon our democracy.'[31]

The *Frankfurter Allgemeine Zeitung* was recovering from its political opportunism of the 1950s, and providing stiff competition. Axel Springer began to take an ever more personal role in the paper's administration, peppering his senior editors with notes and comments and queries on every page of every issue.[32] Springer began investing more money, hiring thirty new journalists to bring the editorial team up to 200, opening new bureaux overseas, proclaiming *Die Welt* as Germany's first 'national newspaper', changing its linguistic rules and style.

'He was my friend, he was my mentor,' Springer was to say of Zehrer, but Springer's opinions began to tell in the late 1950s and early 1960s.[33] Perhaps the key event for the Springer empire, certainly for *Die Welt*, was the building of the Berlin Wall, that symbol of a divided, still-occupied nation. Some critics, notably *Der Spiegel* magazine, suggested that the increasingly hysterical anti-Communism of *Bild-Zeitung* helped to provoke the building of the wall.[34] Springer was certainly throwing his weight around, arbitrarily boycotting newsagents who stocked publications which gave the listings of East German broadcasts.[35]

The restraints on the press baron began to weaken. Heinrich Schulte died in 1963, and in the same year, Zehrer moved to Berlin, leaving the day-to-day running of *Die Welt* in the hands of a younger generation of German-Americans, determined anti-Communists. Springer ordered more expansion, hiring another hundred journalists, partly to replace the steady blood-letting of experienced, respected journalists like George Ramseger, Kurt Becker, Paul Sethe who began to resign in droves.[36] In some (non-political) ways, the paper improved, with new sections like 'Literary *Welt*', and ever more pages printing on a buoyant sea of advertising. *Die Welt* was given a face-lift, a modernized modular layout, an Anglo-American style 'Opinion-Editorial page', more pictures, more arts coverage and new sections like 'School and High School', 'Science and Art'. In a bid to attract readers from the conservatively-designed *Frankfurter Allgemeine Zeitung, Die Welt* began to go down-market. 'We will be a paper full of spontaneity, overflowing with freshness and openess,' it told its readers.[37] Circulation rose to a peak of 290,000 in 1964, but a harsh and strident note began to develop, as the right-wing replacements like Wilfried Hertz-Eichenrode attacked the liberal intelligentsia and supported curious causes like Pastor Evertz's 'Fatherland Christianity'. *Die Welt* ran a bizarre series on the 'Red Orchestra', the anti-Nazi Communist spy-ring of World War II, with headlines like '200,000 [Germans] died through treachery', and demanding a hunt for a new Red Orchestra at treacherous work in modern West Germany. There were understanding articles about the roots of the neo-fascist NPD party, which was gaining a brief flurry of electoral support. And in 1966, with the death of Hans Zehrer, an international row developed over the alleged Nazi past and anti-semitism of *Die Welt*'s new editor, Dr Herman Starke.[38] The row was, in fact, unjustified. Starke (on whose appointment Springer had consulted the President of the Republic) had in fact used Gestapo contacts to warn his wife's Jewish relations, and officers who were involved in the 1944 plot to assassinate Hitler, about their escapes. But *Die Welt* was now a target, a symbol of hysterical and crude anti-Communism.[39] *Die Welt*'s own articles helped to justify the attacks it began to receive. A nasty, but relatively small, student demonstration against the Vietnam war and the visiting US Vice-President Hubert Humphrey was blown up into an international assassination plot by *Die Welt*.

'I got back to Berlin from Asia, after covering the Vietnam war, about 1970,' Friedheim Kremna remembers. 'And not only could you not buy *Die Welt* anywhere on a university campus. You didn't even dare carry a copy. I had had no idea how unpopular we had become. How hated.'[40] The campus boycotts had a dramatic financial impact. Through a student discount scheme, *Die Welt* traditionally sold over 20,000 copies a day to students and thousands more to university teachers. This market disappeared within twelve months, and by 1970 the paper was losing money.[41] The attacks on *Die Welt* were launched by the rebellious students of the late 1960s, but were then taken up and made respectable by the politicians of the SDP. It was the students who launched Springer-boycotts and who physically blocked the Springer delivery vans in 1968, but it was the politicians who started to discuss new laws to reduce the capacity of any one organization to monopolize the German press. From 1969, the Social-Democrats were in power in Germany, and Springer's empire itself became a kind of extra-parliamentary opposition.[42] Cannily, enough of the Springer magazine empire was sold to keep its market share below the 40% that the government called the danger level. But even today, over 45 million Springer publications are bought in Germany every week. His empire still employs 11,000 people, with a total turnover of some $500 million a year.[43]

But whereas the Springer organization could make intelligent compromises on the economic level, the nature of the political changes of the early 1970s, the move to détente and *Ostpolitik*, the growth of terrorism, precluded any change in the press empire's political line. More than that, the traditional conservatives of *Die Welt* panicked at what they thought was the terminal crisis of German democracy. *Die Welt*'s new editor, Herbert Kremp, who had been appointed to soften the paper's sharp political edge, lost his own sense of proportion. When Chancellor Willy Brandt won the Nobel Prize for his *Ostpolitik*, Kremp waspishly noted: 'Nobel did not establish a prize for Freedom,' and compared *Ostpolitik* with Chamberlain's appeasement policy of 1938. 'We are living through a Kerensky era,' Kremp warned, a Social-Democrat phase that he saw leading to a Bolshevik state.[44]

Extreme conservatives like Dr Hans Joachim Schoeps were given whole pages to write on the German plight. 'We are at one minute before midnight,' Schoeps warned. 'Now that no General von Seeckt and no loyal officer corps stand at our disposal, so many of us will turn to the only thinkable "strong man" [Franz-Josef Strauß] who has appeared, who will lead us to take the necessary precautions.'[45] Emergency laws, police surveillance of political suspects, preventive detention – these were small prices to pay to preserve the state against the threat of revolution. This panic response had Springer's firm backing. 'We are moving towards the last battle for freedom. . .the state and the economy stand in the gravest of dangers,' he warned.[46]

Restricted to the opinion columns, this kind of shrill perspective would be little more than a historical curiosity. . .but it began to spill over on to the news pages. On domestic affairs, a governmental proposal would be given ten lines, followed by a hundred lines of critical comment from the conservative Opposition. In a strike, the trade-union position would be curtly dismissed, and management's arguments exhaustively outlined.[47] Die Welt's reports of the bloody military coup in Chile against Allende's Marxist government glossed over the reign of terror that the soldiers introduced. The officers' junta in Greece was praised, its tortures excused or denied. (When the files of Greek diplomats were published after the fall of the junta, showing payments to individual Welt journalists for favourable stories, Die Welt merely insisted that it had every confidence in its staff, and dismissed the evidence.[47]) Die Welt's coverage of the Shah of Iran's authoritarian rule only mentioned SAVAK, the security police, to quote, with approval, from SAVAK files on anti-Shah students, living in exile in Iraq, who had studied in Germany.[48] Communist subversion, in Die Welt's pages, was the cause of all problems. Critical German magazines, like Stern, were accused of being 'used by a KGB disinformation scheme'.[49] When the OPEC nations raised the price of their oil, Die Welt claimed that they had been 'guided by their Soviet advisers'.[50] Its own advertising tried to sell its conservatism, somehow believing it would attract readers at a time when the German electorate was voting for détente and a left-centre coalition government: 'The wind has changed. Many people in our land are sick and tired of ideological ultimatums. They want more preservation of the old tried and tested ways. They long for security from radical violence. They want a state with authority. They demand order within freedom. They turn away from ideology, towards ideals. Die Welt has always been for the preservation of the proven, tried and tested ways. That is why Die Welt of today is the paper of tomorrow.'[51]

The tone grew more shrill as the financial losses of the paper began to mount. The student and Left boycott had reduced sales to a low of 196,000 in 1974, and the cost of printing in three separate places, with special local editions in Berlin and Hamburg, dramatically increased *Die Welt*'s costs, as the economic recessions and inflations of 1971 and 1974 increased the cost of newsprint, of salaries and, above all, of distribution. Springer's determination to make *Die Welt* into a national paper for all Germany was particularly expensive in a country where people buy their newspapers, not on the street, but through subscriptions. To compete in Bavaria meant printing early editions, hauling them to the south of Germany, and establishing an expensive distribution network there for a small circulation, in a market where the traditional dominance of *Suddeutsche Zeitung* meant that little was clawed back in local advertising.

The last profitable year for *Die Welt* was 1970. By 1974, the annual loss exceeded DM 20 million,[52] and the decision was taken to move the headquarters to Bonn, in the hope that this might save some DM 10 million a year, and to bring in new printing technology to cut the labour force. Once based in Bonn, *Die Welt* launched a special Bonn supplement, a local edition, with the announced objective of gaining 10,000 new subscribers in the city. The special edition collapsed within a year.[53] Dismayed by the financial losses, and by the political threats he discerned, Springer pondered giving up *Die Welt*, and merging it with the *Frankfurter Allgemeine Zeitung*.[54] Instead, a series of rationalizations took place. By 1980, a new printing centre, equipped with the latest computer technology, had been opened at Kettwig on the Ruhr, where 75% of the copies were printed.[55] The Berlin printing centre and the Berlin local edition were closed. The Hamburg printing was maintained only because it was feared that the loss of the local edition, with its special 'Hansestadt Hamburg' supplement, would savagely reduce the 65,000 copies sold there each day.[56] The weight of *Die Welt*'s circulation was in the Ruhr, the North-Rhein-Westphalia province, with a bare 5% of its circulation going to Bavaria, 4% to the province of Hesse, 4% to the Saar and Palatinate and so on.[57] But the losses continued. 'I hope to keep the losses down to DM 20 million in 1980,' Peter Boenisch promised, with a new editor's confidence, but the accumulated losses of *Die Welt* in the decade of the 1970s totalled about $100 millon.[58]

A second great rationalization then took place, a fundamental but still formally denied change of political course. 'There is no change of political line,' Peter Boenisch announced in 1979. 'There is, however, me.'[59] It was a guarded admission, one that was made with a wary eye upon the deeply conservative Ernst Cramer and Axel Springer at the SpringerVerlag HQ. But an editor who publicly refused to accept an invitation to South Korea because of its denial of human rights, and who attacked 'the blind anti-Communism which feels it necessary to support every vicious, torturing dictator around the world', represented a startling shift from the hysterical conservatism of the early 1970s.[60]

Peter Boenisch was perhaps the one leading executive within the Springer empire who could get away with this change. Since the 1960s when, as a thirty-four-year-old editor, he took *Bild-Zeitung* to a circulation peak of 5.3 million a day, he has been labelled as Springer's boy-wonder. Then, too, he had to tone down the shrill anti-Communism of the *Bild-Zeitung* of 1960. He was one of the few men in the organization who could flatly contradict Axel Springer. In 1963, at the height of the Starfighter crisis, when the US-built aircraft were falling out of the sky by the dozen and taking their German pilots with them, Springer called Boenisch back from holiday to 'put an end to the crisis'. Instead of taking the government's side, Boenisch made his own investigation and then demanded the resignation of the Minister for Defence in the pages of *Bild*. 'There have been other divergences of opinion since I have been editor of *Die Welt*. But I am not going to gossip about them.'[61]

Under Boenisch's editorship, the *Die Welt* which had seen the Shah of Iran's problems as caused only by Communist subversion began to probe into the economic dislocations of the Shah's policies, into the reasons for his unpopularity. Helmut Schmidt's version of *Ostpolitik* was given guarded support. The Chancellor's visit to Poland in a sailing ship in 1979 won an admiring editorial from Peter Boenisch, who contrasted the event with Hitler's visit to Poland in a battleship in 1939. 'Better a yachting cap than a steel helmet,' Boenisch approved.[62] Its politics were still on the Right, bluntly attempting to make electoral propaganda with its news stories about arms deals with the USSR during the 1980 election campaign.[63] The anti-terrorist police were criticized for not working hard enough, for letting the pathetic remnants of the Baader-Meinhof gang stay on the loose, but the tone changed.

So did the look of the paper, with a bolder use of cartoons and graphics, particularly on the front page, and Boenisch daily supervised the layout of every page. Critics sniffed that it was '*flockig*' – or bitty, and superficial. 'I'd only worry if they said it was boring,' Boenisch retorted.[64]

'If Peter Boenisch were to leave, I think more than half the journalists on *Die Welt* would resign,' claimed Peter Jänsch, the elected shop steward of the journalists' union at *Die Welt*. 'He is too good a journalist to make propaganda.'[65] It seemed a broadly held view, and the steady rise in circulation to 250,000 suggests that the new approach won back some departed readers. An independent survey of readership in July 1979 showed that it had grown by 24% from 660,000 to 820,000, although the number of copies sold had not increased anything like as dramatically.[66] But Boenisch was working with sharply curtailed resources. *Die Welt* had been cut back from fourteen to eight foreign correspondents and, more and more, was having to take its overseas coverage from SAD, the Springer group's combined foreign news service.[67] The number of editorial staff had been cut back from 300 of the early 1960s to 160 in 1979 and then to 120 in 1981. Some days, the paper is a slim version of its fat former self. On the day after the German national election of 1980, it was a mere sixteen pages, three of them devoted to sport, one to foreign news and one to cultural affairs. Advertisements filled only 25% of the paper. *Die Welt* cut its coat according to its cloth. On Saturdays, when circulation traditionally rose by about 15% because of the cultural supplement '*Geistige Welt*' and advertising supplements on property and cars, the paper expanded to 122 pages. From 1979 to late 1980 *Die Welt* deliberately tried to reduce its circulation by cutting out high-cost distribution to outlying areas. 'We just can't afford to make ourselves available to every last village in Germany,' Peter Boenisch insisted. But the prestige foreign circulation, to the 800 British and fifty-one Chinese readers, was maintained.[68]

Few papers have been as bluntly, indeed as politically, treated as *Die Welt*. Used in turn as a method of inculcating democracy and a tradition of press freedom by the British; as a vehicle for reuniting Germany by Hans Zehrer; as Springer's personal 'battle-sheet' to defend conservatism, it was at last being allowed to get on with the business of being a responsible, moderate paper with a national audience and an international reputation. It said much for the skills of its journalists that it emerged from its cumulative ordeals, battered but finally unbowed. And much of the explanation can be found in the curious way that post-war German history has been dominated by a series of quite specific generations. Under Hans Zehrer, Germany was still being run by the generation of men, Adenauer perhaps prime among them, who had come to maturity before Hitler, and who wanted to see Germany recover her 'rightful and respected place' among the nations of the world. After Zehrer's time came the generation of the Herbert Kremps and the Axel Springers, men who had come to maturity as Hitler seized power, who had seen an earlier German democracy crumble before a wave of terror between Left and Right, the threats of inflation and unemployment, and who were determined that the new Germany should never have to face such economic and political challenges – largely because, after Hitler, they found it desperately hard to believe that democracy in Germany was stable and resilient enough to survive such threats. This explains the panic at *Die Welt* from 1968 to about 1975. But Peter Boenisch and the team he assembled at *Die Welt*, its string of outstanding foreign correspondents like the legendary Fritz Werth in London, came from a generation which matured when Hitler had fallen, men whose adult lives had known the success of German democracy and an enviably healthy economy. Political panic was foreign to their experience. It was Fritz Werth, during the successive British crises of the 1970s, who pointed out that they should not be taken too seriously. 'It has become a part of the British season,' he explained, 'we all get back from the summer holidays and the pay-claims begin. Come the winter, we have the strike season, and then the demonstrations and "Can-the-government-survive?" season. And then comes spring, and it is the season for cricket, for strawberries, for Wimbledon again. And it will be the same next year.'[69]

This raises the question of the next generation of *Die Welt*, the journalists who were angry students in the 1960s. 'I imagine most of the journalists on *Die Welt* vote Social-Democrat. The international press tradition has become liberal-left, and that is probably no bad thing,' Peter Boenisch acknowledged in an interview when his liberal-ization of the paper seemed to be succeeding. 'The inward-looking, national-conscious traditions of the Hans Zehrer era of journalism have become international. I don't want this paper to be measured against *FAZ* or *NZZ*, but against *The Times*, the *New York Times*, just as Axel Springer made a revolution in German newspapers by modelling *Bild* after the London *Daily Mirror*. Papers are like actors. We need critics, and preferably we need it from our peers. There is a German tradition that you have to read three or four papers in order to be properly informed. I want *Die Welt* to be the paper where readers can find everything they need.'[70]

One representative of that next generation of German journalists, Springer's son and heir to the empire, who had worked as a news cameraman under the name Sven Simon, committed suicide in 1980, leaving the future of the SpringerVerlag in doubt. There is pre-liminary talk of a Trust after Springer's death, but the decision will rest with the unpredictable Springer. He has the habit of going into a kind of retreat at regular intervals, before returning to regalvanize his publications. 'I have not heard from him for months,' Boenisch said in 1980. 'All through the election campaign, not a word.'[71] His paternal spirit looms over *Aktuelle*, the house-magazine for the Springer staff. It blazons his house slogan, 'Be nice to one another', and reprints Springer's speeches.[72] All Springer's journalists must, when they are hired, sign an agreement that they believe in and support his celebrated four principles: German–Israeli friendship, and Israel's right to exist within secure borders; commitment against totalitarianism of Left or Right; belief in the free market economy; and belief in the peaceful reunification of Germany.[73] Even Lord Beaverbrook never had the nerve to ask his writers to sign that kind of contract.

Axel Springer's final decision on the fate of *Die Welt* and of his overall press empire was reached in the spring of 1981. He decided to fire Peter Boenisch, and to sell a key shareholding in the Springer-Verlag holding company to one of his main German publishing rivals, the Burda group.[74] Boenisch's replacement by the conservative triumvirate of Dr Herbert Kremp, Wilfried Hertz Eichenrode and Matthias Warden was bitterly opposed by the 120 journalists on *Die Welt*, who announced: 'We are fighting not only for our editor but for our professional ethics.'[75] Their arguments made little headway against Springer's complaint that *Die Welt* had lost some £8 million in the previous financial year. The staff response was to mark Peter Boenisch's departure with a newspaper in which the headlines were carefully composed to read: The Good Times Are Over. . .Big Setback For The World. . .The People Don't Back The Junta. . . and. . .Decree From The Top.[76]

The sale of 26% of SpringerVerlag to the Burda group for £43 million gave the purchaser, under German law, the power of veto over Springer board decisions. The deal, which required approval by the national cartel office, envisaged Burda purchasing eventual control of Springer. It brought together two of the dominant media groups in the country. The 1979 turnover of the Springer group was almost £500 million, with profits of almost exactly £10 million. In 1980, the Burda group had profits of £3.5 million on a turnover of £200 million.[77] This was the end of the Springer empire, and of a generation of dominance over the German media which had accompanied and even symbolized the German economic miracle.

The immediate result of the sacking of Boenisch and the Burda merger was a renewed decline in *Die Welt*'s circulation and renewed fears that the paper would revert to the *Kampfblatt* (crusading sheet) politics of the 1960s. *Die Welt's* renewed opposition to the anti-nuclear and peace groups in Germany, its dismissal of the environment movement which Boenisch had begun to take seriously, and its revivified defence of the Israeli government led by Menachem Begin made it plain that Peter Boenisch's editorship had been but a brief aberration, to be reversed at Axel Springer's will. Had Boensich stopped the financial losses, Springer executives argued, then the liberalization of *Die Welt* could have continued with impunity. But the continuing financial losses undermined Boenisch's support. In 1981, as in 1946, *Die Welt* was the child of power.

Notes

1. *Beitrage für Zeitgeschichte*, April/May 1976.
2. *Press Power*, Hans Dieter Muller. Translated from *Der Springer Konzern* (Piper Verlag, Munich) p. 91.
3. *Beitrage, op. cit.*
4. *ibid.*
5. Muller, *op. cit.*, p. 94.
6. *Die Welt*, 2.iv.1946.
7. Muller, *op. cit.* Also author's interview with Bernt Conrad. See also '*Hans Zehrer als politischer Publizist*', by Ebbo Deamnt, *Die Welt* archives. See also '*Die Welt 1946–53. Eine deutsche oder eine britischer Zeitung?*', Karl-Heinz Harenberg.
8. *Die Welt*, 16.iv.1946.
9. *Die Welt*, 14.xii.1946.
10. *Beitrage, op. cit.*
11. Author's interview, B. Conrad.
12. Muller, *op. cit.*, p. 92.
13. *ibid.*, p. 93.
14. *ibid.*, p. 97.
15. Statistics from *Beitrage, op. cit.*
16. *Die Welt*, 28.x.1948.
17. Muller, *op. cit.*, p. 95.
18. *Beitrage, op. cit.*
19. Author's interview, B. Conrad.
20. Karl-Heinz Harenberg, *EDIT*, vol. 2, p. 25.
21. Muller, *op. cit.*, p. 105.
22. *ibid.*, p. 107.
23. K.-H. Harenberg, *EDIT, op. cit.*
24. Muller, *op. cit.*, pp. 15–17.
25. *ibid.*, pp. 58–79.

26. Die Welt, 8.xi.1956.
27. *Beitrage, op. cit.*
28. Quoted in *Beitrage, op. cit.*
29. *ibid.*
30. Muller, *op. cit.*, p. 109.
31. *Die Welt*, 16.vii.1963.
32. Muller, *op. cit.*, p. 110. Also author's interviews with Peter Boenisch and B. Conrad.
33. *Beitrage, op. cit.*
34. See Muller, *op. cit.*, p. 69.
35. *ibid.*, p. 168.
36. K.-H. Harenberg, *EDIT, op. cit.*, p. 25.
37. *Beitrage, op. cit.*
38. Muller, *op. cit.*, pp. 118–20.
39. *ibid.*, pp. 11–15.
40. Author's interview, Freidheim Kremna.
41. Author's interview, P. Boenisch. Also Herr Pötter, *Die Welt* commercial department (author's interview).
42. K.-H. Harenberg, *EDIT* article passim.
43. 'The Publications of Axel Springer'. SpringerVerlag Marketing Department, Hamburg.
44. Quoted in *Der Spiegel*, 22.5.72.
45. *Die Welt*, 11.iii.1972.
46. Speech to Deutsche Atlantische Gesellschaft, March 1972.
47. Author's interview, P. Jänsch.
48. 'Ferngesteuerte Studenten'. *Die Welt*, 4.iii.1972.
49. *Stern*, 10.7.75.
50. *Die Welt*, 1.xi.1973.
51. Quoted in full in K.-H. Harenberg, *EDIT, op. cit.*
52. See *Der Spiegel*, 14.vii.76. Also see *Le Monde*, Paris, 6.xi.1974.
53. Author's interview with Giesel Reiner, and Peter Boenisch.
54. *Der Spiegel*, 14.vii.1976.
55. *The Times*, London, 1.vii.1980.
56. Author's interview, P. Boenisch.
57. See 'Your way into the German Market', SpringerVerlag Marketing.
58. Author's interview, P. Boenisch.
59. *Der Spiegel*, 3.ix.1979.
60. Author's interview, P. Boenisch.
61. *ibid.*
62. Quoted with approval, in *Der Spiegel*, 3.ix.1979.
63. *Die Welt*, 19.ix.1980.
64. Author's interview.
65. Author's interview.
66. *Die Welt*, 7.vii.1979.
67. Author's interview, Friedheim Kremna.
68. Author's interview, P. Boenisch.
69. Author's interview, Fritz Werth. See also the *Guardian*, London, 9.iii.79.
70. Author's interview, P. Boenisch.

71. *ibid.*
72. See *Aktuelle*, November 1980, SpringerVerlag.
73. Quoted in full in K.-H. Harenberg,   *EDIT, op. cit.* Also author's interview, P. Jänsch.
74. *Financial Times*, London, 30.vi.81.
75. *The Times*, London, 5.ii.81.
76. *Die Welt*, 21.iv.81. See also the *Guardian*, London, 23.iv.81.
77. *Financial Times*, London, 30.vi.81.

DIE WELT: EDITORIALS

The independence of India: 14 August 1947

'England gives up the glory of having ruled for two centuries the richest, most muddled and wildest country on earth, for the greater glory of voluntarily giving up that rule, in dangerous times, and stepping back into the role of friendly counsellor.'

The independence of Israel: 15 May 1948

'As the leaders of Jewry in Palestine greet their new state, they stand on armed guard at the doors of their homes. . .The reason for the dramatic sharpening of the Palestinian problem has been, to a great extent, Jewish terrorism. Against Arab and Briton alike, it has become ever more marked since the end of the war. . .With mounting alarm, one must ask what will be the end of a policy which should bring security, but is itself so insecure.'

The Berlin blockade and airlift: 28 October 1948

'The security of Europe against the Communist danger and the ever more expansionist aims of Soviet global policy has forced into existence a wholehearted military alliance of the West European powers, the USA and Canada. . .Moscow will more easily understand the language of a military alliance than the compromise proposals, phrased in weak and yielding terms, that the West has so far deployed.'

The Communists win power in China: 14 October 1949

'All the [American] deliveries of military equipment to Chiang Kai-Shek have hitherto been so much wasted effort – otherwise this catastrophic development would never have happened. He can be dreaming only of [American] military intervention. . .But the USA is now less than ever prepared to plunge its country and the world into a new war.'

The Korean war: 10 October 1950

'Should the United Nations' forces now cross the 38th Parallel, this would not of itself mean a deliberate widening of the war. But should this happen, which God forbid, a widening of the conflict would not have been caused by General MacArthur's authorized mandate, but because Moscow or Peking have from the beginning in Korea been looking for that conflict.'

The Suez invasion: 7 November 1956

'The peoples of the world find the hypocrisy of a great power like Russia to be despicable, to put itself forward as the protector of the freedom of small nations, while even now it is stamping down on Hungary. But equally those peoples cannot recognize the glory of a battle in a righteous cause, which Britain and France are trying to apply to their own armies' banners. Britain and France will not enjoy a speedy police action, but will face a long, hard, bloody war, while suffering the icy hostility of nations who only yesterday were proud to think of them as friends.'

The Russian invasion of Hungary: 25 October 1956

'The Bolshevik governments were imposed on the people of the Soviet zone at bayonet point. The Red Army was in every way a bad preacher and an unbelievable apostle for the new religion of the East. Only with Stalinist methods could the Communist minority seize and cling on to power. The down-trodden people long for real freedom and genuine democracy, for a radical turn away from the USSR, for an ideological, political and economic breach with Moscow.'

The Bay of Pigs assault on Cuba: 20 April 1961

'Kennedy has certified that he has every sympathy for the counter-revolutionaries, whom he has called patriots, while not himself being connected with them. But the unmistakable "Halt" which the young President has conveyed to Khrushchev leaves no more doubt about American policy towards the USSR and its lust to expand. The USSR is fully answered, in the proper form, in an unshakeable manner.'

The Cuban missile crisis: 24 October 1962

'Whoever demands that America stand fast in Berlin, must also understand why America must stand fast against the Soviet arsenal in Cuba. . .As long as it exists, Communism must by its nature strive for world domination.'

The Gulf of Tonkin incident: 6 August 1964

'The peoples who are allied to the US stand behind President Johnson. They know that the struggle for the Indochinese coastline has not broken out because America seeks an adventure in world politics, but because America will lay down the law for a halt to Communist aggression in Asia, just as it will in Europe.'

China's nuclear weapon: 19 October 1964

'No one is ever elected to the nuclear club; members have to appoint themselves. And hardly has a new member emerged, than he stands before the radiation glow of this unholy new power, whose possession leaves no nation unchanged. It will make the Chinese more answerable and less unthinking in their anti-Western mission.

Rhodesia's UDI: 12 November 1965

'By its UDI decision the government of Rhodesia is trying, with its white minority, to block a development which cannot be stopped, and which should not be stopped. . .The day Ian Smith has chosen can lead only to disaster hereafter.'

The Russian invasion of Czechoslovakia: 22 August 1968

'The USSR has slammed down a fist of iron, and with its tanks has crushed the bud of the Czech democratic experiment. But then Russia is experienced in this brutal repression of emerging freedoms. Three times it has used brute force against the weaker. What a record for a world power which trumpets itself abroad as humanity's guardian.'

Israel's occupation of the West Bank: 27 November 1973

'Nothing can replace for the Israelis the sense of security they obtained after 1967 through their occupied territories. . .But US sympathy for Israel now stands in direct opposition to Dr Kissinger's global concept of a peace structure. Kissinger's construction is in acute danger. . .No one is naive enough to think that the US's Middle East policy will not be influenced by the Arab oil boycott. . .Israel has chosen a very hard road.'

The OPEC price rise: 1 November 1973

'The Arabs, expertly advised by their Soviet friends, have declared war on Europe. With the cut-off of Holland's oil, the impertinence of the Arabs towers up, threatening reprisals to anyone who wishes to help Holland. They put before us an extraordinary alternative, either to suffer a cruel winter, or to deny aid to a good neighbour. . .But Europe can mobilize its own troops in this economic war.'

Watergate: 7 August 1974

'The President of the USA has confessed. This is an unprecedented event. The very word "confessed" suggests the status of a defendant, who by the voluntary recital of his sins hopes for a mild response from his judge. The President, and he now says it himself, has led his people by the nose, and obstructed justice. . .It was an intoxicating mix of reasons of state, power madness and a sense of personal mission.'

The fall of Saigon: 2 May 1975

'The fate of these people, in a Ho-Chi-Minh future, should be considered, under the bureaucratic rule of a system which has always hitherto in Asia taken the path of liquidating its opponents – as a natural thing to do – when the world sends back its embassies to a re-opened Saigon.'

Sport and politics: 22 January 1980

'One good has come out of the Olympic row. It has revived the world's suspicions of the world's greatest trouble-maker [Russia]. We may hope that people learn from it. The clanking of medals in the stadium should not drown the clanking of the tank tracks.'

The space venture: 13 April 1961

'The fact that he is called Gagarin, that he is a Russian, should not affect adversely man's joy and satisfaction over a peak of technical and scientific achievement. For once, the whole planet can triumph. . .But the USSR will now reap the harvest of its long-desired goal. Its leadership realized, earlier than the West, that space research and space flight is not only a technological problem, but it also opens up great possibilities for propaganda, political and, one day indeed, military purposes.'

Freedom of information: 18 May 1973

'Freedom of the press is, in reality, the freedom of a publisher to publish. Equally, it is the freedom of an editor, and during a strike by printers this freedom is confounded. It is a right of all people, whether they now publish a newspaper, or merely want to read one. It is a freedom in the face of those who would oppress unpopular views, just as much as in the face of the State, or a trade union which is being replaced by new printing presses. Men who hold their own opinions will fight for this freedom to the last.'

(Translations by the author)

5

Corriere della Sera

Corriere della Sera was founded in 1876 by three wealthy young professional men, with the objective of launching one of the three, Riccardo Pavesi, on a political career.[1] It was a modest enough beginning, with 3,000 copies, on a shoestring capital of 30,000 lire. It was enough to pay three printers' wages for one year – but not to pay anything else.[2] As editor, Pavesi hired an out-of-work and impoverished journalist, Eugenio Torelli Viollier. Born in Naples of a French mother and Italian father, Viollier had a curious past, playing a double game in the dramatic revolutionary year of 1860. He worked for the Interior Ministry of the ramshackle Kingdom of the Two Sicilies, being given the job because of his father's reputation as a liberal constitutionalist, while also secretly supporting the Garibaldi invasion which was to overthrow the Kingdom and propel it into a united Italy under the throne of Piedmont. After Naples, Viollier worked as a journalist, as private secretary to his lifelong friend Alexandre Dumas, and then moved to the biggest, most industrialized and fastest-growing city in Italy – Milan, dominated by its commercial and industrial bourgeoisie.[3]

On the eve of *Corriere*'s launching, the Kingdom of Italy was but fifteen years old. More than two-thirds of the infant State's population of 20 million were illiterate. Regional dialects meant that there was no universally understood language. Roads and railways were being painfully built. The bulk of the nation's army was expensively and cruelly trying to put down endemic regional revolts in the south and in Sicily. Other than in the small, north-western enclave of the old Kingdom of Piedmont, there was no tradition of parliamentary democracy, and little enough tradition of constitutions. There were no great political parties, ony shifting alliances and unstable coalitions in a parliamentary majority that depended on regional loyalties, State patronage and corruption.[4]

The system was not working well when *Corriere* was born, as the front-page statement of the four-page paper acknowledged. 'We are conservatives,' it announced. 'We are conservatives first, and moderates second. We want to conserve the Monarchy and the Constitution because they have given Italy independence, unity, liberty and order. . .but with the government leaning towards meanness, timidity, fiscalism and towards aristocratic ideas, do not we, its supporters, have the right to sound a warning when it looks like toppling?'[5]

The project was dubious enough for its printers to demand payment in full in advance. For their five centimes, the readers had the first-page editorial, a second page of cultural notes and reviews, a page of foreign and national news lifted from other publications and press telegrams, and a page of classified ads. *Corriere* was produced by a colourful team. Viollier himself was going through a brief, tempestuous marriage with one of Italy's few militant suffragettes. Ettore Teodori, having sailed round the world, fought with Garibaldi and been a ranch-hand in the US, was chief sub-editor and wrote everything from weather reports to foreign affairs.[6] Giacomo Raimondi wrote the economic news, perhaps the vital component of any paper in a city which was Italy's industrial heartland. He combined a passionate belief in the Manchester school of *laissez-faire* economics with an ideological bent that carried him towards Socialism and into Karl Marx's 'International'.[7] Viollier followed the tradition of the rest of the Milan press in devoting at least a page to cultural affairs, and in attracting to his paper Italy's small band of intellectual writers. The lack of readers, and the weakness of publishers, led the intelligentsia to depend on the press for money and for the opportunity to publish. This intellectual tradition helped to carry *Corriere* through the grim days of fascism, when all the papers carried the same, authorized news stories, and depended on their literary and intellectual distinction.

The Italian intellectual elite was itself too small to specialize. One of *Corriere*'s early editors was the architect Luca Beltrami who designed the new centre of Milan, as well as *Corriere*'s own offices.

Luigi Capuana, the novelist whom Emile Zola described as 'the maestro of Italian realism', spent most of his life as *Corriere*'s theatre critic. Giovanni Verga, the musician who wrote *Cavalleria Rusticana*, was a regular contributor who through *Corriere* discovered a brilliant talent for photography.[8] The worlds of politics, business, culture and journalism were not just intertwined; they were interchangeable. And *Corriere*'s early success, when it was being heavily outsold by the popular papers like *Il Secolo*, rested on its intimacy with this intellectual elite.

Viollier was also, thanks to Dumas and the example of the lively French press, an editor with a hunger for news. In 1879, when the river Po flooded dramatically, Viollier went himself to cover the disaster – one of the only Milan journalists to bother, and certainly the only editor. This mix of contents found sufficient favour in Milan to be selling almost 10,000 copies by 1880, and to arrange a distribution system for the whole province of Lombardy the following year.[9] *Corriere*'s independent political line also made it stand out from its rivals. Shortly after its appearance, the rightist coalition which had governed Italy for fifteen years fell, and as the bulk of the press took up positions for or against the prospect of a 'Left' coalition government, *Corriere* announced a policy of armed neutrality against any government, and submitted its own list of individual candidates of merit to its readers, irrespective of their party loyalties. This independent line of Viollier led to two of his original publishers withdrawing their money from *Corriere*, and Viollier quickly found replacements among Milan notables, professionals and local aristocrats. They did not last long, as Viollier continued to insist on supporting 'practical men' for the city government, rather than parties, or ambitious individuals who happened to hold shares in *Corriere*.[10]

The difficulties of ownership and finance were resolved in 1885 when Benino Crespi bought the paper – 'the first Italian publisher to consider ownership of a daily newspaper not as a political platform, but as a source of profit and as a public duty'.[11] Crespi, a wealthy cotton magnate, put in 100,000 lire of capital, expanded the print order to 30,000 copies, bought new and larger premises and expanded the workforce to 120. Viollier began to spend the money on news. He sent Paolo Bernasconi to Paris as *Corriere*'s first foreign correspondent. He sent Vico Mantegazza to Africa for five months, at a cost of 18,000 lire, to report on Italy's first colonial wars. Money was used to buy news – Viollier spent 25,000 lire on telegraph bills for the Dreyfus case alone. But the investment paid off. By 1887, circulation had topped 50,000.[12]

Now that *Corriere*'s financial health was secured, Viollier began to spell out, in a series of editorials, his own concept of a free, responsible newspaper – a unique, and even startling development in Italy. 'We have an aversion to political spoutings, to abstract questions, to sterile polemics,' he wrote.[13] 'We are disposed to worship neither our governors, nor the governed.'[14] Viollier strove for the detachment and objectivity which he felt were the hallmarks of the leading European paper of the day, the London *Times*. His aim, he wrote, was 'a truly independent paper, without making any ostentatious fuss about its freedom; which seriously tries to remain cool-headed; which would not want to be right at any cost, having once realized that it was wrong; which would not blow up facts on purpose. And it should lead, not follow, its readers.'[15] His restraint was carried to curious extremes. During the mounting financial scandals of the Crispi government of 1892, Viollier denounced 'that tendency in journalism which scurries to put before the public gaze those private shames, griefs and misfortunes, sacrificing both truth and delicacy in a frenzy of hurried information and dramatic colouring',[16] and his readers had to turn to the reports of the furious parliamentary debates to learn which politicians had been robbing them.

Viollier, given complete editorial freedom by Crespi, tried to steer *Corriere* on to a much wider stage. He opened *Corriere* bureaux in London and Berlin in 1889, to add to the one in Paris. As Italy joined the other European powers in the rush for colonies, Viollier gave the adventure cautious support, agreeing that Italy must show that she was a European power, but sceptical of the rhetoric of Italy's civilizing mission. 'If some Italians want to be seen as conquistadors, let them have the courage to announce themselves as such, without hypocrisy, and without fear of the sacrifices that will be involved,' he commented.[17] And as the economy grew, with the great tunnels being gouged through the Alps to link Italy with Germany and France, Viollier noticed the prime casualties, the industrial working class. He called for an end to the expensive subsidies to the opera of La Scala. The money should be spent on public baths, he claimed.[18] He came back from his retirement in 1898 because his replacement as editor, the drama critic Domenico Oliva, was heartily backing the government's repressive measures against working-class strikers and rioters in Milan. Viollier began with an open letter to Oliva in *Corriere*, denouncing him for 'supporting this repression of constitutional rights and liberties'.[19] Equally, while generally supporting the government in its endless civil war against the peasant rebellions in the south, Viollier sent down a future editor, Alfredo Comandini, to Sicily to see for himself. His bluntly factual reports led to a spontaneous subscription in Milan to raise funds for the victims of the campaigns.[20] At the same time, *Corriere* was tapping new markets, enthusiastically taking up the new craze of cycling in the 1890s, offering cups and prizes, organizing round-Italy races, and helping to found the Touring Club of Italy. In 1901, *Corriere* expanding into organizing Italy's first car race.

By the time of his death in 1900, Viollier had established a paper with a circulation of 70,000 copies a day, many of them outside Italy. He had built a tradition of political independence, a centre-right policy of economic *laissez-faire*, supporting private property and low taxes, but within a strict framework of the constitution and the law, with a belief in education and social reform, and committed to gathering and reporting the news – at almost any cost, and preferably from *Corriere*'s own journalists. *Corriere* was respected and profitable enough for Crespi to invest another 92,000 lire in 1895 in technical innovations and to launch a Sunday edition in 1899. New printing machines were purchased to turn out the extra copies, to produce dramatic front-page photographs of the Milan riots, to introduce the new-fangled telephone as a direct link from Rome to the Milan offices.

Viollier also left behind him his private secretary, an anglophile journalist, who wanted to make *Corriere* into the *Times* of Italy (where he had served a brief apprenticeship), Luigi Albertini. He was to become the most celebrated of all Italian editors. He became editor by a kind of *coup d'état* against the incumbent Oliva.[21] First, Albertini bought two shares in the company through his future father-in-law, a well-known playwright. Then he organized the Milan staff against the increasingly reactionary line of Oliva, quoting Viollier's open letter. Then he persuaded Crespi that he should replace Oliva. Crespi left matters to Albertini, who took advantage of Oliva's visit to Rome to meet the new government, and began publishing editorials which contradicted Oliva's views. Oliva appealed in vain to Crespi, and then resigned.

Albertini's early years saw a spate of reforms and improvements. There was more foreign news, with 'special envoys' like Luigi Barzini being sent to cover the Boxer Rebellion in China, the Russo-Japanese war and Britain's war against the Boers. New foreign bureaux were opened in Vienna, Constantinople and St Petersburg, and steno-graphers were hired to take dictation over the new telephone. *Corriere* began serializing novels, printing more feature articles, and a network of correspondents was established throughout Italy.

By 1902, with circulation topping 100,000, Albertini's new *Corriere* was established. Its political stance was more partisan than under Viollier, more committed to the Liberal group in parliament, and although critical of Giolitti and the Radicals, socially advanced enough to launch the campaign for the eight-hour day, controversial as it was among Milan's prosperous bourgeoisie. For Albertini, social reform was the only way to head off Socialist revolution and the wave of strikes that savaged the economy – some of them organized by the impassioned young Socialist revolutionary, Benito Mussolini.[22]

Albertini was more than a journalist; he saw newspapers as industrial concerns like any other, and he began a fundamental re-organization of *Corriere*, aimed deliberately at founding a publishing empire. Even before he became editor, he had persuaded the com-pany to launch the Sunday edition, less newspaper than magazine, full of pictures – an Italian version of the *Illustrated London News*. He bought the rights to Conan Doyle and started the Italian cult of Sherlock Holmes. He founded a monthly middle-brow culture magazine, *La Lettura*, and began publishing an edition of cheap monthly novels. In 1908, he founded *Corriere dei Piccoli*, a children's magazine full of comics and cartoons. The well-read Italian family, Albertini believed, should be served exclusively by the *Corriere* empire. He sent a team to investigate womens' magazines in France to see if *Corriere* could launch one for Italy, but decided that the market was not yet ready.

Into the new buildings in the Via Solferino came new American Hoe rotary presses, new equipment to handle photographs. He installed the first clippings library and archive in an Italian newspaper, brought in linotype machines, time-clocks and factory discipline. In 1906, *Corriere* became the first Italian paper to give its readers eight pages of newspaper – and he set up a warehousing company to store the extra stocks of paper required. He increased the number of columns on each page, to pack in more advertisements and more news, and to free the pages to take stronger headlines. He designed a crowded, busy layout, using different typefaces to vary the headlines, and started to break the monopolies of the advertising agencies who channelled ads to the various newspapers, setting up a department to design new, bolder ads on the American model, and then offering the designs to the major advertisers. When the newspaper vendors of Milan tried to fight him, demanding more money to handle the heavier papers, and asking for the same high profit margin that they received from the rival *Il Secolo* and *La Stampa* of Turin, Albertini set up his own vendors and launched a drive to get new subscribers, avoiding the street vendors altogether. He brought the industrial revolution to the Italian press.

He also brought a new style of editorship. Traditionally, an editor like Viollier had written the editorials, hired new staff, and then presided over the happy anarchy that was a nineteenth-century Italian newspaper. Albertini ran *Corriere* as if it were an army. He admired military men, and *Corriere* became almost the official journal of the Italian armed forces when in 1904, Albertini began giving almost a page to a regular 'Military Bulletin', with news of promotions and transfers among officer corps. He divided the journalists into separate departments, and appointed subsidiary editors to run the sports section, the economic news and so on. He started the 'terza pagina', a third page devoted to culture, to literary essays, which attracted the best of Italian literary life – including the flamboyant nationalist and romantic poet, Gabriele d'Annunzio, who became a regular contributor and personal friend of Albertini. *Corriere* even paid off the poet's vast debts.[23]

Foreign affairs Albertini kept to himself, recruiting a new generation of journalists, most of them from university, whom he sent to roam the world for *Corriere* stories. During the Libyan war, when Italy invaded the Turkish empire's province, Albertini had teams of reporters in North Africa scurrying their way past the military censors; he sent his '*corrieristi*' into Turkey itself, disguised as tourists with Hungarian and Romanian passports. He loved the pace of modern life, and filled *Corriere*'s pages with stories about aviation, about motor cars, about the promise of the electric future. He dedicated the paper to a spirit of daily excitement and experiment. One memorable day in 1912, he cut the front page in two to print two vast stories – the sinking of the *Titanic*, and the theft of the Mona Lisa in Paris. By the outbreak of the First World War in 1914, *Corriere* was selling 700,000 copies a day – almost 100,000 of them outside the heartland of Milan and Lombardy. And these readers were getting the benefit of foreign news hot from the presses of London's *Daily Telegraph* and Paris's *Le Matin*, with whom Albertini signed mutual agreements to share stories – but Albertini had arranged in advance the telephone links from London to Paris and Paris to Milan which meant that his readers had the same news, in their morning paper, as the English and French readers were scanning.[24]

Within fifteen years Albertini had made *Corriere* into *the* Italian paper, and it had an influence which no other paper could match. Luigi Albertini himself later became a Senator, but his power stemmed from his publishing empire. For most of those fifteen years, *Corriere* had supported the Italian government's Triple Alliance with Austria and Germany. But as Albertini began to question an alliance between powers like Austria and Italy, with such divergent interests in the Balkans, Italy's loyalty to the Alliance began to quaver, until with the outbreak of war in 1914, Italy remained neutral. By 1915, hoping to wrest territory from Austria, to take a share of Germany's colonies, and to join the winning side, Albertini threw the weight of his papers behind an alliance with France and Britain. Having opposed strikes and Socialist demonstrations throughout the politically turbulent pre-war years, *Corriere* began to back the pro-war demonstrations of May 1915. 'The conscience of Italy is speaking loud and clear,' *Corriere* said of the angry war-riots in Rome. Once war was safely declared, *Corriere* looked back at the popular tumult and judged: 'The days of May were a sign, not of anarchy, but of political maturity among the people.'[26] Albertini's militarist tendencies, the contacts he had developed in the army through his 'Military Bulletin', and the Italian nationalism which had led him to support the wars for Empire, all combined to swing him towards war against the old Austrian enemy. The glamour of war itself was an attraction. Luigi Barzini, prince of his *corrieristi*, had been the first journalist into Belgium as the German army invaded in 1914. By the start of 1915, Albertini had deployed twenty foreign correspondents around the war zone. Six months later, with Italy at war, *Corriere* itself began to suffer as 380 men from a workforce of 700 were mobilized into the army. Alone of all Italian newspapers, *Corriere* undertook to carry on paying their wages to their families.[27]

Elected to the Senate, with his newspaper selling up to a million copies on days of battles, victories, defeats and the lengthening casualty lists, Albertini felt on occasion the need to rein in his *corrieristi*. When his foreign editor, Oreste Rizzini, sent back a long and pessimistic article from army HQ, suggesting that the army was exhausted, under-equipped and in no state to withstand an Austrian counter-attack, Albertini suppressed the piece, and wrote back to Rizzini that *Corriere*'s influence was now so great that it could even depress the government.[28] A month later, stiffened by six German divisions, the Austrians launched the great attack of Caporetto, inflicting a humiliating defeat on Italy. The very word Caporetto later became Mussolini's catch-phrase to condemn parliamentary government, the betrayal of the army, the need for a national, military resurgence.

Just as Italy had reneged on its Triple Alliance in 1914, so France and Britain reneged on the secret Treaty of London of 1915, which promised Italy parts of Turkey, of the Balkans, of Austria and of Africa in return for joining the war. This betrayal, forced largely by the American President Wilson and his commitment to the ideal of national self-determination, became another injustice in the speeches of Mussolini, who founded his Fascist Party in 1919. Mussolini's forces grew as the post-war recession and unemployment ravaged Italian society, and provoked a wave of Socialist agitation, factory occupations and what looked like a Bolshevik threat in Italy. Mussolini hired out his Fascists as strong-arm gangs to break strikes, to evict workers occupying their factories, and to protect the property of the rich. Like most of the rest of the Italian bourgeoisie, Albertini and his chief political writer, Luigi Einaudi, at first welcomed the Fascists as protectors against Red revolution.[29] But in the course of 1922, as Albertini saw the Bolshevik threat receding, he judged that the remedies of an emergency were no longer required. The constitutional State itself, and not Mussolini's thugs, should rule the streets. He refused to accept a Fascist membership card. Although full of praise for the Fascists in the summer of 1922, when they evicted a Socialist junta who had taken over the municipal government of Milan, *Corriere* began to oppose them and call for the State to resume its authority. Mussolini himself saw Albertini as a key opponent. 'There are still some in Italy, Senator Albertini for example, who delude themselves about the capacity of the liberal state to recover its prestige and its authority,' Mussolini sneered.[30] And *Corriere* was still terrified of the Left. In September 1922, *Il Secolo* attacked 'the reactionary bougeoisie of *Corriere*, for impeding, at the last minute, the formation of a centre-left coalition against the Fascists'.[31] Luigi Einaudi replied in an editorial: 'This is a Socialist manoeuvre to take control of the police and the army and use them first against Fascism, but then against the nation itself.'[32]

It was too late. The King had already summoned Mussolini to form a government, even while his Fascists prepared to march on Rome. Mussolini himself chose to travel by train, wearing a top hat and spats rather than a black shirt. Once in power, however, Mussolini began to transform the constitutional, parliamentary system into a dictator-ship. Press laws were prepared, waiting to be enacted. A wave of Fascist terror began, burnings of Socialist offices, beating of left-wingers, arbitrary arrests. *Corriere*'s hesitant support switched to firm opposition as Albertini saw the liberal, constitutional state in which he believed eroded by terror and dictatorship. Ironically, it was at this time that Albertini's control over the paper reached its peak. The death of old Benino Crespi in 1910 had divided his majority share-holding between his three sons. In 1920, faced with an incipient civil war in Italy, the other minority shareholders sold out, leaving the Crespi brothers with seventy shares, and Luigi Albertini and his brother with fifty shares, in a company capitalized at 250,000 lire. The real value was perhaps a hundred times as high. When Mussolini finally forced Albertini to go, and to surrender his shares, he sold them to the Crespis for 10 million lire.[33] By that time, Albertini's *Corriere* had become the most powerful opposition voice to the dictatorship. With the murder of the Socialist leader Matteoti by Fascist thugs in 1924, *Corriere* began a series of investigations. It unearthed and published Mussolini's direct orders to his provincial chiefs to 'make life intolerable for the dissidents'. *Corriere* placed reponsibility for the murder firmly upon Mussolini. 'Matteoti was not one isolated incident, but simply the latest, the most monstrous example of a series of deliberate criminal acts aimed at suffocating the legitimate voice of opposition,' *Corriere* thundered.[34] The blackshirt gangs, while Mussolini dithered over whether or not to introduce total press censorship, began a campaign of intimidation. Bombs were thrown at the *Corriere* building and newspaper kiosks were smashed if they displayed *Corriere*. Copies to subscribers were stopped in the post. Advertisers were threatened with reprisals if they used the columns of *Corriere* rather than Mussolini's *Popolo d'Italia*. Circulation fell sharply, but Albertini continued the campaign, calling on Carolo Sforza, the only Italian ambassador to resign in disgust at Mussolini's march on Rome, to write a powerful series on 'The freedom of the press and the lessons of history'.[35] By early 1925, the intimidation of the paper, the beatings of its journalists and the Fascist attacks combined to defeat Albertini's courage. He resigned, sold up his shares as Mussolini insisted, and retired into private life.

Corriere ceased to be an independent newspaper. Like the rest of the Italian press, it printed what the dictatorship instructed. When Mussolini's two sons joined the army, the order came from Rome: 'headline across two columns on front page'.[36] Papers were not simply told what they must publish, but also what they must avoid. Remarque's famous anti-war novel *All Quiet on the Western Front* was ignored by the Italian media – by order. In the early years of Fascism, before the ideology and the totalitarian structure had congealed, there was still some room for manoeuvre. The first editors under Fascism were respected journalists whose political views were broadly acceptable to Mussolini. They could publish the speeches of a semi-Fascist like Giovanni Gentile, who praised Mussolini himself, while criticizing his court. Mussolini's traditional alliance with Italian big business meant that *Corriere*, property of the Crespi family, would be manipulated and controlled, rather than crudely taken over.[37]

There was even scope for the old *Corriere* skills. Mussolini's foreign wars, in Albania, in Ethiopia and in support of the Franco military coup and civil war in Spain, brought out the old traditions of the war correspondents. Mario Massai, a veteran of D'Annunzio's bizarre 'invasion' of Fiume, was *Corriere*'s aviation correspondent and covered the Ethiopian war by flying over the front lines, returning to a radio, and transmitting his stories so that they were printed in *Corriere* even before the official announcements. He died in 1939, lost on an inaugural flight from Rome to Rio.[38] Aldo Borelli, a convinced Fascist since 1922, joined *Corriere* to bring Fascist discipline to the cultural pages, and volunteered to fight in Spain in 1936, at the age of forty-six. 'By the mid 1930s, there was a new generation of journalists, brought up in Fascism, who did not need censors. They could censor themselves and believe in it,' *Corriere*'s own historian explained. 'They were professional journalists, very brave and skilled, but working inside a framework of faith that they accepted.'[39] In some senses, they succeeded. *Corriere* retained its position as the dominant newspaper, selling a regular 500,000 copies, and peaking at a million on days of battles and disasters. The old layout skills that Albertini had introduced were mobilized for stunning headlines. After the Munich conference of 1938, when Britain and France surrendered Czechoslovakia to Hitler, *Corriere*'s headline read 'Il Duce saves the peace'. After the Ethiopian invasion, it had run 'Il Duce founds the Empire'. During the disastrous war, *Corriere* men froze to death on the Russian front. Indro Montanelli, later to become editor of *Il Giornale Nuovo*, sent back a remarkably polite message from Helsinki: 'I would be extremely grateful if you could do a note to Piccoli in Stockholm to send me urgently something to eat (chocolate, fruit, etc. Anything will do) because I am literally dying of hunger.'[40]

Within *Corriere* there remained a group of anti-Fascists and political neutrals, who seized the chance with the Badoglio armistice of 1943 to hang the old Italian flag from *Corriere*'s balcony. Ettore Janni, the literary editor, former deputy and translator of D'Annunzio, called the journalists together round Albertini's vast editorial table and said, 'The lion has returned; the old *Corriere* is back.'[41] The lion did not last long. With the Anglo-American armies stuck far in the south, the German army occupied the north and re-established a rump of Mussolini government with the Salo Republic. The news came to *Corriere* in the form of a squad of German troops, whose officer delivered a brief written statement saying that it must be printed in the next issue.[42] As the Allies fought their way north, *Corriere* continued to appear in truncated form, with circulation that twice touched 1,000,000, while being ordered to run front-page stories, with gruesome pictures, of the shooting by firing squad of 'traitors to Mussolini'.[43] Mussolini had put his own commissioner, Ermano Amicucci, in charge of the paper. Janni had fled to Switzerland. But even with official backing, Amicucci found it hard to produce a paper, as the journalists steadily disappeared. 'There is clearly some kind of literary-journalistic sabotage afoot,' Amicucci concluded.[44] In his editorials, he brooded over the doom of Fascism. 'The tribe of Israel bears the major responsibility for this war,' he wrote.[45] It was a confusing time, with Mussolini trying to organize some kind of popular support by claiming to be still a Socialist, and arresting industrialists – among them, *Corriere*'s part-owner Mario Crespi, who was released after protesting his loyalty to the regime.[46]

In April 1945, as the Allies advanced on Milan and the partisan raids grew bolder, Milan exploded into insurrection. At *Corriere*, an elderly anti-Fascist journalist, Mario Borsa, who had worked briefly with Janni in the 1943 Armistice and who had partisan support, published 'The New *Corriere della Sera*' with the headline 'Milan revolts against Nazi-Fascists'.[47] It was a single-page broadsheet, with news of the revolt, statements from the liberation groups, and packed with news of the wider war, all taken from BBC radio broadcasts from London. An editorial from the National Liberation Committee of *Corriere* announced the paper was 'at the immediate disposal of the anti-Fascist cause', and recounted the 'clandestine struggles' of the anti-Fascist cells within the paper.[48]

Borsa and his colleagues had to struggle to keep the paper alive. The various political factions on the Liberation Committee wanted either to punish *Corriere* for its service to Mussolini or to suppress it, so that its readership would be available (or forced) to buy other newspapers, the Communist *Unita* or the Socialist *Avanti*. Borsa's key ally was a British officer, Major Michael Noble of the Psychological Warfare Branch. From the appearance of the 'New *Corriere*', on 24 April, until 22 May, when Borsa was allowed to publish '*Corriere d'Informazione*', the *Corriere* offices and their type were used to produce *Avanti* and *Unita*. Noble and the US Army Colonel Poletti took over the building to produce another paper, *Giornale Lombardo*, the official voice of the Allied Military Government, but then arrangd for Borsa to revive *Corriere*. Just as *Die Welt* in Germany and *Le Monde* in Paris were founded by act of conquest, so *Corriere* was saved by the same conquerors.

Borsa did not last long. Technically, the paper was still owned by the Crespi family, but their demands for the return of their property had to wait until they had been cleared of their collaborationist past. The Crespis argued that they had always been monarchists, and they determined to fire Borsa when he began using *Corriere* to campaign vigorously against the return of the Italian monarchy, and for a democratic republic.[50] An anglophile who believed in British journalism and British parliamentary democracy, Borsa also campaigned for a realignment of Italian politics into two great parties, one of the left, and one of the centre. This lost him any chance of support from the established political groupings, and left him on weak ground to withstand the Crespi family, as the looming Cold War and the threat of a Communist takeover in Italy began to rally that vast coalition of the rich, the Church, the moderate and the alarmed which became Christian Democracy. By August of 1946, Borsa had been forced out. He asked his replacement, Guglielmo Emanuel, what he intended to do with the paper. 'Exactly the opposite of what you have done,' Emanuel replied.[51]

A gentle purge followed. Borsa's supporters on the paper, and journalists with Communist sympathies, were demoted.[52] *Corriere* took a stern anti-Communist line in domestic and international affairs, and the paper was a loyal enough son of the Church for Emanuel to apply formally to the Archbishop of Milan for a dispensation permitting his journalists to read 'prohibited journals' such as Communist papers, for professional reasons.[53] It was still a two-page paper, carrying a half-page of small ads, doubling in size to four pages on Sundays – even by 1947. By 1949, four pages were the norm, sometimes six, and the economy had revived enough to provide two pages of ads, some profits to the Crespis, and a circulation of 460,000. It published under Borsa's original title 'The New *Corriere della Sera*', but Borsa's second title, '*Corriere d'Informazione*', was used for an evening paper. In 1951, the share capital was rearranged for tax reasons and to take account of inflation. The share capital rose from 180,000 lire to 90 million, of which 87 million were held by Vitorio Crespi's widow, Maria Bernasconi, and the remaining shares by the other Crespi brothers.[54] Eleven years later, the share capital rose to 900 million lire, and the ownership was disguised among three holding companies, Cema, Alpi and Viburnum, which were to be the vehicles through which Giovanni Agnelli of the FIAT fortune (who also owned Turin's *La Stampa*) and Angelo Moratti, the oil magnate, bought into *Corriere*.[55]

'If the *Corriere* of the 1950s seems to be cautious or quiet, you must not forget what a tender plant Italian democracy then was,' Glauco Licata, *Corriere*'s own historian, points out. 'In the wake of Mussolini, with the world's largest Communist Party after those of Russia and China, responsible journalists could believe that their main duty lay in safeguarding democracy, and write accordingly.'[56] *Corriere* supported NATO, the EEC, a united Europe, and the Christian Democratic Party in Italy. Symbolizing the link between *Corriere* and the state, Luigi Einaudi, Albertini's old editorial partner, became President of the Italian Republic in 1948. *Corriere* was again the paper of the Italian Establishment.

Corriere quietly prospered. Its economic and cultural pages remained the best in Italy, and it began to increase its sports coverage, to establish special sections, like Motoring, that would generate more advertisements. The Italian press as a whole became more dependent on advertising because of strict government controls on the selling-price of papers, which formed part of the national price index. Even in 1980, *Corriere* can only charge 400 lire for its thirty-two pages, while the Communist *Unita* charges 400 lire for its ten pages. One effect of this deliberate government policy has been to weaken newspapers, which retain a political independence, to the benefit of television, which the politicians control.[57] *Corriere*'s political stance therefore, while in broad sympathy with the Christian Democrats, was critical. The paper prided itself on being 'the paper of quality and seriousness, which serves no particular interest, whether party or private, but promotes exclusively the common good, the well-being of the nation'.[58] It attacked political scandals, the corrupt Christian-Democratic fiefdoms which had emerged in Florence, in Naples and

Sicily.[59] It warned the Christian Democrats that 'a party which depends for almost half of its votes on workers and peasants cannot but move to the left', and supported the cause of the centre-left politicians like Mario Scelba who fought against the Vatican wing of the party who tried to move it to the right.[60] While opposing the Communist Party, it acknowledged the dramatic success of Communist local governments in cities like Bologna, and contrasted their work with the corrupt incompetence which was ruining 'the cultural shrines of Venice and Florence'.[61] It continued to campaign, in spite of law suits and political pressures, to expose the politicians who were corruptly stealing money from the fund to save Venice. *Corriere* prided itself on its honesty, refusing to let its journalists go anywhere unless *Corriere* paid the bills.[62] It proved an expensive restraint, as *Corriere*'s management, unable to raise money by increasing the cover-price, tried a series of loss-making expansions into the crowded magazine market. *Amica*, a women's magazine, succeeded. Few others did and, by 1970, *Corriere*, together with the rest of the Italian press, moved into a state of financial crisis.

The Italian economic crisis, which was to be made the sharper by the OPEC price rises of 1974, depressed advertising revenues in *Corriere* by almost 30%, while the costs of paper almost tripled and wages and overheads rose dramatically. Having made modest profits in the first two post-war decades, *Corriere*'s publishing empire began to collapse. In 1974, the deficit was £4.625 million, and £7.164 million the next year, and almost exactly £9 million in 1976.[63] The underlying reason for this was that the later directors of *Corriere* had never been able to repeat the success of Luigi Albertini in expanding the newspaper-buying market. Through his other titles and his early promotion of sport, before 1915 Albertini had transformed *Corriere* from being the paper of the industrial borgeoisie of Milan into a popular, national quality paper. After 1945, *Corriere* was never able to expand from this market and find new readers. In 1975, only one Italian in ten bought a daily newspaper – the lowest figure in Europe. There was (and remains) a vast potential market for new readers, if only it could be tapped. This, at least, was the view of the Crespi family, living as they still did under the shadow of Albertini. Partly because they saw a way of expanding the readership, and partly because Italy was undergoing a fundamental political and social re-alignment, the Crespi family in 1972 appointed Pierro Ottone as editor, with a mandate to move *Corriere* to the political left, and to recognize that powerful wing of moderate Communism which was moving the Italian Communist Party towards its 'historical compromise' with government. Ottone's *Corriere* was to identify with that equally potent wing of social reform which was bringing the issues of divorce and abortion on to the national agenda, to the horror of the Church and the traditional Christian Democrat Party.

The Ottone experiment was successful in that it attracted new readers and created a new spirit of involvement and democracy among *Corriere*'s journalists. It was a disaster in that it took place in the worst possible economic climate, and it provoked the resignation of a group of senior journalists who felt that the *Corriere* of old was being sold out to the Left. Ottone's new *Corriere* made a point of covering the views of strikers, as well as of management, of reporting the anger of students on demonstrations, as well as the disgust of their professors. In a full-page report on the military coup in Chile, it condemned what it saw as 'a Nazi-style dictatorship'.[64] It called editorially for reforms in the divorce and abortion laws, and began to publicize the views of moderate Communists. The series of scandals, of Ministers taking bribes from the Lockheed Corporation, were exhaustively probed in *Corriere*. Whereas the growth of the Italian political-investigative magazines like *Panorama* and *Espresso* had followed the unwillingness of the established press to probe too deeply into the murk of the Christian Democrats' fiefdoms, *Corriere* was now belatedly trying to tap that market.

Indro Montanelli, one of the veteran *Corrieristi* and the man who almost starved in Helsinki, resigned noisily, to start a rival paper, *Il Giornale Nuovo*, in order, as he told *Le Monde*, 'to combat the demagogic attitude of the new *Corriere*, which slides to the Left, to the distress of the middle classes of Milan'.[65] Montanelli's resignation, in which his frustration at being passed over for the editorship may have played a part, was backed by another of the major industrialists who were taking advantage of the press recession to control ever wider swathes of Italian publishing. Eugenio Cefis, head of the vast Montedison combine, guaranteed Montanelli's paper with a promise of 12,000 million lire of advertising.[66] These manoeuvres took place against a background of worryingly rising votes for the MSI neo-Fascist party, a sudden spate of left- and right-wing terrorism, and endemic political crises which even the half-hearted support of the Communist Party for the government could not resolve. And *Corriere* continued to lose money. In 1974, ending an associaton which had begun ninety years earlier, the Crespi family sold their shares in *Corriere* to the vast Rizzoli publishing empire which itself was linked to the Montedison group through a complex series of bank guarantees. In the weeks before the sale, the *Corriere* journalists, inspired by the example of France's *Le Monde* and London's *Guardian*, tried to establish a trust company run by the journalists themselves. The Crespi family considered the idea, and rejected it. The Crespi shares, and those of FIAT and Moretti, went to Rizzoli. Rizzoli himself promised to retain Ottone as editor, and to continue the 'democratic, laical, anti-Fascist and progressive line of the new *Corriere*'.[67] Interviewed about the change by *Le Monde*, editor Ottone said: 'We know that certain of our stands have displeased the Milan bourgeoisie, who are accustomed to believing our paper to be rather close to the Establishment. But Signor Rizzoli, who is above all a publisher, has leftist sympathies, and we believe that our good faith will sustain our development.'[68]

Circulation fell a little, under the rivalry of Montanelli's *Giornale Nuovo* and the national daily, *La Reppublica*, but the financial losses continued to mount, aggravated, albeit inevitably, by Rizzoli's investment in new technology, in cold type and photo-composition, and above all by the establishment of a teletransmission line to Rome. Rizzoli believed that *Corriere* had to expand to survive, and the teletransmission meant that *Corriere* could publish a special Roman edition, from which *Corriere* could be more quickly distributed to the centre and south of Italy. The new Rome edition, with its own staff, contained seven pages of specifically Roman news, as well as the backbone of *Corriere*'s foreign, economic, political and sports reports. By 1980 the expansion had paid off, to the extent that the *Corriere* group was breaking even once again, with *Corriere* itself showing a healthy profit, and supporting the loss-makers like the evening paper *Corriere d'Informazione*.[69] In 1980, 23% of *Corriere*'s sales were of the Roman edition – rather more than the 22.5% of sales in Milan itself. The eternal nagging distribution problem of the Italian press, based on a profusion of sales-points, still meant that 18% of copies printed were returned unsold, but *Corriere*'s steady purchase of distribution agencies meant that it received 75% of the sale-price of each paper. With a steady circulation of 600,000 and a healthy 17 million lire for a full page of advertising (which accounted for almost exactly half of the paper's income), *Corriere* is financially healthy and poised to grow. The group has successfully launched new sports and youth magazines, using the old editorial staff.[70]

One casualty of the modernization and expansion was Pierro Ottone, the most forceful and courageous editor the paper had known since Albertini. In 1977, he was asked to resign and was replaced by the former crime and news editor, Franco di Bella, who was working for a Bologna newspaper at the time. To break his Bologna contract, the personal intervention of Prime Minister Andreotti was required, leading to speculation about the renewed control of the Christian Democrat Party. There was even speculation in the Italian press that Rizzoli had been enabled to pay off his debts to FIAT by new loans from Swiss and Bavarian banks, supporters of the right-wing German Christian-Democrat, Franz-Josef Strauß. The price of the loans, it was said, was Ottone's head. These rumours are authoritatively denied by *Corriere* executives, but Ottone's 'window to the Left' has certainly been closed. Ottone's deputy editor, Michele Tito, resigned at the same time.[71]

Corriere's financial crisis led to new controversies and manoeuvres in 1981. In April, Angelo Rizzoli and his managing director, Bruno Tassan Din, decided to sell 40% of their shares to Roberto Calvi, a controversial banker, for £65.3 million.[72] Since Rizzoli had just announced that the group's debts of £114 million for 1980 amounted to 41% of the value of annual sales, this appeal to the banks did not seem unreasonable. It meant that Rizzoli still held a controlling 50.2% of the shares, with the Rothschild Bank of Zurich holding the remaining 9.8%[73] But in Italy, finance and politics (and newspapers) are incestuously entwined. The banker Calvi was seen as a supporter of the Italian Socialist Party, and was rumoured to be one of its major financial supporters.[74] The proposed sale to Calvi came under immediate political fire, which was the hotter since Calvi was facing a police investigation for alleged foreign-currency deals.[75]

While this furore was under way, Italian political life was rocked by a new conspiratorial scandal. A secret lodge of freemasons, said to include almost all influential Italians in public life, was brought to light. Among the members of the P-2 lodge were Roberto Calvi, Angelo Rizzoli and his aide Bruno Tassan Din, Franco di Bella, the editor of *Corriere della Sera*, and three of his senior journalists.[76] Shortly after the scandal broke in May, Franco di Bella announced that he was taking an extended holiday, and in June he resigned. The sale of *Corriere* plummeted by over 100,000 copies in the course of the scandal's first month. He was replaced by Alberto Cavallari, who was described by his *Corriere* colleagues as being 'as non-political as it is possible for an Italian journalist to be'.[77]

Thanks to the political upheaval of the P-2 scandal, the Italian government fell. The new Prime Minister, Giovanni Spadolini, was the former Professor of Politics at Bologna University who had been from 1968 to 1972 the editor of *Corriere della Sera*. Spadolini was the leader of the Republican Party; the Party's President, Bruno Visentini, was also President of Olivetti and the very man whom Rizzoli had named as the guarantor of *Corriere*'s editorial independence when he announced the sale of shares to Calvi.[78] In October of 1981, the battered Angelo Rizzoli and the banker Robert Calvi announced that they wanted to sell their 90.2% shareholding to the guarantor, Visentini. The Socialist Party, a key component of Giovanni Spadolini's governing coalition, announced that they would walk out of government if the sale to the President of the Republican Party went ahead.[79]

While these financial-political-journalistic debates were under way, the Italian press as a whole was becoming even more bankrupt than usual. Total losses were officially stated (in a debate in the Chamber of Deputies in July) to amount to £180 million. As the deputies spoke, the 133-year-old *Gazetta del Popolo* of Turin was formally closed by court order because of its bankruptcy. The Italian government voted to subsidize its failing press (which was a disguised subsidy to the political parties) at a cost of £90 million in the scheme's first year.[80] But the subsidy contained one condition: it was limited to those press groups which did not control more than 20% of the market. In effect, this meant that the Rizzoli group would have to be broken up. To the battered staff of *Corriere* this was a welcome development. Their distaste for the Rizzoli style of management had reached a furious peak with the P-2 scandal, the consequent fall in circulation and the damage done to *Corriere*'s reputation. They welcomed the Visentini takeover.[81] While non-Italians saw the Visentini purchase as emphasizing once again the subjugation of the Italian press to political interests, Italian journalists saw it as an improvement, a move from discredited politicians to acceptable and, above all, solvent men of influence, who happened, in the inevitable Italian way of things, to have useful political weight.

Largely because of the intimate role that the press plays in Italian political and cultural life, the fate of *Corriere della Sera* has mirrored to an uncanny degree the state, and the endemic crises, of Italian history. A paper as dominant as *Corriere* is a participant rather than an observer. Its very editorial system mirrors the crisis-structure of the Italian state. Whereas other international newspapers, like *Le Monde* or *The Times*, endeavoured to maintain correspondents in key overseas centres, *Corriere* maintained the tradition of keeping a core of up to sixty 'special envoys' in Milan (out of 210 journalists), who would fly out to trouble-spots at a moment's notice, reacting to crises, rather than preparing for them. Some areas of *Corriere*'s coverage, notably Iran in the 1970s, suffered lamentably as a result. 'We have the journalism of the present tense in Italy – it is exciting, but not always wise,' commented one of its leading 'special envoys'.[82] But equally, this crisis-management meant that on the major Italian story of the 1970s, the wave of urban terrorism, *Corriere* was unrivalled in its coverage. Its journalists paid the price for their skills, being prime targets for the shooting through the legs which became the terrorists' classic vindictive strike against their critics.

In May 1980, one of *Corriere*'s most brilliant young journalists, an expert on Italian trade unions, and secretary of the Milan journalists' union, Walter Tobagi, was shot dead by terrorists outside *Corriere*'s office in the Via Solferino. His replacement signs his articles with the initials of the paper itself, and is provided with two full-time body-guards by *Corriere*. As *Corriere*'s biographer stated: 'Historically, the role of the journalist is different in Italy. He is an intellectual, a man of letters, a man of influence, a man of possibly dangerous ideas. As a journalist, a believer in a free press, he is by definition a man of democratic, liberal views. He is therefore a symbol. In Mussolini's time, and in our own, he becomes a target. It is within these con-straints that one must live and work. Walter Tobagi died for them.'[83]

Notes

1. *Storia del CdS*, Glauco Licata, p. 19.
2. *ibid.*, p. 22.
3. *ibid.*, p. 14.
4. *Storia di cento anni di vita Italiana, visti attraverso il CdS*, Denis Mack Smith, pp. 17–40. Also see '*Cento anni del Corriere della Sera*', special supplement of *CdS* 13.x.1976, under year entry 1876.
5. *CdS*, 5.iii.1876.
6. *CdS*, supplement, *op. cit.*, see year 1878.
7. Licata, *op. cit.*, p. 24.
8. *CdS*, supplement, *op. cit.*, see year 1894.
9. *ibid.*, Introduction.
10. Licata, *op. cit.*, p. 32.
11. Mack Smith, *op. cit.*, p. 42.
12. *CdS*, supplement, *op. cit.*, see year 1887.
13. *CdS*, 9.xii.1887.

14. *CdS*, 26.viii.1889.
15. *ibid.*
16. *CdS*, 10.ii.1892.
17. *CdS*, 18.viii.1888.
18. *CdS*, 10.vii.1890.
19. *CdS*, supplement, *op. cit.*, see year 1898.
20. *ibid.*, see year 1891.
21. Licata, *op. cit.*, pp. 74–9.
22. *Mussolini*, Christopher Hibbert, pp. 30–33.
23. Licata, *op. cit.*, pp. 93ff.
24. *ibid.*, pp. 105–6.
25. *CdS*, 16.v.1915.
26. *CdS*, 12.xii.1915.
27. Licata, *op. cit.*, p. 173.
28. *CdS*, supplement, *op. cit.*, see year 1917.
29. Mack Smith, *op. cit.*, pp. 252–87.
30. *Opera Omnia*, Mussolini, vol. XVIII, (Rome, 1936), p. 362.
31. *Il Secolo*, 2.ix.1922.
32. *CdS*, 8.ix.1922.
33. *CdS*, supplement, *op. cit.*, Introduction.
34. *CdS*, 30.xii.1924.
35. *CdS*, 21.i.1925.
36. *CdS* supplement, *op. cit.*, see year 1935.
37. Author's interview, Glauco Licata.
38. *CdS* supplement, *op. cit.*, see year 1939.
39. Author's interview, Licata.
40. *CdS*, supplement, *op. cit.*, see year 1941.
41. *CdS*, supplement, *op. cit.*, see year 1943.
42. Licata, *op. cit.*, pp. 345ff.
43. *CdS*, supplement, *op. cit.*, see year 1944.
44. Mack Smith, *op. cit.*, p. 418.
45. *CdS*, 1.xii.1943.
46. Mack Smith, *op. cit.*, p. 419.
47. *CdS*, 26.iv.1945.
48. *ibid.*
49. Licata, *op. cit.*, p. 391. Also author's interview, Licata. Also *CdS*, 7.v.1946.
50. Mack Smith, *op. cit.*, pp. 426–30.
51. Licata, *op. cit.*, p. 415.
52. *ibid.*
53. *CdS*, supplement, *op. cit.*, see year 1946.
54. *ibid.*, Introduction.
55. *ibid.*, also author's interviews, Glauco Licata *et al.*
56. Licata interview.
57. *ibid.*, see also *Le Monde*, 3–4.xi.1974.
58. *CdS*, 4.iii.1951.
59. *CdS*, 16.iv.1966. and 24.x.1966, Ottone's articles.
60. Mack Smith, *op. cit.*, p. 507. See also *CdS*, 20.ii.1966.
61. *CdS*, 7.ii.1969. See also *CdS*, 4.ii.1971, Montanelli's articles.

62. Author's interview, Ettore Mo.
63. *Financial Times*, 1.viii.1980.
64. *CdS*, 1.xi.1973.
65. Quoted in *Le Monde*, 3–4.xi.1974.
66. *Financial Times*, 1.viii.1980.
67. Mack Smith, *op. cit.*, p. 575.
68. *Le Monde, op. cit.*
69. Author's interview, Gianni d'Angelo, *CdS* Financial Director.
70. *ibid.*
71. Author's interviews. See also *Financial Times, op. cit.*
72. *The Times*, London, 24.iv.1981.
73. *Economist*, 17.x.1981.
74. *ibid.*
75. *The Times*, 24.iv.1981. *The Times* also announced that Signor Calvi's passport had been withdrawn by the Italian police.
76. *Economist, op. cit.*
77. Author's interview, anonymous *CdS* source.
78. *Guardian*, 12.x.1981.
79. *ibid.* See also the *Guardian*, London 14.x.1981 and the *Economist, op. cit.*
80. *Guardian*, 3.viii.1981.
81. *Economist, op. cit.*
82. Author's interview, Ettore Mo.
83. Author's interview, Glauco Licata.

(Translations by the author and Julia Watson)

CORRIERE DELLA SERA: EDITORIALS

The independence of India: 6 September 1947

'The new free and independent India, which has been so much declaimed and for which Gandhi fasted for so long, has been born badly. It has been born in violence and blood. . .The issue is that the Indians have not obtained freedom because they have become mature enough to make use of it, nor because they have become strong enough to defend it, but because England has become too weak to keep India in its dominion.'

The independence of Israel: 22 May 1948

'The UN may have approved of partition, but it could not provide the force required to effect it. And thus Israelis and Arabs have remained alone, confronting one another. But basically, they are only pawns in a game more vast than Palestine, because behind one and behind the other stand the Great Powers, their interests and their intrigues.'

The Berlin blockade and airlift: 1 July 1948

'In Berlin, there is now a showdown. Whichever of the two sides pulls back or gives in will lose prestige and lose face, as they say in the Orient. Prestige is not simply a question of national vanity or pride. If the Western allies retreat from Berlin, the Berliners,who have just been at war with the Communists, will be abandoned to the mercy of their enemies, as the liberals and democrats of Poland, Romania, Hungary, etc., were abandoned at the Yalta Conference. And after that, what faith could the German people ever have again in the power of the Allies, or in their resolve?'

The Communists win power in China: 27 December 1949

'China is too vast to become a satellite of anybody. In the course of its thousands of years of history, China has always digested its conquerors, but no conqueror has ever been able to swallow China. . .China now needs capital that it can only get from America, industrial plant and machines that it can only get from America and other Western countries. . .Mao will become a new Tito. There is no reason why Mao and the Chinese Communist Party should bow to Moscow. There are no Russian troops in China, and China is immense, and its strength to resist is infinite.'

The Korean war: 15 September 1950

'The United Nations must not stand idly by as France did when Hitler invaded the Rhineland, and as all the powers did (including the then ambivalent Italy) when the German devil invaded Czechoslovakia. If the peace of the world is to be saved, it will be because President Truman honourably accepted the challenge, on behalf of the peace-loving world, as soon as the UN denounced North Korea's hypocritical violation of world peace.'

The Suez invasion: 1 November 1956

'The Americans have taken a position against Britain and France at the UN for two reasons that are easily understood, but hard to justify. President Eisenhower, facing elections in a few days, wants to be the man who kept his country at peace. Second, America wants to gain the support of the Arab countries and to secure their supply of Middle-East oil. . .But this means that the Atlantic Alliance has reached this point: that its leading members are looking at each other, not as friends from whom one can expect assistance and support, but as untrustworthy adversaries to stand on guard against.'

The Russian invasion of Hungary: 6 November 1956

'Moscow is right to be afraid. The days in Budapest have given blunt proof that the civilized world is appalled by Communism, and that liberation from Communist oppression is always a possibility. . .Only the intervention of tanks and outside armies could have re-imposed Soviet imperialism, faced with the people's heroism, who rose in revolt in the august causes of nation and liberty.'

The Bay of Pigs assault on Cuba: 21 April 1961

'The attempt by the Cuban rebels has failed. This failure is a tragedy. A tragedy for that courageous band of men who went to fight against a bloody tyranny, and who are now, in part, its prisoners.'

The Cuban missile crisis: 24 October 1962

'President Kennedy's decision is, in itself, grave. The more so because, in the way it was conceived and announced, it does not allow Moscow, nor does it allow the American government, any other options but either a humiliating retreat or a show of strength. . . President Kennedy has burnt his boats. He has left himself no possibility of retreat. An appeal to the UN Security Council would at least have left open one way out.'

The Gulf of Tonkin incident: 6 August 1964

'Why did Hanoi's Communist gunboats attack the American fleet? Because the Communists of Hanoi and Peking are not frightened of

American reprisals. They calculated that American democracy, however powerful it may be physically, lacked the necessary courage to take a firm stand, and that American resolve would be paralysed this year by elections.'

China's nuclear weapon: 17 October 1964

'One should acknowledge a relationship between China's atomic bomb, and the fall of Khrushchev. On Russia's borders has emerged an immense Communist state three times as strong in population, who has become its political and ideological adversary. And now that state has the atom bomb, which gives it much greater power and prestige. . .In this uncertain time, with so many imponderables, with a Russia facing possibly fundamental political changes, and with an atomic China which could ally itself again with Russia, the unity and vigilance of the free nations are the truest guarantees of international peace and order.'

Rhodesia's UDI: 13 November 1965

'Despite everything, there is one hope. However strong Rhodesia may be militarily, she is vulnerable on the economic front. And certainly the Rhodesians are not fighting in the name of any ideal, unless it be the shortsighted racist ideal which could yet, in the most dangerous course of events, drive all the whites from southern Africa altogether. The Rhodesians are simply defending their racist privileges.'

The Russian invasion of Czechoslovakia: 22 August 1968

'The violence has been repeated in Prague, just as in Budapest. The betrayal is renewed under the Czech skies with the same squalid cadence as in Hungary twelve years ago. A Communist country has been invaded overnight by the Red Armies, its autonomy stamped on, its rights put to the stake according to the cruel logic of Tsarism, and without even the apparent 'balance of power' justifications which accompanied the invasion of Hungary.'

Israel's occupation of the West Bank: 6 November 1973

'A dramatic political reality has come to light, a vulnerable reality of an Israel whose origins are contested by its neighbours, and which is yet deprived of any real demographic base from which to wage war. . .Israel now gives the impression of searching for a new psychological and cultural dimension, as well as a political solution. This crisis could yet lead to a coup by the Right, taking flight into that myth of total territorial and military security, which simply cannot exist.'

The OPEC price rise: 8 November 1973

'The Europeans now find themselves confronted by a dilemma, between the necessity of supplies of Middle-Eastern oil, and the convenience of supporting American global strategy. It will not be easy to decide between the dependence of their economies on Middle-Eastern oil and their dependence on the security of American military protection.'

Watergate: 9 August 1974

'Men of other countries and other systems might be surprised by the gravity which America has attributed to episodes which in their origin and by their nature seem futile if compared to the criminal acts which have blotted, and are blotting, other politicians in countries not very far from America. But the problem is not in the relative triviality of Watergate, which pales beside the horrors of dictatorship, violence, terrorism and the arrogance of power of other systems and other democracies. The shining principle which emerges from the tragedy is the impossibility of betraying, on whatever level, the solemn oaths to govern a democracy along the principles of justice.'

The fall of Saigon: 1 May 1975

'Even now, if the reunification of Vietnam by force corresponds with the needs of essential justice, the world is not everywhere just in the same way. If from today there are no longer two Vietnams, there are still two Germanies. . .And in the end, if the American purpose in Vietnam has failed, the Soviet purpose in Czechoslovakia and Hungary did not fail only because there cannot be a guerrilla war without jungles, marshes and rice-fields. There cannot be a guerrilla campaign in streets, in industry, in a country of towns.'

Sport and politics: 19 January 1980

'However encrusted with impurities they have become, sport in general and the Olympic Games in particular stem from an idealism which has nothing to do with political and ideological conflicts, but which is important for everybody's co-existence. Once link that ideal to intolerance, to anger, to implacable hatreds, and you begin to fray that thread of hope which we should strive to protect, even in the worst adversity. This is not to argue for neutralism in sport, but to call for sport to participate actively in the improvement of international relations. The cannon should not have to roar when the Olympic nations quarrel.'

The space venture: 13 April 1961

'Our utter incompetence prevents us from appreciating, in any precise scientific way, the range of the latest great Soviet space venture. . .But given the very real intransigence into which Soviet foreign policy has stiffened, its invitation to space peace seems more like an invitation to surrender and, without doubt, it was made as an exercise in propaganda.'

Freedom of information: January 1980

'The Italian press today is not burdened by the suppressions of the Fascist period. The press is threatened instead by financial difficulties through the government's controls on the price at which newspapers may be sold, to the degree that papers are not able to cover their costs, and by other burdens deriving from artificial restrictions on a free market economy.'

(Note: this editorial of freedom of the press in Italy was published the day after *Corriere*'s editor and two of its journalists were summoned before a court to explain why they had published information about, and from, the Italian 'Red Brigade' terrorists. The article went on: 'It would be serious indeed if the Italian people got the impression that they could find information in the uncritical broadsheets of political factions, which the authentic newspapers did not dare to print.'

(Four months later, one of those *Corriere* journalists, Walter Tobagi, was murdered by terrorists in the street outside his office.)

6

Pravda

The political career of Nikita Khrushchev got under way when he was asked to put his name to a letter in *Pravda* in 1930, denouncing an attempt by anti-Stalin 'rightists' to take over an obscure Communist Party congress.[1] A generation later, in 1964, that career came to an end with a front-page photograph in *Pravda* of Brezhnev and Kosygin, his replacements. The following day, without referring to Khrushchev by name, *Pravda* published the only official criticism of his years of power: 'Wild schemes, half-baked conclusions and hasty decisions, bragging and bluster – these are alien to the party.'[2] From that date onward, Khrushchev became a non-person. The official party newspaper, which had mentioned his name an average of 160 times per issue during his years of power, ignored him. His death was marked by a two-line story, noting the death of 'a pensioner'. *Pravda* serves the party, and the party leadership of the day. News is tailored to suit the party line. Khrushchev could hardly have complained at *Pravda*'s treatment of his fall. His own key promotion, to become General Secretary of the party central committee in the Ukraine, had been signalled with a front-page picture in *Pravda* on 28 January 1938. The caption said that he had been 'elected to the position by a plenum of the central committee of the Ukraine'. This was not in fact possible. The entire central committee of the Ukraine had been physically liquidated four months before *Pravda*'s 'election' took place.[3]

Throughout its seventy-year history, *Pravda* and the Communist Party have been one. Its first offices in St Petersburg in 1912 were also the HQ of the illegal Bolshevik Party. To this day, some 35% of the party's own income comes from the profits made by *Pravda*, and its associated magazines, the theoretical journal *Kommunist* and the *Economic Gazette*.[4] *Pravda*'s own editorials on each 5 May, the USSR's Press Day (which in itself commemorates *Pravda*'s first issue) stress that Soviet newspapers exist to serve the party. 'The press is the strongest weapon in the hands of our party,' it said on Press Day in 1950. The message was unchanged for Press Day in 1968: 'It is the most important duty of our press to wage an offensive struggle against bourgeois ideology and to oppose actively the efforts of certain literary, artistic and other works to intrude with views alien to the Socialist ideology of Soviet society.' The battle metaphors of *Pravda*'s definitions of the press role are not accidental. They stem from Lenin's early definitions of the role of a Communist publication, and from his conviction that the press, Communist or capitalist, is a weapon in the class struggle. In July 1956, *Pravda* reprinted Lenin's early writings on the press. He made two fundamental points, first: 'freedom of the press is freedom for the political organizations of the bourgeoisie. To give these people such a weapon as the press is to help our enemy', second: 'in the capitalist world, freedom of the press represents the freedom to buy the newspapers and those who edit them, as well as the freedom to buy, corrupt and mould public opinion in the interests of the bourgeoisie'.[5] (It is worth recalling, before dismissing the argument as Bolshevik exaggeration, that George Orwell makes precisely the same argument in his essay on the political effect of boys' magazines in Britain.[6]) But in a *Pravda* article (12 September 1918), Lenin took the argument further: 'We have not learned to wage the class struggle in our papers as skilfully as the bourgeoisie did . . .Remember how they used to hound their class enemies?' This theme, of newspapers at war, is a constant and conscious directive of the Soviet press to this day. As *Pravda* put it more recently (27 July 1965): 'A journalist is an active fighter for the cause of the party.'

Thus, the editor of *Pravda* is always a member of the Central Committee of the Communist Party of the Soviet Union. His loyalty is to the party, and the current editor, Viktor Afanyasev, makes no secret of the limitations this imposes: 'We are not interested in scandals in private life or in discrediting an official. We do not do anything that can hurt our way of life, our system, our principles.'[7]

Alien as this may be to journalists brought up in the Western tradition, loyal Soviet editors feel neither discomfort nor embarrassment at putting the party's needs first; they are simply its organ. As Afanyasev put it in an interview: 'Our aim is propaganda, for our party and our State. We do not hide this. . .We work under the leadership of the Central Committee. There is a mistaken idea in the West that all our material has to be approved. This is not so. The Central Committee trusts us, and we make the paper so that it answers the needs of the party and country, conforming to party policy.'[8]

This fundamental obedience to the party involves *Pravda* in sudden reversals of line which appear monstrous to Western eyes. Until late December 1979, President Hafizullah Amin of Afghanistan was 'a loyal and progressive friend of the Soviet Union'. The day after his assassination in a coup, he became 'an agent of Western imperialism'.[9] (It should be borne in mind that a number of Western newspapers made similar somersaults in June 1941, when Hitler's invasion transformed Russia from a frightful enemy to loyal ally overnight.)

But we cannot begin to compare *Pravda* with the newspapers of the West. *Pravda* does not exist in the same competitive milieu; it does not depend on advertising income; it does not have to deliver the news quickly; it does not even define 'news' in the same way. The official Soviet line is quite clear: 'News is agitation through facts. News must be didactic and instructive.'[10] It is not *Pravda*'s job to entertain, nor to win readers by appealing to their tastes. More than nine million of *Pravda*'s circulation of eleven million is guaranteed by subscriptions to party members, to institutions. The distribution system of *Soyuzpechat* is so unwieldy that even news-kiosk sales have to be ordered more than a month in advance.[11] To look at *Pravda* in the capitalist marketplace, we have to go back to before the First World War, to the first of the successive stages of *Pravda*'s history.

The first *Pravda* was produced in 1908, in Vienna, by Leon Trotsky.[12] It was an organ of the Menshevik (or minority) Party, and critical of the Bolshevik (majority) wing of the Communists, led by Lenin. The argument between the two groups was based on their differences over the pace and organization of the Russian revolution against the tsar in which they both believed. In 1910, after an attempted reconciliation between the two wings, an agreement was reached that the Bolsheviks should help finance Trotsky's *Pravda*, but Lenin, who controlled the party funds, steadily starved it of capital, even though it remained the most popular of the revolutionary papers smuggled into tsarist Russia.[13] In 1912, after a wave of strikes, the tsar's government liberalized enough to permit opposition papers to be published. Although Lenin was to remain in exile, he grabbed at the opportunity, stole the name '*Pravda*', and on 5 May 1912 the official Bolshevik *Pravda* was launched in the city which was to become Leningrad. Its publisher was a Menshevik named Malinovsky, and its editor one Chernomazov – both men were later to be exposed as tsarist police agents.[14] Circulation quickly reached 40,000, with a regular fare of verbatim speeches from Socialist deputies in the *duma*, the tsar's consultative parliament, exhaustive reports of labour disputes, and letters and notes from leading factories. Lenin and Zinoviev sent articles from their exile in Cracow, then part of the Austro-Hungarian empire. Partly because sectarian politics were endemic on the Left, and partly because the *okhrana*, (the tsarist secret police) wanted to divide the Left, *Pravda* steadily became more shrill and more critical of the Mensheviks. Circulation declined to about 25,000, according to the well-informed *okhrana* archives, which also noted that *Pravda* did better when it examined the workers' plight rather than spouted revolutionary ideology.[15]

Pravda's first Bolshevik editor was Stalin, until he was arrested at a charity ball to raise funds for the paper. Of its 645 issues under tsarism, almost one issue in three was confiscated or fined. A total of thirty-six *Pravda* editors were sued, and they served a total of four years in prison; a series of illiterate nominal editors were appointed for this purpose.[16] *Pravda* itself was barely legal; the Bolshevik Party was banned. Bolsheviks were therefore described in its columns with the code phrase 'consistent and staunch labour democrats'. Because of state harassment, *Pravda* was re-launched eight times with slightly different names. There was *Put Pravda* (Path of Truth) and *Rabochaya Pravda* (Workers' Truth). It was however able to orchestrate political campaigns. In December 1912, the five Bolshevik deputies in the *duma* raised the issue of persecution of trade unions, while *Pravda* simultaneously chronicled examples of such persecution, under the guise of recording *duma* speeches. From his Cracow exile, Lenin sent a constant spate of orders, pleas, letters and articles. He used his personal friendship with Maxim Gorky to persuade the great writer to send articles to *Pravda*, and organized a section called 'Peasant Life' to widen the paper's appeal beyond the urban proletariat. Workers and peasants themselves were encouraged to become part-time correspondents, or *Rabeslkor*; in *Pravda*'s two years, they contributed some 17,000 items. As the Communist Party's official history puts it: 'A whole generation of revolutionary proletarians, which later carried out the October Socialist revolution of

1917, grew up with *Pravda*. On *Pravda* were tried out most of the revolutionary methods, journalistic and otherwise, that later became standard Soviet mass communications theory and procedure.'[17] In a sense it was too good to last. On 8 July 1914, the eve of the First World War, *Pravda* was suspended for the duration of the war.

But the war itself was a revolutionary force, undermining tsarist authority as the ramshackle regime suffered disastrous losses and defeats. When the February Revolution of 1917 toppled the tsar and brought in the provisional government of Kerensky, the liberals and moderates, *Pravda* was back on the streets within five days, edited by Molotov who followed what he believed to be Lenin's line of opposing the provisional government and the war itself. Within a week, Stalin and Kamenev had returned to St Petersburg from Siberian exile, taken over the paper, and changed the line, supporting the Kerensky government. 'The mere slogan "Down with the war" is impractical,' Stalin wrote (28 March 1917). 'The Russian soldier must stand firmly at his post.'

In mid-April, with the connivance of the German authorities who believed that he could weaken the Russian war effort, and almost certainly with German gold to finance *Pravda* and the Bolsheviks through the summer of 1917, Lenin returned to Russia from his wartime place of exile in Switzerland.[18] Immediately, he changed the Stalin–Kamenev line. He published his 'April Theses' in *Pravda*, demanding an end to the war and a new workers' revolution to overthrow the moderate Kerensky government. On one of the few occasions in its history, *Pravda*'s columns saw a debate within the party. The following day, 21 April, Kamenev and Stalin attacked Lenin, saying that his line was: 'unacceptable in that it starts from the assumption that the bourgeois revolution is ended'. Lenin had more support, and he had the money to start printing 200,000 copies a day, and his view prevailed. But *Pravda* became perilously exposed. In July, the Bolsheviks' first abortive attempt at a *coup d'état* to seize power failed, *Pravda*'s presses were smashed, and Lenin went into hiding. Twice during the July days, *Pravda* appeared with large gaps on its front page, ready to publish a proclamation that the Bolsheviks were taking power. Each time, the proclamation was held out as the Kerensky government rallied to its own defence.[19]

But in November, with the continuing war sapping at Kerensky's support, the Bolsheviks, their supporters in the army and their own Red Guard militia were strong enough in Moscow and St Petersburg to take power. It was more a *putsch* than a revolution. But it was carried out by determined men. Within three days of taking power, Lenin published a decree closing all opposition papers. 'As soon as the new order becomes stabilized, all administrative restrictions on the press will be lifted,' *Pravda* said (10 November 1917). This decree was never revoked, and became the basis for the continuing censorship, administered by the Glavlit office. Glavlit was the one tsarist state office which continued to function under Communism with an unchanged name. Once power was achieved, Lenin forbade polemics, sensationalism and advertisements in *Pravda*. He ordered that it change from a paper which 'primarily reports the political news of the day into a serious organ for the economic education of the mass of the people'.[20]

These orders were swiftly amended under the pressures of civil war, as the Whites (and their Western capitalist allies) tried to overthrow the Bolshevik government. *Pravda* became the battle-cry. 'The rule of capital will die with the last breath of the last capitalist, nobleman, priest and army officer,' it thundered (4 August 1918). 'The hymn of the working class will be a hymn of hate and revenge. Workers! if you do not destroy the bourgeoisie, it will destroy you,' (31 August 1918). The two-page paper was distributed free wherever the Bolsheviks could send the propaganda. There were special sections of the paper for the Red Army, for women, for youth. The numbers of copies published fluctuated dramatically, between 50,000 and 200,000, depending on the paper shortage and the fortunes of war, as the White armies pressed the Bolsheviks back to an enclave around Moscow.

When the civil war was finally won, the Bolsheviks were left with a barren, war-torn, impoverished land. One of the first peacetime decisions of Lenin was to lay down a structure for the Soviet press. In April 1921, the Central Committee issued guidelines for what the press should contain: how many lines for arts and industrial news, what proportion of foreign news, of ideology and so on. Lenin's blueprint could still clearly be seen in the structure of *Pravda* as late as the 1940s. It was a design for total party control over the press.[21] Ironically, in the doomed revolt of the sailors of Kronstadt in 1921 (once among the Bolsheviks' staunchest supporters), one of their demands was for a free press.[22]

It was with Lenin's stroke and death in 1924 that the great weakness of a party-controlled press became apparent: unless the party leadership itself is secure, the press can drift. As Lenin lay on his death-bed, writing the testament that was meant to guide the party in choosing his successor, he asked for a copy of it to be sent to *Pravda*. It remained unpublished as his rival heirs, Stalin, Zinoviev, Trotsky and the rest, were uncertain whom it would benefit, whom it might harm.[23] As the rivalries continued, it became plain that Stalin, who controlled the party secretariat, had occupied the key position, not least because *Pravda* was the party's paper. *Izvestia*, by contrast, is the paper of the Soviet government, a different and, in a sense, lesser organ in the Soviet state.

Throughout 1924, *Pravda* ran a pro-Stalin campaign. When *Leningradskaya Pravda*, run by Zinoviev (the Leningrad party boss) criticized Stalin, Stalin was able to use the party machinery to get the Fourteenth Party Congress to pass a resolution ordering 'a change and improvement of the *Leningradskaya Pravda* editorial staff'.[24] Stalin's strategy was complex. In the mid-1920s, he made a tactical alliance with the gifted young theorist Bukharin (author of *The ABC of Communism*) who was the editor of *Pravda*. Having used Bukharin to defeat Trotsky and Zinoviev, Stalin later turned on Bukharin. But the party machinery, through its Central Committee secretariat and the *orgburo*, enabled Stalin to impose his own grand design upon the Soviet press as a whole, and to create a publishing structure which survives to this day. Stalin's design was for four layers of newspaper throughout the country: a national press, a press for each of the Soviet Republics, a regional press and then a local newspaper. Effectively this was a horizontal structure. Cutting across this, almost on a vertical basis, were the specialist newspapers, for farmers, industrial workers, women, the military, and so on. As a matter of course, each editor of each paper was an ex-officio member of the central committee of his local Communist Party, whether on local, regional, national or all-Union level. In effect, this gave Stalin a dominant role throughout the Soviet mass media.[25] He extended this influence by means of the *Rabselkor* system of part-time and amateur correspondents which had been a feature of the *Pravda* of tsarist days. In 1924, there were about 100,000 *Rabselkor*, 216,000 in 1925, and 500,000 in 1928. Stalin defined their role and purpose precisely: 'It is not only that the press agitates and criticizes, but above all it has a large network of workers, agents and correspondents throughout the country, so that the thread from the party through the paper extends to all worker and peasant districts without exception, so that the interaction between party and state is complete.'[26]

Stalin dragooned the press, as well as the party, into the service of a total and centralized authority, which meant, in terms of 1920s Soviet reality, into his own service and support. The keystone of this edifice was *Pravda* itself with its monitoring function over the press as a whole. In October 1929, Stalin instructed *Pravda* to begin a regular 'review of the press', in which it examined the work of the press throughout the USSR, under the rubric: 'The proletarian press must relentlessly and consistently fight for the party line.' In effect, *Pravda* policed the rest of the Soviet press.[27]

Significantly, *Pravda* was given this role three months after it had launched Stalin's press campaign against his former ally, Bukharin. And ironically, Bukharin himself was nominally editor of *Pravda*, a post he used to publish, in the course of September 1928, the only complete statement of the views of the 'right-wing' opposition to Stalin. Bukharin's articles argued against Stalin's forcing through the programme of the collective farms, and his persecution of the *kulaks*, the richer peasants. Bukharin suggested that a healthy and prosperous farming community like that of the USA provided a vital consumer market for industrial goods, was more productive, and that allegations of food hoarding by the *kulaks* were exaggerated.[28] This represented a challenge that Stalin quickly moved to quell, replacing Bukharin as editor of *Pravda* with L. Z. Mekhlis, a Stalin loyalist who was to become a general in the NKVD, the secret police. Under Mekhlis, *Pravda* turned to attack Bukharin and to claim that the collective farm programme was a success. As Khrushchev later commented: 'We had been living under the illusion promoted by *Pravda* that collectivization was proceeding smoothly.'[29]

The 1930s were a savage decade in Soviet Russia, marked by purges and show-trials and a political repression that rivalled, and may well have exceeded, that of Hitler's Germany. *Pravda* under Mekhlis was a loyal participant in the process. It was *Pravda* which launched the attacks on the hitherto sacrosanct figure of Maxim Gorky (28 January 1935); *Pravda* again which prepared the ground for the great purges in the army, running a curious series on espionage, spies and their dangers, mainly culled from the sensational press of the West. As the series began, with an article on the military vulnerability of a country that allowed spies to penetrate its secrets, *Pravda* ran a typical editorial: 'The punishing sword of the proletariat has become neither dull nor rusty. It will descend on the heads of those who want to tear our beautiful country to pieces and subject it to the yoke of German-Japanese fascism' (5 June 1937). As the series ended on 11 June, *Pravda* announced the arrest and forthcoming trial of Tukachevsky and the first batch of the Red Army's generals, the first phase of a purge that was to decimate the officer corps. When it was not savaging his enemies or lauding the economic drive of Stalin, *Pravda* was the cheer-leader for the cult of personality which surrounded him: 'Stalin, the genius of the new world, the wisest man of the epoch, the great leader of Communism,' ran a typically fulsome editorial of 25 November 1936.

The tragedy of Stalin's 1930s produced its own elements of farce. After extolling the vast productivity of a Ukrainian coalminer and holding him up as an example to all Soviet workers, *Pravda* named the 'hero of labour' as Nikita Izotov. An apologetic note came from the Ukraine to say that, in fact, the man's name was Nikifar. Rather than admit to having made a mistake, *Pravda* arranged for Nikifar to appear in court and formally change his name to Nikita.[30]

Pravda reflected all that was worst, the servility, the slogans, the betrayals of friends and colleagues, the vindictiveness of Stalin's purge years. *Pravda* correspondents working abroad, above all in Spain during the civil war, served as military advisers, diplomats and propagandists, as well as reporters. Their reports followed the serpentine courses of the party line. Nikhail Koltzov, the *Pravda* correspondent in 1936, helped to organize the defence of Madrid. On his return to Moscow in 1938 he was shot, although his name was rehabilitated in Khrushchev's Twentieth Party Congress speech of 1956.[31] Ilya Ehrenburg, who went out to Spain as *Izvestia* correspondent and then began writing for *Pravda*, veered from anti-fascist polemics to 'stretching out the hand of conciliation to the Spanish patriots' of the old *Falange*, the fascist party itself, under Stalin's later 'Spain for the Spaniards' policy (17 June 1938). The same somersaults had to be turned in August 1939, when Stalin signed the Non-Aggression Pact with Hitler's Germany, and again with Hitler's invasion.

Pravda's role in the war changed little. The glories and immediacies of war reporting were left largely to the soldiers' paper *Krasnaya Zvyezda*, and indeed *Pravda*'s privileged access to the better-quality paper stocks meant that it was unpopular among the troops – the thick paper was unsuitable for rolling cigarettes.[32] *Pravda* conveyed the orders and perspectives of the party. When Italy capitulated in 1943, *Pravda*'s readers were not informed. As Stalin kept up the pressure on Britain and the US to open a second front in Western Europe, *Pravda* printed allegations that the British were negotiating secretly with the Nazis for a separate peace and a Nazi-capitalist alliance against the Soviet Union.[33] And Stalin's grim internal terror continued. When the mass deportations from the Baltic states began in 1941 and of the Crimean Tartars in 1944, they went unreported in *Pravda* (although *Izvestia* did mention the Crimean Tartar deportations two years later).[34] *Pravda*'s job was to inspire and, under the pressure of war, the occasional flash of imagination was permitted. With the battle of Stalingrad at its height in the winter of 1943, almost a whole issue of the paper was devoted to printing the text of a play 'The Front' by Alexander Korneichuk, which criticized the old-fashioned commanders who had lost the early battles and hailed the spirit of the new Soviet men who were taking their place.[35]

The exigencies of war saw an even further tightening of the party's grip upon the press through the *Perechen* system, the list of topics that journalists were not allowed to mention. In 1940, the *Perechen* booklet was 220 pages thick; by 1950 700 pages.[36] Still in force in the 1970s, the current *Perechen* topics include information on the organs of censorship, the amount of crime and numbers of arrests, information on the correctional labour camps, the number of illiterates and of drug addicts, and reports of the consequences of natural disasters, or on the human victims of accidents. Long after Stalin's era, in March 1961, the disastrous breach of Kiev's river dykes, when 145 died and vast damage followed in the flood, saw no report in *Pravda* for eighteen days, because of *Perechen* directives. A construction accident during the rebuilding of *Pravda*'s own offices in 1974, when at least five men died, has never been reported.[37]

Given the opportunity, some of *Pravda*'s reporters could do impressive work. In August 1948, Yuri Korolkov published the result of weeks of investigation into an explosion at a factory at Ludwigshafen in Germany. By questioning factory workers and digging into old records, he was able to establish that the explosion had followed French, American and British efforts to re-establish the German V-2 missile manufacturing site, that several workers had been killed, and that the explosion itself came from hydrate of hydrazine, part of the V-2's propulsion fuel.[38] On the domestic front, *Pravda* investigations twice almost aborted the young Leonid Brezhnev's political career before it had properly got under way. Brezhnev was in charge of the reconstruction of the Zaporozhe steel plant, and he and his administrative team were criticized in its pages for project delays: 'They do not seem very interested in this vital reconstruction,' (7 February 1947). Brezhnev, who saw the criticism as part of an internal party campaign against his own patron, Khrushchev, fought back on *Pravda*'s own terms and in its own pages, sending regular progress reports to the paper, and claiming a three-column front-page space in October 1947 to report that the plant was back in production. Five years later, promoted to be party boss of the Moldavian Republic, Brezhnev came under fire in *Pravda* once more, after a *Pravda* investigation into corruption within the party secretariat. 'The Moldavian Central Committee has received serious warnings but has given the matter no real attention,' *Pravda* charged. After Brezhnev's formal report to the party congress, *Pravda* virtually accused him of lying: 'his report does not reflect the true state of affairs'. Brezhnev was perhaps fortunate that Stalin's era was about to die with the man, and his patron Khrushchev to reach a position to protect him.[39] Again the pattern emerges, as it did in 1917 and again in the 1920s, of *Pravda* as the weapon of the dominant group in the party becoming evidently blunt when the party leadership was confused, or undergoing change.

Pravda's history reflects a recurrent pattern within the Soviet State itself. After each interregnum, be it the summer of 1917, the years after Lenin's death, the years after Stalin's death or after Khrushchev's fall, *Pravda* begins to act like a Western newspaper, reflecting different thrusts of debate within the party establishment without being dominated by a single voice. However, once the leadership is established, whether it be that of Lenin, Stalin, Khrushchev or Brezhnev, *Pravda* falls back into monochrome, monolithic conformity. The last years of Stalin's life were no exception. From his seventieth birthday, on 21 December 1949, when *Pravda* ran twelve pages of messages of congratulation, the litany of loyal 'happy birthdays' lasted without pause for two years.[40] Just before his death in 1953, *Pravda* once again signalled the beginning of a new purge, with an 'exclusive' report on the celebrated 'Doctors' Plot'. Stalin's death aborted both plot and purge, and the subsequent changes within the Kremlin left *Pravda* floundering. It was too uncertain of developments even to announce the fall of Beria, Stalin's chief of the secret police. Western diplomats and Russians too first learned of it when Beria's name was left out of a list of Kremlin leaders at a particular reception.[41]

The fall of Stalin and Beria marked the beginning of the most fascinating period of change for the Soviet press. Whereas Stalin had dragooned the press into his own service to establish his party authority, Khrushchev almost wooed the press to gain its support for his ambition. Within months of Stalin's death, Khrushchev promised the press a new start. *Pravda* quoted his speech to a conference of newspaper editors (4 December 1953) with evident approval: 'Well-worn methods by which everything is written to a single pattern must be vigorously driven from the newspaper pages . . .material must be more varied and more thought given to content and to presentation.'

In 1956, with Khrushchev's personal backing, the Union of Journalists was founded, its goals set out in the usual dreary slogans, but there was a clear policy to increase the status of journalists and to boost the popularity of the press.[42] In the same year, a newsy, photo-filled popular paper was launched, *Sovetskaya Rossia*, which quickly reached a circulation of two million. Advertisements began to appear in the press, and Khrushchev's son-in-law Adzhubei, as editor of *Komsomolskaya Pravda* and later of *Izvestia*, began to brighten the layout and style of the press as a whole. There were fits and starts in Khrushchev's thaw, since he never commanded the personal, ruthless authority of Stalin. The Soviet press never published his Twentieth Congress speech, denouncing Stalin's purges, for example, and *Pravda*, as the stern voice of the party, occasionally fulminated against 'the blind imitation of scandal newspapers', but it sympathized with the general direction of the changes.[43] 'Soviet newspapers are insipid, lifeless, deadly dull and difficult to read,' it acknowledged in its Press Day editorial of 1960.

The Khrushchev thaw was a very real presence for Soviet journalists, however chill it may have seemed in the West. When the magazine *Novy Mir* began to publish Solzhenitsyn and its bold young editor Tvardovsky came under public attack, it was *Pravda* which published Tvardovsky's defiant reply and his attack upon the censorship bureaucracy,[44] and it was Khrushchev himself who asked *Pravda* to print that classic poem of the thaw, Yevtushenko's denunciation of the old dictator, 'Stalin's Heirs'.[45] Pavel Satyukov, *Pravda*'s editor, and Adzhubei at *Izvestia* were presiding over a kind of mild cultural revolution in Russia, and the Soviet papers improved as a result. They also had real issues to debate. Even after Khrushchev had decisively asserted his authority over his main rivals, Bulganin and Malenkov, there were still major policy debates taking place within the *politburo*, between the 'metal-eaters' of the armed forces and heavy industry and the advocates of co-existence; between the pro- and anti-Chinese factions. It was in *Pravda*'s pages, for example, that the debate about liberalizing the economy and introducing the profit motive took place. The first article was published by Professor Liberman in 1962. There was silence until 1964, when Professor Trapeznikov replied, and *Pravda* announced that the debate was now open, and asked

other experts to contribute articles of their own.[46] The relaxation
went far beyond *Pravda*. In 1960, the TASS news agency was allowed
to send its news direct to radio and TV, bypassing *Pravda*. And in
1961 a new, much more informal features agency was opened, the
Novosti Press Service, with Adzhubei's personal backing.

In many key ways, however, the subservience to party and national
policy needs continued unchanged. Foreign policy was perhaps the
most sensitive area, and during the Cuban missile crisis for example,
Pravda's editorials swivelled from missile-rattling bluster to conciliation and back to bluster again, to claim at the end of the crisis a
Soviet victory in Kennedy's promise not to invade the Caribbean
island. A less predictable example of the partisan nature of *Pravda*'s
foreign news came with the Indian-Chinese war of the same year. Five
days after the first reports of hostilities from Delhi and Peking,
Pravda published its first story: the Chinese government's statement
in full, but no Indian comment. That was the limit of the coverage on
the foreign news page. In its editorial, on the same day, *Pravda*
blamed 'imperialist circles in the West' for the war, and then proposed
a ceasefire and truce 'at the line of de facto control'. This way of
putting it had the advantage of not needing to specify the fact that
Chinese troops had advanced into Indian territory. For two weeks,
Pravda was silent on the war, a silence that was broken by another
editorial calling for a truce. For over a month of active hostilities, that
was the full extent of *Pravda*'s coverage. *Pravda*, along with the rest
of the Soviet press, then reported the ceasefire and subsequent
settlement.[47] In *Pravda*'s pages, unwelcome news is simply screened
out. One of the few content analyses of the paper shows strikingly
how this process worked over China. In the 1950s, China was an ally,
a Communist little brother. In the 1960s, the Sino-Soviet split meant
that China almost disappeared from *Pravda*'s pages. The following
figures refer to percentage of space, in column inches, devoted to
China in particular years: 1956: 6%; 1959: 5.2%; 1962: 0.7%;
1965: 0.1%.[48]

With the fall of Khrushchev in 1964 and his replacement by the
triumvirate of Brezhnev, Kosygin and Podgorny, *Pravda* became
once again a weapon in the struggle for primacy within the Kremlin.
Kosygin, whose power base was the government itself, was supported
by *Izvestia*, the government paper now newly purged of Adzhubei,
Khrushchev's son-in-law editor. Brezhnev, the party figure, had the
support of *Pravda* and of *Kommunist*, the party's theoretical journal.
Brezhnev's key cheer-leader in the press, Stepanov, edited

Kommunist and was given *Pravda*'s pages to publish pro-Brezhnev pieces.[49] One of the symbols of Brezhnev's growing dominance was the way in which the newsprint allocations to *Pravda*, and consequently its circulation, began to soar ahead of *Izvestia*. Under Adzhubei, the process had been briefly reversed. *Pravda*'s circulation rose from 5.8 million in 1963 to 7 million in 1965, to some 11 million in 1980. Brezhnev's era saw an end to the thaw in Soviet literary life and, with the appointment of Mikhail Zimyanin (the former deputy foreign minister) to the editorship in 1965, *Pravda* began to take a harder line in foreign affairs, becoming particularly critical of the US role in Vietnam.[50]

The recipients of *Pravda*'s propaganda are on the whole the elite of Soviet Russia, the Communist Party members. The only readership survey of the paper which has been available in the West took place in 1970. It found that 75% of the readers were party members, that their average age was forty-two, that 25% lived in rural areas, and that 39% had been through some form of higher education. But, for party members, they had some curious priorities in their reading. The table of their choice of articles went as follows:

Official communications	81%
Events overseas	74%
International themes	63%
Themes on morals and the upbringing of children	57%
Satirical articles	57%
Lead editorials	45%
Party themes	41%

The readers reported themselves 'least satisfied with the completeness of information' on moral themes, on education and everyday life, on consumer services and on economics. The interest shown by *Pravda* readers in international affairs was matched by a similar survey of readers of *Izvestia* and of *Trud*, the trade-union paper.[51]

The sheer inefficiency of the *soyuzpechat* distribution system means that readers do not have a great deal of choice in what they buy. A Russian does not simply hand over his kopeks at the news kiosk. Orders for papers have to be placed in advance and, on *Pravda*, a circulation drive takes place at the end of each year, when party cells, *komsomol* groups, and trade unions combine with the *soyuzpechat* to persuade fellow citizens to take out subscriptions for the papers. In December 1962, when it felt that Adzhubei's *Izvestia* was drawing too far ahead in circulation, *Pravda* ran its own campaign under the slogan 'Newspapers and periodicals in every family' – but even this campaign was tempered by the fixed allocations of newsprint available.[52]

The people who decide what *Pravda*'s readers will see in the paper meet each day at 11 a.m. in *Pravda*'s Moscow office. They go by the name of the *redkollegiya*, and they are composed of the kind of people who would make up the editorial conference on any paper. There is the editor-in-chief, his two deputies (one of whom is the foreign editor), the various department editors and the managing editor, or 'responsible secretary' whose job on other papers is to make sure that censorship rules are being followed. *Pravda* alone is exempt from the need to submit each month advance plans of subjects to be covered and themes of main articles, and thus the managing editor's role is much more administrative.[53] Much of his work is involved in the complex and technologically sophisticated process of transmitting *Pravda*'s pages by satellite to the forty-three cities around the USSR in which *Pravda* is printed, thus ensuring delivery around the vast country on the same morning.

The thirty or so senior journalists who meet each morning control a network of 180 editors and writers in Moscow, sixty staff reporters around the country, and forty foreign correspondents. Just under half of *Pravda*'s journalists have come from the journalism faculties of the universities. The rest have been promoted from smaller papers, or from party positions.[54] As editor-in-chief, Afanyasev earns a basic salary of some £400 a month, to which are added generous expenses, bonuses, extra bonuses for each article of his which is printed, freelance earnings (from radio and TV commentaries, for example) and the usual consumer privileges of a senior party official. By contrast, a typesetter on the paper (all of whom are women) will earn approximately £140 a month as a basic wage, with generous bonuses for night work. A compositor can make up to £200 extra a month through bonuses.[55]

The main oddity of the *redkollegiya* meetings for a Western journalist is that they are concerned less with discussing the next day's paper than with the *Pravda* of two days hence. Up to 60% of *Pravda*'s columns are planned more than two days in advance. When a journalist from the London *Times* visited *Pravda* in 1977, he was startled to note that three front-page columns of a paper two days from publication had been reserved for a report on the talks between President Assad of Syria and Brezhnev.[56] Irrespective of whether the talks went well or ill, whether major decisions were made or not, the three columns were to be filled. Nor are the front pages reserved for late news. They are devoted almost exclusively to party news, editorials, economic achievements and the visits of foreign dignitaries. A typical front-page story (27 August 1967) will begin: 'The agricultural workers of Sumi province, having developed Socialist emulation so as worthily to meet the 50th aniversary of the Great October Socialist Revolution, on 25 August fulfilled the plan for the sale of grain to the State by 123%.'

Pravda usually runs to six pages, occasionally to eight, and to four pages on Mondays; it is the only Soviet paper to appear seven days a week. A fairly typical issue will run as follows (the example is taken from 6 October 1965, but a parallel study in 1979 showed only minor differences):

Page One: A four-column story at the top of the page, headlined 'Labour watch of millions', describes the efforts to bring in the harvest, with stories on how the miners must dig extra coal to feed power stations to increase production for the harvest. The main picture is of a Sudanese-Mali delegation visiting the Kremlin. There is a two-column editorial, headed 'To complete the work in the fields successfully', on the relationship between productivity and party decisions. The rest of the page is taken up with small items on the US troops in Vietnam, cement shipments, and the visit of a Hungarian delegation to Mongolia.

Page Two: More than half the page is devoted to readers' letters and to reports of the official action taken in response to the letters, under the heading 'To *Pravda* they reply – Measures taken'. The rest of the page is taken up with a list of Central Party Committee resolutions, headed 'Faith in the Party inspires', and small items on productivity targets met in various industries.

Page Three: A half-page survey of Soviet foreign policy since 1945, a quarter-page feature on 'Native Peoples', or ethnic communities within the USSR, a photo of an oil refinery and the formal report of the chairman of a collective farm.

Page Four: World press reports on the recent plenary meeting of the Central Committee, printed verbatim. Arrangements for the celebration of the sixteenth anniversary of the DDR (one column), and small items on economic news from Comecon nations, the arrival of an African ambassador and Russian trade links with Cyprus.

Page Five: Foreign news stories, taken direct from the TASS wire, datelined Ankara, Warsaw, Jakarta, Bonn, Helsinki and Saigon. A feature on Rio de Janeiro, brief reports on the shooting-down of a US aircraft in Vietnam and Indo-Pakistan border incidents, and a small feature on the first issue of *Granma*, the Cuban newspaper.

Page Six: A short story, a poem, a photo of the countryside. A feature section, headed 'Through the mother country', of farm stories written in nostalgic vein. One small story from a police court. The sports section contains two small reports on chess games, and there is a two-column section, headed 'Our information department', which contains TV and radio listings and theatre notes.

The changes that do take place in *Pravda*'s coverage, seen over a period of years, are overwhelmingly those of proportion; how much space is devoted to various categories of news. Since the 1950s, for example, there has been a dramatic reduction in the space given to foreign affairs, another fall in the space given to economic news, slightly more space given to sport, and a great deal more space devoted to science and education. Tables from separate studies have been combined to give the following breakdown:

	1947–8	1956	1959	1962	1965
International news	42.3%	47.5	41.8	37.1	29.7
China	2.3	6	5.2	0.7	0.1
Domestic news	57.7	52.5	58.2	62.9	70.3
Arts/Literature/Cultural	3.5	3.7	11.6	7	6.8
Sport	0.6	1.4	1.6	1.5	2.4
Economics	31.1	25.7	34.8	27.7	21.3
Politics	18.5	15.7	5.5	18.5	18.6
Science/Education	1.7	1.6	2.8	3.7	11

Note: Figures refer to percentage of space allocated[57]

The finances of *Pravda* are complex and obscured by official secrecy. For over fifty years, the cover price was maintained at two kopeks, but by 1970 the price had risen to three kopeks for a six-page *Pravda* and four kopeks for eight pages. At a circulation of 11 million, that gives a minimum annual income of 120.45 million roubles. *Pravda*'s own costs breakdown has never been formally published, but *Pravda* sources point researchers to the published breakdown of *Izvestia*'s costs, made public in 1968, and say that the *Pravda* proportions are broadly parallel. According to *Izvestia*, the costs are as follows, as a percentage of total income: Newsprint 30%; circulation and distribution costs 25%; mechanical expenses (mainly printing) 30%; editorial and management 3%; and profit 12%.[58]

These figures are inherently unreliable. It is difficult to believe that
the wage costs alone, let alone the hard-currency costs of maintaining
forty foreign correspondents, could be held down to 3% of income, or
some 4 million roubles. Many salary costs are clearly hidden inside
that 30% for 'mechanical expenses'. Still, the profit figure of 12% is
not unreasonable, although one would like an answer to the key
question – given that these were the years of *Pravda*'s establishing its
satellite printing hardware (and its development), were these investments internally generated or furnished from outside? The figures
also suffer from other statements made by senior Soviet press
officials. In 1955, *Izvestia*'s editor claimed a profit of 40 million
roubles on a circulation of some 4 million – although total income
from those sales would be about 36.5 million roubles, and this at a
time when *Izvestia* ran almost no advertising.[59] Similarly, in 1966,
Pravda's editor told one Western researcher that *Pravda* was making
a profit of 'about $US 50 million a year'.[60] It is hard to see how these
profits were generated on the sales figures for that year, which would
suggest a total sales income of some 51.1 million roubles. *Pravda*
executives are broadly parallel. According to *Izvestia*, the costs are as
follows, as a claim that the figures are distorted, by not allowing for
the profits *Pravda* makes from printing other newspapers, such as
Komsomolskaya Pravda, but clearly the Western researcher is here at
a classic disadvantage. *Pravda* is not keen to provide definitive
figures.

The part of *Pravda* which Soviet journalists are most keen to
display to the West is the celebrated 'Letters' section. In 1979, *Pravda*
received more than 600,000 readers' letters, and answered each of
them – although it printed fewer than 1,000.[61] On the third floor of
the newspaper building in Pravda Street, sixty of the 180 home
journalists are concerned with reading, answering and deciding
whether to publish a reader's letter. Each letter is checked for
accuracy with the individual, and the party committee, the factory,
the office or the union involved in the complaint being made – and
usually the letters do contain complaints, the press being one of the
few safety valves in Soviet society. Army officers write in to complain
that parental money orders to conscript sons are used for drinking
bouts; consumers complain about the quality or design of samovars.
Very occasionally, a letter alleging official (if local) corruption will be
printed, with accompanying reports from *Pravda* journalists. The
example of the criticism of Brezhnev in the Stalin era, however,
suggests that allegations of official wrongdoing have been officially

inspired, and editor-in-chief Afanyasev insists: 'We are not interested in scandals in private life or discrediting an official.'[62]

In fact, to a striking degree, individual personalities and their defects are absent from *Pravda*'s pages – even in the case of hostile foreign leaders. *Pravda*'s cartoonist, Vasily Fornichev, who is usually allowed more latitude than most, had a cartoon of the exiled Shah of Iran banned from publication. It had shown an unctuous Sadat of Egypt welcoming the Shah to exile. Behind Sadat was a pyramid with a tiny door, big enough only to crawl into. 'I knew *Pravda* could not print it,' Fornichev commented in an interview. 'They don't like caricatures of ruling heads of state, whatever our country's relations with them are.'[63]

This respectful attitude to foreign leaders was perhaps best displayed during the Watergate crisis of Richard Nixon's presidency. A comparison of the Watergate coverage of *Pravda*, the London *Times*, *Le Monde* and *Die Welt* made by the Political Science department of Ohio's Cleveland State University showed *Pravda* by far the least critical of the four papers. Using the Jani-Fadber co-efficients of imbalance to measure pro and con attitudes, the study gave *The Times* a negative index of 155; *Le Monde* a negative index of 93; *Die Welt* a negative index of 37, and *Pravda* a *positive* (or pro-Nixon) index of 192. *Pravda* referred throughout to 'the so-called Watergate affair' and described it as an affair 'fabricated by certain circles to remove a President committed to US-Soviet détente'.[64] Once again, *Pravda* gives the party line.

Where there is no definite party line, or where that line may be changing, *Pravda* becomes the vehicle for new ideas, the floating of new policies. On 1 October 1976, *Pravda* ran a seven-column article calling for a restoration of normal relations with China. There was no mention of Mao or Maoism, praise of Peking's achievements and policies until 1960, and it concluded that 'relations had deteriorated but not through the fault of the Soviet side'. *Pravda* insisted that Moscow was prepared to hold talks on border disputes without prior conditions, and that the USSR had no 'economic, territorial or other claims on China'. This was clearly a foreign policy breakthrough of enormous significance. The signal of its death also came in *Pravda*, eight months later, with a vitriolic editorial headed 'Peking is preparing for a new global slaughter', accusing China of allying with the imperialists and threatening world peace. It concluded: 'We must prepare for war,' (15 May 1977). The idea had been floated, and it had sunk. *Pravda* is the party's voice authorized to make public statements on issues which the other newspapers have carefully refused to explore. Soviet press coverage of the Afghan campaign of 1979–81, for example, had been limited to a bare dozen references in military publications like 'Red Star' and 'Military Banner'. In July 1981, the first eye-witness account of the counter-insurgency war in Afghanistan appeared in *Pravda*, under the by-line of Ivan Shchedrov. 'It is difficult to recall the details of the battle, but it ended in a [Government] victory,' he reported. 'Much happened during the four hours of battle. Having lost four people, the detachment with thirteen wounded drove the column to the capital.'[65] He went on to describe the hailing of three Afghan soldiers as heroes and their instant promotion to sergeants' rank. But as Britain's *Guardian* noted: 'This sketchy battle report raised more questions than it answered. If Government forces won, what were the enemy losses? Were Soviet troops involved? Did Soviet helicopter gunships, only a few minutes' flying time from Kabul, intercede? If so, why did the battle last four hours?'[66]

During the Polish crisis of 1980–81, *Pravda* was deployed as the threatening organ of the *politburo*. While Soviet troops signally failed to intervene, *Pravda* gave every indication that they might, and every 'justification' why they should. A Polish memorial at the site of the massacre of some 10,000 Polish officers in 1939, which is widely accepted to have been committed by Soviet killer squads, was dismissed in *Pravda* as 'an anti-Soviet witches' sabbath. . .Nazi propaganda. . .a Hitlerite version of events'.[67] (The Soviet Union has consistently claimed that the officers were murdered by the Nazis.) But *Pravda*'s coverage quoted only those hard-line Communist cadres who called for the restoration of party authority and the denunciation of the Solidarity movement. The widespread public support for Solidarity, and its justified criticisms of corruption within the Communist Party, were withheld from *Pravda*'s readers.

It is *Pravda* which has consistently given the official line on Solzhenitsyn and the dissidents, *Pravda* which gives the formal response to Western accusations of Moscow's denial of human rights and breaking of the Helsinki agreements.[68] *Pravda* regularly runs articles on trials in the US which are said to be trials of dissidents, or of blacks whose human rights have been denied. There is a regular feature headed 'Society of violated rights' about the US, and another about the West headed 'World of Capital – social problems'. *Pravda*'s report of the British steel strike of 1979 had a correspondent on the picket lines talking to the strikers 'for whom the class struggle is a daily reality, a necessity, a duty'.[69] Articles such as these are printed not only for the Soviet audience, but because *Pravda* is seen to be the Soviet Union's public and international voice. *Pravda*'s editorials are sent as a matter of course not only to every newspaper in the USSR, but also to Moscow Radio to be beamed overseas. As the Communist Party paper, *Pravda* is also published for Communist parties abroad – which has some curious results. In 1977, *Pravda*'s publication of a series of articles by Italian Communists on Eurocommunism and the tactical possibilities of working, in elections and government, with bourgeois parties, amounted to the most subversive political writings legally available to Russian readers for many years. Similarly, during the World Communist Conference of 1969, held while memories of the invasion of Czechoslovakia still ravaged Communist parties in the West, Moscow agreed to an ultimatum from the Italian and Romanian parties that their speeches to the conference be printed verbatim in *Pravda*. The result was that *Pravda* readers read the most bitterly critical denunciations of Russian policy and of the Czech invasion ever legally seen inside the Soviet Union.[70] For a week, *Pravda* read like a *samizdat*. And then it went back to being *Pravda*.

Notes

1. *Khrushchev Remembers*, N. Khrushchev, pp. 20ff.
2. *Pravda*, 17.x.1964.
3. *Brezhnev*, John Dornberg, p. 63.
4. *Mass Media in the Soviet Union*, Hopkins, p. 184.
5. *Pravda*, 8.vii.1956. Also quoted in *The Press in Authoritarian Countries*, International Press Institute.
6. 'Boys' Weeklies' from *The Collected Essays*, George Orwell.
7. *Time* magazine, 23.vi.1980, p. 37.
8. *The Times*, 22.ii.1977.
9. *Time* magazine, *op. cit.*
10. N. G. Palyunov, TASS director, lecture at Moscow University in 1956. Quoted in IPI, *op. cit.*
11. *How the Communist Press Works*, Buzek.
12. *The Communist Party of the Soviet Union*, L. Schapiro, p. 129.
13. *ibid.*
14. *Lenin*, D. Shub, p. 149.
15. 'Pre-Revolutionary *Pravda* and Tsarist Censorship', W. Bassow, *American Slavic and Eastern European Review*, vol XIII, 1954.
16. *Voices of the Red Giants*, J. W. Markham.
17. *History of the All-Union Communist Party*, Rothstein *et al.*, p. 171.

18. Shub, *op. cit.*, pp. 243–8 and 341–3.
19. *ibid.*
20. *Collected Works*, V. I. Lenin, vol. XXIII, Moscow, 1959, pp. 225–7.
21. Markham, *op. cit.*, p. 71.
22. Hopkins, *op. cit.*
23. *Lenin and the Bolsheviks*, A. B. Ulam, p. 740.
24. Hopkins, *op. cit.*, p. 87.
25. *ibid.*
26. *J. Stalin*, O. Pechati (Izdalestvo Proletarii, 1925) quoted Hopkins, *op. cit.*, p. 87.
27. Hopkins, *op. cit.*, p. 98.
28. *Pravda* 13 and 21.ix.1928.
29. Khrushchev, *op. cit.*, p. 72.
30. *Russia*, R. G. Kaiser, p. 217
31. *The Spanish Civil War*, H. Thomas (Pelican, London, 3rd edn, 1977) pp. 319, 393.
32. *The Last Battle*, C. Ryan (NEL, London, 1968) p. 313.
33. *Bodyguard of Lies*, A. Cave Brown (Star Books, London, 1977) p. 597.
34. IPI, *op. cit.*,
35. Khrushchev, *op. cit.*, p. 287.
36. Markham, *op. cit.*, p. 123. See also Kaiser, *op. cit.*, pp. 215–16.
37. Kaiser, op. cit., p. 221.
38. *Pravda*, 18.viii.1948.
39. Dornberg, *op. cit.*, pp. 113–22. See also *Pravda*, 5.ii.1947 and 3.x.1947.
40. IPI, *op. cit.*
41. Markham, *op. cit.*, p. 132.
42. See Markham, Hopkins, Khrushchev, *op. cit.*
43. The nearest *Pravda* came to reporting the Khrushchev speech was 6.vii.1956, in an editorial against the cult of the individual. It ran: 'Many acts of Stalin, particularly in the sphere of the violation of Soviet Law, became known only after his death, mainly in connection with the exposure of the Beria gang and the establishing of Party control over the organs of State security.'
44. Markham, *op. cit.*, p. 246.
45. *ibid.*
46. Hopkins, op. cit., pp. 185ff.
47. *Pravda*, 26.x.1962. See also Markham, *op. cit.*, p. 240.
48. *Soviet Political Indoctrination*, Hollander, p. 43.
49. Dornberg, *op. cit.*, pp. 203–5.
50. *The Elite Press*, Merrill, p. 101.
51. Hollander, *op. cit.*, p. 62.
52. Buzek, *op. cit.*
53. Markham, *op. cit.*, p. 123.
54. *Time* magazine, *op. cit.*, p. 37.
55. *ibid.*, and also *The Times, op. cit.*
56. *The Times, ibid.*
57. Hollander, *op. cit.*, p. 43, but also *Public Opinion in the Soviet Union*, Alex Inkeles. Percentages and comparisons by the author.
58. Hopkins, *op. cit.*, p. 184.
59. Markham, *op. cit.*, p. 137.

60. *ibid.*
61. *Time* magazine, *op. cit.*
62. *ibid.*
63. *Guardian*, 2.viii.1980.
64. *The Times*, 23.iv.1975.
65. *Pravda*, 16.vii.1981.
66. *Guardian*, 21.vii.1981.
67. See the *Guardian*, 16.iv.1981.
68. See *Pravda*, 1975, 'The Way to Treason' (on Solzhenitsyn), and 13.ii.1977, 'They Represent Nobody' (on dissidents).
69. *Time* magazine, *op. cit.*
70. Dornberg, *op. cit.*, p. 232.

PRAVDA: EDITORIALS

The independence of India: 29 August 1947

'The British plan is directed against the liberation movement of the Indian people. It aims not at the departure of the British, but at the retention in their hands of the maximum number of economic and military positions. Inasmuch as the plan is based on the partition of the country, it does not serve to unite India but rather to fan the flames of religious strife.'

The independence of Israel: 4 May 1948

'It is the governing Anglo-American circles who bear all the responsibility for aggravating the Palestine crisis. It is their aim to solve, not the national problem in Palestine, but the oil problem – a deliberate transfer to the road dictated by the selfish interests of the US oil monopolies.'

The Berlin blockade and airlift: 27 June 1948

'The Anglo-US-French plan for the splitting and dismembering of Germany is doomed to failure. Nothing can stop the forward march of history. Germany can exist only as a single entity . . .Does not history teach that the conspiracy of Anglo-US monopoly capital with the Ruhr magnates can have but one result – a repetition of German aggression?'

The Communists win power in China: 5 October 1949

'The broad masses of the Chinese people, led by the working class and by its fighting Communist vanguard, supported by the mighty camp of Socialism and democracy, have dethroned the rotten bourgeois Kuomintang regime, the regime of national treachery, feudal oppression and colonial exploitation. . .The historic victory of the Chinese people represents a new and stronger blow to the whole system of imperialism, a new defeat for the camp of reaction and the warmongers.'

The Korean war: 11 September 1950

'Dr Goebbels first frightened his own countrymen and then the inhabitants of the occupied territories with his propaganda about the Red Peril, about Asiatic expansion and Communist uprisings. Are not President Truman and his European satraps using precisely the same phrases today?'

The Suez invasion: 2 November 1956

'The entire responsibility for the dangerous consequences arising out of the aggressive intentions against Egypt lies fully upon the governments of Britain, France and Israel, who have embarked on the road of violating peace and security, upon the road of aggression. The whole world now sees the worth of the false assurances of the imperialists regarding their alleged loyalty to the cause of peace and their hypocritical statements about their care for the freedom and independence of peoples.'

The Russian invasion of Hungary: 4 November 1956

'The actions of the reactionary forces in Hungary, as facts amply prove, are the fruit of subversion by the imperialist powers over a long period of time. . .The reactionaries, who have run amok, are blowing up the monuments to the Soviet soldiers who gave their lives to liberate Budapest from the Hitlerite hordes. . .To bar the road to reaction in Hungary is the urgent task dictated by events.'

The Bay of Pigs assault on Cuba: 20 April 1961

'The strings of this plot against the Cuban revolution lead to the USA. The counter-revolutionaries set out for their expedition from American territory. The landings in Cuba were effected under the cover of the USA's warships and air force. . .The time has passed forever when the USA could brandish its stick in the belief that it was the biggest and longest, because the other side now has equally long and heavy, and no less weighty, sticks.'

The Cuban missile crisis: 24 October 1962

'The actions of the US military are gross blackmail, which might lead to disastrous consequences for all mankind. . .The imperialist aggressors would do well to remember that if they seek to set alight the conflagration of a world war, they will inevitably perish in the fire.'

The Gulf of Tonkin incident: 6 August 1964

'The events preceding the raid show that the USA was seeking a *casus belli*. . .Was not the US fleet performing a covering operation during the time when those South Vietnamese warships kept firing on North Vietnam? Accusations of aggression against North Vietnam will be laughed at abroad.'

China's nuclear weapon: 24 October 1964

'To this day, the ruling circles of the USA are preventing the People's Republic of China from taking her lawful part in the organization of the UN. . .Soviet disarmament proposals have once more demonstrated to the world that general and complete disarmament is possible, provided that new efforts are made and goodwill displayed.'

Rhodesia's UDI: 12 November 1965

'London is trying to reduce the Rhodesia crisis to an internal, almost a family problem of relations between the British Crown and the 'rebellious' refractory Rhodesians who have taken this rash step. British propaganda is doing its utmost to draw a veil over the main thing – that a crime has been committed against four million Africans in the land of Zimbabwe and an insolent challenge thrown down to the whole of independent Africa. . .This amounts to collusion with Smith by the British imperialists.'

The Russian invasion of Czechoslovakia: 21 August 1968

'Relying on the fraternal support of the peoples of the Soviet Union and the other Socialist countries, the Communist and working people of Czechoslovakia are striking a crushing blow at the forces of counter-revolution, defending the freedom and the independence of their homeland and sovereignty.'

Israel's occupation of the West Bank: 16 October 1973

'Who is the aggressor in this war which is the continuation of the June war of 1967? The aggressor is he who seizes the territories of other states. Struggle against foreign occupation is not an act of aggression. A war to keep the occupied territories belonging to other states is not a national defensive war but an anti-national aggressive war.'

The OPEC price rise: 29 October 1973

'The energy crisis in the West is not only an economic problem but also a political one. . .the genuine prospect of the use of oil as a political weapon by the Arabs compels Western European countries increasingly to disassociate themselves from the pro-Israeli policy of the USA. . .A constructive solution to the energy crisis in the West will depend on the consideration given to the interests of the Arab peoples who are waging a just struggle for the restoration of their lawful rights.'

Watergate: 11 August 1974

'The change of Presidency is an internal affair of the USA. . .the thing to do now is to adhere unswervingly to the agreements already concluded, and fulfil pledges already given in order to improve Soviet-US relations and make the process of détente irreversible.'

The fall of Saigon: 3 May 1975

'The victory of the patriots in South Vietnam has demonstrated how the possibilities for imperialism have narrowed in our time. . .the end of hostilities signifies that one of the most dangerous seats of international tension has been eliminated. Conditions are thereby created for a further improvement in the overall international atmosphere.'

Sport and politics: 6 August 1980

'The success of the 22nd Olympic Games struck a crushing blow against the futile attempts of the American administration to wreck these Games, and demonstrated the bankrupt and futile nature of the efforts of certain forces to make use of sport for mercenary political aims, and to destroy the time-honoured traditions of international sports co-operation.'

The space venture: 17 April 1961

'You wish to know what Communism is, gentlemen? Then open your eyes to the heavens and you will see that Labour has become master of a considerable part of the world – and behold what it produces. . .A Soviet man has left the confines of the earth. This sentence alone, as a mathematical formula, sums up the preceding history of human society, the harnessing of the mighty forces of nature and the growth of man himself.'

Freedom of information: 6 July 1956

'In our country there is not and cannot be any freedom to buy or to bribe the press. . .It is the inalienable and basic right of millions of workers to use the press as a platform for criticism, business-like proposals and the discovery of fundamental State problems. . .the essence of democracy does not lie in formal outward signs but in whether political authority does in fact reflect the vital interests of the majority of the people, the interests of the workers.'

7

Al-Ahram

The Egyptian press was born of Christian midwives. The first news-paper in Egypt was founded in 1799 by Napoleon Bonaparte, on his brief and abortive expedition of conquest. Printed on the world's first Arabic printing press, which was brought in the French army's baggage train, *Al-Hawadeth el-Yawmiyah* ('Daily Events') launched a tradition of a press under firm government control which has lasted to this day.[1] Throughout the early part of the nineteenth century, the Ottoman masters of Egypt and their Khedives maintained a tight rein on the infant press. But in 1863, Khedive Ismail, French-educated and liberal in inclination, came to power at a time when the authority of the Ottomans had waned, and the French and British were assuming economic control, a process that was to be intensified by the building of the Suez Canal. Ismail's Egypt became a magnet for the free-thinking intelligentsia of the Ottoman world; among those who flocked to Alexandria were two Maronite Christian brothers, Salim and Bishara Taqla from Beirut. They were not wealthy but one had been a schoolteacher, and they launched their newspaper *Al-Ahram* ('The Pyramids') on loans from former pupils.[2] A four-page weekly of foolscap size, it began mainly as a newspaper of commercial and shipping news, rooted in the port of Alexandria. There was no short-age of rivals; in the six years after *Al-Ahram* first appeared on 5 August, 1876, another thirty newspapers were launched in Egypt.[3]

There were limits to Ismail's liberalism. Hostile voices were suppressed, and even the cautious Taqla brothers were arrested briefly. Thereafter they avoided political comment and decided to base their newspaper's appeal upon a timely, reliable and comprehensive news service. *Al-Ahram* was a pioneer from the beginning. In 1881 it became the first Arab newspaper to print a photograph; it was the first Egyptian newspaper to have its own correspondents overseas, in Istanbul and Paris, and the first to use interviews as news-gathering tools.[4] In 1881, it was successful enough to become a daily paper, and in 1890 it increased to broadsheet size. It still had an amateurish look, with hand-drawn advertisements, but the Taqla brothers had become powerful enough to attract influential support.

After the British invasion of 1881, Britain and France operated a condominium in Egypt, thinly veiled by the claim that they simply advised the palace. *Muqattam* was the newspaper backed by the British, and *Al-Ahram* was subsidized and protected by the French. It was strictly forbidden to write about any of the affairs of French North Africa, on pain of losing its subsidy from the French consul.[5] But as the British steadily became the dominant partner in the condominium, *Al-Ahram* began to detach itself steadily from the French camp and begin hesitantly to follow the more independent line of the newspaper *Mu'aiyad*, and of the openly nationalist *Liwa*. At this time, the political stances of the various newspapers were matters of nuance rather than of firm editorial stands. But the celebrated Dinashawni affair of 1906 served to define the various positions. A group of English officers out hunting set fire to a threshing floor and did other, probably accidental damage to the village of Dinashawni. The angry villagers killed one of the officers, and the British demanded and secured heavy judicial reprisals. The English-language *Egyptian Gazette* condemned the villagers as 'African savages'; *Liwa* saw them as 'innocent souls', and *Al-Ahram* very circumspectly described the events and the trial and declined to comment on the merits of the case. It noted, however, the real implication of the trial. After Dinashawni, said *Al-Ahram*'s editorial, no Egyptian could seriously dream of driving out the British from Egypt. The imperial masters were there to stay.[6]

The First World War, with Egypt as a base for the British campaigns against the Turks in Sinai and Palestine, seemed to prove *Al-Ahram* right, as the British tightened their military grip upon the country. But the British backing for the Arab revolt against the Turks (assisted by Lawrence of Arabia, whom *Al-Ahram* helped to make into something of a hero) stirred Egyptian nationalism. In the wake of the war, Sa'ad Zaghlul founded the Wafd Party and the Wafd's own newspaper,

Al-Balagh, to campaign for full independence and an Egyptian constitution. Banned from reporting Zaghlul's speeches as political events, *Al-Ahram* printed them on its society page, where they may well have been more widely read.[7]

Al-Ahram had forty years' experience of publishing under restraint, and part of its success lay in the realization of the Taqla brothers that profitable newspapers did not have to be filled with political news. Society pages, literary columns, articles on Egypt's archaeology could all be presented as bland features, while they still carried a powerful, if almost subliminal, message. The revival of Arabic poetry amounted to a cultural revolution with nationalist overtones; the glories of ancient Egypt that the archaeologists were revealing became a focus for an Egyptian national pride. As a policy, it was more profitable than brave but, for the next thirty years, *Al-Ahram* continued to pick its way between the various political forces of the palace, the Wafd, the British, the Muslim Brotherhood and the infant Communist Party.[8] The paper increasingly leant towards the Wafd, but the failure of Zaghlul's popular uprising of 1919 and his arrest by the British seemed to justify *Al-Ahram*'s caution. Nor were the British heedless of *Al-Ahram*'s suggestions of cautious reform. In 1922, the British granted a limited degree of independence, a constitution, and endorsed the monarchy. The constitution guaranteed press freedom – except 'in the interests of the social system', a condition that seemed permanently to apply.

When the Wafd Party overwhelmingly won the first elections of 1924 and Zaghlul became the first elected head of government, *Al-Ahram* warned him against his more radical supporters. After Zaghlul's death in 1927, the pro-Wafd papers found themselves banned and suspended, but *Al-Ahram* was merely cautioned.[9] The economic depression and endless political riots led to a new and conservative constitution in 1931, which was roundly condemned by all the press save for *Al-Ahram*. Its caution became the more obvious in 1936 when the Fath brothers founded *Al-Misri*, an openly pro-Wafd paper which quickly reached a circulation of 100,000 and began to topple the staid *Al-Ahram* from its long dominance of the Egyptian press.[10] Ironically, *Al-Misri* was given the political room to manoeuvre by the government of Ali Mahir, the one Prime Minister to win *Al-Ahram*'s wholehearted support.

Ali Mahir was perhaps the first Egyptian Premier to realize the full potential of the press and to learn that there were other ways of winning its loyalty than bribes. He established a Press Association, instituted a prize for journalism, started courses in journalism at the university, exempted journalists from paying for their telephones and gave them reduced fares on the railways. 'How can a Minister have achieved so many things in a few months?' asked *Al-Ahram*'s admiring editorial. 'He has made his Ministry the living heart of the revolution.'[11] Ali Mahir strongly backed *Al-Ahram*'s campaign for 'Egyptness', a national identity that was as rooted in the Pharoahs as in Arabism. If this was a thinly veiled method of promoting nationalism against the British, then *Al-Ahram*'s campaign for the translation and broadcasting of the Koran was a barely disguised attack upon the religious fanatics of the Muslim Brotherhood.[12] But Ali Mahir apart, it was hard to define the precise political stance of the paper, perhaps because its main market, the literate and prosperous Egyptian middle class, was equally uncertain. Since the founding of *Al-Ahram*, the ability to read a newspaper, even published in Arabic, was a skill limited to fewer than one in six of the male population. In the city, reading a newspaper marked a man as a prosperous and even intellectual member of the middle classes; in the rural areas, it marked him as a landowner and a village notable.[13] These were the classes that had done reasonably well out of the British occupation, who feared the accumulation of too much power in the hands of the King, of the Muslim Brotherhood, or even of the Wafd. *Al-Ahram* spoke, in its characteristically muted way, for them and their desire for a quiet and stable life. They bought the paper for its unrivalled coverage of Egyptian and foreign news, for the sober reliability of its shipping and cotton price reports and its Stock Exchange listings. But beneath that complacency a troubled nationalism was stirring. Egypt's middle classes still took most of their culture from Europe, a Europe which had been redrawn after the First World War on the principle of national self-determination. Why should these principles not be applied to Egypt? This rather pensive, even wistful radicalism was often expressed in the letters to *Al-Ahram*. To take only one example, a young Egyptian returning from Europe wrote that the Nile seemed to run blood in his dreams, and that as he looked at Europeans in the trains: 'In Europe I respected and esteemed these people, but here, wherever I behold them, I can only think in terms of independence and slavery.'[14]

Once again, the British met the challenge with reforms. In 1936, Premier Nah'has, the new leader of the Wafd, negotiated the Treaty of London, which gave the British Army continuing rights of occupation, but gave the Egyptians a wider measure of independence, including an Egyptian to run the army, to run military (which also meant internal and political) intelligence and to man their own embassies abroad. *Al-Ahram* generally supported the Treaty, but also gave a platform to its critics, on the grounds that if this Treaty was to define the nature of the Egyptian state for the next generation, then it deserved wide discussion. But while advocating public debate, *Al-Ahram* went on to argue for political stability through a reconciliation between Nah'has and the palace.[15] It was not to last long. The outbreak of Britain's war with Germany in 1939 brought Egypt under open military rule once more, but the war in North Africa against the Italians and Germans brought the prospect of an end to British occupation. At first, *Al-Ahram* continued on its profitable way, beginning to offer advertisements in colour in early 1940. Circulation was still slightly ahead of *Al-Misri*, the main rival, at 130,000 copies a day. The paper ran 10–12 pages a day, almost half of them advertisements, and it enjoyed a healthy sale in the Arab world beyond Egypt.[16]

But the 1940s were to prove a disastrous decade for *Al-Ahram*, partly because its political independence (or indecisiveness) before 1940 meant that it had few powerful friends to help steer it through the corrupt maze of newsprint rationing which wartime controls had created. *Al-Misri*, for example, was allotted very large allowances of newsprint at one-tenth of the market price, and made large profits from selling its surplus on the black market.[17] The political atmosphere was sharply polarized. The palace held up news to give scoops to its favourite weekly, *Akhbar el-Yom*. *Al-Misri* became stridently nationalist, a stance which easily shifted to shrill anti-Zionism as the Jewish State struggled into existence after the war. *Al-Akhbar* was launched, a sensational but capable newspaper which emphasized crime, sex, headlines and pictures and which quickly established a near dominance of the youth market. The death of *Al-Ahram*'s publisher Gubrael Taqla (son of Bishara Taqla, the founder) in 1946 was a blow, and when the veteran editor Antoin el-Gumayel died in 1949, the paper reached its lowest ebb. Circulation had sunk to 68,000, and advertising was dwindling. The only healthy advertising section was the death notices, and since many of them contained the names of traditional *Al-Ahram* subscribers, the future seemed bleak.[18]

Al-Ahram insisted on maintaining its standards, proud of its reputation as 'the *Times* of the Arab World'. It disdained the commercialism of *Al-Akhbar*, and rejected the political partisanship of *Al-Misri*. Its economic pages continued to be the best in the Middle East, and it was thoughtful about the economic implications of America's new global power and Britain's plain intention to dismantle its Empire. It was *Al-Ahram* which coined the Arabic phrase for neo-colonialism 'Al-Istimar al-Hadith', and *Al-Ahram* which led the campaign for laws to increase the proportion of local industries in Egyptian hands.[19] Its news coverage continued to be thorough, with a new regular feature on page two, 'The situation in the country', which recorded the wave of riots and unrest in that sad year of 1947, when war loomed against Israel and revolution bred within Egypt. Newsprint continued to be rationed, and *Al-Ahram* as a four-page newssheet was still a shadow of its pre-war self. In the decade after the war ended, the paper lost £1,500,000 Egyptian ($3.5 million). Its advertising manager, Salvator Adjeman, had to turn advertising away, because he could not get the newsprint to run it.[20] In 1951, the Taqla family, in something close to desperation, offered the control of the news and features pages to the brightest young star of Egyptian journalism, the roving political correspondent of *Al-Akhbar*, Mohammed Heykal.

Mohammed Heykal had been born in 1923 to a middle-class landowning father who was also a cotton merchant. He studied economics at Cairo University, and journalism at the city's American University. He began his career as an unpaid trainee on the English-language *Egyptian Gazette* at the age of nineteen, and one of his first assignments was to cover the battle of El Alamein. In 1944, he joined *Akhbar El-Yom*, and his facility with languages and his own skills quickly made him its leading journalist. In 1948, during the doomed war against the new State of Israel, the young Heykal wrote a series of articles on the siege of the small post of Falouja, one of the few examples of Egyptian heroism and success in the war. The commanding officer was Gamal Nasir, who was wounded in the action. The friendship between the brilliant young journalist and the man who was to become Nasser was born during the battle of Falouja. Three years in a row, Heykal won the Farouk prize for journalism. A grant from the US State Department allowed Heykal to visit the USA, and to stop off in embattled Korea on the way. As the only Egyptian journalist regularly covering foreign affairs and regularly travelling, he had an authority without parallel in the Egyptian press. One trip to Iran led to a book *Iran Fawqa Burkan* – 'Iran on top of a volcano' – which attacked Mossadeq's anti-Western stance for its dependence on Soviet support, and which led to Heykal's own arrest in Egypt, under a law which forbade the criticism of a friendly monarch. He was soon freed and, indeed, King Farouk's last Prime Minister offered the young journalist the official post of chef-du-cabinet in his office. Heykal refused all such political offers; he preferred journalism. He also decided not to accept *Al-Ahram*'s first offer of a job in 1951. The following year, he secured one of the great scoops of his life. Nasser consulted him before the coup on the likely response of the British. When the coup against the monarchy was unleashed on 23 July, Heykal alone was in a position to write about the personality and objectives of its leader.[21]

The main daily papers reacted to the new regime in their traditional ways. *Al-Masri* called for a swift move to rule by political parties; *Al-Akhbar* gave uncritical backing to Nasser, and *Al-Ahram* was its traditional cautious self. It had thrived by giving offence to none, but it found even this impossible when faced with the army's young officers. One army censor bluntly ordered *Al-Ahram* to cease writing about the cotton trade, because he knew nothing about it and was taking no chances.[22] The easy way out, taken in almost all the columns except those written by Heykal, blamed everything upon the ousted monarchy. Heykal objected; the problems of Egypt reflected the weaknesses of an entire society, of an 'Egyptness' that could neither define nor inspire itself. The new government was at first equally unclear. In 1954, Nasser and the army shouldered aside Neguib and his policy of bringing back the political parties. For a brief month, Nasser lifted press censorship, and then restored it. He launched a new, official newspaper, *Al-Gumhuriyeh*, edited by Anwar Sadat, and closed down *Al-Misri* and had its publisher, Mahmoud Abul-Fatah, tried *in absentia*.[23] The Press Syndicate was closed, and fourteen journalists and seven managers were accused of having taken bribes from the previous regime. *Al-Ahram* tamely argued that Nasser's aim was worthy enough; to force the Egyptian press to be more responsible, to fill its pages with inspirational articles on development and educational essays on politics, rather than the sensationalized sex and crime stories which had made up the staple diet of most papers.

Were it not for the closure of its rival, *Al-Misri*, *Al-Ahram* would probably have collapsed in 1955. On the verge of bankruptcy, its owners offered Heykal the untrammelled editorship – an offer which Nasser endorsed. He started on the remarkable salary of £500 Egyptian a month, and he confidently demanded that a clause be added to his contract to guarantee him 2½% of any profits made by the paper. When he signed, there were no profits. The contract also spelled out, for the first time in the history of the press in Egypt, what kind of paper Heykal was expected to produce: '*Al-Ahram* is a nationalist and independent newspaper which stands for respect of public order, state authority, laws, religion and ethical standards. It does not believe in attacking religions and stands against atheism. In its support of local justice, *Al-Ahram* resists Communism as an ideology. It is committed to the principles of truth, moderation, sympathy, politeness and independence in opinion, with respect for opposing views.'[24]

Heykal called in the two previous joint-editors, Ahmed el-Sawy and Aziz Merza, told them he had nothing but respect for their work and asked them to stay on. When they asked him what changes he had in mind, he replied: 'I want tomorrow's paper to be exactly like yesterday's.' He explored the venerable building in which the newspaper was produced and was appalled. It was a rabbit warren of tunnels and basements and bridges between pokey, darkened offices. 'I had a feeling the building was filled with ghosts,' he wrote later. 'They were scared of development and chose to hide behind their superiority complex.'[25]

Heykal took over at a time of political turmoil. The Anglo-French invasion of the Suez Canal in 1956, in collusion with the Israeli assault through Sinai, had redrawn the strategic map of the Middle East. Abandoned by the US, bullied by Britain and France, Nasser felt he could turn only to Moscow for help. In Algeria, Arabs were struggling to free themselves from French occupation, and in the Gulf a more sedate movement was easing out the British colonialists, while another kind of sovereignty, rooted in the US, was replacing them. The energy with which Heykal hurled himself into every kind of challenge was dramatic. As the Anglo-French troops advanced from Suez, Heykal made plans to flee Cairo with Nasser, taking a portable printing press to inspire a guerrilla war against the occupiers. As Russia saw an opportunity for challenging Western influence in the Middle East, Heykal secured another scoop, a long and revealing exclusive interview with Khrushchev which introduced to the world the Russian leader's vision of competitive, but peaceful, co-existence.[26] In the same month, he presented to Madame Taqla, the owner of *Al-Ahram*, his plans for the future of her paper.

Al-Ahram had to retain that strongest tradition of its past success, he insisted. It had to be known as the most reliable and most informative of the news organs. He rejected the 'official paper' mantle of

Al-Gumhuriyeh, and the sensationalizing style of *Al-Akhbar*. He wanted a special fund to purchase new printing presses and equipment, and to hire and train new staff. He presented a long-range plan for a new building, based upon his observations of what the new technology of popular mass newspapers could do at Axel Springer's *Bild* plant in Germany, and at Britain's *Daily Mirror*. He closed *Al-Ahram*'s overseas bureaux, and persuaded Associated Press to cut its news service fee from £2,000 a month to £300. He hired fifty fresh university graduates, and started an in-house school of journalism. The difficulties of printing the flowing Arabic script had always meant that long or dramatic headlines had to be hand-drawn by a calligrapher, a lengthy and complex process. Heykal helped his engineers to design a new machine that could do the job more flexibly and much faster. The layout of the paper changed, with a dramatic style of bolder and larger pictures, particularly on the front and back pages. Page two became devoted to foreign news, and he stated an op-ed page, which his own opinionated articles and reputation made into the new *Al-Ahram*'s greatest asset.[27]

Egyptian officials, the foreign press, the diplomatic corps, all knew that Heykal was close to Nasser. As a result, his every printed word was studied and analysed for the clues it might offer about the thinking of the head of the most powerful State in the Arab world. But this special relationship alone does not begin to explain the kind of influence that Heykal began to wield. Other Arab journalists, particularly Tareq Aziz of Iraq's *Al-Thawra*, enjoyed a similar intimacy with their heads of State, without ever approaching Heykal's international reputation. It was the combination of Heykal's relationship, Nasser's unique importance in the Arab world, and Cairo's growing role as the centre of the Middle East, that combined with Heykal's own remarkable talents to produce the phenomenon of his eighteen years with *Al-Ahram*. Nasser was the apostle of Arab unity, of Arab liberation, of Arab radicalism. He was the first Arab leader to play a major role on the world stage, and one of the first of the Third World's new leaders to confront the appalling problem of retaining a kind of independence in a world dominated and carved up by two competing superpowers.

By 1958, Heykal had almost doubled circulation to 120,000 a day, and at the end of that year, he was able to demand his 2½% share of the first profits *Al-Ahram* had seen since the war. The paper had made £23,000 that year.[28] One result of his success was disaster for the official newspaper, *Al-Gumhuriyeh*, whose circulation had collapsed from 160,000 in 1957 to 40,000 by 1958, with accumulated losses of just over £1 million.[29] But Heykal's success was flawed by the framework of government control in which it had been achieved. As the International Press Institute reported in 1959: 'There no longer exists in the Egyptian press a single newspaper which could really constitute a menace to the new regime, and one can go so far as to say that all of the press has become an instrument of propaganda for the regime.'[30]

That control was to be modified the following year. The original intention of the 1960 Press Law was to bring the newspapers even more firmly under political direction, by fully nationalizing them and vesting control in the Arab Socialist Union which, in the words of the decree, 'embodies the will and authority of the people'. In a private letter to Heykal, Nasser wrote that the press was 'an authority whose function is to guide the people actively to participate in building their society', and that as a result, the purpose of the new law was 'to restore ownership of the media of social and political guidance to the people'.[31] In the pages of *Al-Ahram*, Heykal welcomed the new law, even though he was critical of its provisions for all journalists to be licensed to work (or not) by the ASU, and wary of the direct political and bureaucratic control of the papers that the new law clearly implied. By lobbying Nasser, by force of argument and persuasion, he succeeded in significantly modifying its terms. The ASU was empowered to appoint a board of directors who would then appoint an editor, thus putting one vital buffer between editor and political masters. Heykal also convinced Nasser that the press should be non-profit-making, or at least that any profits made be equally divided between the staff as a bonus, and a re-investment and equipment fund. The five major publishing houses had to surrender their ownership to the ASU, and journalists needed its licence to work, but matters could have been very much worse without Heykal's intervention. Moreover, Heykal used his privileged, indeed unassailable position, to criticize ASU directives and policies in print, and to support any of his staff who fell foul of the ASU bureaucracy.[32]

Heykal had enough opportunities to argue his case before Nasser. He tutored the semi-educated President in Arab poetry, art, history and philosophy. At 8 a.m. each morning, over the private phone that connected Heykal's office to Nasser's bedroom, the two men discussed the state of the world and Heykal briefed Nasser on the news of the day. Nasser told his security staff that Heykal had access to every file in the presidential office. The relationship was curious one. They could argue and differ about policies, and Nasser could be so offended by Heykal's articles that the two men felt forced to reach a private agreement never to discuss them. Nasser constantly pressed Heykal to work in and for his government; but in 1955, 1958, 1961 and 1967 Heykal turned down ministerial office. When Nasser in 1970 appointed Heykal Minister of Information, without consulting him, the new Minister's first act was to abolish censorship on cables leaving Egypt. But on the same day, Nasser had Heykal's personal secretary and *Al-Ahram* columnist Lufti el-Kholi thrown into jail. What held them together was personal affection, the fact that they had shared so much of each other's and Egypt's history, the commitment they both felt to the political dream of a united Arab nation with its own parliament, and a quite remarkable degree of personal trust. Nasser relied upon Heykal for his discreet communications with the US Embassy in the 1950s (which led to vicious suggestions that the editor was a CIA agent), for opening communications with the PLO, for sounding out the new regime of Colonel Muammar Gadafy in Libya, for persuading Brezhnev to supply anti-aircraft missiles in 1970, for a kind of private diplomacy and counselling service. It was the very intensity of this relationship which made *Al-Ahram* into the most significant newspaper in the Arab world.[33]

Remarkably, Heykal found time to transform Egyptian journalism in the process. In 1960, he launched *Al-Ahram*'s Friday supplement, and the presence of his article 'Bishara' ('Frankly Speaking') on its front page made it required reading. He hired Egypt's leading literary figures to write for *Al-Ahram*. Lewis Awad became literary editor, Naguib Mahfouz the novelist began writing a regular column, and Tawfik al-Hakim, the leading Arab playwright, became a regular critic for the paper. Not only did they make *Al-Ahram*'s coverage of culture and the arts supreme in Egypt, they launched a trend in Arab journalism as a whole.[34] In 1964, Heykal gave the paper a face-lift, a new design and two extra pages. There was enough money to re-open the overseas bureaux in London, New York, Paris and in key Arab cities. The paper began printing a minimum of two pages of foreign news a day. He began *Da'irat Ma'aref*, the daily encyclopaedia of *Al-Ahram*, based on the work of 100 Egyptian specialists co-ordinated by three university professors. He began *Al-Ahram*'s private think-tank, a group of scholars and consultants who produced in-depth reports on economic, political and diplomatic issues of the day, and published their findings on a full page each week. The quality of news coverage, in the hands of those fifty university graduates whom Heykal had personally trained, improved sharply, and the finances of the paper's marketing and advertising were improved. In 1963, The Ahram Ad Agency was formed by a consortium of press companies, but managed by *Al-Ahram*, and Heykal's improvements in the printing plant meant that the paper could offer regular four-colour ad pages. Heykal aimed at a regular proportion of 40% advertising, but this figure was usually exceeded, in spite of Nasser's almost total ban on ads from foreign countries or companies. (In 1959, Nasser found that the Communist countries were spending over £200,000 a year in the Egyptian press, and resolved to reduce this potential influence.) In 1965, *Al-Ahram*'s circulation was 650,000 on weekdays, and a million on Fridays, a staggering testimony to the changes that Heykal had brought to the moribund paper of ten years earlier.[35]

By 1968, *Al-Ahram*'s financial health was sturdy enough to have accumulated more than £4 million in profits, money which was invested in the luxurious new building which Heykal had been planning for a decade. Having persuaded Nasser to let the nationalized newspapers retain half of their profits for investment, Heykal then persuaded his own staff to surrender half of their profit bonus to the *Al-Ahram* development fund. 'We can prove that social ownership can be as creative as private ownership,' Heykal told them, and issued bonds in the company to its 4,000 employees.[36] The lavish new building contained its own mosque, its own doctor and free clinic, its own art consultant to choose the 200 oil paintings which were to be 'a museum for contemporary Egyptian art', as Heykal put it. Orchestral concerts and lectures were scheduled in the vast, marble entrance-hall. The publishing empire was expanded with monthly economics and politics reviews, and in 1965 Heykal hired a group of young left-wing journalists to produce *Al-Talia*, ('Vanguard') a monthly magazine on current affairs. Heykal authorized them 'to preach their Marxist views within the framework of Nasserism'.[37] In periodical as well as in daily journalism, everything that was new or adventurous in Egyptian journalism seemed to stem from Heykal. He had something of a fetish about innovation, but his fetish made sense. When *Al-Ahram* began paying £4,000 a month to hire an IBM computer, it earned £32,000 a month in time-renting the computer to outside clients. Having invested in overseas distributors and arranged air freight, Heykal found that foreign sales of *Al-Ahram* were earning £250,000 a year by 1970; the newspaper had outgrown Egypt. It was the nearest thing to an international Arab daily.

If one effect of the 1960 press law had been to make journalists a

privileged and even wealthy section of the new Nasserite elite, there
was still no doubt that the press existed on the sufferance of the
government. The Amin brothers, publishers of *Al-Akhbar*, fell from
favour in 1965. Ali stayed in exile, and Mustafa was sentenced to life
imprisonment on spurious charges of spying for the CIA.[38] But
Heykal was privileged to speak out and criticize. In 1967, after criticizing the secret police, the General Intelligence Agency, two bullets
were fired at him as he left his office. Rather than silencing him, this
provoked an angry denunciation on the policy of arbitrary arrests
carried out by 'the visitors of dawn'. Heykal protected his staff, saving
Lewis Awad from arrest when his literary editor attacked the education system, and supporting Tawfiq al-Hakim when his satirical play
'Market of Donkeys' was rather too obviously a satire on the Arab
Socialist Union. When Gamal el-Otaifi was arrested after writing a
highly critical series on the judicial system, Heykal provoked a row
with Nasser, insisting that he be released. And again, when Vice-
President Ali Sabri tried to establish a Supreme Press Council to
'co-ordinate' the various newspapers, Heykal went to Nasser to have
the idea scrapped, and campaigned publicly against the scheme,
charging that 'if the government imposes somebody on top of us, then
freedom of expression will come to an end'.[39]

There was little enough such freedom anyway, and Heykal's privilege was the more remarkable for its very uniqueness. He was able to
make it clear, as a new Israeli war loomed in the summer of 1967, that
he was against resorting to arms and against provoking the Israelis by
closing the Gulf of Aqaba to Israeli shipping. He warned in his
column that this struck at 'the whole philosophy of Israeli security.
Hence I say that Israel must resort to force of arms. Therefore I say
that an armed clash between Egypt and the Israeli enemy is
inevitable.'[40]

When the war was lost, Heykal launched a forensic examination of
the whole of Egyptian society. It was no use blaming the generals or
the soldiers, he argued; the explanation for defeat lay much deeper.
When General Mahmoud was tried and sentenced to twenty years for
incompetence, Heykal attacked the sentence. 'Our officers' initiative
should not be paralysed by the feelings of angry masses in the streets,'
he wrote, thus provoking an angry student demonstration outside
Al-Ahram itself.[41] But Heykal's personal sense of disillusion ran
deep, and the following year, as the culmination of his disaffection, he
wrote an extraordinary editorial on the inefficiency and evils of the
government and concluded, 'If the regime cannot change itself, it

must be changed' – which provoked yet another row with Nasser.[42]

For Heykal, the success of his newspaper, the role of an independent press, the rigidities of Egyptian censorship and the inefficiencies of the Egyptian State and its Arab allies had all become part of a single pattern. He used his editorial column as a pulpit to denounce the dangers and present his own solutions, breaking every Arab precedent about the role of the press: 'There exists in the Arab world a crisis of confidence, a credibility gap. Somehow there is a feeling that the truth is being lost. The only remedy is to propagate clarity and truth as much as possible, regardless of its bitter-sweet taste. If circumstances do not permit us to tell the whole truth, we should not, in any circumstances, permit ourselves to say anything that contradicts the truth. . .We should never be able and never prepared to erect crematoria for them [the two million Jews of Israel] as Hitler did. We should never be able and never prepared to throw them into the sea. The actual struggle in Palestine is not between the Arab nation and the two million Jews, but between the Arab nation and the Zionist State, as an embodiment of racism and aggression linked with world imperialism,' (23 August 1968).

Heykal and the newspaper he had restored had become symbiotic; no other Arab journalist had the stature, and few had the courage and originality, to put forward ideas about the future of the Middle East such as these, and in no other newspaper would his views have been given the prominence and the international exposure which *Al-Ahram* guaranteed. But with the death of Nasser and the succession of Anwar Sadat, Heykal's position began slowly but inexorably to be undermined. At first Sadat depended on Heykal, insisting that he remain in the Cabinet, and support the new President against the Opposition faction in government, led by the Vice-President, Ali Sabri, who had earlier tried to impose stricter controls on the press. While supporting Sadat during the abortive coup of May 1971, Heykal found bugs on his phone at *Al-Ahram*, and was placed under full surveillance.[43] Having supported Sadat in part because he and *Al-Ahram* were against too close a relationship with the Russians and against a renewed war with Israel, Heykal increasingly found himself at odds with Sadat's policy shift towards the US. Since the late 1950s, *Al-Ahram* had consistently argued (within the limits of free expression in Egypt) for a watchful non-alignment, with Egypt committing herself to neither side of the great-power rivalry. His editorials criticized the presence of Soviet military advisers in Egypt, until their expulsion in 1972, and he also argued against Sadat's purge of the leftist intelligentsia in 1971 – a purge which included several of Heykal's colleagues and protégés. This was hardly new. What was different under Sadat was the new President's growing conviction that Heykal had built at *Al-Ahram* a potentially dangerous personal power base, and Sadat's consequent resolve to chip away at the privileges to which Heykal had become accustomed in Nasser's day. In 1972, Sadat ordered all his ministers to encourage a greater flow of news from their offices and to give statements and press conferences to all papers equally, without favouring *Al-Ahram*. It was presented as a move to more open government in Egypt, but it also struck at the very root of *Al-Ahram*'s supremacy. 1972 was Sadat's 'year of decision' – a slogan which Heykal dismissed as rhetoric. *Al-Ahram* also supported, or at least sought sympathetically to comprehend, the anti-Sadat student riots of that year. And Heykal's blunt editorial series 'No peace; no war' (which argued that the Soviet Union had an interest in maintaining tension without resolution in the Middle East, with an eye on naval bases in Egypt) re-affirmed Heykal's insistence to comment on Egyptian policy as he saw fit. Heykal was trying to impose a classic Western concept of the role of the journalist upon an authoritarian State. Sadat's first answer, delivered when Heykal was interviewing Chou En-lai in China in February 1973, was to have sixty-four intellectuals, most of them in the media, dismissed from the Arab Socialist Union, and thus from their jobs. Among them were *Al-Ahram*'s literary editor Lewis Awad, and the columnist, Ahmed Baha'el Din.[44]

On the eve of the Yom Kippur war, looking for Heykal's support, Sadat reprieved the dismissed men, and Heykal found himself committing perhaps the most questionable act of his career. To lull Israeli suspicions, he printed false stories in *Al-Ahram*, suggesting that a group of senior Egyptian officers were about to leave to make a pilgrimage to Mecca. When the war came, Heykal insisted on reporting it honestly. Against the orders of the censors, he printed the news of the Israeli counter-strike across the Suez Canal and, in defiance of Sadat's personal instruction, he printed the terms of Dr Kissinger's six-point ceasefire proposal. Suspecting that Sadat's patience was all but exhausted, Heykal used *Al-Ahram* as a bludgeon for his own views in those tumultuous weeks after the ceasefire. In November, his editorials argued passionately for a wary independence between the superpowers. In January, in the celebrated article, 'The Israeli style of negotiation', he warned of the limitations of American friendship when the Jewish lobby in the US was so powerful. On 1 February he warned once more against pinning too many of Egypt's hopes on to an American president who was tarnished and indeed doomed by Watergate. On 3 February, Sadat had Heykal dismissed as editor of *Al-Ahram* and appointed, without even asking him, as a presidential adviser. He was replaced as managing editor by Ali Amin, one of the brothers who had owned *Al-Akhbar* and whom Nasser had driven into exile.[45]

It was the end of an era. *Al-Ahram* began to flounder, as Ali Amin sought to prove that it was under new management by ordering shorter, more dramatic stories, with a less restrained layout and more pictures. He had learned his trade as publisher of the sensationalist *Al-Akhbar*, and *Al-Ahram* began to go down-market. But Heykal had left a magnificent legacy behind him. The daily circulation was 772,000 in the year that he left, reaching over 1,100,000 on Fridays. Kuwait, Saudi Arabia, Libya, Sudan, Syria and the Emirates were importing over 10,000 copies each, every day. Europe was taking 6,500 copies a day and North America 4,650. With a staff of 5,000 publishing the paper, books, an economic weekly, monthly and quarterly journals, the *Al-Ahram* corporation virtually embodied Egypt's intellectual rebirth. There were foreign bureaux in New York, Moscow, Rome, Paris, Bonn, London, Kuwait, Riyadh and Dubai, with part-time correspondents in Frankfurt, Athens, Tokyo, Hong Kong, Beirut and Washington. In Salah Jaheen, Heykal had brought on to *Al-Ahram* the finest cartoonist in the Middle East.[46]

Political appointments meant that *Al-Ahram* was directed by five managing editors in the next five years. One of them, Ahmed Baha'el Din who succeeded Ali Amin, was in the chair long enough to write one critical editorial before being fired. The week after Heykal was dismissed, Sadat announced a liberalization of press censorship, suggesting that the papers could write about anything except military secrets – but few journalists took this seriously as the controls were steadily re-applied. There was pettiness in the treatment of Heykal: he was banned from writing in Egypt, forbidden to travel abroad, not invited to the hundredth-anniversary celebrations of *Al-Ahram* in 1976, and finally, in September 1981, during President Sadat's purge of his critics and Egypt's religious leaders, Heykal was arrested.[47]

Heykal was not the only victim of the Sadat years. From 1975, there was a wave of officially inspired criticism of Nasser and his policies, a campaign which Ali Amin (quite justifiably) supported. He had knowledge of that 'Nasser's Archipelago' of concentration camps in

the western deserts, and in his weekly editorial column, 'An Idea',
designed to replace Heykal's 'Frankly Speaking', he enthusiastically
backed Sadat's move towards the US, the new emphasis on free
enterprise and the critical approach to the Nasser years. Sadat himself, while professing to believe in press freedom, hired and fired key
editors, established a Supreme Press Council to control them, and
used the columns of *Al-Ahram* to make two revealing statements on
the role of the press in his Egypt. 'I want freedom of the press, but at
the same time I want a dedicated press,' he announced in September
1973, on the eve of war. But in May 1975, he succinctly phrased his
own priority: 'If freedom of expression is sacred, Egypt is more
sacred.' In 1978, as the new government of Mustapha Khalil was
announcing an end to State supremacy over the press, the police were
seizing copies of the banned leftist paper *Al-Ahaly*. In the same year,
out of favour once more, Ali Amin was banned from writing on
politics. When *Al-Ahram*'s new editor, former Minister of Culture
Youssef Sebai, was killed by terrorists in Cyprus, Ali Hamdi El-
Gammal was brought in to preside over the faltering paper. It became
impossible to get reliable circulation figures for *Al-Ahram*. Sami
Mansour, a veteran commentator, reckoned that the daily had lost
200,000 in circulation by the end of 1978, and that the Friday edition
had fallen to 750,000. El-Gammal claimed, to the contrary, that
circulation had never been higher for the daily, although he acknowledged that the Friday edition's sales had fallen. Heykal himself has
claimed that Friday circulation had fallen by a disastrous 65%, and
that daily circulation had been maintained by an aggressive marketing
campaign giving readers a free chance to compete in a lottery.[48]

Certainly it was not the paper it had been under Heykal. Most of his
improvements had remained: the superlative foreign and domestic
news coverage, the stress on the newspaper as an organ of education,
with long and detailed research studies, the best of the new Arab
culture – all these remained. But the sharpness of comment had gone,
the marvellous and startling arrogance of an Egyptian journalist who
felt that his views were just as worthy of public attention as those of his
government. For most of its career, *Al-Ahram* had proved that a
discreet caution was the way for an Egyptian newspaper to survive.
Briefly, Heykal showed that there was another way. Even if Heykal's
courage and independence flickered, rather than burned with an even
constant light, he had single-handedly given the Arab press a different
and more inspiring tradition. And supreme professional that he is, he
had increased circulation sixfold in the process.

His critics are right to stress that there was another and more questionable side to his journalism. 'Heykal built a pyramid and buried the press in it,' is the view of Mustafa Amin and, certainly, so much of Egypt's journalistic energy was pumping through *Al-Ahram* that the other papers seemed rags by comparison. That bitterness comes through in the verdict of Mousa Sabri, *Al-Akhbar*'s editor, that Heykal 'wanted to rule, not write'. And there is no gainsaying the verdict of one of Heykal's successors at *Al-Ahram*, Ali Hamdi El-Gammal: 'He mixed his roles as a journalist and as a politician.'[49]

Notes

1. *Press, Politics and Power*, Munir K. Nasser, ch. 1 *passim*.
2. *ibid*. See also *Daily Journalism in the Arab States*, Tom McFadden, (Ohio State Univ. Press, 1953). p. 5.
3. McFadden, *op. cit*. See also 'Government control of the press in the UAR' A. Almaney, *Journalism Quarterly*, vol. 49, 1972.
4. Nasser, *op. cit.*, pp. 36ff.
5. *Egypt: Imperialism and Revolution*, J. Berque, p. 208.
6. *ibid.*, pp. 237–8.
7. *ibid.*, p. 409.
8. *ibid.*, p. 437.
9. Nasser, *op. cit.*, p. 4.
10. Almaney, *op. cit.*
11. *Al-Ahram*, 1.iv.1936.
12. *Al-Ahram*, 3.iv.1936.
13. Berque, *op. cit.*, p. 207.
14. *Al-Ahram* 6.iv.1936.
15. *Al-Ahram* 10, 11.viii.1936.
16. Almaney, *op. cit.*
17. 'The Press in Authoritarian Countries', International Press Institute (*IPI Survey No 5*, Zurich, 1959) pp.175–7.
18. Nasser, *op. cit.*, p. 37.
19. *Al-Ahram*, 20.i.1947; 21.ix.1947; 1.x.1947.
20. McFadden, *op. cit.*, p. 27.
21. Nasser, *op. cit.*, ch. 2.
22. IPI, *op. cit.*, p. 177.
23. Almaney, *op. cit.*
24. Nasser, *op. cit.*, p. 39.
25. *ibid.*, p. 40.
26. *Nasser*, Robert Stephens, p. 189.
27. Nasser, *op. cit.*, p. 108.
28. *ibid.*, p. 41.
29. IPI, *op. cit.*, p. 180.

30. *ibid.*, p. 183.
31. Quoted in Nasser, *op. cit.*, p. 9.
32. *Al-Ahram*, 28.v.1961; I, 3.vi.1961. But see also Heykal in *Al-Amal*, Tunisia, 21.xii.1968.
33. See *Cairo documents*, M. Heykal. See also Nasser, *op. cit., passim.*
34. *The Arab Press*, William A. Rugh, p. 32 and pp. 74–5.
35. *The World's Great Dailies*, John C. Merrill and H. A. Fisher, chapter on *Al-Ahram.*
36. Nasser, *op. cit.*, p. 47.
37. *ibid.*, p. 50.
38. *Sunday Times*, 10.ii.1974.
39. Nasser, *op. cit.*, p. 60.
40. *Al-Ahram*, 26.v.1967.
41. Nasser, *op. cit.*, p. 58.
42. *ibid.*, pp. 58–9.
43. *ibid.*, p. 75.
44. *ibid.*, p. 79.
45. *The Road to Ramadan*, Mohammed Heykal (Fontana, London, 1976), pp. 30–1; see also *Al-Ahram*, 14.xi.1973; 18.i.1974; 1.ii.1974. See also *The Times*, 4.ii.1974.
46. Merrill & Fisher, *op. cit.*
47. *Guardian*, 3.ix.1981.
48. This difference of opinion is thoroughly rehearsed in Nasser, *op. cit.*, p. 114.
49. Nasser, *op. cit.*, pp. 107–9.

AL-AHRAM: EDITORIALS

The independence of India: 24 June 1947

'Egypt would be the first country with which the new Pakistan State would open diplomatic relations, President Jinnah affirms. This will be the first symbol of independence, the first symbol of the new world which opens.'

The independence of Israel: 4 June 1948

'All the Arab nations prefer to have the Palestine question resolved by peaceful means. . .With the Arab armies at the gates of Tel Aviv, the Arabs know the right way to achieve their aims, but they have left the matter in the hands of the UN during the truce period, the responsible body dealing with international affairs, so as to avoid disturbing the peace of the world.'

The Berlin blockade and airlift: 15 March 1948

'There is a great danger threatening the Arab countries – Russia – who gives open support to the Zionists in opposition to the Arab nations. Be warned against the lying propaganda planned for the realization of Russia's ambitions in Europe, for the Arabs will be the next victims, since the USSR desires the invasion of all the Arab nations and is exploiting Communism to achieve her aim.'

The Communists win power in China

No relevant editorials.

The Korean war

No relevant editorials.

The Suez invasion: 1 November 1956

'It is difficult to see whether the actions of the British and French are prompted more by weakness than injustice, or more by injustice than weakness. The existence of injustice has been clear since the Canal crisis started. Now they have become shameless; today they have announced to the world that they support aggression.'

The Russian invasion of Hungary

No relevant editorials.

The Bay of Pigs assault on Cuba: 18 April 1961

'The invasion of a small independent nation such as Cuba by a great power and its agents must bring comparisons to any thoughtful Arab mind with the invasions at the time of Suez. Then as now, such injustice is a threat to world peace. Then as now, speedy action will be needed to save the innocent victims of aggression. The friends of freedom will not stand idly by.'

The Cuban missile crisis: 24 October 1962

'Is President Kennedy simply trying to kindle the enthusiasm of the American voting masses before the November Congress elections? The enthusiasm of the American masses may be kindled, but the entire globe may catch fire – atomic fire – at the same time.'

The Gulf of Tonkin incident: 6 August 1964

'No matter whether President Johnson is prompted by genuine conviction or whether his action forms part of the fight for the presidency between him and Goldwater so as to win the votes of extremists and those pressing for a widening of the war, world peace should not rest like this, at the disposal of any one individual.'

China's nuclear weapon: 30 October 1964

'The great problem is that China rejects the new theory of the impossibility of war under the present balance of nuclear terror, on the grounds that the conflict between capitalism and Communism could prove too strong a factor for war to be neutralized by the nuclear balance.'

Rhodesia's UDI: 13 November 1965

'As Britain leaves her colonies, she intended to leave in them a white minority to rule the national majority, to control its freedom and its resources. . .but unanimity in condemning British policy in Rhodesia requires no genius. It is obvious that although Britain proclaimed her rejection of racial rule in principle, she did not try to do anything concrete about Ian Smith and his hateful band, and their disregard of the rights of four million Africans.'

The Russian invasion of Czechoslovakia: 30 August 1968

'In principle, intervention by any State in the affairs of another is unacceptable. If this intervention takes the form of military action, the matter becomes even more serious, irrespective of the reasons leading to it. In the case of Czechoslovakia, what was announced about the Czech Communist system being in danger is no sufficient reason. . .But I am not in favour of condemning it. The Warsaw Pact members have at least listened, understood and responded to the Czechs. And no Arab can forget that one of the decisions at Bratislava was that Czechoslovakia should adhere to the Warsaw Pact policy with regard to Israel.'

Israel's occupation of the West Bank: 26 October 1973

'The basis of peace in the Middle East will not be established by encouraging Israel's expansionist ambitions, not by Israel's consolidation of its occupation of Arab territory – nor by replenishing Israel's military arsenals so Israel can freeze anew every solution to the crisis by relying on its absolute military deterrent power.'

The OPEC price rise: 18 November 1973

'Oil is a source of wealth which the Arabs put at the service of progress and the prosperity of the peoples of the world. It is their right that the world which benefits from this wealth should support their legitimate rights.'

Watergate: 1 February 1974

'The shadow and the glitter – the Nixon presidency will not last six months.'

The fall of Saigon

No relevant editorials.

Sport and politics

No relevant editorials.

The space venture: 13 April 1961

'The possibilities opened by science, and the limitless space which science has started to invade will first and last serve the cause of life itself – on earth and in space. The sincere congratulations expressed to the USSR by its friends and its foes round the world indicate that the spirit of true science has started to dominate. Scientific rapprochement between the two camps may be able to remove the last of the conflicts between them and bring about an atmosphere of understanding and co-operation.'

Freedom of information: 23 August 1968

'There exists in the Arab world a crisis of confidence, a credibility gap. Somehow there is a feeling that the truth is being lost. The only remedy is to propagate clarity and truth as much as possible, regardless of its bitter-sweet taste. If circumstances do not permit us to tell the whole truth, we should not, in any circumstances, permit ourselves to say anything that contradicts the truth.'

8

Asahi Shimbun

One Japanese in three – more than 35 million people – is a regular reader of *Asahi Shimbun*.[1] Its morning edition sells 7,400,000 copies, and its evening issue another 4,640,000. Some 8,800 people work for the paper, more than 3,000 of them journalists. To buy a full page of advertising space in the national edition costs up to £60,000.[2]

When one of those journalists wants to cover a riot, he uses *Asahi*'s own riot van which drives to the edge of the tumult, extends a long telescopic arm from its roof, and a closed-circuit TV camera begins to scan the scene. At the push of one button, a still photograph is taken. At the touch of another, the photo is transmitted back to the news-room, ready to print. On 28 October 1979, when a long-dormant volcano erupted in central Japan just after 8 a.m., *Asahi* scrambled one of its own fleet of seven aircraft to take photographs. By 11 a.m., the front-page exclusive pictures were on sale.

Strikingly, for a paper of its circulation, it is a serious, quality publication, concentrating on politics, economics and foreign affairs, with twenty-four overseas bureaux. More than half of all Diet (National Assembly) members, university professors and physicians are *Asahi* readers. More than 40% of senior managers, government officials and professionals read *Asahi*.[3] The paper's daily diet of newsprint fills 208 six-ton trucks.[4]

The *Asahi* group has investments in forty-eight of Japan's 107 commercial radio and TV companies. It is majority shareholder in fifteen other enterprises, including property companies, printing industries and cultural centres. Its English-language daily, *Asahi Evening News*, dominates the expatriate market. Its Asahi Building Company is said to be Japan's third largest. Revenues for the six months to March 1979 were £217 million.[5] It publishes four weekly magazines, five monthlies, two quarterlies, ten annuals, and about 200 books a year.

And yet there are signs that this mammoth among newspapers is also something of a dinosaur. It is faced with the same problem of overmanning, of new technology and job redundancy, of staff morale, of shrinking profits and rising costs, leading to the same evolutionary imperatives and threats of extinction, which beset the dinosaurs of Fleet Street.

The profits on those revenues of £217 million were £700,000 – or 0.3%. In 1980, *Asahi* moved into a vast new purpose-built building which cost over £80 million – most of which had to be borrowed from the banks. Even Japan's low interest rates will impose a £5 million a year burden on company profits. And the advance to fully computerized, cold-type printing in the new HQ means that at least 500 and perhaps 800 printers will become redundant. They will not lose their jobs, but their probable redeployment into work as security guards and delivery staff is testing the traditional loyalty of *Asahi*'s company trade union.[6]

'Journalists at *Asahi* have seen a steady erosion of their real wages since the oil crisis of 1973,' Masaki Sata, chairman of the union's Tokyo branch, said in an interview. 'In the last two decades, the vast differential which journalists enjoyed in their salaries, compared to public officials and private industry, has entirely disappeared. The best of university graduates used to compete to join *Asahi* – and the standard of recruits is now falling. There is anger and uncertainty among the staff. The structure of our company union weakens us – the differences of interests between printers and journalists. We don't want to go the way of Britain, with its unions, and we know that the company is not making enough money to pay us well. We hope that the economy will improve, that perhaps another newspaper will collapse and we can grow by taking its market share. I am pessimistic about the future.'[7]

Japanese newspapers face a number of constraints upon the conventional solutions. It will be difficult to expand the twenty-four-page paper and print more advertisements, because more than 90% of *Asahi*'s copies are home-delivered. Bigger and heavier papers will boost distribution costs. These are already paralysingly high. Labour laws and growing prosperity have eroded the number of school-age delivery boys. Young students can now get a dormitory room, two meals a day, their tuition fees paid and £120 a month in return for delivery stints, morning and evening.[8]

Asahi executives fear that they have reached a circulation ceiling, that the Japanese market has been saturated, with 45 million daily newspapers already being published for a national total of 35 million households. A bitter circulation war led to agonized and abortive peace talks between the main competitors in October 1979. All the parties recognized that much of their post-war circulation growth came from the effect of industrialization breaking up the old extended families, particularly in rural areas, and leading to smaller, 'nuclear family' units. But this process now seems to have peaked.[9]

Part of the reason for the huge circulation figures of Japanese newspapers is the furious competition between distribution agents, who give out free gifts or help families moving into new flats, in return for subscriptions. *Asahi* has also sub-contracted an unknown number of highly controversial task-forces to win new subscriptions, on a payment-by-results basis. There have been a number of embarrassing accounts of their activities, including bribery and even violence among these task-forces, in Japanese investigative magazines.[10] The *Nihon Shimbun Kyokai*, the Newspaper Editors' and Publishers' Association, acknowledge that up to 10% of subscriptions may be ghost clients, listed by the distributors to get bonuses.[11] *Asahi* alone has almost 4,000 exclusive delivery agents who employ 70,000 people and, in a high-wage economy, such a labour-intensive system will inevitably bite deeper into *Asahi*'s revenues. Already in 1979, the distribution system takes more than 50% of the cover-price of each newspaper sold.[12]

There is also a limit to the revenue available from advertising. Until Japanese economic growth began its take-off in the early 1960s, the Japanese press had traditionally taken 45% of its revenue from ads, and 55% from sales. In 1962, ad revenue overtook circulation receipts, until the economic recession of the oil crisis reversed those proportions in 1975 (when subscription rates were increased by 50%). In that year, newspapers earned £820 million from advertising, but TV earned some £840 million, and broadcasting's share of the market is growing.[13] In 1978, TV took 35% of all advertising expenditure, and newspapers only 30%.

Nor is *Asahi*'s own investment in broadcasting helping its balance sheet, which for the half-year to March 1979 showed that 'other interests' (including property, radio and TV) contributed only 0.5% (or £1,850,000) to group revenue. In 1978–9, *Asahi* was losing money in TV and radio.[14]

A Western management would look for savings among the over-manned (and over-worked) journalists, where *Asahi*'s insistence on collecting its own news is so wasteful that it angers its own reporters. *Asahi* has three reporters stationed permanently at the Bank of Japan. About two-thirds of their working time is spent monitoring, minute by minute, financial exchange rates, and phoning them back to the economic desk.[15] In any other country, this kind of clerical work is left to the wire services, and journalists are paid for their analytical ability to assess – rather than simply list – these movements. Throughout Japan, *Asahi* has a larger newsgathering staff than the national press agencies. The Tokyo economic desk alone has fifty journalists. *Asahi*'s editorials are written by a special department of thirty journalists[16] (larger, for example, than the London *Guardian*'s Home and Economic news teams combined). With twenty-four pages in the morning edition, twelve in the evening, and even counting the 130 specifically local editions (which means 2–4 pages of local news inside the national edition), *Asahi* has an embarrassingly low productivity rate among its 3,308 journalists. Many reporters aged forty or more who have not been promoted to desk or administrative jobs simply do not work at all; but Japanese tradition has, so far, made it impossible to fire them, or to assign men of such seniority to the humble tasks of newsgathering.[17]

An *Asahi* journalist gets his job through an intensely competitive examination. In 1979, 1,281 graduates sat for thirty places. Sample question: 'Place in chronological order the British, Italian, Canadian, Japanese and Swedish general elections.' They also had to pass at least one graduate-level language examination, in Chinese, English, French, Spanish, Russian or German; write essays, and write sample articles to a deadline after hearing a lecture. But it is after they are hired that the real test of their vocation begins. After a two-week training scheme, they are sent to one of *Asahi*'s 197 local bureaux around Japan, to cover police news. For three years they stay in the small provincial offices, reporting intensely local news for regional editions. If they do well, they then spend two or three years in a larger prefecture office. Only then are they screened for possible admission to one of the main offices in Tokyo (with 1,224 journalists), Osaka (759), Seibu (423) or Nagoya (270). Once at the centre, they can expect another five grinding years as a member of that quintessentially Japanese institution, a press club attached to a government office or ministry. 'There are few resignations, but many lose heart,' one veteran of the system, now a senior editor on the Foreign Desk, confided.[18]

A press club is an exclusive body of Japanese-only reporters, who spend their working lives in the ministry press-room, receive the same government handouts and press conferences and briefings, and phone in their identical news to the desk at HQ. Even so, Japanese newspapers regularly run identical word-for-word stories, on official news. Some Ministries, such as MITI, make a practice of writing their news releases in specific *Asahi* or *Mainichi* styles, which need only subbing to be transmitted directly in to the paper. This is the culmination of news management.[19] Once at the HQ desk, the story can be re-written and correlated with reports from other clubs. Only then do reporters begin the frantic competition for scoops, through the traditional 'night and morning visits' to the homes of senior officials and politicians. *Asahi* provides a chauffeur-driven car for such trips, and they mean that the average reporter's day starts at 8 a.m. and he rarely gets home before midnight. Wives are accustomed to seeing their husbands only on Sunday, or the occasional Saturday off.[20]

It is considered a sign of laziness to take the full allocation of twenty-five days' annual holiday. Journalists based in Tokyo are not normally paid expenses for entertaining their contacts, nor are their home telephone and newspaper bills reimbursed by the company. Salaries and promotion are linked tightly to seniority within the company. A twenty-five-year-old graduate reporter can expect to earn £240 a month. A journalist in his late thirties earns a basic £6,000 a year, with two annual bonuses to bring a real annual income of almost £10,000. A senior journalist aged fifty (and retirement currently arrives at fifty-five) can expect salary and bonuses to combine at about £18,000 a year. These are *Asahi* pay scales, which tend to be 5% higher than Japan's other two major dailies, *Yomiuri* and *Mainichi*. The average basic salary at *Asahi*, including print workers, is £6,000 a year, boosted by bonus and overtime to almost double that amount. The average pension (a supplement to the state pension) for *Asahi* workers is £135 a month.[21] Like the rest of Japan, *Asahi* has a slowly ageing workforce, which means steadily rising wage costs in a society where pay reflects seniority. The average age of an *Asahi* employee has risen from 37.8 years to 39.7 years in the last decade. Each worker also benefits from a social wage, averaging £1,600 a year; 55% of this pays for the health, unemployment and pension insurance demanded by law; the rest is *Asahi* contributions to the employees' pension payments, its housing loans and subsidies, canteen and recreation facilities, including sports grounds, ski lodges and country cottages. Total labour costs in 1979 were almost exactly £120 million.[22]

This empire began in January 1879, eleven years after the Meiji restoration which aimed at (and succeeded in) bustling Japan from feudal isolation to industrial modernity within the space of a generation. The samurai technocrats of Meiji saw newspapers, under strict control, as part of the modernizing and educative process. In the year of the restoration, eight newspapers were founded in Tokyo, and one editor was jailed for saying that the vaunted restoration meant but a transfer of power from one noble family to another. In 1869, the first press law was enacted to forbid 'indiscreet criticism of laws'. By 1875, it had been extended to forbid discussion of the law, obstruction of the law (a deliberately vague provision), publicity for foreign laws, or slander of national policy.[23]

Asahi Shimbun ('Newspaper of the morning sun') was founded by Ryohai Murayama (a nobly born samurai) and the Kimura family of wealthy merchants in the country's economic-industrial centre of Osaka. Its first issue proclaimed that: 'the newspaper will be edited for easy reading, even by children, with illustrations and other devices for the guidance of the common people, to teach them social justice'. The first issue sold 2,940 copies, which fell within a month to 922, but rising within eighteen months to 2,586.[24]

The fall of circulation reflected the early disenchantment with the press, both official and public, which was a feature of the Meiji years. Officials wanted an educative press, but not a critical one; readers wanted an educative press, but quickly became cynical of government propaganda disguised as an independent publication (which Meiji officials deliberately tried to establish). In January 1881, with circulation above 10,000, *Asahi* asserted its independence by being closed for three weeks on government orders for printing a series on 'Easy lessons in parliamentarism' – eight years before the National Assembly was founded. By this time, the Kimura family had abandoned the venture, and Murayama had brought in as partner Riichi Ueno, son of another Osaka merchant. The Murayama family (with 44% of the shares) and the Ueno family (with 20%) control the company to this day. *Asahi* staff members own the other 36% of shares through a Trust system which forbids newspaper stock sales outside the members.

Asahi's early success was based on the rapid economic expansion of its Osaka market and on its determination to win new, barely literate readers by simplifying the complex mass of 7,000 variously pronounced ideographs which made up the cumbersome Japanese language. *Asahi* printed phonetic symbols alongside the formal ideographs until 1946, when a national reform cut the number of ideographs to 2,000. *Asahi* was also well enough financed (and quickly profitable) to avoid the need for private subsidy, which turned so many of its competitors into mouthpieces for particular families and political cliques. By 1887, *Asahi* had the largest circulation of any Japanese paper, 34,000 a day.

Most of all, the paper had a lively and adventurous sense of news. On 11 February 1889, Murayama was in Tokyo to attend the announcement ceremony for the new Japanese constitution. He then made Japanese press history by getting *Asahi*'s Tokyo staff to send Japan's longest-ever press telegram: 10,730 ideographs (which took from 11.25 a.m. to 4 p.m. to transmit to the Osaka office) which were published in a special edition. By 1899, the *Asahi* laid, at its own expense, Japan's first long-distance telephone line, to link the Osaka and Tokyo newsrooms.

Murayama was also a Japanese pioneer in printing technology. His first machine was a 300 sheet per hour flatbed, manned by a chanting crew of *sake*-fuelled labourers. By 1885, he had bought a steam machine, and in 1890, be bought the first modern printing machine in Japan, a French Marinoni. Ignorant of the special formula for printing ink, Murayama had to find it by trial and error. It was all part of his and Ueno's almost messianic urge to expand and grow. In 1888 he had bought an ailing Tokyo paper, which he re-launched as the Tokyo *Asahi Shimbun*, sharing national news and editorials with the Osaka *Asahi*, but with pages of local news. (The pattern is maintained today, with 139 different editions of *Asahi* for different localities.)

In 1891, the paper suffered its sixth suspension by government, for publishing a critical open letter to the Home Minister. On the day the ban was lifted, Murayama hired every horse-drawn bus in Tokyo to give free rides all day, and make the re-opening into a city-wide celebration. He made his papers into an unusual (for Japan) mixture of information, opinion and entertainment. He persuaded some of Japan's best-known writers to overcome their distaste for a mass market and write for *Asahi*. For the serialization of one such novel by Bunkai Udagawa, the Osaka paper was banned for a week as 'dangerous to public safety'.[25]

By 1900, the Osaka paper had a circulation of 100,000, and the Tokyo *Asahi* had passed 50,000. Murayama had signed an exclusive agreement with Reuters to get the best foreign news coverage in Japan. And by this time, *Asahi*'s own reporters were stationed abroad. Keitaro Murai was the only Japanese newsman inside the Peking Legation for the long siege during the Boxer uprising of 1900. In 1904, the Russo-Japanese war showed not only the success of the Meiji restoration in modernizing Japan, but also the news-hungry, competitive spirit of the equally-modernized Japanese press.[26] *Asahi* sent twenty-six reporters to cover the war in Manchuria, and hired a seventy-five-ton ship to communicate with the Japanese battlefleet. The Russians sank the ship, captured the sixteen crewmen and reporter Hiroshi Miyamura – who then scooped the world with his 'Behind the enemy lines' series on his release.

When America mediated a peace treaty at New Hampshire, the great issue was whether Japan would or would not be paid war reparations by the defeated Russians. The Japanese government, worried at public reaction to the treaty, imposed strict censorship of all cables. Murayama cabled to his American correspondent: 'What prospects Texas rice harvest?' and got the reply: 'No prospect Texas rice harvest for Japanese emigrant.' *Asahi* immediately ran an extra edition with its world scoop 'No Russian Reparations'. The paper's subsequent criticism of the peace treaty led to a twenty-four-day ban in Osaka, and a fifteen-day ban on its Tokyo editions.

The paper's independence and readiness to criticize government and military slowly established a series of pragmatic principles into a coherent political position. *Asahi* was for modernization and economic growth, for parliamentary democracy based upon universal suffrage, against militarism and controls on the press. This political stance emerged as a reaction to government measures; in 1909, a new press law gave the Home Minister the right to seize and block distribution of articles he deemed 'a threat to peace, order or public morals'. The same law gave the Army, Navy and Foreign Ministers the right to prohibit articles on their affairs. In 1914 alone, 453 editions of newspapers were confiscated. And this was a time of political confusion, with the old Meiji technocrats dying off, and new civilian and military political groups competing with the old aristocracy to fill the vacuum.[27]

The press became a key battleground. In 1912, the arbitrary assumption of office by the government of Prince Katsura was criticized, and eventually defeated, by the massed editorials of the press and the public opinion they mobilized. *Asahi* acted as a rallying point for the 'Constitution Protection Movement', a loose coalition of opposition groups, merchants, officials and political groups which opposed the increasing military presence in government.[28] Violence and brutality began to emerge. In 1914, *Asahi*'s opposition to the government of Admiral Yamamato led to its reporters being waylaid and beaten by hired thugs. In August 1918, two *Asahi* reporters were imprisoned for reporting on a mass-meeting of protest against the then Prime Minister, General Terauchi. (Terauchi had been a bitter opponent of *Asahi* since a series of articles in 1911 exposing the brutality of his rule in occupied Korea.) In September 1918, the aged founder of *Asahi*, Ryohei Murayama, was attacked by right-wing thugs in an Osaka park, beaten with clubs and left tied to a tree for *Asahi*'s coverage of the anti-government rice riots. The following year, Murayama was ordered to resign from *Asahi*, on pain of the government's withdrawing its licence to publish.

Asahi battled on. In 1921, at the time of the Washington Naval Conference on limiting naval building, *Asahi*'s editorials supported international disarmament, and went on: 'Domestically, we would like to see the destruction of the *gunbatsu* [military clique] which is now attempting to gain power.'[29]

Asahi, and the rest of the press, continued to campaign for universal suffrage, which finally came in 1925. And they continued, as papers must, to fill their pages and entertain their readers. None did a more professional job than *Asahi*. In 1919, the only Japanese to talk his way on to the Graf Zeppelin airship for its round-the-world flight was *Asahi*'s Kichinai Kitamo. Over Tokyo, he persuaded the captain to fly low over the central Hibiya Park, where Kitamo dropped his flight diary and photographs to the waiting team of *Asahi* messengers. By 1923, *Asahi* had its own air fleet of nine planes for special deliveries and photographs. They were just in time to cover – and photograph – the great Tokyo earthquake.

By the 1920s, *Asahi* had become, even in appearance, a modern, almost Western paper. Its City Editor, Bunshiro Suzuki, claimed that the First World War had seen a shift away from the rather staid British tradition of layout and design to the more dramatic American model.[30] Advertisements became bolder and larger, with a pronounced shift towards display rather than classified. In 1924, sales of *Asahi* reached a million copies, during a tough circulation war which saw bloodshed between delivery agents, and a rival newspaper, *Jiji*, declaring formal war on *Asahi* in its editorials. Western visitors saw the confident, expanding press in almost heroic terms. 'Journalism today is the dominant power in the Japanese Empire,' declared Walter Williams, dean of the University of Missouri's celebrated School of Journalism.[31] And Bunshiro Suzuki, among other Japanese commentators, agreed. 'No Cabinet has been able to remain in power against general opposition from the press,' he was able to write, as late as 1931.[32] But the controls were tightening. In 1925, yet another press law prohibited articles which could be interpreted by the government as 'undermining the existing governmental and economic system'. In the same year, right-wing thugs assaulted Nagataka Murayama, the owner's son-in-law, and managing editor Taketora Ogata, with rocks and razors. Although arrested, one of the attackers was quickly released by the police. In 1928, there was a series of attacks by gangs on both the Osaka and Tokyo offices. Furniture was wrecked, sand thrown in the presses, and there was an abortive campaign to start an advertising boycott of *Asahi*. These attacks were 'justified' on the grounds that a typographical error had disrespectfully suggested that the Empress had died.[33]

As military influence in government increased throughout the 1930s, *Asahi* was identified as the stronghold of liberal opposition. Its Osaka and Tokyo editions were selling more than two million copies, and in 1935 a new office was opened on the southern island of Kyushu to print a separate edition which quickly reached a circulation of over 200,000 a day.

Influential and financially healthy, *Asahi* campaigned steadily against Japanese military ambitions in China, for the League of Nations and, in January 1936, it opposed the election of Admiral Osaka on the old issue of military intervention in civil affairs. On 26 February, in a bizarre and eventually abortive military coup, some 1,400 troops of the crack 1st Division occupied central Tokyo. Their first target was *Asahi*, which they ringed with machine guns, and called on the editor to come out. 'I thought it was my last hour,' recalled Taketora Ogata. 'I was very nervous, but my spirits were restored by our lift attendant, who asked me which floor I wanted in the usual way as I went down to face the soldiers.'[34]

The guns did not fire. But the troops wrecked the offices, smashed the composing room and threw the type out of the window. The printers sorted through the type, and with the loss of only one edition *Asahi* was back on the streets the same day.

It was a brief respite. In the same year, the militarized government began to control news at source, by establishing a new national news agency, *Domei*, to feed the press with government-approved stories. *Asahi*'s business managers took advantage of the centralizing trend to conclude a series of price-fixing agreements on subscription and advertising with its major rival, *Mainichi*, in a successful attempt to crush smaller rivals such as *Hochi* and *Jiji Shimpo*. *Asahi*'s editorials were still bold enough to oppose the new mobilization law, giving extraordinary powers to the army, in 1938. But at a quiet celebration for the 20,000th issue of *Asahi*, Ogata broke down as he told his staff in Tokyo: 'Recently it has been said that the newspapers have lost courage. Personally I do not have the courage to deny this.' It was the week before Pearl Harbor.[35]

From 1940, the military censors at the Bureau of Information had begun telling newspapers what *must* be printed as well as what had to be omitted. In 1941, total control over all news and press articles was given to the Japan Press Authority, which reported to the Bureau of Information and the Home Ministry.[36] Thenceforth, Japanese papers were little more than printing presses for the army. The one break in the control came, typically, from *Asahi*. A former editor and politician, Seigo Nakano, published a guest column on 1 January 1943 which angered General Tojo. *Asahi* was banned for a day, and Nakano was arrested. While his army guards slept in the next room, he committed traditional suicide in total silence.[37]

Asahi has always believed in high-density journalism. Both before and after the Second World War, *Asahi*'s own newsmen outnumbered the Japanese news agency reporters on the grounds that *Asahi* wanted to print its own news. Even the truncated two-page *Asahi* which was published after the surrender in 1945 employed almost 6,000 people. And in the course of the war, more than a thousand *Asahi* reporters went with the troops to the battlefronts. Their stories were limited to homely interviews and features on the soldiers, and war news – successes and disasters alike – was in the hands of the Japan Press Authority and the armed forces. 'Tiger' Saito, one of *Asahi*'s war correspondents who survived to become the model for the head of Japanese Intelligence in Ian Fleming's *You Only Live Twice* novel of James Bond in Japan, had a celebrated row with General Tojo over his blunt refusal, as a journalist, to wear military uniform.[38]

But the paper he came back to after the war found itself under a new and very different form of censorship: that of the American military authorities, known as SCAP, from General MacArthur's title, Supreme Commander Allied Powers. On 15 September, *Asahi*'s editorial accused the Allies of a breach of international law in their use of the atomic bomb on Hiroshima and Nagasaki. Two days later, commenting on US reports that Japanese atrocities in the Philippines had cost them potential popular support, *Asahi* said: 'This point applies also to the Allied Forces now in Japan.' It was banned for two days. One month later, on 24 October, SCAP called in all Japanese editors and publishers to order them 'to fulfil your obligations to establish a free press'.[39]

A former vice-president of *Asahi*, Hiroshima Shimomura, was one of fifty-nine military and civilian officials put under arrest in December 1945 as war criminals. Up to 1947, a total of 351 Japanese newspapermen were purged with the backing of the Allied powers. Pressure from newspaper staff and from SCAP combined to force out senior *Asahi* officials who were identified with the war policy. *Asahi* owners threatened to fire journalists who were demanding the resignation of the president, chairman and ten directors in October 1945. Under the threat of a total strike, the Murayama and Ueno families (who occupied the company presidency and chairmanship) agreed to resign, on condition that they retain 60% of the stock.

SCAP organized weekly conferences for the Japanese press on their duties under a democracy and American newspaper design – at a time when *Asahi* was limited by newsprint rationing to a two-page broadsheet. And SCAP pressure for democratic reforms throughout the Japanese press and government opened the way for a headily democratic period of worker control, near revolution, trade-union militancy (led by *Asahi*'s Katsumi Kikunami, later to join the Communist Party) and American confusion, until the hardening Cold War and the Korean conflict reversed American policies. By 1951, all the 351 purged journalists had been reinstated, and in June 1950 SCAP ordered the dismissal of seventy Communist Party 'members and sympathizers' from the pro-Communist daily *Akahata*. When the Korean war broke out, SCAP banned *Akahata* indefinitely, and a further 700 'Communist sympathizers' were purged from the Japanese press. At the height of the left-wing movement, a general strike was called, supported by all the major papers except *Asahi* whose members voted behind police guards, by 324 votes to 153, not to support the strike. The strike failed. 'The *Asahi* employees running the paper were too greatly tempted by the chance to make circulation gains while the other papers went on strike,' commented William Coughlin, the American historian of the press under the occupation.[40]

Part of the union militancy at *Asahi* is explained by the thorough re-organization which cut into the workforce on the shrunken post-war papers.[41] And the paper began a series of technological developments to overcome some of the problems of the Japanese language itself. Japanese newsrooms are thoroughly familiar places to Western journalists, except for their relative silence: there are no hammering typewriters. Stories are still written in longhand – since typewriters for the 2,000-odd ideographs would be grossly complex. There are telex machines, by which holes are punched in tape to symbolize each character, but by far the most vital development for the Japanese press was the facsimile transmission system developed in Britain shortly after the war for the *Manchester Guardian*. It is basically a copying machine, with the copy coming out hundreds of miles away. In 1959, *Asahi* began to transmit its whole newspaper to the northern Japanese island of Hokkaido in this way, and to extend its system of local editions so that for the first time a national newspaper was also able to compete effectively with the regional dailies, providing both national and local news. The importance of this local newsgathering competition is the main reason why *Asahi*'s 3,000 journalists are still reasonably optimistic that their jobs are secure.

By 1956, Japanese industrial recovery was well under way. *Asahi*, with a circulation of 2,300,000 for its morning edition, was more influential than ever.[42] That same Taketora Ogata who had faced the soldiers in 1936 was the leader of the ruling Liberal Democratic Party, and about to become the next Prime Minister when he died of a heart attack. Ogata's political eminence epitomized the role *Asahi* played within the post-war Japanese Establishment. It had always drawn its recruits from the prestigious Tokyo University which produced the bureaucrats and business executives of the *zaibatsu*, the great industrial concerns. (And *Asahi* had always paid its journalists rather better than government or industry.) But as Japan turned effectively into a liberal one-party state under the LDP (or a corporate state, given the enormous power of industry and the bureaucracy), *Asahi* became, in the words of one Japanese critic, 'a trade journal for the political Establishment'.[43]

But the Establishment had its own bitter internal debates; *Asahi*'s proclivity for being on the leftist side of those debates won it the nickname 'Red *Asahi*'. It probably deserved the title during the ferocious attacks it (and other Japanese papers) made on Premier Kishi's government when he clumsily forced a controversial new US-Japanese security treaty through the Diet in 1960. Kishi locked

Socialist deputies out of the chamber for the vital vote. *Asahi*'s bitter editorials certainly helped provoke the wave of riots which swept through Japan. When one demonstrator was trampled to death, *Asahi* joined with other major papers in publishing a joint statement calling for non-violent demonstrations and saying that the national outrage (and, by implication, its own campaign) had gone too far.[44] Premier Kishi, whose flouting of the traditional Japanese systems of political consensus had eroded his own party's support, quickly resigned. His resignation statement said: 'Violence is not only that of pistols and fists, that of the pen is the more dangerous.'[45]

This peak of *Asahi*'s radicalism led to hesitant efforts by the owning Murayama family to recover a degree of editorial control. In 1964, five directors threatened to resign if the family pressure was maintained, and an Osaka court directed both parties to agree on a peaceful settlement.[46] Today, *Asahi* executives say that the paper 'is like a constitutional monarchy – the Murayamas sit on a throne, but below the throne we are a republic'.[47] But the 'Red *Asahi*' charge was echoed by the US State Department in 1965, which claimed that *Asahi* (and *Mainichi*) was Communist-dominated after it printed a series of articles criticizing America's role in Vietnam and accusing the US Air Force of repeatedly attacking civilian targets.[48] 'We think we were right on that – even the State Department might agree with us at last,' the then Foreign Editor said in an interview.[49]

Most criticism of *Asahi*'s editorial stance, however, accuses it of being too tame, too soft when Japanese national interests are at stake. Perhaps the most dramatic example, which is now universally regretted by *Asahi* editors, is the remarkable series of conditions which they accepted from the Chinese Communist government in return for keeping a correspondent in Peking in the 1960s: no criticism of the Chinese government, no support for Taiwan, and 'no articles which might impede normalization of China-Japan relations' were permitted. The Chinese interpreted these conditions harshly. Five of the original nine journalists were expelled; another was jailed for espionage; one TV reporter was banned because his network had shown a programme on Taiwan. *Asahi* neither complained nor withdrew from China. The national interest called for normalizing relations with China, and *Asahi* co-operated – while keeping its readers in ignorance of the chaos and disaster of China's Cultural Revolution.[50] Even the journalists back in Tokyo were not immune: Yuichiro Kominami, editor of the prestigious *Asahi Weekly Journal*, ran an article which was mildly critical of China and received a letter from *Asahi*'s man in Peking, insisting on a formal apology to the Chinese government.

'*Asahi* is a part of the Japanese Establishment, part of the bureaucracy,' Kominami said in an interview. 'When I ran articles criticizing the automobile industry, Nissan threatened to withdraw advertising. The drug companies made similar threats when they were criticized – and I was asked to stop my "negative comments". It is a matter of self-censorship, rather than censorship from the outside. Similarly, we barely write, and never editorialize, about minority problems in Japan. There is discrimination against the Koreans who live here, against our own outcasts – but you would hardly know it from the press. Our society has a series of taboos, and the press conforms by its silence, or by a quiet voice.'[51]

(In fairness, it should be noted that British newspapers share similar taboos. Scandals about the Royal Family, for example, are rarely covered unless the foreign press has already broken the story and, in the case of King Edward and Mrs Simpson before the Abdication crisis of 1936, not even then. And the cosy, closed world of British parliamentary reporting, with its vows of silence and anonymity through the lobby system, is strikingly similar to the restrictive practice of the Japanese press club. But in Britain, the competition and disparity which is Fleet Street's most dramatic feature usually finds a way to sidestep its own limitations. Not in Japan.)

The scandals of corruption surrounding the Tanaka government, even before the Lockheed bribery scandal of 1976, were common knowledge among Japanese journalists. It took a monthly magazine, *Bungei Shunju*, to publish the story, and even then the Japanese daily press did not take up the story until Tanaka had been hammered at a press conference for foreign journalists.[52] Once the story broke, *Asahi* did well, getting the classic scoop of an on-the-record interview with the Lockheed vice-president, which spelt out the pattern of corruption. But the failings of the Japanese press at this time have led to widespread, and often justified, criticism. They have the influence and the power, but they seem to lack the will to use it.

'When the major Japanese newspapers began their concerted reporting of Tanaka's financial connections, the political world was rocked and the Tanaka Cabinet fell in less than a month,' noted Seizaburo Sato of Tokyo University, adding that this showed the power of the Japanese press, compared to the two years it took before President Nixon resigned.[53] The fact is that the tradition of Japanese political reporting, whereby a journalist is assigned to cover in enormous depth a political faction or even a personality, leads to dangerously close relationships. It is commonplace for political correspondents to act as speechwriters and advisers (and thus as protectors) to the men they are supposed to cover.[54] The secretary of the now discredited ex-premier Tanaka, for example, could regularly take political correspondents to expensive dinners, and then play mah-jong with them, for large stakes of money. He always lost.

It leads to a curious style (to Western eyes) of news reporting. To offer one example, chosen by a Japanese critic of the press, of a news report on a local government election in Nagoya in April 1973: the headlines read: 'Righteous indignation elects a progressive mayor. Commodity prices and pollution push voters to the limit. A weak populace rises up: "We won't allow them to ignore the public interest".' The body of the news story read: 'Crowds of young people and housewives rushed through the streets in the big drive to strike a blow at the kind of conservative politics, inexorably allied to big business, that ignores the people's interests. The progressive forces finally came out on top all over the city. The conservatives were decisively routed.'[55]

The nearest Japan has recently come to a clear issue of press freedom was the arrest of *Mainichi* journalist Takichi Nishiyama in April 1973 for obtaining secret government cables on the Okinawa treaty with the US. But Nishiyama had sat on those cables for nine months, and when they were published it was through an Opposition deputy in the National Assembly – not in the press.[56] The Japanese press generally attacked Nishiyama's arrest on the grounds of the public's right to know. *Asahi* was unusual in criticizing *Mainichi*'s decision to make the story public, not in its pages, but in the Diet. But even at *Asahi*, editors say they see no need for a freedom of information law, on the grounds that 'we are not a society of law, of contract. These things are done differently here.'[57]

Japanese society is based upon consensus rather than confrontation, upon seniority at least as much as merit; whereas in the West the phrase 'the national interest' is usually a government excuse to cover its own embarrassment, in Japan it is a nationally shared concept and ideal. Within these cultural limitations, Japan has a free and brave press, and *Asahi* is universally acknowledged as its flagship. By all other standards, *Asahi* is outstanding for the scope and quality of its coverage. The general mix of its articles works out in the following proportions:[58]

Politics	
(including foreign news)	32%
Culture and entertainment	
(including TV and radio listings and features)	21%
Economics	15%
City news	15%
Home news	8%
Sport	9%

The proportions have changed over the years. A survey in 1956 (but based on 2 November, at the height of the Suez crisis and when Russian tanks were ringing Hungary) showed that 38% of *Asahi*'s stories were of foreign news.[59] But a more thorough survey of seventy-two issues over an eleven-year period showed foreign news taking the most space, with economics, sports and politics following on, until 1968. From 1969 onwards, foreign news had fallen to second place, with economics taking the most space.[60] Later studies have shown foreign news taking between 10% and 15% of editorial space, depending on world events.[61]

Under the threat of growing costs and falling profits, and a bitter circulation war with the rival paper *Yomiuri*, *Asahi* is deliberately starting to go down-market. 'We have to move towards the character of a more popular paper,' deputy managing editor Toshiharu Shibata said in an interview. 'We have to keep our vast market, and also keep our authority as a leading paper. The proportion we are heading for will be twelve pages, half of the paper, with a popular character, with the rest very serious and authoritative. Market research suggests that in more and more households, women choose which newspaper is bought. The husband can read a paper of his choice in his office. So we will have to appeal to women – and hire more women. So far we have about twenty women journalists – out of 3,000. One is assistant editor of our science magazine, one is a bureau chief in a suburban office. Last year, six of our thirty new recruits were women; this year, three out of thirty. They still have to pass our entrance examination – but this change will have to come.'[62]

In 1980 *Asahi* moved from its old, cramped and grimy office block, between the Palace and the bright lights of Ginza, to a vast new purpose-built twenty-storey block down by Tokyo harbour. Disturbingly, *Asahi* received a government subsidy to buy the nationally owned land at a fraction of its market value. *Yomiuri* and *Mainichi* also owe their buildings to this kind of government generosity. Ex-

Premier Tanaka specifically reminded political correspondents of this, and of his distribution of commercial TV franchises to newspapers, shortly before he was forced to resign.[63]

Asahi will have its pages designed and its stories set by *Asahi*'s self-developed computer system, and the traditional hot-metal printing process will be fully replaced by a computer-controlled cold-type system, feeding batteries of high-speed web-offset printing presses.[64] It will be the most modern printing process in the world and the future economics of *Asahi* will depend, in large part, upon the 800 jobs the new technology should save. The company's plan is to reduce the number of employees, eventually, to 6,500 (the number employed by *Yomiuri*).[65] It will be a long and difficult business, threatening traditional Japanese employment patterns and loyalties, just as oil price rises and falling growth rates and threats of unemployment threaten Japanese society as a whole.

'These are problems which are facing all newspapers, around the world,' Shoryu Hata, editorial managing director, said in an interview. 'And when we are criticized by some for being too restrained, too much a part of the Establishment, we note that we are also criticized by the Establishment as being too left-wing. We are called 'the pinko paper' by conservatives. This balance of criticism is important.'[66]

But the changes and challenges which Japan and *Asahi* now face must be seen in the context of the traditional resilience and flexibility of Japanese society. It is a culture which has, in the last three generations, passed through a savagely swift modernization, the militarist takeover of the 1930s, the overwhelming defeat of 1945, and the stunning economic transformation of the last twenty years. *Asahi* was born of this process, and grew and survived in spite of the crises, fighting for its independence even throughout the merciless 1930s. This tradition is of enormous importance to *Asahi* today. It has been Japan's predominant newspaper since the 1880s; perhaps the best guarantee of its future is that its staff are determined to maintain that tradition.

Notes

1. See 'The Meiji Roots and contemporary practices in the Japanese Press', James Huffman, *Japan Interpreter*, vol II, No. 4, Spring 1977.

2. ABC, Jan–June 1979, for circulation. Advertising charges supplied by Masateru Shiga, assistant to the president, Asahi company.
3. Marketing Research Associates Inc., June 1979.
4. Figures given by Mr Shiga.
5. Company balance sheet, and interview with Mr Shiga.
6. Interview with Zenjiro Doi, chairman Asahi Labour Union.
7. Interview with Masaki Sata, chairman Tokyo branch, Asahi Labour Union.
8. Interview with Yoshiyuki Wada, deputy chief, International Affairs Department, Japan Newspapers' and Editors' Association (*Nihon Shimbun Kyokai*).
9. Interview with Shoryu Hata, managing director for editorial affairs, *Asahi Shimbun*.
10. Interview with Takashi Tachibana of *Bungei Shunju* magazine, and *Bungei Shunju*, 1979, *passim*.
11. Interview with *Nihon Shimbun Kyokai*.
12. Interview with Mr Shiga.
13. See 'The Japanese Press 1976', published by *Nihon Shimbun Kyokai*; also *ibid.*, 1978.
14. Interview with Mr Shiga.
15. Interview with *Asahi* journalists Eiichiro Kirimura, Yuichiro Kominami, Tomohisa Sakanaka.
16. Interview with editorial board director, Junnosuke Kishida.
17. Interview with T. Tachibana, already cited.
18. Interview with Yasunori Asai. Statistics from Mr Shiga. See also 'A National Newspaper in Japan', Hisashi Maeda, pp. 9–10.
19. There are a number of critiques of the press club system. See Huffman, *op. cit.*; 'Competition and Conformity', Nathaniel B. Thayer, (in *Modern Japanese organization and decision-making*, ed. Vogel, Univ. of California Press, 1975), pp. 284–303; 'Japanese Newspapers, their approach to the news', Richard Halloran, in *Asahi Evening News*, 6.xii.1973, and 7.xii.1973. See also *Japan: Images and Realities*, R. Halloran. Also *Japan, The Fragile Superpower*, F. Gibney, pp. 243–63.
20. Interviews with *Asahi* journalists and union officials, already cited.
21. Interview with Shoichi Ueno, Welfare Service Manager, *Asahi Shimbun*. Mr Ueno is the heir to the Ueno family's 20% share in *Asahi* ownership. He has worked as an *Asahi* journalist before moving to management.
22. See Halloran, *op. cit.*, pp. 170–83.
23. *The Asahi Story*, Asahi Shimbun Publishing Co. Tokyo, 1965.
24. *ibid.*
25. See *The First Casualty*, Philip Knightley, Quartet, 1982.
26. I am indebted to Richard Storry's *A History of Modern Japan*, for a basic history of these times.
27. See 'Japanese Journalism', Bunshiro Suzuki, in *Western Influence in Modern Japan*, ed. Nihobe.
28. See *The Asahi Story, op. cit.*
29. Suzuki, *op. cit.*
30. Quoted in Suzuki, *op. cit.*, p. 210.
31. *ibid.*, p. 207.
32. See *The Asahi Story, op. cit.*

33. *ibid.*
34. *Japanese Press, Past and Present* (*Nihon Shimbun Kyokai*, Tokyo, 1949), p. 12.
35. *The Asahi Story, op. cit.*
36. See Halloran, *op. cit.*
37. See *The Asahi Story, op. cit.*
38. Interview with Richard Hughes, the celebrated Asian correspondent for the *Sunday Times* of London, a personal friend of Fleming and Tiger Saito.
39. *Conquered Press*, W. J. Coughlin. Mr Coughlin's book is the basis for my information of the 1945–51 period.
40. *ibid.*
41. *Japanese Press: Past and Present, op. cit.*
42. See *One Day in the World's Press*, ed. W. Schramm, p. 105.
43. See Jun'ichi Kyogoku in *Bungei shunju*, January 1975 (translated into English in 'Japan Echo', vol 11, No. I, 1975).
44. See *The Press in Japan today*, E. P. Whittemore, 'A Case Study'.
45. Quoted in 'Japan's big dailies', the *Economist*, 22. v. 1965 p. 15.
46. See *The Elite Press*, J. C. Merrill, p. 281.
47. Interview with Toshiharu Shibata, deputy managing editor, *Asahi Shimbun*.
48. See 'Japan, The Two Rerrchaners', A. Axelbank (*New Republic*, 13.xi.1965) p. 11.
49. Interview with T. Shibata, already cited.
50. Interview with T. Shibata and with J. Kishida (already cited). And see Gibney, *op. cit.*, p. 256.
51. Interview with Yuichiro Kominami, editor of *Japan Quarterly* (*Asahi* publication), and former editor of *Asahi Weekly Journal*.
52. See Huffman, *op. cit.*, p. 451.
53. 'Tanaka's resignation and the Japanese press', Seizaburo Sato.
54. See J. Kyogoku,*op. cit.* And interview with T. Tachibana, already cited.
55. Cited by Masaomi Omae in *Bungei Shunju* magazine, quoted and translated by Gibney, *op. cit.*, p. 247.
56. *ibid.*, p. 254.
57. Interview with T. Shibata, already cited.
58. *Characteristics of the Japanese press*, Susumu Ejiri, p. 13.
59. *One Day in the World's Press, op. cit.*, p. 137.
60. 'Comparative contents analysis of two Japanese papers', Sheji Hoshino.
61. *ibid.*, and personal observation and analysis by the author, 1979.
62. Interview with T. Shibata, already cited.
63. See *Bungei Shunju*, March 1974. Also, interview with T. Tachibana, already cited.
64. I am indebted to Masateru Shiga for guiding me around the *Asahi Shimbun* newsroom, print shops and computer department. See also '*NELSON – a new editing and layout system of newspapers*', *Asahi Shimbun Publications*.
65. Interview with S. Hata, already cited.
66. *ibid.*

Note: The interviews with *Asahi* journalists and executives took place between 3 and 16 November, 1979, in Tokyo. I am indebted to the staff of *Asahi Shimbun* for their courtesy, and to the other Japanese journalists and non-Japanese correspondents who gave me the benefits of their insights.

ASAHI SHIMBUN: EDITORIALS

The independence of India: 7 June 1947

'The principle of democracy is based on self-determination of the individual and of the nation. However, it is a prerequisite that the individuals unite for a higher-level co-operative society, rather than divide into unintegrated units, such as India and Pakistan.'

The independence of Israel: 1 May 1948

'When a fight is taking place, one must first restrain the flailing arms, not start a debate on its causes. Similarly, in Palestine, the ceasefire must be given priority. The United Nations General Assembly and Security Council must try for a ceasefire, and put an end to the anguish and torment of people who are suffering from a racial struggle which is also a tribal conflict.'

The Berlin blockade and airlift: 8 July 1948

'It seems that the prospects of a Four-Power Council meeting to discuss the whole issue of Germany's future were increasing, when the Berlin blockade crisis arose. The UK/US/French side will neither approve nor acknowledge any alterations of any points determining West Germany's future even should there be a Four-Power agreement, and it is doubtful that any of the Soviet demands will be accepted. Consequently, the promise of a Four-Power meeting is unlikely to relax the Soviet blockage.'

The Communists win power in China: 3 October 1948

'We cannot tell whether the revolutionary ideologies of Communism will be able to cope with the hard realities facing China. Not, at least, from a simple reading of that ideology. But to anticipate immediate class confrontation and class war would be too pessimistic a view – or even dangerous wishful thinking.'

The Korean war: 10 October 1950

'It is clear that the objective of the governments of the United Nations forces is nothing but world peace. And we hope that not only North Korea, but also China and the Soviets will also straightforwardly accept the UN resolution for free general elections throughout North and South Korea, and a withdrawal of non-Korean military forces.'

The Suez invasion: 2 November 1956

'For a great power to create a *fait accompli* by resorting to military action constitutes an intolerable threat to those small nations which have newly achieved independence, and indeed, it goes against the whole trend of the world today. It would be no exaggeration to say that if a great power goes so far as to use the veto in the UN Security Council so that it can take armed action, then the very existence of the UN is in peril.'

The Russian invasion of Hungary: 5 November 1956

'All these developments show that the Soviet Union is unwilling to permit the existence of a government which displeases it or which tries to be too independent. Worse than this, it is undoubtedly attempting to overthrow such a government by military force. Its action here is different in nature and far more serious in its implications than the military action taken by Britain and France against Egypt.'

The Bay of Pigs assault on Cuba: 10 April 1961

'It is absolutely impossible to believe that the US government will resort to direct armed intervention in Cuba's internal affairs.'

The Cuban missile crisis: 24 October 1962

'It is our belief, however, that even if there were such dangerous excesses (i.e. missile bases) by Soviet Russia and Cuba, it would not give the US justification for engaging in the same kind of dangerous excesses. . .If a Soviet ship is sunk, what will happen? We shudder even at the mere idea.'

The Gulf of Tonkin incident: 4 August 1964

'The action of the US 7th Fleet, from the time that it was first sent out, was fraught with the danger of developing into a situation that could not be dismissed simply as defensive action of the high seas. It would be more correct to say that an anticipated incident occurred.'

China's nuclear weapon: 31 December 1966

'It will be impossible to expect any actual results by trying to make any country suspend nuclear tests and nuclear arming while shutting that nation out of international society. We must increase efforts to bring China into world society, whether we like it or not.'

Rhodesia's UDI: 15 November 1965

'It is nothing but a continuation of the absolute control and oppression of the 4,000,000 African natives by their 220,000 white masters. In other words, the continuation of a colonial form of government.'

The Russian invasion of Czechoslovakia: 24 August 1968

'By treading underfoot the banner for putting an end to domination and oppression among nations and peoples – as well as such principles as complete equality among the various Socialist nations, national sovereignty, respect for independence and non-interference in domestic affairs – the Soviet Union has severely damaged with its own hands its reputation as the apostle for 'peaceful co-existence' which it has built up over the years.'

Israel's occupation of the West Bank: 25 October 1973

'Can't the Arabs, who have withdrawn their demand for the extermination of Israel, go one step further and officially recognize the existence of Israel? As for Israel, cannot it withdraw its one-sided argument that territory taken from other countries is necessary for its own safety?'

The OPEC price rise: 27 December 1973

'Inasmuch as oil and oil products today are being used in every aspect of Japanese economic life, rapid increase in the price of oil poses serious problems that could very well lead to the bankruptcy of the nation's economic fabric. . .The time has come for the Japanese to start thinking in dead earnest about how rapidly to convert their eco-social structure into one that depends less on oil and conserves energy resources.'

Watergate: 24 October 1973

'The core of the problem involves the question of the extent to which the President's executive privileges can be condoned.'

The fall of Saigon: 2 May 1975

'From beginning to end, the Vietnam war was a war of national liberation. The fact that the final victory was won by the liberation forces is proof that the era of suppression of nationalism by the big powers has come to an end. This, we feel, is the greatest significance of the war. . .In the long run, those who attempt to obstruct the aspirations of a people seeking independence are defeated.'

Sport and politics

No relevant editorials.

The space venture: 18 July 1969

'Many people voice doubts about why such huge amounts of money and energy have to be used to land two astronauts on the moon. Actually, unbalanced progress can't be avoided. If mankind cannot go out into space until all the problems on earth are solved, the opportunity will be lost for ever. . .What is important is whether distributions of this are balanced. Looking at the way the US has been doing things, the impression is that over-excessive emphasis has been placed on the Apollo project.'

Freedom of information: 5 July 1976

'Leaving aside those cases which clearly violate the laws and regulations on crime and punishment, the propriety of newsgathering should be left up to the conscience of the journalistic world and to the criticisms of the people.'

Note: From 1954 onwards, when *Asahi*'s own translations of its editorials began to be published in the English-language *Asahi Evening News*, I have used the *Asahi* English text. For the quotations before that date, I am indebted to the professional translation service of Capital Enterprises Inc. of Tokyo, and to the skill and kindness of Ms Eiko Tsuzuki, the company's director.

9

The New York Times

The city of New York had seen the birth and death of seven newspapers called the *New York Times* by the mid-point of the nineteenth century. As if to ward off the ill fates which had attended its predecessors, Henry J. Raymond, founder of the eighth attempt in 1851, called it the *Daily Times*. There were few young newspapermen in the city better fitted to make the venture. He had worked with the legendary Horace Greeley to produce the first *Tribune*, and he had spotted a gap in the city's market. His first issue observed that immigration had doubled the literate population of the city in the last five years. Moreover, he cannily observed, Greeley's *Tribune* was 'too radical' for the New York middle class (although it was making an annual profit of some $60,000) and James Bennet's *Herald* was 'too sensational'. Raymond acquired a wealthy partner, a former banker, George Jones, and his first editorial announced that: 'The *Times* would seek to allay, rather than excite, agitation. . .There are very few things in this world which it is worth while to get angry about, and they are just the things which anger will not improve.'[1] Raymond's prospectus, widely circulated in the business section of the city, maintained the moderate, non-radical, non-sensational stance: 'the *Times* will seek to be CONSERVATIVE in such a way as shall best promote needful REFORM'.[2] But however bland his editorials, Raymond was a man in a hurry, committed to expansion. He quickly founded an evening edition, a Sunday edition, and a West Coast edition published whenever a ship sailed for California; by 1856, he was publishing a European edition. His energies were rewarded. After ten days on the streets, his New York *Daily Times* claimed 10,000 subscribers; at the end of his first year, 25,000.[3]

Part of Raymond's success was his hunger for news. In 1854, he stole a scoop on a New York shipwreck from the rival *Herald* by sending a reporter to purloin the *Herald*'s page proofs, and then Raymond's printers beat the *Herald* on to the streets. For the Austro-French war of 1859, Raymond himself sailed to the Lombardy battle-fields to send back reports. When Darwin's *Origin of the Species* was published in New York in 1860, Raymond gave it half a page, and a powerful editorial which attacked Darwin's critics.[4] But Raymond's sense of news values was conventional. His paper began with two or three columns of European news, followed by items of American news (the lead item in the first issue was about fugitive slaves from the South), and only the last columns on the front page ran New York news. For the first issue, the city news was the death of a Baptist missionary, the execution of two convicted murderers, and the first appearance of bloomers in New York. They caused, the *Times* observed, 'hostility and derision'.[5]

The major explanation of Raymond's success lay in his political career. He was known as the Godfather of the Republican Party, giving the keynote speech at the party convention of 1856, and being elected as a Congressman in 1862. Raymond's *Times* was effectively a party organ, in favour of business, commerce, growth and against slavery and the South. The *Times*'s economic crisis of the 1880s came when Raymond's successor abandoned the Republican Party, and its subscribers abandoned the *Times*. But in the 1860s, Republican politics meant that the *Times* was 'stout for the war', the Civil war. Raymond himself reported the first battle of Bull Run, and he organized a news team so effective that Stanton, Lincoln's Secretary of War, read of Sherman's plan to march through Georgia to the sea in the *Times*, fourteen days before he was informed through official channels.[6] Sam Wilkinson's report of the battle of Gettysburg for the *Times* is one of the war's more poignant documents; the reporter described finding the body of his eldest son on the battlefield. And there was a kind of war back in New York itself, when the riots against conscription led to mob assaults on the pro-war *Times*. Raymond's political connections secured the loan of two government machine guns, and he manned one of them himself. The *Times*'s defences were secure enough for Raymond to send an armed squad of sixteen *Times* employees to relieve the besieged offices of the *Tribune*.[7]

When Raymond died in 1869, his *Times* was so successful that his partner, George Jones, refused an offer of a million dollars. He employed thirty-six reporters, one of them a woman, Maria Morgan, who covered livestock, dog shows and racing. Still a staunchly Republican paper, Jones's *Times* became the most vocal critic of the corrupt city administration of Boss Tweed's Tammany Hall Democrats. Both Tammany and the *Times* were products of the city's surging growth, but whereas the *Times* prospered on the growth of commerce and the middle class, Tammany Hall depended on the votes of the tides of immigrants arriving from Europe, and on corruption, 'No Caliph, Khan or Caesar has risen to power or opulence more rapidly than Tweed. . .and there he sits today, pocketing our money and laughing at us', ran the *Times* editorial for 25 September 1870. The war was on, and by July of 1871 Tweed was alarmed (but rich) enough to offer Jones $5 million to drop the campaign. And then Tweed's own rivals within Tammany Hall brought Jones the doctored account books. For the first time, the *Times* ran a front-page story with a headline across more than a single column. The Tweed revelations covered three columns, and Jones also printed 500,000 copies of a four-page supplement on the documented frauds – one copy for every second New Yorker. And to make sure that the immigrants knew the story too, Jones printed them in German and in English, and the Tweed gang was broken.[8]

For a decade, the *Times* was in an unassailable position, powerful, respected and profitable. By 1883, it was making $188,000 a year. But the next year profits fell to $56,000, and down to $15,000 by 1890.[9] The honesty which led Jones to reject Boss Tweed's $5 million led him throughout the 1880s to attack corruption in the Republican Party. In the 1884 election, the *Times* refused to support the official Republican candidates and backed Grover Cleveland. A haemorrhage of ads and subscriptions followed as angry New York Republicans refused to do business with a paper which they saw as a traitor to the party. Jones stuck to his guns, and supported Cleveland again in 1888. He died in 1891, and the paper was dying too, its presses antiquated, with accumulated debts of $300,000 and losing $75,000 in 1892. Circulation had collapsed to 9,000 a day, and Jones's honesty was not solely to blame. He had changed the *Times* little since the Boss Tweed days, and the *Times* was facing dramatic competition from the new mass papers of Hearst and Pulitzer.

It was bought by a near bankrupt, the son of a German-Jewish immigrant who had learned his trade as a printer's devil on the

Knoxville Chronicle of the 1870s.[10] In 1878, with $37.50 of borrowed money he started the *Chattanooga Times*. By the 1890s, he was a prosperous Southern publisher, who had lost large amounts of money on land speculation. The $75,000 of his own money which he paid to buy the *New York Times* was itself borrowed. The controlling share interest in the paper was held in escrow by the bankers, to be turned over to the young Adolph Ochs as and when he made the paper profitable. But he had won the support of the bankers, including the legendary J. P. Morgan and Marcellus Hartley of Equitable Life Assurance Society. Ochs solicited testimonials from everyone he knew or could think of, from President Cleveland to Wall Street. He succeeded through sheer nerve; every other letter he wrote at this time was to hold off another creditor. But there was a fundamental honesty about the man. Even when desperate for money, he rejected $36,000 of advertising from the city government on the eve of the 1896 election, and opposed the traditional practice by which $200,000 of city taxpayers' money was channelled to the New York papers every election. It was a principled stand, and his exposure of the practice in his newspaper probably did the paper good.

But more important were the changes in the content of Ochs's *New York Times*. His support had come from the bankers, and the *Times* became a bankers' paper. 'The neglected and non-sensational departments of news were quietly and unostentatiously improved,' Ochs commented.[11] Every Monday, there was a special financial section. His City Editor, who backed the plan for more financial news, began a weekly column called 'The Merchants' Point of View'. Another daily column was started, headed 'Arrival of Buyers' – simply a list of visiting businessmen. It became a permanent *Times* feature, running 2,000 names a day by 1946. Ochs dropped the short stories and the fiction department and began a weekly book section. He ran a light daily feature, 'Topics of the Times', and increased the letters section, deliberately soliciting opposing views to his bland editorials. He made the paper easier to read, widening the spaces between lines, and used better newsprint. He made staff cuts in every department except the editorial, and after seven weeks running costs were down by $2,000 a week. But the main change was in the expanded financial section. Real estate transactions, stock market reports, commercial news and law reports – Ochs made the *Times* into the businessman's paper, and business responded. Within two months, he was rivalling Pulitzer's *World* and Hearst's *Journal* in the length of his daily advertising columns. By the end of his first year, circulation had improved to

22,000, and the year after that he had doubled the number of advertising lines to 4 million a year.[12]

It was barely enough. He was still selling a fraction of the circulation of Hearst and Pulitzer, and in 1898, the two giants threatened to swamp him with their coverage of the Spanish-American war – a war which Hearst always claimed to have inspired through his sensational papers. His *Journal* even ran a front-page banner headline: 'How do you like the *Journal*'s war?'[13] It was not the best of atmospheres for the survival of Adolf Ochs's paper, predicated as it was on a belief in the public's need for a non-sensational paper. The tone Ochs sought was clear from the winner of the competition he launched to find a slogan for the paper. It ran 'All the World News but not a School for Scandal'. Wisely, Ochs preferred to use his own slogan – 'All the News That's Fit to Print'.[14] So he chose not to try and beat Hearst and Pulitzer at their own game. Instead, he stunned New York by dropping his price from three cents to one cent a copy. Circulation rose from 25,000 to 76,000 in the course of a year. Two years later, its shares the bankers held in escrow were formally given to Ochs. He had made the paper profitable. Indeed, within six years of taking over, his *Times* was making $200,000 a year. By 1904, he was borrowing another $2,500,000 to build a new headquarters for the *Times* on its current premises on 43rd Street, and he persuaded the city fathers to name the nearest crossroads Times Square. But his financial foundations were still flimsy. The controlling shares he had been given were already pledged to the Equitable Assurance Society as security for a $250,000 loan for working capital. When that company's scandal broke in 1905, Ochs went to Marcellus Dodge, owner of the Remington Arms Company, borrowed $300,000, paid off the Equitable debt and gave the controlling shares to Dodge. So when, in 1915, the *Times* was accused of being British-owned (so partial had its editorials been on the First World War), Ochs was misleading his readers when his editorials claimed (17 March, 1915) 'Mr Ochs is in possession, free and unencumbered, in controlling and majority interest of the stock of the *New York Times*'. Not until the next year was the Dodge loan repaid and the controlling shares back in Ochs's hands.[15]

By then, the paper was dramatically healthy. To the solid Ochs foundation of business news and sober reporting had been added the genius of Carl van Anda. In 1904, he joined the *Times* from Bennet's *Sun*. He was a formidable man. It was he who comprehended the work of Albert Einstein, and promoted his theories of relativity in the

Times. And it was van Anda who spotted a mathematical mistake in Einstein's equations.[16] When van Anda did a deal with the London *Times* for exclusive American use of the story on the discovery of Tutankhamen's tomb, he could not only read the hieroglyphics, but detected within them a 4,000-year-old forgery. Fascinated by technology, some of the first US scoops he arranged came by radio dispatch from the London *Times*. He arranged with Marconi for wireless transmissions to the *Times* across the Atlantic. Radio was one way to beat the Hearst–Pulitzer scoops. Another was organization. Van Anda ran the *New York Times* as if he were running the Prussian general staff.[17] He helped to finance and organize the Peary expedition to the Pole, and the *Times* got the scoop. The first aviator to fly from Albany to New York was covered by a special train hired by van Anda to follow his route and to take exclusive photographs. Perhaps his greatest scoop was the sinking of the *Titanic* in 1912. Van Anda had monitored the radio reports and the *Times* splashed the (unconfirmed) news that the 'unsinkable' ship had gone down. When the rescue ships came in to New York, van Anda had the whole staff deployed on the quayside, a battery of hired rooms and telephones to get the story back, and every reporter had an assigned task; to get aboard the rescue ships, to interview particular survivors, rescuers, and so on. The sober seriousness of Ochs's *Times* was the perfect foundation for van Anda's pyrotechnics; the paper combined scoops and exhaustive coverage, exclusives and weighty business coverage; the *Times* was a quality paper that was also run with the verve and dash of Hearst and Pulitzer at their best.[18] It was van Anda, for example, who decided that the man to cover world championship boxing for the *Times* was John L. Sullivan, the greatest champion of them all. It was van Anda who organized a code for his reporters covering the Western Front in the Great War, to enable them to beat the censorship; van Anda who spent without a second thought $75,000 a year on cables alone to cover the wars in the trenches; van Anda who organized the scoop which published the British and German White Papers on their version of the war's outbreak; and when that war was over, van Anda organized a bank of twenty-four telephones for the *Times* to receive perhaps it most dramatic exclusive: the full text of the Versailles Treaty. By the war's end, circulation was 487,000 on Sundays and 352,000 in the week – twenty-four times higher than when Ochs had bought the paper, and with seven times as many ads.

The paper had been modernized. Its layout had assumed the form it was to retain for the next sixty years. It had a Sunday magazine supplement, multi-column headlines, front-page photographs and, again thanks to van Anda, a growing clippings library arranged by subject-matter as well as the standard biographic files. It had become the pre-eminent American newspaper, but it operated – at Ochs's insistence – within a code of self-imposed responsibility. One of its great scoops remained unpublished, after consultations with the President and the US Ambassador in Berlin, because of Ochs's code. In 1908 William Hale, a *Times* correspondent, was granted an interview with the German Kaiser. The Kaiser was more than frank; he threatened war against Britain, alleged the British were 'traitors to the white race' because of their recent alliance with Japan, and called for a white, Christian alliance between the USA and Germany. It was bellicose, racist stuff, and the *Times* suppressed it – until thirty-one years later, on the eve of the Second World War, it was published in the Sunday magazine.[19] Ochs's argument was that his paper 'so far as possible consistent with honest journalism, attempts to support those who are charged with responsibility for government'. It was a policy that was to be maintained into the 1960s, when the growing evidence from Vietnam, and in particular from the Pentagon Papers in 1971, convinced a new generation of *Times* journalists that their government was no longer worthy of trust, that it lied and cheated and broke the rules – and it was the responsibility of the press to expose that.

But in 1918, the *New York Times* was not the solid institution it was to become in the 1970s. Ochs himself feared that one incautious editorial could kill the paper. As the First World War drew to a close, an Austrian peace-feeler, calling for a peace conference, inspired a war-weary editorial from the editor, Charles Miller. 'Only the madness or the soulless depravity of some of the belligerent powers could obstruct or defeat the purpose of the [peace] conference,' it said. The next day, Ochs received 3,000 telegrams of complaint, and he suggested that he retire, leaving the paper in the hands of trustees. When dissuaded from this, he suggested that the *Times* should thenceforth appear without editorials. The storm, which saw accusations from other papers that Ochs had taken 'Austrian gold', soon passed, but it helped to bring on the depression that Ochs was to suffer from for the rest of his life.[20]

There were other, better-founded, criticisms which bit almost as deep. In August 1920, Walter Lippmann, fast becoming the most respected of all American journalists, and Charles Merz, later to become a *Times* editorial writer, published in the *New Republic* a devastating critique of the *Times*'s coverage of the Russian Revolution. On ninety-one occasions between November 1917 and November 1919, they recounted, the *Times* had reported that the Communist regime had fallen or was about to fall – almost one such erroneous report a week. Four times Lenin and Trotsky were reported to be preparing to flee; three times they were said to have fled; twice Lenin was handing in his resignation; three times he was reported in prison – and once he was reported dead. 'The news about Russia is a case of seeing not what was, but what men wished to see,' said Lippmann and Merz.[21] Perhaps because of this proven bias, the *Times* was to maintain, throughout Stalin's pre-war years, a reporter in Moscow whose bias was so pro-Moscow that, a generation later, Scotty Reston was to claim that Walter Duranty had been an agent of Russian intelligence. Duranty suppressed news of the famines that followed collectivization, apparently believed the flagrantly untrustworthy evidence of the purge trials, and it was his reports, more than anything else, which won the *Times* its 1930s nickname as 'the uptown *Daily Worker*'.[22]

Flaws such as these appear larger in retrospect than they did at the time. They are eddies at the riverbank; the mainstream history of the *Times* flows honourably on: exhaustive reporting, a commitment to being the newspaper of record, publishing the full texts of treaties or of presidential news conferences and statements; technological advances, its own radio mast in 1919, its own radio transmitter (call-sign 2-UO) by 1924; a worldwide photo-news service that had a hundred cameramen around the globe in 1925; an extra $500,000 invested in foreign news coverage alone in 1922. Flashes of the old van Anda hunger for scoops still illuminated its pages – like the exclusive contract the *Times* signed with the young aviator Charles Lindbergh and the *Times* exclusive in obtaining Lenin's political testament. In the first twenty-five years of Ochs's ownership, six other New York papers had died. The *Times* had increased its advertising tenfold; it had earned total profits of almost exactly $100 million – of which only 4% had been paid out in dividends. The rest had been ploughed back into the paper.[23]

The 1920s was a decade of growth and prosperity. In 1926, the *Times* had over 3,000 employees, 309 of them reporters. Its income was $27 million, and it was publishing an average of thirty-two pages of news, and thirty-four pages of ads every day. There was a new generation of the family to manage the paper – Arthur Hays Sulzberger, who had married Ochs's daughter Iphigene. Among the few clouds on the horizon were the gloomy reports on the booming stock market by the *Times*'s financial editor, Alex Noyes. When the Harrimans of Wall Street protested to Ochs that Noyes's reports could lose him advertising, Ochs replied: 'One of the most rigid rules of the *Times* is that no editor must be interested in, or seek, or solicit advertising.' Perhaps the old man had forgotten his instructions to his first Washington correspondent, W. C. Dunnell, that part of the Washington job was to solicit ads on the side.[24]

The Wall Street crash of 1929 hurt the *Times*. Circulation fell by 2,000, but ads dropped by 20% in 1930. Ochs felt secure enough to continue with his expansion plans, embarking on a $2 million new printing plant in Brooklyn. Other papers suffered more. Pulitzer's *World* faced collapse, and although Ochs turned down a suggestion that he buy it, he offered the *World* journalists $5 million to keep it running on a co-operative basis. But by 1932, the Depression was biting. All the *Times* employees had to take a 10% wage cut, and the paper shrank to forty pages and less. By 1935, revenue had shrunk to $16.8 million, (against $27 million in 1926), and ads had been cut by a third. But circulation was healthy, at 460,000, an increase of 100,000 on 1926, and the *Times* used its cash reserves to improve the paper. In 1933, it began colour printing in the magazine, and in 1936 it incorporated the old rotogravure picture section. The previous year, the 'Week in Review' section was launched, part of a planned improvement of the Sunday paper that took its circulation over 700,000.

Ochs had died in Chattanooga in 1935, and his successor, Arthur Hays Sulzberger, who had helped to develop the *Times*'s own wirephoto technology, began to change the traditional formula. 'I saw the effect the radio commentators were having,' he explained. 'I wanted the paper to move editorially out of the ivory tower.'[25] The paper became more combative, more partisan in its coverage of the fascism that had emerged in Europe. Ochs himself had been sensitive enough to charges of his Jewishness to refuse to print letters denouncing Hitler and his persecution of the German Jews.[26] He did, however, send Fred Birchall to report on Germany, and there win a Pulitzer Prize with his reports on Nazism, including a scoop on the concentration camps. Perhaps more impressive than Birchall's work was Simeon Strusky's cool analysis of German national, and German middle-class, incomes from 1911 to 1931. His contemporary judgement has never been bettered: 'The middle classes were supposed to have been driven into Hitler's arms by their bitter economic condition at a time when they were really growing wealthy. . .It is not really a case of their seceding from democracy, but of their never having been converted.' This was reporting of a remarkably high order.[27]

Under Sulzberger, the *Times*'s anti-fascism became more strident. Eight days in a row, the *Times* denounced Italian aggression in Ethiopia. In 1938, an historic editorial by Charles Merz made it clear that the *Times* had chosen sides: 'We shall be fully prepared, if war on a large scale envelops Europe, to choose the side of the democracies,' it said.[28] When that war broke out, while America was still neutral and Roosevelt was fighting a third re-election campaign on a peace platform, the *Times*'s editorial on the British evacuation of Dunkirk was couched in the language of a co-belligerent: 'This shining thing in the souls of free men Hitler cannot command, attain or conquer. It is the great tradition of democracy. It is the future. It is victory.'[29]

But it was still the *Times*, and caution of a kind continued to rule in the editorial chair. The *Times*'s coverage of the Spanish Civil War was measured out with rulers – the same number of column inches from Franco's side as from the Republic. A later academic study of the difference between the published stories of Herbert Mathews, the *Times* man on the anti-Franco side of the lines, and the dispatches he had originally sent, showed that the *Times*'s editing had been 'seriously biased'. Sulzberger was under considerable pressure from the Roman Catholic Archdiocese of Brooklyn, and from Catholic readers, to give Franco's side (which was backed by the Church) a sympathetic hearing.[30]

Domestically, the whole business of New York journalism was being transformed by the growing importance of Washington as a news centre, a process that accelerated with the Roosevelt presidency and the New Deal. Arthur Krock, who took over the *Times*'s Washington bureau in 1933 from the veteran Richard Oulahan, was building what amounted to a separate power base in the capital. The *Times*'s editorials supported Roosevelt in the 1936 election; Krock opposed him. Krock's Washington column made him one of the most influential political correspondents in America, but he nurtured a resentment against the New York masters that was to be bitterly documented in his memoirs.[31] But Krock and the *Times* editorials joined to condemn Roosevelt's plan to pack the Supreme Court with his own nominees, and thus outflank the judicial controls imposed upon the executive by the constitution. The *Times* ran fifty separate editorials on the issue. For the *Times*, at least, there was another source of hostility for Roosevelt – the question of *Times* finances and the family control. When Ochs had died, the *Times* was still a private company, accountable only to Ochs. Even before his death, there had been fears that death duties might force the *Times* to seek money from, and perhaps lose control to, the banks. A family Trust was established, and under its provisions, the family Trust sold some $6 million of controlling stock in the *Times* back to the New York Times Company itself. The cash was to be used by the Trust to pay death duties and legal fees, and the family lost almost $500,000 in annual income. 'We were unwilling to have any bank, or group of banks, hold the control of the *Times* and we were prepared to make any sacrifice to avoid that,' Sulzberger later explained.[32]

To Roosevelt, this was 'a dirty Jewish trick', aimed at evading taxes. There is strong evidence to support the *Times*'s own view – that Roosevelt hoped to use the tax laws to bring the *Times* under government influence, if not control.[33] This did not happen. When the Trust finally lost voting control of the stock, in 1971, it was a matter of choice, selling shares to buy the Cowles publishing group of magazines, TV and radio stations. It was part of a corporate strategy to turn the *Times* into the flagship of a publishing empire, and to guarantee its income irrespective of newspaper strikes or falling profits on the *Times* itself. The *Times* was part of an eponymous corporation that was one of the 500 biggest business groups in the country.

It was during the Second World War that America became a global power, a fate that the nation had resisted after the first war, refusing to join the League of Nations. The *New York Times*, which had seen the war coming and chosen sides in advance, became a great international newspaper at the same time; the authoritative voice of the Pax Americana. On the one hand, it was a newspaper, gutsy and independent and hungry for news, breaking the story of the D-Day landings by monitoring the German radio and with a pre-written series of features on invasion, German defences, the tactics of amphibious operations and the strategy of fighting across France, all ready to be printed on 7 June, the deadline after the landing.[34] There were ten *Times* men on the Normandy beaches. On the other hand, it was an American institution, the paper of record for the era that America was making the world's history. While the scientists were setting up the atomic pile and the Manhattan Project, the FBI was scouring the nation's libraries, removing those copies of the *Times* from 1940 in which William Laurence, the science correspondent, had written about the theory of the atomic bomb – they might have been useful to the Germans. And when the time came to drop the bomb on Hiroshima, Laurence was flown out to the Pacific as the journalist of record to write the story. He and the *Times* were trusted enough to be given time to prepare ten pages of history, of background, of description and scientific analysis, for the copy of the *Times* which recorded man's first use of nuclear warfare against man. The American State chose to make its history under the eye of the *New York Times*.[35]

The *Times* of 1940 had been the creation of two men; the worthy, good, grey *Times* of Adolph Ochs, and the vibrant, brilliant, organized news machine of Carl van Anda. The war added something else, a kind of national recognition of the *Times* as an institution. Although he had long retired , the van Anda elements remained – the planning of the D-Day coverage testified to that. And the worthy *Times* of Ochs was plain in the way there was a special weekly edition of the paper for the troops, the way the *Times* boasted of carrying more war news that any other paper on earth, its average 250,000 words each Sunday representing more reading-matter than the best-seller of the day, *Gone With the Wind*. The scoops still ran. Scotty Reston, who had made his name reporting the London Blitz, obtained and printed the Dumbarton Oaks agreement, the blueprint for the post-war world. And the economic muscle of that world after 1945, the Marshall Plan, was another Reston scoop, 25,000 words of it cabled to him in Washington from his source in Paris. And perhaps another legacy from the canny, money-conscious old Ochs was that while the *Times* had prospered during the war, it had not profiteered. Although the paper had begun to recover from the doldrums of the Depression, its 1944 profit was just over $1 million, almost exactly what it had been in 1935, although revenue had increased from $17 million to $22.5 million. Two-thirds of that income came from advertising, which had grown by less than 5% since 1935 – still barely two-thirds of the 1926 level. In 1944, as in 1935, the *Times* made an annual profit of $2.13 for each paper it sold – by 1969, it was making over $30 per copy sold, 8½ cents per copy per day. The 1944 daily circulation had fallen by a few thousand from 1935, but its Sunday circulation had grown by over 100,000 to 815,000. However powerful the *Times* might be, it was far from being rich.[36]

The Korean war boom was to improve matters, although the growing threat to advertising revenues and the growing rivalry in the provision of basic news from radio and TV were to alarm young executives like Turner Catledge, whom Sulzberger had groomed for high office in a hard-travelling – and harder-drinking – Pacific tour during the war.[37] It was Catledge who insisted that the old Ochs rule of 'I want it all' had to go; stories had to be shorter, tighter, and there had to be more of them. If a daily paper could not compete in immediacy with the radio and TV, it could swamp them with volume. During the month of March 1955, there were 762 different US date-lines and 288 different foreign datelines on *Times* stories, and Catledge insisted that the depth of *Times* coverage could and should make all competitors seem trivial. It was under Catledge that the *Times* began to brag of its sheer size, of the 200 acres of forest needed to supply the newsprint for the Sunday edition. Revenue climbed to $56 million in 1951, to 85 million in 1956. By 1951, the two major circulation hurdles had been cleared — over 500,000 copies a day and over a million on Sundays. And discreetly, another change had taken place. In 1935, the *Times* had run 104,000 columns of news, and 64,700 of ads. In 1951, those proportions were reversed: 83,000 columns of news, and a staggering 137,000 columns of ads. Profits were $2,663,000 in 1951. It was a fatter, richer paper, but the fat was ads.

But if the years of the war had not brought profits, they had brought prestige. The *Times* as an institution gave Sulzberger remarkable influence. In 1952, Sulzberger's was one of the trusted voices which persuaded General Eisenhower to run for the presidency, and the *Times* backed him – even though Iphigene Sulzberger and the bulk of the *Times* staff were for Stevenson, Ike's opponent.[38] Sulzberger wrote some of Eisenhower's speeches but, significantly, the President chose not to declaim one Sulzberger passage in praise of General Marshall at a time when Marshall was under the vicious fire of Senator Joseph McCarthy.[39] It is too often forgotten that McCarthy was staunchly backed by reactionary Southern politicians like Eastland, who used the venom of McCarthy to attack the *Times* for its stands on other matters. As the *Times* itself observed in a courageous editorial: 'because we have condemned segregation in the Southern schools. . . because we have insisted that the true spirit of American democracy demands a scrupulous respect for the rights of even the lowliest individual'.[40] Not that the *Times* was, in the jargon of the day 'soft on Communism'. That same editorial stated: 'We would not knowingly employ a Communist Party member in the news or editorial depart-ments of this paper, because we would not trust his ability to report the news objectively, or to comment on it honestly.'[41] The *Times* conducted its own internal purge. Two employees were fired, and one resigned under pressure.[42] But the *Times* denounced McCarthy and his works, denounced the system of trial by congressional committee, and came out of the appalling affair with perhaps more credit than – in view of that internal purge – it deserved. Ironically, the fact that it was chosen for McCarthyite attack was a kind of praise, a recognition even by the gutter of American politics that it was now an integral part of that East Coast, liberal Establishment, like the State Department itself, which the American right-wing populist tradition loathed even more than Communism.

It was in an attempt to dilute that East Coast character (and label) that the *Times* launched a West Coast edition in 1963. It was a bold, if abortive and ill-planned experiment; it was on target for its circulation goal of 100,000, but an almost total lack of advertising support (inevitable, given the steadily improving *Los Angeles Times*) and the disruptions of the 1963 New York newspaper strike killed it.[43] The strike lasted for 114 days, produced a classic *bon mot* from Reston: 'How do I know what I think if I can't read what I write?'; and did wonders for the *Times*'s competitive position by killing off the *Mirror* and forcing mergers among the *Herald–Tribune*, the *World–Telegram and Sun* and the *Journal–American*, before they too withered on the vine. In 1961, before the strike, the *Times* had but a 30% market share of New York daily advertising; after the strike, it had 55.5%. Its daily circulation climbed by 20,000 to 740,000 by 1969, and its Sunday circulation was but 12,000 copies short of 1½ million. During the sixties, *Times* revenue almost doubled, to $223 million, with profits of $31.3 million.

The East Coast Establishment character that had so provoked McCarthy had another, darker side to it. The war had not only made the *Times* into a national institution, it had also fundamentally changed the character – and the social roots – of serious American journalism. Part of the change was the way Scotty Reston ran the Washington bureau, hiring journalists from the Ivy League colleges, men who had been to prep school and college with America's future politicians, bankers, diplomats. James Angleton, the CIA's head of counter-intelligence, McGeorge Bundy of Kennedy's White House, and the *Times*'s Walter Sullivan had all edited the *Yale Literary Magazine* together.[44] The CIA was a part of that Ivy League Establishment, and the *Times*'s chief foreign correspondent, Cy Sulzberger, was an old and close friend of Frank Wisner, the CIA's head of operations, and of Richard Helms, later to run the Agency.[45] During the Second World War, American Intelligence was called the OSS and John Oakes (a member of the Ochs family and later the *Times* editorial page editor) and Ben Welles, later a senior *Times* man, served in the same Intelligence section as James Angleton.[46] The OSS, like the Ivy League colleges, was a stage of growing up for one

generation of the American elite. *Times* men were part of that process, and so, to a lesser degree, were *Washington Post* men.
Journalism had become, in Dan Moynihan's words 'a profession
attractive to elites'.[47] A similar process took place in France, where
Le Monde was to be staffed with men who had served de Gaulle, and
in Britain, where men from *The Times* and the *Manchester Guardian*
and the BBC worked in and with government departments, some of
them secret, that were all mobilized in fighting a total war against
Nazism. As the Second World War merged into the Cold War, and
honest, decent men could believe that a new, if undeclared, total war
was under way against Communism, the old friendships and the old
loyalties persisted.

It is within this perspective that the *Times*'s curious relationship
with American Intelligence during the CIA's Guatemala coup, during
the Bay of Pigs and the Cuban missile crisis should be seen. When
Cord Meyer, later CIA station chief in London, spoke of 'a relationship of trust between the CIA and *Times* correspondents', and when
Sulzberger permitted the CIA to scan the off-the-record personal
letters his correspondents sent back to him, when *Times* men
regularly drank and lunched and wenched and exchanged gossip with
Intelligence officials, it was not a conspiracy to pervert the free flow of
news, but an easy socializing that the men had known since they were
all at college together.[48] To a later generation, which had not known
the crucible of the Second World War but which had known Vietnam
and Watergate and the CIA's illegal domestic Intelligence programme, it all looked very much more sinister, very much more
organized.

The CIA did arrange with Sulzberger to have the *Times*'s Central
American correspondent, Sydney Gruson, transferred out of
Guatemala as the CIA was preparing its coup there.[49] *Times* men did
know in advance of the U-2 flights across the Soviet Union before the
Russians shot one down and aborted the Eisenhower–Khrushchev
summit – and the *Times* men did not run the story. The *Times* did
know in advance of the CIA plan to invade Cuba's Bay of Pigs, and
the story was censored to keep out the imminence of the operation
and the role of the CIA.[50] As President Kennedy wrote to the publisher of the *Times* when the paper held back on the scoop that there
were Soviet missiles in Cuba: 'An important service to the national
interest was performed by your agreement to withhold information
that was available to you.'[51] When the *Times* ran a major and critical
series on the CIA in 1966, it asked John McCone (later a director of

the CIA) to vet the manuscript and suggest some amendments. The
service worked the other way, too.[52] The *Times* got the world scoop of
Khrushchev's 1956 speech denouncing Stalin's crimes because the
CIA leaked it to Harrison Salisbury.[53] Cy Sulzberger's column listing
KGB men around the world using diplomatic cover came from his
CIA friend, Richard Helms.[54] Where the *Times* had held back, it
argued that it did so from a sense of responsibility and an awareness of
national security. There was no formal alliance. Even during the
Second World War, Sulzberger turned down point-blank an OSS
request for secret agents to use *Times* credentials and cover.[55]

It was less a matter of institutions, of the *Times* identifying with the
American State, than a matter of individual friendships and trust. And
perhaps the most dramatic feature of the process was the way in which
that trust was broken by Vietnam and Watergate, and the American
press, led by the *Times* and the *Washington Post*, found themselves
forced into a new role as institutional, or constitutional, critics of
government itself. The understanding between *Times* men and CIA
men was based upon an assumption that they were on the same side, a
partnership of the morally just. The *Times*'s increasingly critical
editorials on the Vietnam war, and the way in which the Nixon
administration tried to control the press and stop the publication of
the Pentagon Papers, were the thesis and antithesis of the process.
And Watergate was the synthesis, confirming and justifying the press
in its adversary role against government. The process was not inevitable. It took courage on the part of the press – the *Times* in particular
felt betrayed by a part of the Establishment when its traditional
law firm refused to defend its publication of the Pentagon Papers
in the courts.[56]

American newspapers are in a uniquely enviable position. The First
Amendment to the Constitution says bluntly that Congress shall
make no law abridging the freedom of the press. That has not stopped
successive governments, state and federal, from trying. The *Times*'s
coverage of the slow revolution of civil rights for black citizens in the
South, and a series of articles by Harrison Salisbury on the mood and
the racism of Birmingham, Alabama, brought a series of libel writs for
$6,150,000 against the *Times* itself, and for $1,500,000 against
Salisbury.[57] The writs were brought by state officials with the
objective not simply of making money but of using the writs and the
threat of writs to emasculate reporters determined to try to cover the
South. In the local courts, the *Times* lost; on appeal to the federal
courts, they won and established a series of precedents in libel law in

America which reinforced the First Amendment. Henceforth, public officials could only sue for libel when newspapers had maliciously printed lies, knowing them to be lies, about officials. The Pentagon Papers judgement went further. It effectively prohibited the government from censorship, from preventing a newspaper from publishing. Once published, a newspaper could be brought to law if it had offended the Espionage Acts or betrayed vital national secrets. But there could be no control in advance of publication. These two landmark cases, in each of which the *Times* was the protagonist, did more than simply widen press freedom; they symbolized the new relationship between press and government. That hoary old description of the press as the Fourth Estate of the Realm, which had little enough force when Burke coined it in the eighteenth-century British House of Commons, was given life. The press had become, with legal support, an equal and established institutional critic, a permanent and not necessarily loyal opposition to all the arms of government. It says little for modern democracy that such a status was needed; it says more that such a status was achieved.

It would be tempting to assume, in this high-flown constitutional theory, that the press, or at least the *New York Times*, was somehow infallible. Far from it. As a human institution, trying to make sense of a whole world overnight, every night, and getting it right and written for the next morning, it was bound to be flawed. One of the most remarkable features of the whole Pentagon Papers story is the way in which the *Times* and the *Post* seemed to forget and ignore the four key volumes, those on the diplomatic history of the Vietnam war, which were not unearthed until a *Times* reporter, on his own initiative, launched a legal action to make them public.[58] During the long investigations of Watergate, when one might have assumed the *Times* to be straining every nerve to catch up on the lead of the *Washington Post*, *Times* reporters simply forgot, even though twice reminded, to interview Larry O'Brien, the victim of the original Watergate bug and one of the key sources for the story.[59] The *Times* did a disappointing, almost lazy job on one of the biggest stories on its own doorstep, the bankruptcy of New York City. With the largest staff of foreign correspondents of any paper in the world, with senior executives and journalists flying in to Tehran regularly, it myopically insisted on writing the story of Iran as the oil-rich, loyal friend of the West, rather than the squalid, ill-managed, brutal and doomed dictatorship, doing the West more harm than good, which it was.[60]

Part of the difficulty in judging the work of newspapers lies in the cursory way in which they tend to be read. Editorials, headlines, prominent feature articles are remembered, and the essential drudgery of the news columns is too often forgotten. The saga of the *Times*'s hostility to Vietnam, the Pentagon Papers, the criticism of the Nixon–Agnew government appears, in retrospect, to take coherent form; the bold *Times* against bad governments; impassioned and partisan journalism taking firm sides in a battle in which history would justify the newspaper. It was not like that at all. The *National Review*, a highly conservative magazine, embarked on a lengthy and penetrating survey of the *Times*'s 'fairness' in the wake of the campaign of Vice-President Agnew against 'the East Coast Establishment press'. The survey found that at the height of the battle, the *Times* had run ten stories, totalling 15,150 words, with a pro-Agnew emphasis; five stories, totalling 4,450 words, with an anti-Agnew emphasis, and eight stories, totalling 10,450 words, in which the emphasis was even. Five of the pro-Agnew stories made the front page, but only one of the anti-Agnew articles. At the time, the *Times*'s editorial ran: 'Agnew has exacerbated the division among the people of this country. . .and has undermined the basic principle of freedom of speech'. In a survey of five major news stories, including Agnew, Vietnam and campus unrest, the *National Review* concluded: 'The *Times*'s news performance, in terms of balance between Right and Left, may not be flawless, but it must be rated very high.'[61] This was praise indeed and proof, if it were needed, that the good grey *Times* of Adolph Ochs was still, in an essential and fundamental way, alive and well and doing its journalistic duty.

The mercurial role of Carl van Anda on the modern *Times* was played by Abe Rosenthal, brought back from covering Japan in 1963 to be Metropolitan Editor, to cover 'the magnificent disaster' that was New York City. Individual stories, like the police report of a woman's murder within earshot of thirty-eight apathetic witnesses became a series, a grim symbol of social change, of New York's new mood of fear and isolation. But the city was changing in more ominous ways for the *Times*. Its middle-class readers were moving out to the suburbs, and the retail stores, the backbone of *Times* advertising, were moving out with them. New papers, like Long Island's *Newsday*, were founded for the suburban market and reached 62% of Long Island households in 1974, compared to the *Times*'s circulation to only 14% of households in the New York metropolitan area. Daily circulation fell by 80,000 copies between 1969 and 1973, and profits collapsed from the $31.3 million of 1969 to $4.6 million in 1975.[62] And the *Times* was no longer a private company; it was now answerable to disturbed shareholders, as interested in profit as in quality.

The two main problems were getting, or holding on to, readers who had moved out of the city, and reducing the *Times*'s production costs. The publisher, Arthur Ochs Sulzberger, son of Arthur Hays, told shareholders in 1977 that the *Times* employed 50% more production workers than its competitors – and this was a reason why the *Times* provided 66% of the revenue of the parent corporation, but only 24% of the profits.[63] The unions, understandably, were suspicious, but through a series of negotiations, lifetime job guarantees and a strike in 1978, the manning levels were cut down, from over 800 composing-room staff in 1974, to fewer than 500 in 1980, with a target of less than 100 by 1985. Total manning levels at the *Times* were cut from 6,223 in 1969 to 4,700 by 1978.[64] And the new cold-type technology was introduced in 1978, the year of the strike. The reporters even lost their typewriters, now writing directly on to computers. The *Times* based eighteen reporters in the New York outer suburbs, running a regular three columns of suburban news a day, and forty columns on Sundays. The Connecticut special section is profitable, the Long Island and New Jersey sections break even and, in 1980, the Westchester section was still losing money. The sections do not yet generate enough ads to cover the full costs, 'but the money is less important than saying we care for those areas, those readers. It is an investment,' commented Jonathan Friendly, editor of the suburban sections.[65]

But there are other ways of wooing readers, and the *Times* had been pondering them since the late 1960s, when it planned an abortive evening paper.[66] In the course of 1976, what became known as the new *New York Times* began to emerge, a four-section paper: one section of national and international news; another of metropolitan news; a business section; and a different advertising-generator section each day – Sports, Science, Living, Home, Weekend – each of them a daily magazine, each of them winning new advertising, and each of them a target for parody among traditionalists. There was a joke among *Times* men that soon the most prestigious job would be restaurant critic. The *Times* hungrily chased and celebrated the new leisure industries – within limits. Other papers had run a Food section; the *Times* called theirs Living. The ads department had said that a Science section could never work and wanted a section of fashion; the editorial staff said it would, and were proved right. The slogan for the new *Times* was 'More than just the news' – which proved less embarrassing than the *Times*'s short-lived publicity slogan of the 1960s, which ran 'Without it, you're not with it'. 'To maintain the *Times* as it was, to maintain the concept of the paper as a trust for news, we had to change,' Abe Rosenthal commented. 'We were not looking for new kinds of readers, but more of our traditional kind, to generate the revenues that would allow us to keep the quality of the *Times* as a world institution. A lot of people were not doing their patriotic duty of buying the *New York Times*, or were not buying it regularly enough.'[67]

There was no loss of editorial space or of quality in the news and editorial sections to which the *Times*'s editors were committed. Business coverage and local news expanded in the new *New York Times*. An average day would see 200 columns of editorial matter: ninety columns of news, sixty columns of business (more than half of them stock market tables), and fifty from the new 'lifestyle' sections.[68] The new mix worked. The Weekend section alone put on 35,000 new circulation within a year. Other changes were made less obtrusively. The type script was increased from 6-point to 8.5-point to make the paper easier to read. The column-format was changed to six columns for news space, nine columns for ad space, which packed in more ads and saved 5% on the *Times*'s newsprint bills.[69]

The circulation slide was halted, the finances began to recover. After a loss of $12.6 million in the strike year of 1978 (the strike lasted eighty-eight days), the *Times* made a profit of $27.4 million in 1979, on a revenue of $394 million. Over 75% of that revenue came from ads. On the daily paper, space in 1980 averged 58% for ads, 42% for editorial, but 75% for ads on Sundays. The number of journalists increased, from one employee in nine in 1969 to one employee in four in 1980. With a profit ratio of not quite 7% on revenues, the *Times* of 1979 was doing only moderately well by US business standards; with an annual profit per paper of $29.01 in 1979, it was one of the most profitable of the world's great papers, part of a corporate empire with three TV stations (two of them bought in 1979) and total earnings of over $650 million.[70]

The purpose of this edifice was to sustain a newsgathering operation without parallel on the globe. The editorial budget for the *Times* of 1980 – the money spent on reporters, foreign correspondents, cables, columnists, features, but not including the costs of production, was a munificent $53 million – more than the entire annual budget of a paper as worthy and prestigious as Britain's *Guardian*.[71] It keeps thirty-three foreign correspondents around the world, with twenty-four bureaux. It employs over 600 reporters, another 120 copy

editors, with fifty-one reporters spread across the USA in ten
bureaux, and another forty-seven in the Washington office. There are
fifteen journalists in the Science section alone, thirty-nine in sports,
forty-nine financial reporters, and fifty in the Cultural section.[72] They
turn out over 100,000 columns a year – which amounts to each *Times*
journalist producing the equivalent of two full-length novels in the
paper every year. This is editorial wealth beyond the dreams of
avarice.

And the journalists run the paper. When the Pentagon Papers were
to be printed, and when New York suffered an electricity blackout, all
the high-paying prestige ads in the first ten pages of the paper were
scrapped to make way for news. 'We report directly to the publisher,
not to the business side of the paper. We are independent of financial
questions or problems,' claims executive editor Seymour Topping,
and the business managers agree.[73] 'I think it is in our interests to
stress that the *Times* is different, that news comes first. We are
selling quality. It is as simple as that,' commented business manager
John Pomfret.[74]

Nonetheless, the statistics show that the *Times* has changed its
traditional character from the days of Adolph Ochs. It was probably
inevitable, given the role of advertising in American society and the
nature of newspapers, and it certainly became inevitable once the
Times became a public corporation. But between Ochs's last year,
1935, and 1978, the number of ad columns rose by 320%; the number
of news columns fell by 29.8%. (Although 1978 was a strike year, the
relative proportions of ads and editorial must remain constant.) Even
before the financial crisis of the mid-1970s really broke, when the
circulation and profits slide had begun, the figures tell the same story.
Ad columns between 1935 and 1973 rose by 409%, news columns
increased by 0.6%. In the same period, ad revenue increased by
1360%, while circulation increased by 187%. 1951 was a good year for
the *Times*, yet between 1951 and 1973, profit per employee rose by
728.8%, and profit per copy sold rose by 540.7% – several times faster
than inflation. The figures show the *Times* making more money,
printing less news.[75]

Against those startling figures must stand the fact that in those
years, the *Times* transformed the role of the press in America – and in
the Western world as a whole. Whatever suspicions might be aroused
by the CIA–*Times* relationships of the Cold War, it must be recognized that when its trust in government was undermined, the *Times*
rose to the new challenge. When radical journalists queried the role of

the CIA and the *Times*, the *Times* launched its own investigation and published the results, interviews and documents, for all to see.[76] And it was the *Times* which exposed the illegal CIA operations against Americans who had opposed the Vietnam war, exposing the illegal burglaries, the harassment, the phone tappings, the panoply of a secret police that the Intelligence establishment was spreading over the nation which claimed to lead the free world. When Abe Rosenthal says that his role is 'to keep the *Times* straight', he understates the case; the role of the American press, led by the *Times*, has been to keep America straight, to add an independent set of teeth to those freedoms which successive American governments and Intelligence services tried to undermine, in defiance of the Constitution.[77]

Perhaps because it has achieved so much, expectations of the *Times* are higher. As the paper which had led the press campaign for civil rights for blacks, the *Times* seethed in 1979 when a legal complaint for racial discrimination was filed against it by its own employees – backed by the most distinguished black journalist on the *Times*, Roger Wilkins.[78] And in 1978, when the *Times* women employees had filed a similar discrimination suit, the *Times* chose to settle, setting up a $233,500 annuity fund for its 584 women employees, and promising to hire more women in future.[79] The *Times* had to live up to the standards set by its own editorials. And human nature being what it is, the *Times*'s very prestige made it a natural target for criticism, for sniping, for *Schadenfreude* from its press colleagues. 'There seems to be a subliminal attitude of antagonism towards the paper and towards its power. People trust it, but have to resent it too,' commented Arthur Gelb, whose control of the new 'lifestyle' sections made him a natural target for those who attacked the *Times* for becoming a daily magazine.[80]

Just as New York has been the ultimate of the world's cities, the richest, brashest and most extraordinary, so its dominant newspaper, with the richest readership and advertising and news base to plunder, became the ultimate in its own field. It was an irony that as New York began to crumble in the 1970s, the *Times* reached a peak of independence and courage as a paper. But newspapers need their bases. The shredding of New York has forced the *Times* to widen its constituency. In 1980, the new national edition of the *Times* was launched, a two-section paper of news and financial affairs, transmitted by satellite to Chicago. Computerized typesetting makes it easy and attractive for advertisers to choose where to display their wares, in the national section, the suburban editions, the city section, or any blend of these. And already in the pipeline is a third tier to the *Times*, a Bos-Wash edition to circulate in the 500-mile corridor between Washington and Boston, crammed as it is with academics, bureaucrats, managers, students, politicians, corporate head-quarters, the very stuff of the *Times*'s circulation manager's dreams.[81] The paper has outgrown New York.

Notes

1. E. H. David, *History of the New York Times*, pp. 15ff. See also *The story of the New York Times*, Meyer Berger, Chapter 1, p. 7.
2. Berger, *ibid*.
3. *ibid*. See also *Henry J. Raymond and the New York Press*, A, Maverick.
4. Berger, *op. cit.*, p. 44.
5. *New York Times*, first issue. See also *One hundred years of famous pages from the New York Times*, ed. H. S. Commagher.
6. Berger, *op. cit.*
7. *ibid*; see also Maverick, *op. cit.*
8. Berger, *op. cit.*
9. Until 1935, all financial and circulation figures are taken from Berger, *op. cit.*; in this instance, p. 95.
10. *Without Fear or Favour*, H. E. Salisbury, p. 25.
11. Berger, *op. cit.*, pp. 108–9.
12. *ibid.*; see also Salisbury, *op. cit.*, p. 26.
13. Quoted in Salisbury, *op. cit.*, p. 26n.
14. *ibid.*
15. *ibid.*, pp. 99ff.
16. Berger, *op. cit.* See also *The Kingdom and the Power*, Gay Talese.
17. A comment that emerged in author's interview with A. M. Rosenthal, editor of the *New York Times* in 1980. Mr Rosenthal agreed that he too was running 'a general staff operation'.
18. Talese, *op. cit.*
19. Berger and Salisbury, *op. cit.*
20. Salisbury, *op. cit.*, pp. 250ff.
21. *New Republic*, 4.viii.1920.
22. Salisbury, *op. cit.*, pp. 459–66.
23. Berger, *op. cit.*
24. Salisbury, *op. cit.*, p. 27.
25. Berger, *op. cit.*, p. 423.
26. Salisbury, *op. cit.*, p. 30.
27. *New York Times*, 21.viii.1932.
28. *New York Times*, 15.vi.1938.
29. *New York Times*, 5.vi.1940.
30. Salisbury, *op. cit.*, p. 453.

31. *Memoirs*, A. Krock (Funk & Wagnalls, New York 1968) p. 94.
32. Quoted in Salisbury, *op. cit.*, p. 109.
33. *ibid.*, pp. 110–11.
34. *New York Times*, 7.vi.1944.
35. *New York Times*, 7.viii.1945.
36. Statistics from 1935 are taken from annual reports, and from *The New York Times, Its making and its meaning*, ed. *New York Times*. Also from occasional untitled internal reports circulated to *New York Times* staff, on file in *New York Times* archives.
37. See Talese, *op. cit.*
38. Salisbury, *op. cit.*, p. 469.
39. *ibid.*
40. *New York Times*, 5.i.1956.
41. *ibid.*
42. Salisbury, *op. cit.*, p. 472.
43. A lengthy account of the West Coast experiment is given in Talese, *op. cit.*
44. Salisbury, *op. cit.*, p. 517.
45. *ibid.*
46. *ibid.*
47. *Commentary* magazine, March 1971.
48. Salisbury, *op. cit.*, p. 579.
49. *ibid.*, p. 481.
50. *ibid.*; see also, *My Life and The Times*, Turner Catledge.
51. *New York Times* archives, letter from President J. F. Kennedy to Orvil Dryfoos, 25 October 1962.
52. Salisbury, *op. cit.*, pp. 522ff.
53. Salisbury, author's interview.
54. Salisbury, *op. cit.*
55. *ibid.*, p. 454.
56. *ibid.*, p. 245.
57. *ibid.*, p. 382.
58. *ibid.*, p. 347.
59. *ibid.*, p. 430.
60. Author's interview, Charlotte Curtis, *New York Times* op-ed page editor, Robert Semple, foreign editor.
61. *National Review*, 15 September 1972.
62. Annual reports.
63. Annual report, 1977.
64. Author's interview, John Pomfret, *New York Times* business manager.
65. Athor's interview, J. Friendly.
66. Author's interviews, A. M. Rosenthal, Arthur Gelb, Seymour Topping.
67. Author's interview, A. M. Rosenthal.
68. Author's interview, Alan Seigal, news editor.
69. *ibid.*
70. Annual report, 1979.
71. Author's interview, S. Topping.
72. Author's interview, R. Semple.
73. Author's interview, S. Topping.

74. Author's interview, J. Pomfret.
75. Author's calculations, from annual reports.
76. *New York Times*, 25.xii.1977; 26.xii.1977; 27.xii.1977.
77. Author's interview, A. M. Rosenthal.
78. Salisbury, *op. cit.*, p. 588.
79. *ibid.*, p. 31.
80. Author's interview, A. Gelb.
81. Author's interview, J. Pomfret.

Note: All interviews were undertaken at the *New York Times* offices in New York, in March and April of 1980.

NEW YORK TIMES: EDITORIALS

The independence of India: 4 June 1947

'From the British standpoint the new settlement represents a magnificent achievement of statesmanship. It ends the grandeur but also the misery of Empire and promises to make the British Empire a true commonwealth. It lifts the "white man's burden" from the backs of his brown brothers and recognizes the right to freedom in one crucial part of the world.'

The independence of Israel: 16 May 1948

'As the General Assembly itself has pointed out forcefully, a State of Israel cannot hope to exist and prosper without economic unity of the whole of Palestine. But while these things are true, it is also true that a new State judged worthy to receive recognition must also be judged worthy to have an opportunity to defend itself in action.'

The Berlin blockade and airlift: 28 June 1948

'A Western surrender of Berlin would be such a blow to the democratic forces and give such an impetus to further Communist expansion that the loss of Berlin would inevitably lead to the loss of Germany. And the loss of Germany would in the end mean the loss of Western Europe, which would confront Britain and the United States with at least as grave a menace as was ever posed by Hitler.'

The Communists win power in China: 10 October 1949

'We can at the very least make it plain that we support the Nationalist Government of China and that we do not propose to 'traffic' with the aggressor. . .We shall have to answer to our own consciences and to history if we sacrifice principle to expediency.'

The Korean war: 1 October 1950

'The end of this small but terrible war may be peace not only in Asia but around the world. It is for that purpose that the war was fought. Through this tragic episode we may be able to prove that the free nations are not merely against aggression but that they are also positively for the well-being of their neighbors.'

The Suez invasion: 2 November 1956

'If the military actions of Israel, Britain and France are violations of the United Nations Charter, then so are the prior actions of Egypt.'

The Russian invasion of Hungary: 5 November 1956

'We accuse the Soviet Government of murder. We accuse it of the foulest treachery and the basest deceit known to man. We accuse it of having committed so monstrous a crime against the Hungarian people yesterday that its infamy can never be forgiven or forgotten.'

The Bay of Pigs assault on Cuba: 20 April 1961

'The struggle now going on for Cuba is like a battle in a long, complicated and spread-out war. The Cuban battle will be won or lost in the next few days, but the "war" will continue for years. The United States is engaged in an all-out struggle to save the Western Hemisphere for democracy and freedom.'

The Cuban missile crisis: 28 October 1962

'It was a resumption on a new scale and in a new place of Soviet Russia's unremittingly aggressive effort (that has already subjugated Eastern Europe and half of Asia) to advance world Communism by any means. . .President Kennedy's reaction was inevitable and proper. The offensive build-up in Cuba could not be tolerated by the United States.'

The Gulf of Tonkin incident: 5 August 1964

'The attack on one of our warships that at first seemed, and was hoped to be, an isolated incident is now seen in ominous perspective to have been the beginning of a mad adventure by the North Vietnamese Communists. . .United States determination to assure the independence of South Vietnam, if ever doubted before, cannot be doubted now by the Communists to the north or their allies.'

China's nuclear weapon: 17 October 1964

'Peking's feat may have no immediate military importance, but it creates important political and psychological pressures on other countries to attempt to obtain similar capability. . .there is need for agreement among the United States, the Soviet Union, Britain, France and China to stop all atomic testing, to halt the production of materials for fission and fusion weapons and to provide the verification procedures needed to assure that any such agreement is faithfully executed.'

Rhodesia's UDI: 12 November 1965

'The trouble is that Britain and everyone else involved must manoeuvre with great skill to prevent racial war from erupting and to minimize the danger to innocents, white as well as black, in Central Africa. . .There is no moral or political choice for the United States. We must give Britain full support.'

The Russian invasion of Czechoslovakia: 22 August 1968

'The most pressing need goes far beyond mere verbal denunciation of the Soviet outrage. The need is for effective UN action to force the prompt evacuation of Czechoslovakia by the occupying troops and the restoration of the legal government of Czechoslovakia to its full freedom of action and sovereignty.'

Israel's occupation of the West Bank: 28 November 1973

'The latest conflict had demonstrated once again that the Arabs are not prepared peacefully to yield their lost territory, and there is no indication that they ever will be. The Arab attack on October 6 shattered the illusion that peace could be preserved indefinitely by the presence of Israeli deterrent forces along the 1967 cease-fire lines.

'Those borders have not been secure for Israel in the past, nor – even if they should be reinforced and doggedly maintained – can they be in the future.'

The OPEC price rise: 28 October 1973

'The Western, industrialized world is up against a quasi-monopoly possessing unprecedented ability to halt most areas of economic life in Western Europe and Japan. . .For the long run, Arab oil blackmail is intolerable and ways to break that grip on the throats of Europe and Japan must be found. Finding alternative sources of energy is a must, but for the short run the need is for a campaign of energy conservation unprecedented in peace-time history.'

Watergate: 4 November 1973

'The visible disintegration of President Nixon's moral and political authority, of his capacity to act as Chief Executive, of his claim to leadership and to credibility leads us to the reluctant conclusion that Mr Nixon would be performing his ultimate service to the American people – and to himself – by resigning his office before this nation is forced to go through the traumatic and divisive process of impeachment.'

The fall of Saigon: 30 April 1975

'The United States left Vietnam with the same confusion and lack of direction that took this country there in the first place. The scenes of agony and tumult in Saigon yesterday, as the helicopters lifted American diplomats and panic-stricken Vietnamese away, add up to one more sorrowful episode at the conclusion of an American – and Vietnamese – tragedy.'

Sport and politics: 7 July 1976

'Politics and the Olympic games have been all too frequently intertwined for many years, and each time the cause of sports has suffered. . .The Olympics would be turned into a shambles if the principle of political discrimination were to be legitimatized.'

The space venture: 21 July 1969

'Man is still a pathetic creature, able to master outer space and yet unable to control his inner self; able to conquer new worlds yet unable to live in peace on this one; able to create miracles of science and yet unable properly to house and clothe and feed all his fellow men; able eventually to colonize an alien and hostile environment and yet increasingly unable to come to terms with the nurturing environment that is his home.'

Freedom of information: 11 March 1979

'Should a magazine be free to publish an article on how to make a hydrogen bomb?. . .Under the Constitution, Government bears a "heavy burden" to prove extreme and immediate danger if it seeks to silence a magazine. It is that claim by Government that is on trial, not the wisdom, value, maturity or patriotism of the article.'

10

Washington Post

Lord Northcliffe, the British press magnate, once observed that 'of all the American newspapers I would prefer to own the *Washington Post* because it reaches the breakfast tables of the members of Congress'.[1] But given the enormous advantage of being the President's local daily, perhaps the most remarkable feature of the *Post*'s career is how long it needed to become even an adequate international newspaper, let alone a great one. Not until 1957 did the paper open its first bureau overseas, in London. Not until the mid-1960s did it begin to establish a network of staff correspondents abroad. In 1961, when a science correspondent called Howard Simons became the ninth member of the *Post*'s national desk, he asked if he could hire a car in Florida to cover a space launch. He was told it would cost too much, and it was suggested that he hitch a ride from the rival *Baltimore Sun*.[2] It took the courageous decision to print the Pentagon Papers in 1971, and then to pursue the Watergate inquiries, to establish the *Post*'s credentials as a great newspaper, worthy of comparison with the *New York Times*. Not until 1972 did the *Post* consider its own columns of sufficient historical importance to publish a regular index.

Much of the blame for this can be laid at the door of the McLean family, father and son, whose appalling stewardship from 1905 to 1933 drove the *Post* into bankruptcy and to the humiliation of reporting its own sale, at a public auction on the office steps, for $875,000. It took ten years, and the loss of a further $20 million of the Meyer family's money, to restore the *Post* to financial health and journalistic credit. A Leo Rosten study of the Washington press corps in 1935 polled ninety-three Washington-based reporters who voted the *Post* as one of the seven 'least fair and reliable papers in the USA'.[3]

But then the *Washington Post* had faced an uphill battle from its very beginning, when it was launched to compete against five other daily newspapers in a city of only 130,000, a third of them black and but lately arrived from Southern states still devastated by war and reconstruction. In the words of Horace Greeley, the most eminent newspaperman of his day, it was a city 'of high rents, bad food, disgusting dirt, deep mud and deplorable morals'. His celebrated advice, to 'go West, young man', was aimed at the city's clerks.

The *Washington Post* was founded in December 1877 by Stilson Hutchins, who had founded and published newspapers in Iowa and Missouri, all of them devoted to the cause of the Democrat Party.[4] The *Post* was launched to be the party's voice in the capital. The first issue vowed 'to do what it can to uphold the Democratic majority in the House and the majestic Democratic minority in the Senate'.[5] Hutchins used the *Post* as a bludgeon to belabour the Republican President Hayes, and invariably referred to him as 'the bogus President' or 'His Fraudulency'.

Political passions aside, the new *Post* had three great merits. First, it reported politics, not just from Washington, but across the nation, and regularly held its presses until dawn to print the latest telegraphs on elections in California or political appointments in New York. Second, it wrote about politics in a cynical and knowing, but entertaining way. In its first week, the *Post* informed its readers: 'Nothing very well calculated to curdle the blood of the Nation occurred in any of the brain workshops of the Government yesterday. The meeting of the Cabinet was not important.'[6] Third, and most unusual for Washington, it covered foreign news. The first issue carried a front-page story on the Turko-Russian war, and by 1883 Hutchins had hired his first foreign correspondent, a Mrs Lucy Hooper, who filed social and cultural news from Paris.

Hutchins hired good reporters, and he wrote the best stories himself. His illustrated front-page story of 1880 on Edison's invention of the electric light bulb was a model of its kind. The article described the bulb, explained the principle on which it worked, described Mr Edison's laboratory, and analysed the profits he could expect to make and how long the bulbs lasted. It went on to assess the cost advantages of electric as against gas lighting, relating this to the cost of coal in Washington and New York, and speculated on the possible fate of gas shares on the stock exchange.[7] The *Post*'s passion for detail could be gruesome. For the execution day of President Garfield's assassin in 1881, the whole front page was deployed to recall the crime, the trial and the irony that on the day of the murder, the assassin's unpaid landlady had advertised in the *Post* for his whereabouts. Most striking of all was the dramatic layout of the front page, styled around a group of engravings which depicted the scaffold scene, the last walk to the gallows, the death watch, the last prayer in the prison cell, a landscaped view and a map of the prison itself, all topped up by two portraits of the assassin and one of his clergyman.[8] When the *Philadelphia Times* said that the *Post* was 'the first real newspaper that Washington has ever had', Hutchins proudly reprinted the praise on his front page.

Within a year of the first issue, Hutchins had reached a circulation of almost 12,000 copies a day, and had bought up a rival Republican paper, *The Union*. Success brought a moderation of tone. For President Garfield's inauguration, the *Post*'s editorial warned: 'If to be Democratic is to be stupidly and brutally partisan, then the *Post* is not Democratic.' The partisan Democratic paper of 1877 became an independently minded and rather complacent publication in the 1880s. The *Post* was cautious, and safely middle-of-the-road in its views. Fifteen years after the Civil War tempers still ran high on race, and the *Post* stepped warily: 'As a rule, the negroes of the South are rude and ignorant. Their personal manners and habits are disagreeable. . .But the work of education will go on, the negro will continue to improve.'[9] The *Post* could be firm enough when few of its readers were likely to disagree: 'The nomadic Indian must disappear. . .To the savage who will not submit to the inevitable, we should show the mailed hand of martial power.'[10]

Hutchins later reckoned that he had made between $25,000 and $40,000 profit in each of the *Post*'s first ten years. He did well enough to double the number of pages, from four to eight, and to buy yet another competitor. But once the *Post* had absorbed the fiercely partisan *National Republican*, there was less and less in Hutchins's paper likely to offend a Republican voter.[11] Hutchins had found a formula, one which was to be the essence of newspaper success in Washington. He had to satisfy two different audiences. There were the professional politicians and the civil servants who wanted a full account of political and administrative news. And then there were the Washingtonians, the people who wanted to know about street lamps and bad roads, and who wanted their newspaper to campaign on behalf of the city itself. Hutchins duly fought for the completion of the Washington Monument and to reclaim the Potomac marshes. Local issues could bring the fire back to his editorials: 'Must we be bathed in sewage, flooded with Potomac overflows and killed by malaria through lack of interest on the part of our lawmakers in the welfare of the Capital and its people?' Hutchins's local interest was not always so high-minded. The *Post*'s first special edition was devoted to the scandal of a New York Senator being driven at gun point from the Washington home of an ex-Governor of Rhode Island, after paying overmuch attention to the Governor's wife.[12]

By 1899, with circulation over 16,000, Hutchins had a new passion. After seeing a demonstration of a new linotype machine, he joined a syndicate to promote it, sold the *Post*, and went on to become a millionaire for his linotype investments. For $175,000, the *Post* was sold to a partnership. Frank Hatton was a Republican and a newspaperman and Beriah Wilkins was a Democrat and a banker, and the two of them agreed that their *Post* would follow, broadly, the Hutchins formula.[13] It was a profitable decision. By 1894, the *Post* was making over $100,000 a year. Hatton ran the editorial side of the paper and was professional enough to bring out at least two extra editions with the help only of the janitor. Wilkins ran the business. And the growth of the city of Washington almost guaranteed commercial success for the newspaper. Even financial depressions left Washington relatively untouched. As a *Post* editorial put it: 'This city is less dependent than any other on those branches of business that were crippled by the panic of '93.'[14] Washington's main employer was the federal government, and the steady growth of the federal payroll has been the backbone of the capital's prosperity.

That prosperity was reflected in the *Post*. By 1900, the daily paper was twelve or fourteen pages, more than half of them advertisements. The big Sunday paper, with thirty-six or forty-four pages, was over 60% advertising. Or, as the *Post* proudly said of its pre-Christmas *Sunday Post* in 1901: '122 columns more advertising than ever carried in a single issue by any of the *Post*'s contemporaries!' And the *Post* stuck to the Hatton formula of appealing to both the political and the local market. In the 1890s its own advertising announced that it was 'read at home, on the streetcars, and in the offices. It is ubiquitous.' By 1905, daily circulation was up to 34,000 and the *Sunday Post* sold 45,000.[15]

Both Hatton and Wilkins agreed that the *Post* was and should remain a more serious, more thoughtful newspaper than most of its rivals. The 1890s were the great days of the New York yellow press, with the *World* and the *Journal* battling for circulation with sensational stories from China and Cuba, and jingoistic appeals for America to follow its 'manifest destiny' as a great power. The *Post* was more cautious, counselling against war with Spain up to the day when Congress declared it. During the Boxer rebellion with China, the *Post* attacked the yellow press for calling the Boxers 'rabble'. To the *Post*, they were 'devoted patriots'.

And the *Post*'s editorials rejected the fashionable cant about the justifications for America's empire: 'All of the gabble about civilizing and uplifting the benighted barbarians of Cuba and Luzon is mere sound and fury, signifying nothing. Foolishly or wisely, we want those newly acquired possessions, not for any missionary or altruistic purposes, but for the trade, the commerce, the power and the money there are in them.'[16]

But the *Post* was still a relatively small paper. For reports from Cuba, it depended on printing the cables of the *New York Herald*. It was able to cover the assassination of President McKinley only because its managing editor, Scott Bone, happened to be in Buffalo on business. 1892 was the first year that the *Post* sent its own reporter to the national conventions which chose the presidential candidates. The *Post*'s sense of news was relaxed. When it received a cable from a Virginia local reporter about the Wright Brothers' early experiments with powered flight, the *Post* sat on the story for a day, and then printed a cautiously re-written version on page one. The *Post* asked for no further reports, and did not bother to send one of its own reporters to look into the story. The *Post* then ignored the Wright brothers until 1908, when other newspapers were printing sensational eye-witness accounts of the flights. The *Post* doubtfully printed an account, and then apologized in its editorials in case the story was a hoax.[17]

In other spheres, the *Post* was an adventurous, innovative paper. In 1891, it ran its first halftone photograph and by 1905 it was printing news photos of a Chicago strike. Hatton and Wilkins commissioned John Philip Sousa to write a 'Washington Post March' for one of its prize-giving ceremonies. The Sunday paper began to print fiction by Conan Doyle, Emile Zola and Bret Harte. Massive promotional editions were published for conventions and meetings in the city. When the Grand Army of the Republic held its reunion in Washington, the *Post* printed an eighty-eight-page special edition, which sold 283,105 copies. Two full-time cartoonists, George Coffin and Clifford Berryman, were hired and promoted as major features. It was Berryman who coined the national catch-phrase of the Spanish-American war, 'Remember the *Maine*', in a cartoon about the explosion of the American warship in a Cuban harbour.[18]

In 1905, after the death of Beriah Wilkins, the *Post* was bought by John McLean, publisher of the *Cincinnati Enquirer* and the major financial backer of the Democrat Party in Ohio. A close friend of William Randolph Hearst, McLean brought Hearst's taste for sensationalism and political influence to the *Post*. Crime and scandal stories became prominent in the paper, with special sports and colour comic sections in the Sunday edition. The *Post*'s name had been made on hard, political news, but McLean preferred to use the cheaper wire services, rather than invest in his own reporters. His own sense of news values was expressed in a letter to his Cincinnati editor in 1912: 'I would always try my best to print the good about the city – both in the news and editorial departments – for the people don't want to read or hear unpleasant news, no matter how true.'[19] The policy may have worked in Ohio, but the Washington audience wanted more from their papers; by 1911, circulation had drifted down by a third, to about 20,000, and McLean cut his price to two cents to win it back. The only feature of Washington life that was covered obsessively was the local baseball team. No reporters could be spared to cover the 1908 party conventions, and a 1912 report of the theft of the Mona Lisa from the Louvre was illustrated by the wrong picture. The *Post*'s standards were falling with its circulation. It ran fewer columns of foreign news, perhaps explained by a peevish 1906 editorial on the Algeciras Conference: 'this thing of being a "world power" is annoying; it is expensive; it may be dangerous'.[20]

The *Post* still had some journalists of quality. President Theodore Roosevelt's attempt at spelling provoked the headline: SUM FU WURDZ, FONETIC, AS TU THE NU SPELIN. But the general level of the staff had declined. In 1912, with but thirteen reporters in the city room, the City Editor Edward Rochester posted a notice that read: 'Two men were dismissed last week for inaccuracy and carelessness. Two others this week are to follow for the same reason.' But then, the *Post* had sunk to third place in Washington circulation, even though the city and its newspapers were growing fast. The automobile boom helped to keep up the advertising revenues, and to pay for the $154,000 which the McLean family spent on buying the fabulous Hope diamond. It was worn by the wife of Ned McLean, the publisher's son. The young couple's taste for extravagance was established by the $200,000 honeymoon. By contrast, the best profit the *Post* ever made under their stewardship was the $183,000 of 1919, fed by the post-war boom.

During the first three years of the First World War, the *Post* advocated neutrality for America, based its reports upon the propaganda sheets of both sides, but leant enough in the German direction for the British mission in the US to list it as the only influential paper in the Eastern USA to be pro-German. After the war, documents alleged to have come from the Germany Embassy suggested that the McLeans tried to sell or lease the *Post*'s services to the German Ambassador, but the family denied this.[21] And the *Post* became bloodthirstily patriotic enough once the US declared war. The editorial of 27 March 1918 catches its mood: 'The German nation will feel these losses for a generation to come. Well, let them die. German science, religion and culture have culminated in a race that worships evil.'

John McLean's death in 1916, and the inheritance of his son Ned led to no improvements at the *Post*, although the war's near-doubling of the capital's population boosted circulation. The *Post* had no reporter at the war (although one made two brief visits to France, mainly to take photographs), sent no reporter to cover the presidential campaigns of 1916, nor to the Paris peace conference with President Wilson in 1919. The only out-of-town reporting that McLean encouraged was for sporting events. He preferred news that broke conveniently on the *Post*'s doorstep. The Washington race riots of 1919, however, were undoubtedly fanned by the *Post*'s provocative reports of where and when the white vigilantes were gathering for the 'clean-up' which led to some forty deaths. Russia's 1917 Revolution led to pro-Bolshevik demonstrations in Washington, and the *Post*'s editorials gleefully joined the Red-baiting of the day, claiming that any 'whine about free speech and liberty is buncombe', and that 'all anarchistic speech and action are treasonable'. The *Post* lacked even the virtue of consistency, welcoming the first proposals of the League of Nations as 'a magnificent, a glorious dream. May it be realized', and then launching a bitter attack upon President Wilson himself and the League in particular.[22]

Behind these lurches of policy lay the increasing Republican fervour of Ned McLean. His father's Democratic loyalties gave way to Ned's growing friendship for the Republican presidential candidate Warren Harding, who put Ned in charge of his inaugural celebrations in Washington and stayed at the McLean home before moving into the White House. McLean's friendship with the Republicans led to his involvement in the Tea Pot Dome oil scandal, when Ned falsely claimed to have been the source of a mysterious $100,000 'loan' to Secretary of the Interior Albert Fall. He then had to retract the lie before a Senate investigating committee when it became clear that Fall's $100,000 had been a direct bribe from oil interests.[23]

The *Post*'s reputation had fallen miserably. The liberal editor Oswald Villard wrote that Washington journalists 'despise, dislike and distrust it; to them it is not only a poison sheet, it is also a contemptible one and they question its moral integrity'.[24] Between drinking bouts, Ned McLean flailed about for a solution. He paid the former Ambassador to London, George Harvey, $75,000 to edit the *Post* for a year. Harvey nailed the *Post*'s colours more firmly to the Republican mast, coining the election slogan 'Coolidge or chaos' in the *Post*'s columns, and instructing *Post* reporters to come round to the White House to pick up his editorials. He was a regular house-guest there, and wrote *Post* editorials one day and Coolidge's campaign speeches the next. By 1924, with the *Daily News* providing more competition on the streets, the *Post* began to lose money. Pillaging his father's estate, Ned McLean himself was still rich enough to be Washington's biggest income-tax payer that year.[25]

The *Post* had its redeeming features. Part of the reason for its circulation growth during the First World War was the wider use of cartoons, including the brilliant and savage Dutchman, Raemaekers. During the 1920s, George Rothwell Brown wrote a light, funny front-page column under the heading 'Post-scripts'. One classic example, on election funding in 1926, ran: 'The question in the Illinois primaries is not so much the amount contributed by the utility boys as how they expect to get it back.' In 1927 Brown himself did most of the work in compiling the 156-page anniversary issue, commemorating the *Post*'s fiftieth birthday. Within two years, Brown had left the *Post*, McLean had raised the cover price to three cents and the Wall Street Depression was upon the nation. The *Post* was but one of the victims. Its advertising revenues collapsed. On Roosevelt's election day, in 1932, there were precisely ten insertions in its 'Help Wanted' columns, and one of those was placed by the Empire barber shop which advertised 'Men wanted – for a haircut'. By 1933, with five daily newspapers competing in Washington, the *Post* had 12% of the city's circulation, less than 14% of its much-reduced advertising, and almost $500,000 in debts. Ned McLean's wife sued for divorce, and the bank sued to remove Ned as a co-trustee of his father's estate. In

1933, with circulation at 51,728 (much of it dubious) and its advertisement columns half empty in spite of repeatedly cut rates, the bankrupt paper was sold lock, stock and barrel for $875,000. In 1929, Ned had refused a $5 million bid from the same buyer, Eugene Meyer, investment banker, founder of Allied Chemical, and a former director of the War Finance Corporation.[26]

Meyer began the process of resuscitation. He bought new type, spent $367,000 on extended premises and improved presses, hired Felix Morley from the Brooking Institution to run the editorial page, and summoned Elliot Thurston from the *New York World* to build a national news team. One of the first jobs was to assign a full-time reporter to the White House, where Roosevelt's New Deal was being launched. Meyer had a legal fight that went up to the Supreme Court to keep the *Post*'s comic strips from the rival *Washington Herald*. Meyer later recalled that 'in my first two years I made every mistake in the book', but the revival had begun. In 1935, Felix Morley's editorial won the *Post* its first Pulitzer Prize, and Meyer's decision to print and promote the revolutionary new Gallup polls brought new readership. But the cost was stunning. Meyer lost over $1,191,000 in 1934, and almost $1,280,000 in 1935. In Meyer's first sixteen years, he ran through thirteen circulation managers. But by 1938, with Meyer digging deeper into his pocket to hire fifteen new columnists, including Walter Lippmann, circulation was up to 100,000 copies a day, and the *Post* had the second biggest share of the city's press advertising, led only by the *Star*. The editorial and opinion pages were the flagship of the reviving *Post*, and the news columns depended heavily on the wire services. But Roosevelt's New Deal tripled the number of federal employees in Washington, and Meyer's wealth kept the *Post* afloat, even though in one year the *Post*'s losses exceeded his own income.[27]

Meyer himself was an asset. The *Post*'s greatest scoop of the 1930s, the King of England's plan to marry Mrs Simpson, even at the cost of abdication, came from the future British Ambassador Lord Lothian, a guest at Meyer's home.[28] And the increasingly strident editorial warnings of the dangers of fascism and war in Europe came at Meyer's insistence, even though they led in 1940 to the resignation of his senior leader-writer, Felix Morley.[29] The outbreak of war in Europe had Meyer reaching into his pocket again to buy the *New York Times*'s news service, and the cost sent the *Post*'s annual deficit soaring over $1,000,000 again. But for Meyer, the need to prepare America for what he saw as an inevitable war took on the intensity of a crusade. By October 1940, each day's front page was headed 'It's later than you think', and the editorials urging military aid for Britain became thunderous: 'We are in a state of war, whether we call it war or defence or what have you. . .the only alternative open to us is surrender or resistance.'[30]

America's entry into the war brought newsprint rationing and a dilemma for publishers: whether to cut back on advertising and increase circulation or to reduce sales but wax fat on the advertisers. Meyer took the second decision. In 1941, advertising had taken only 40% of the *Post*'s pages. By 1944, the paper was 50% advertising, spurred by Meyer's idea that advertisers could get tax rebates on 'public service' ads. This policy brought the first *Post* profits since Meyer's purchase – $249,000 by 1945. But the wartime shortage of staff helped to force his decision. By late 1942, it was a rare day when more than two of the average eight front-page stories were written by *Post* reporters. Eugene Meyer's wife Agnes was called in to help fill the columns. But the war had helped to cut production costs. The 1,700 employees of 1933 had been cut to fewer than 800 by 1945, with conscription and full employment.[31]

With the end of the war, the *Post* became even more a family affair, with Philip Graham, the husband of Meyer's daughter Katherine, brought in as associate publisher. Graham had been one of Washington's bright young men of the 1930s, law clerk to Supreme Court Justice Felix Frankfurter, then an attorney with the Lend-Lease office, and he spent his war in Military Intelligence. His Washington connections, and his intense drive to become one of the key policy-makers in this new Washington that was the capital of the free world, set the *Post* on a dramatic new course. Graham wanted influence, and he wanted profits. When he tried to recruit the leading columnist of the day, James Reston, Graham told him: 'I want a miniature *New York Times*.'[32] But in 1945 the *Post* was barely holding its own. One of four daily papers in the city, it had only 24% of the circulation, 22% of the advertising. With Meyer's firm backing, Graham began buying radio and TV stations and publishing a fold-in tabloid TV guide, which became the Sunday edition's biggest circulation booster. Graham hired Russell Wiggins from the *New York Times* to be managing editor, and gave him a news budget of $670,000 a year. By 1948, Graham was in sole charge.[33] Meyer had transferred the bulk of the shares to his son-in-law's name, and in 1954 Meyer guaranteed the *Post*'s future with an $8.5 million payment for the major morning rival, the *Washington Times-Herald*. By keeping all of the *Times-Herald*'s comic strips, all of its experienced sports writers, almost all of the columnists, the *Post* hung on to 85% of the *Times-Herald*'s circulation. The newsprint cost went up 250% but it was a small price to pay for having a monopoly of the city's morning readership. The *Post*'s circulation soared up to 380,000, the ninth highest in the nation. Phil Graham had spent eight years painfully hauling circulation up from a wartime level of 160,000 to 200,000 by the time of the purchase. He had used every trick he knew to increase sales. The *Times-Herald* ran a popular bloodthirsty and salacious page three. Phil Graham brought a similar page three to the *Post*, known to his staff as 'the blood, guts and semen page'. He knew comics were popular, and he began printing forty strips every Sunday, more than any other American paper. But it took the *Times-Herald* merger to make the *Post* profitable, and it took profits to begin the process of expansion which Phil Graham desperately needed to give him the political influence he craved. The year after the purchase, the *Post* began to make a steady $2 million profit a year.[34]

And Graham had not only absorbed a rival paper – he had swallowed a critic. Throughout the long domestic agony that became known as McCarthyism, the *Times-Herald*, along with the rest of the ultra-conservative press, had sneered at the *Post* as 'the Washington edition of *Pravda*'. The very phrase 'McCarthyism' was coined in one of Herblock's bitter cartoons, and the *Post*'s editorial attacks on the witch-hunting and the mood of fear in Washington gave it a reputation for courage that it did not really deserve. Sometimes the courage gave way to Graham's desire for influence. In the last weeks before the 1952 presidential election, Graham stopped Herblock's cartoons, beginning with a cartoon which showed McCarthy and the vice-presidential candidate Richard Nixon with pots of tar in their hands, ready to smear.[35] Graham cultivated Nixon, played golf with him, and wrote an editorial which praised Nixon's notorious 'Checkers' speech and said that Nixon had spoken 'eloquently and movingly'. The *Post* was backing Eisenhower in the election; indeed, Eugene Meyer had flown to Europe to persuade Eisenhower to stand and had raised support and funds for him in Washington; and the *Post* had serialized a hagiographic biography of Ike, 'The man from Abilene', in the election year. Graham himself was master of ceremonies at a fund-raising show for Eisenhower and Nixon on the eve of the election.[36]

Phil Graham's own political position was that of a hard-line cold warrior. When the *Post* ran an editorial on the idea of co-existence with the Russians, he sent down an angry memo which read 'Co-existence is every ounce a bastard idea, sired by Wish and mothered by Cold War weariness'.[37] He opposed the witch-hunting tactics of Senator McCarthy, but had to be dissuaded from firing his liberal editorial writer Alan Barth, who had commended a Communist for not betraying his friends to a congressional investigating committee. Graham's undoubted skills and his personal charm and intelligence gave him an influence in Washington which recalled that of the British press barons in London, an American Lord Northcliffe and Lord Beaverbrook. It was Graham, for example, who brought the John Kennedy–Lyndon Johnson ticket together for the 1960 presidential election.[38] But his influence put him so much at the centre of Washington life that the independence of the *Post*, on several occasions, suffered directly. Ben Bradlee, later to become the *Post*'s most celebrated editor, was a young reporter in 1950 when a series of race riots broke out over the city's segregated swimming-pools. He wrote a powerful story, then found it savagely cut and the riots scaled down to 'disturbances' on Graham's authority. Graham used the threat of publishing the story to force Washington officials to promise to desegregate the pools the following year.[39] The ends may have justified the means. But in 1959, before the ill-fated flight of the U-2 spy-plane over Russia which doomed the Paris summit, the *Post* knew about the flights and knew that the government was lying, or prevaricating about them. It decided, in the national interest, not to print.[40] The *Post* took the same decision (and Phil Graham killed a critical editorial) in 1961, when it had foreknowledge of the disastrous Bay of Pigs invasion of Cuba. Graham himself and a number of his senior journalists were so close to the machinery of government, and so convinced that the US was locked in a Manichean struggle with the evils of Communism, that they compromised the paper's independence. The conventional morality of the day would certainly have supported them, and one of the journalists involved, Chalmers Roberts, later wrote that he and Graham 'found no fault with such a CIA operation and hoped it would succeed in what they perceived as the national interest'.[41] Even more surprisingly, in 1954 at a semi-public dinner with several reporters present, a former chief of the CIA, Bedell Smith, related in a speech how the CIA had spent (in vain) some $200,000 in bribes in the French parliament, trying to buy support for the European Defence Community. The reporter, Chalmers Roberts, sent Graham a memo on the incident, but neither even considered printing it.[42]

The late 1950s were fat years for the *Post*, as it overhauled the *Star* to seize the majority of press advertising. Making more than $2 million a year from the *Post* and another $5 million from radio and TV, the *Post* was curiously slow to plough these profits back into the improved paper which Graham insisted he wanted. In 1953, he had written to Meyer from a European tour: 'What I wouldn't give to have $100,000 a year to spend on three or four good correspondents overseas. We won't be doing a proper job in the capital until we can manage that.' In 1956 he told *Time* magazine (who outlined a cover-story on him and the new *Post*) that he wanted to see the *Post* as internationally famous and respected as the London *Times* or *New York Times*.[43] But the *Post*'s national desk still had only seven men (the *New York Times* had more than twenty on the same job – in the *Post*'s own city), and his first foreign correspondent was only sent abroad, to London, in 1957. It took another five years for the next foreign bureau to open, in New Delhi.[44] A major reason for the hesitant growth of the *Post* was Phil Graham's growing mental illness, which harassed executives began discreetly to call 'Problem A'. His suicide in 1963 came after erratic years of drinking, adultery, scandals which threatened to become public, hysterical phone-calls to his friend President Kennedy, and some periods of brilliant, creative rationality.[45] It was in those rational interludes that he laid the foundation for building the *Post* into a vast, conglomerate publishing empire, by buying *Newsweek* magazine in 1961, for $15 million (only $75,000 of it was paid for in the *Post*'s cash).[46] In the same year, Graham agreed to a suggestion from the publisher of the *Los Angeles Times* that the two papers unite to provide an international news service, which seemed like a way of building a network of foreign correspondents on the cheap.

At the time of Graham's death, James Reston told Katherine Graham that she had inherited 'a mediocre, erratic paper that had no discipline', and Walter Lippmann added that the *Post* was 'sluggish and not adventurous'. On particular stories, where the *Post*'s advantage of intimacy with government was useful, it could do magnificent work. Perhaps the best example was the Cuban missile crisis of 1962 where the *Post*'s well-informed analytical features on the management of the crisis were spread around the nation through the new joint news service. Interestingly, the *Post* had a scoop with its first article, saying that a crisis was brewing over Cuba, before any statement had come from the White House. Significantly, the *Post*'s scoop was printed only because the White House had thought to call only the *New York Times* to ask them not to print any advance speculation – it had not thought the *Post* of 1962 worth warning off.[47]

Mrs Graham, who had gained reporting experience covering the waterfront and labour struggles for the *San Francisco Post* in the 1930s, had then chosen to stay in the domestic background while her brilliant husband ran the *Post*. As soon as she took over, the Washington seduction process began. The new President Lyndon Johnson invited her down to his Texan ranch. She wrote to a friend that she felt 'like the heroine of one's childhood fairy tales' and stunned her editorial page editor by gaily telling Johnson, just before the 1964 election: 'We are for you 100%.' But 1964 showed up some of the *Post*'s weaknesses. The race riots in the cities of the North were covered for the *Post* by the wire services, not its own reporters. And the growing war in Vietnam, where American 'advisers' had been fighting and dying for almost three years, received little attention until 1964, when the *Post* belatedly opened a bureau in Saigon.[48]

In 1965, Mrs Graham began to rebuild the *Post* in her own image. She hired Ben Bradlee from *Newsweek* to come as the new editor, and she began to spend money. The news budget in 1962 had been $2.9 million. By 1969 it was $7.3 million. In the same period, the staff was increased by 35%, the average number of pages in the paper almost doubled from fifty-six to 100 a day, circulation rose by 15% and the annual profit on each copy of the *Post* sold rose from $10.86 to $17.2. The very shape of the *Post* had changed. By 1969, the proportion of editorial space (to advertising) had fallen to only 31% and annual profits had almost doubled, from $4.6 million to $8.8 million. Mrs Graham's *Post* bought into paper-mills in Canada, into warehousing in Washington and TV stations in Florida. Between 1963 and 1978, the income from TV soared from $7.6 million to $52.3 million. Some of the money was being ploughed back into newsgathering. By 1976, the *Post* had sixteen foreign correspondents working abroad. And by 1980, Bradlee presided over a $24 million budget for news and an editorial team of 445 reporters and aides to fill the expanded *Post*. The nine-man national desk of 1961 had become a department of forty-nine people by 1980. The *Post* had become the flagship of a corporate fleet under Mrs Graham, with newspaper division profits increasing almost tenfold from $4.6 million in 1963 to $41.4 million in 1978.[49]

That process of growth created its own internal contradictions. They were seen most clearly in the widening gap between the critical way the news columns reported the Vietnam war and the rigid anti-Communist commentaries of the editorial pages. 'They are worth two divisions to me', the beleaguered President Johnson said of the *Post*'s editorial pages, as domestic and press criticism of the war became more strident.[50] The *Post* tradition is that the editorial columns are wholly independent of the rest of the paper. The effect, until the veteran Russ Wiggins left the editorial chair for one of President Johnson's last appointments as lame-duck Ambassador to the UN, became almost schizophrenic. When the Reverend Martin Luther King came out against the Vietnam war, the *Post*'s editorial thundered: 'He has diminished his usefulness to his cause, to the country and to his people.' And when Harrison Salisbury of the *New York Times* began reporting from Hanoi on the effect of American bombing upon North Vietnamese civilians, the *Post* sneered that Salisbury was simply being used by Ho Chi Minh as a new tactic – 'one as clearly conceived as the poison-tipped bamboo spikes his men emplanted underfoot for the unwary enemy'.[51] By contrast, on the news pages Ward Just was reporting that the war 'may be unwinnable' and that: 'We are here defending freedom as we understand it for people who don't.'[52]

But Bradlee hired new blood by the gallon, and the new *Post* overwhelmed the old. David Broder came as political correspondent from the *New York Times*. Stan Karnow, Ward Just, Art Buchwald, Nicholas von Hoffman, all were summoned to the new *Post* whose layout and design were being transformed and modernized by Dave Lavanthol, using pictures sent back from Vietnam by the *Post*'s own photographers, dispatched at last by Bradlee. The new men, on occasion, ran rough-shod over the old. After three vain years fighting off Bradlee's demands for a bigger news budget, veteran publisher John Sweeterman took early retirement. And another of Bradlee's recruits, Richard Harwood, informed the old hands that they had run 'a schlock newspaper'. In its hiring and its presentation, the *Post* of the late 1960s was a very hungry paper. But it was still sloppy in its sub-editing and typography, still woefully erratic in its reporting. In 1965, it suffered the humiliation of being judged 'less fair and reliable' than its now-humbled rival, the *Washington Star*, in a poll of Washington correspondents.[53]

These internal tensions were not simply the *Post*'s growing pains but part of a wider national process. The *Post* of the 1950s had seen itself as classically liberal: against race segregation, against McCarthyism and, rather than saying simply that it was anti-Communist, it would have argued that it was against totalitarianism of both Right and Left. In the 1960s, such political definitions became more complex. The *Post*'s editorial attack on Martin Luther King

illustrates the point. The *Post* under Phil Graham had been committed to civil rights and to rehabilitation of Washington's slum areas,
inhabited mainly by blacks. Phil Graham had put his and the *Post*'s
energies and prestige behind an ambitious plan to rehabilitate
Anacostia, one such area. The real social effect of this well-
intentioned campaign was to make black families homeless as affluent
young whites moved into a newly fashionable area. Phil Graham's
historic policy of minimizing the race issue in riots was applied yet
again in 1962 when thirty-two people were injured as blacks fought
whites after a Washington football game. The story of the fighting
made page one, but the fact that 'the racial element was involved' was
buried deep in the story. Simeon Booker, the *Post*'s first black
reporter who had resigned ('I was only allowed to use one bathroom
on the editorial floor at the *Post*'), told the facts of the riot – in a letter
to the editor.[54] The old policy of sanitizing news in the interests of
racial harmony was no longer tenable. The *Post* began to hire black
reporters (spurred on, like so many papers, by the need to have black
newsmen who could cover a rioting ghetto with at least a degree of
impunity), and found themselves, in 1972, facing a new kind of race
problem. By 1972, almost 10% of the 400 newsroom employees were
black, a higher proportion than on any other paper in the country.
But a group of black writers argued that the *Post* was not doing
enough, that its hiring policy smacked of tokenism, and that black
writers were deliberately sidetracked on to minor stories. Finally they
filed formal charges of discrimination against the *Post*. The paper's
respected black columnist, Bill Raspberry, commented in his column
that the paper 'has done more than any other white newspaper in the
country both in terms of its editorial policy and in terms of its newsroom hiring practices. And when you do more, more is expected of
you. The expectation is, in fact, a compliment.'[55]

But the *Post* was facing attack from another direction. The Nixon
presidency was the spur which drove the paper on to greatness. It
began with a defensive battle. Vice-President Spiro Agnew launched
a series of attacks on the 'effete elite' media of the East Coast, the TV
networks and the liberal press. His attacks led the *Post* to appoint its
own ombudsman, Richard Harwood, who acted as house critic of the
Post's performance and lightning-rod for the public complaints (and
cancelled subscriptions) which followed the Agnew criticisms.
Harwood began an unprecedented process of newspaper introspection, analysing the *Post*'s columns for their selection, presentation and writing of the news. Some of his findings were striking. The

Post's coverage of the 1970 congressional elections turned out to be stunningly biased – in favour of Nixon's Republican Party. The *Post* ran thirty front-page stories, totalling 268 column-inches, on the Republican campaign, and only six page-one stories, of thirty-five inches, on the Democrats. Harwood concluded: 'We salivated over the Republicans for one reason only – the President was out campaigning for them.'[56]

But the Nixon attacks on the *Post* were not limited to rhetoric. The *Post*'s purchases of TV stations and its corporate ambitions had left the organization vulnerable. Licences to operate those stations depended on federal approval, and Nixon's White House planned deliberately to punish the *Post* by withdrawing those licences. The onslaught drove the *Post*'s Stock Exchange price down from $38 to $21.[57] This consideration was an unseen but leading character at the *Post*'s first great drama of the Nixon years, the decision whether or not to follow the lead of the *New York Times* in publishing the Pentagon Papers. Not only were the TV stations at risk, but the *Post* was also about to become a public company, offering its shares for sale on the Stock Exchange. The underwriters of that stock offer would have been entitled to withdraw their support if the *Post*'s decision to publish had been condemned by the courts. The final decision, at a party with Ben Bradlee on one phone and her business manager on the other, was taken by Mrs Graham alone.[58] It was the most courageous, because the most concentrated, decision of her publishing career. It could have bankrupted the corporation. The *Post* was still running second, behind the *New York Times*, but publication of the documents, when the government had already invoked 'national security', broke decisively with the old tradition of automatic support for government. 'It could not have happened without Vietnam,' Ben Bradlee commented. 'Vietnam changed all the rules. They rammed it down our throats that they lied, lied and lied again.'[59] It should be added that the Nixon administration, dominated by Californians and scornful of the traditional East Coast elite, did not have the personal contacts with the *Post* that sweetened press–presidential relations in the 1950s and 1960s.

The *Post*'s courage, dedication and tenacity in its Watergate coverage is too well known to need re-telling. It was a landmark of modern journalism, and it established the *Post* firmly as a great and courageous newspaper. But had the *Post* of 1972 not already achieved a rare degree of prominence and repute, the slow encroachment of its revelations might have been brushed aside. Had the Bradlee era not built up the international network and name of the *Post*, had those steady investments in staff and talent not been made, or had the utter determination to make the *Post* into a great national institution not been there, then the whole interlocking process of congressional inquiry, of Judge Sirica's court and the moves towards Nixon's impeachment might never have taken place. And the *Post* was mature enough, vast enough, to nourish many views. The ever-independent editorial page, which had always insisted that only a proven crime should topple a President, did not finally call for Nixon's resignation until the morning of the day that he resigned.

But in the words of Bradlee: 'Watergate was a helluva act to follow.' The paper's Metro desk, whose deadlines had been pushed back to 5 p.m. by the priority of Watergate coverage, suffered a great fall in morale. 'Every reporter starts looking for Watergates everywhere, and all the editors get cautious,' Bradlee recalled.[60] But the energies of the paper were distracted by a series of industrial disputes that culminated in a dramatic strike of the men who operated the giant presses. Since about 1970, newspapers have been living with the promise and implications of two technological revolutions in their industry. The first, in photo-typesetting and offset printing, known as the cold-type process, can save up to 30% of production costs. The second revolution, using lasers to engrave offset plate directly, rather than setting the traditional type, can save another 25% in production costs. The bulk of those savings comes in the wages of redundant printers. In 1972, the *Washington Post* employed just over 1,000 men in the printing process. By 1980, they employed 480. In 1990, they plan to employ fewer than 150.[61] This means the death of an ancient and skilled craft, and the understandable anger this generated among the *Post*'s printers led not only to a strike but to an attack upon the printing presses themselves, with axes and acid and fire, and further assaults upon *Post* executives and foremen. Tom Wilkinson, the assistant managing editor, has a bullet-hole in his office window as a reminder of the passions that were aroused.[62] The *Post* management had prepared for the strike, sending employees to a 'scab school' where they learned how to publish a newspaper without printers. The *Post* lost only one day's papers. Plates were helicoptered to outside presses, advertising supplements were trucked north from Florida. And in the callous words of the *Post*'s President, Mack Meagher, when the strike had been broken it left 'one union dead on the battlefield and others that have been chastened by the combat'.[63]

Productivity went up 20%, overtime worth $1.2 million a year was eliminated, and as publishing costs fell profits began to soar, from 10.4% of revenue in 1973 to 17.1% in 1978. In 1978, after the victory, the *Post*'s payroll cost as a proportion of revenue was 29.7%, compared to over 40% on the *New York Times*. Between 1973 and 1978, the *Post*'s profit per employee went from a healthy $4,781 a year to a stunning $17,250.[64]

Those profits reflected not only a union 'dead on the battlefield', but also a different, and more profitable, kind of paper. The paper was fat with advertising: two out of every three pages were sold to advertisers in 1978. And the *Post* was no longer simply a newspaper. Since 1969, it had a 'Style' section for features, gossip, aimed at the affluent young reader whose lifestyle needed grooming and direction. The *Post* also spawned a 'Weekend' section, dedicated to leisure, listings of theatres, and to advertising. The first section of the *Post* was a national and international newspaper, the second was a local newspaper for Washington, and the rest was a daily magazine. Traditionalists grumbled, but the advertisers and the readers endorsed the changes. Since the launch of 'Style', circulation has risen by 15%.

By 1980, the editorial mix of the paper had settled in the following proportions. The figures are in columns per day:

Style	17
National news	14
Sports	15
Comics/Features	12.5
Financial news	10
Metro news	12
Foreign news	8

Interestingly, in a readers' survey in 1979, it was found that readers enjoyed the *Post* most for its foreign news.[65]

The future of the *Post* is now in the hands of Phil and Mrs Graham's son Don, a young man who fought in Vietnam, worked as a policeman in Washington, reported for the *Post* and *Newsweek* and won his managerial spurs for his devoted work in bringing the paper out during the strike. He is determined to improve the *Post*'s local city coverage, and insists that he runs, not an elite national paper, but 'a big city daily. Some of our readers are in the White House or State Department, but a lot more of them are poor blacks, or struggling middle-income people in the suburbs.' He speaks eloquently of his time as a policeman: 'The city I saw out there in the streets was not adequately reflected in the news columns of the paper. We have to improve that.' But Washington is a peculiar city. The average black-household income in the *Post*'s area is higher than the average white-household income in the US as a whole. The *Post* had become a suburban newspaper, with less than a quarter of its circulation being sold inside the District of Columbia itself. And as one *Post* readership survey put it, 'With every price increase, we whiten the readership another shade.'[66]

The *Post*'s policy, as expressed by its editors and its publisher, is to reverse that process. But the *Post* is unusual in having its own resident futurologist, Chris Burns, vice-president for planning. He is a man who talks in millions of dollars, pointing out that the *Post* has already spent $25 million on the new printing technology, with plans to spend another $100 million in the next decade. But at the end of that decade, instead of the current 100-page *Post*, fat with classified ads and selling 600,000 copies at twenty-five cents, he foresees a forty-page paper, only one-third of it advertising, selling for up to a dollar a copy. Competition from data-banks, he believes, will rob the news-paper of the bulk of its classified ads. (This process had begun in London in 1978, when used-car buyers and sellers began to make contact through a computer rather than the classified columns.) The loss of classified would remove half the *Post*'s revenue and force it to attract high-price advertisers by delivering a more precisely defined and affluent readership. Such readers would want a lot of news, and a lot of expert comment and analysis, and they would be prepared to pay for it. The *Post* would still make money but, more important, it would generate prestige which would allow the corporation as a whole to make more money from other ventures, in information packaging, making TV programmes and the software of the coming information revolution. 'We are in the news centre of the world. There is a growing market for the information and the stories that we don't even bother to print. Our objective is to be the dominant source of inform-ation about the US government, world diplomacy and America. We'll cede Stock Exchange information to the *Wall Street Journal*. But that's our future.'[67]

But the *Post*'s future began to look considerably more complex in 1981, as the paper's senior journalists began an internal competition to succeed the almost legendary Ben Bradlee. Keenness and ambition were evidently at the root of the shattering scandal which saw the *Post* win, and then lose, the prestigious Pulitzer Prize for one of its new, young and black reporters, Janet Cooke. Her eye-witness account of watching an eight-year-old child become a heroin junkie was an invention. Once alerted by a wire agency to the fact that Ms Cooke had lied about her academic credentials, the *Post* interrogated Ms Cooke intensively until she confessed that her story was untrue.[68] Beginning its leading article with the words 'We apologize', the *Post* also printed a full report by its ombudsman which acknowledged that there had been 'a total systems failure' in the paper's internal mechanism for defining and judging its stories.[69] He also judged that Bob Woodward, the editor in charge of local news, had been 'negligent'. (Woodward's reputation was to be partially redeemed later in the year by an article on CIA misbehaviour which saw a CIA deputy director resign within forty-eight hours.) The ombudsman went on to suggest that the doctrine of bitter rivalry among young *Post* reporters, the follow-Watergate syndrome, was also to blame.

The scandal provoked a mood of guilt, introspection and defiance at the *Post* which led to a further embarrassment, a story in the 'Ear' gossip column which claimed that outgoing President Jimmy Carter had bugged the incoming Reagans. Under the threat of a million-dollar libel writ, the *Post* publicly apologized for the story in a front-page retraction signed by Donald Graham.[69] But if the *Post*'s reputation had suffered, its financial position was enhanced. In August 1981, its only rival for the abundant local retail advertising market, the *Washington Star*, closed with losses of some $40 million.[70] The economics of American big-city newspapers, as much as the merits of one newspaper over another, meant that the *Post*'s profits were secure enough for it to consider launching a new evening paper in Washington, even while its failure as a reliable newspaper had undone so much of the good name which Watergate had won. As the *New York Times* commented: 'When a reputable newspaper lies, it poisons the community. Every newspaper story becomes suspect.'[71]

Notes

1. *The Washington Post, the first 100 years*, Chalmers M. Roberts, p. 76.
   A recent survey of US Congressmen showed that 82% read the *Washington Post* each day, 67% read the *New York Times*, and 31% the *Wall Street Journal*. No other paper approached this breadth of congressional readership. See 'What America's leaders read', *Public Opinion Quarterly*, 38, Spring 1974.
2. Author's interview, Howard Simons.
3. Quoted in *Lords of the Press*, G. Seldes, pp. 295–7.

4. Roberts, *op. cit.*, ch. 1, *passim*.
5. *Washington Post*, 6.xii.1877.
6. Roberts, *op. cit.*, p. 8.
7. *Washington Post*, 2.i.1880.
8. *Washington Post*, 6.xii.1927, fiftieth anniversary supplement.
9. *Washington Post*, 23.ix.1879.
10. *Washington Post*, 8.x.1879.
11. Roberts, *op. cit.*, p. 13.
12. *ibid.*, p. 12.
13. *ibid.*, pp. 42ff.
14. *ibid.*, p. 44.
15. *ibid.*, p. 77.
16. *Washington Post*, 14.i.1900.
17. Roberts, *op. cit.*, p. 76.
18. *ibid.*, p. 81.
19. Quoted *ibid.*, p. 88.
20. *ibid.*, p. 90.
21. *ibid.*, pp. 125–6, 146.
22. *ibid.*, p. 156.
23. *ibid.*, pp. 170–81.
24. *ibid.*, p. 162.
25. *ibid.*, pp. 176–9.
26. *Washington Post*, 18.xii.1977, *Centennial*, supplement to *Washington Post*. See also *Eugene Meyer*, M. J. Pusey, pp. 242–8.
27. Roberts, *op. cit.*, p. 218.
28. Pusey, *op. cit.*, p. 270.
29. Roberts, *op. cit.*, p. 231.
30. *ibid.*, p. 233.
31. See *Keeping Posted*, ed. L. L. Babb. See also Roberts, *op. cit.*, pp. 241–2.
32. *The Powers That Be*, D. Halberstam, p. 224.
33. Pusey, *op. cit.*, pp. 356–380.
34. *ibid.*, pp. 382–4. See also Roberts, *op. cit.*, pp. 315ff.
35. Halberstam, *op. cit.*, p. 193.
36. *Pillars of the Post*, H. Bray, pp. 7–10.
37. Bray, *op. cit.*, p. 31.
38. Halberstam, *op. cit.*, p. 314.
39. *ibid.*, p. 161.
40. Roberts, *op. cit.*, p. 325.
41. Roberts, *op. cit.*, p. 350. See also Halberstam, *op. cit.*, p. 375.
42. Roberts, *op. cit.*, p. 324.
43. *ibid.*, p. 315. Pusey, *op. cit.*, p. 386.
44. Roberts, *op. cit.*, p. 286. Also author's interviews, Phil Foisie, Ben Bradlee.
45. Roberts, *op. cit.*, p. 363.
46. Halberstam, *op. cit.*, p. 364.
47. *ibid.*, p. 520.
48. Roberts, *op. cit.*, p. 372. See also Halberstam, *op. cit.*, p. 530.
49. Roberts, *op. cit.*, pp. 377–9. Also author's interviews, B. Bradlee, Howard Simon.

50. Halberstam, *op. cit.*, p. 529.
51. *ibid.*, p. 534. Also author's interview, Meg Greenfield, editorial page, *Washington Post*.
52. Roberts, *op. cit.*, p. 385.
53. Author's interview, Richard Harwood. See also Roberts, *op. cit.*, pp. 379ff. Halberstam, *op. cit.*, p. 536.
54. *Washington Post*, 26.xi.1962.
55. Roberts, *op. cit.*, p. 427.
56. Author's interview, Richard Harwood. See also Babb, *op. cit.*, p. 91.
57. Roberts, *op. cit.*, p. 428.
58. Halberstam, *op. cit.*, pp. 577–8; Roberts, *op. cit.*, p. 419.
59. Author's interview, B. Bradlee.
60. *ibid.*
61. Author's interview, Larry Wallace, *Washington Post* vice-president, labour relations.
62. Author's interview, Tom Wilkinson, assistant managing editor. *Washington Post*, 29.ii.1976, Outlook supplement on the strike, by Robert G. Kaiser.
63. Kaiser, *op. cit.*
64. Author's interview, Donald Graham, *Washington Post* publisher. See also *Update, facts about the Washington Post Company*. See also *Facts about the Washington Post Company*, undated.
65. Author's interview, Howard Simons, managing editor.
66. Author's interview, Donald Graham.
67. Author's interview, Chris Burns, vice-president for planning.
68. *Guardian*, 18.iv.81.
69. *Washington Post*, 17.iv.1981. See also the *Guardian*, 18.iv.1981.
70. *ibid.*
71. *The Times*, 7.iv.1981.
72. The *New York Times*, 17.iv.1981.

Note: Interviews took place in Washington, DC, during March 1980.

WASHINGTON POST: EDITORIALS

The independence of India: 5 June 1947

'The statesmanship that attended the union of the American or the German states is only a tithe of the statesmanship that is needed to cement an independent India. This country, we are sure, will watch its exercise with sympathy and prayerful anxiety, for a great deal is at stake for all of us in the liberation of the great and populous subcontinent of India. . .

'At any rate, the British have fulfilled their pledges handsomely. In the light of what has happened of late in India, they may now be acquitted in the eyes of our Anglophobes of "divide and conquer" administration in India.'

The independence of Israel: 10 May 1948

'The low estate to which American foreign policy has been dragged by all these manoeuvres is pretty shocking. Equally disturbing is that our backing and filling has injured the United Nations. What is happening at Lake Success is a reminder of the Ethiopian dispute of 1936. That dispute killed the League of Nations. In Lake Success, talk: in Palestine action. . .Wisdom is said to be attention to realities, and the time has long since passed when we ought to catch up with realities. We suggest that instead of lagging behind history, we get in front of it. That is to say, we should make history, as our world power requires.'

The Berlin blockade and airlift: 5 April 1948

'To retreat under threats. . .would be gravely to undercut our influence in Europe and virtually to invite Moscow to go ahead with its conquests.'

The Communists win power in China: 5 January 1949

'Mao Tse-tung is like Tito in this: he owes precious little to Moscow in a positive way for his success. . .Mao Tse-tung is his own architect of his Communist victories. And, if the present has any relation to the past, he is a nationalist.'

The Korean war: 28 September 1950

'The U.N. exercised trusteeship over all of Korea and supervised elections designed for the whole country; the artificial division arose because Russia flouted the General Assembly. There is not the slightest reason for the United Nations to modify its original stand for a united Korea if military forces find it necessary to go north of the parallel.'

The Suez invasion: 1 November 1956

'Over the long run history is likely to judge the British-French military intervention in Egypt by whether it succeeds. . .But if their gamble fails, they will have plunged not only themselves but also their European neighbors into an oil drought. . .But if they are wrong, what they will have unleashed is unending religious and racial war against the Western white man, with ramifications to the tip of Africa and the end of Asia. . .Even if they "win", they have damaged the Western moral base for protest against Soviet imperialism.'

The Russian invasion of Hungary: 2 November 1956

The flame of freedom and independence burns in Budapest and beckons to the free world to save it from extinction.'

The Bay of Pigs assault on Cuba: 19 April 1961

'The sternness of the warning bears some resemblance to the rattling of rockets by Mr Khrushchev at the time of Suez. If now the invasion should fail, it would appear to the world as if the Soviet Union had saved his Cuban stooges by intimidating the United States. That is the unlovely prospect that may confront this country unless the effort to deliver Cuba from the Communists quickly catches hold.'

The Cuban missile crisis: 23 October 1962

'The actions outlined by the President are not extreme. He has proclaimed a "strict quarantine" on all offensive weapons destined for Cuba. . .This much is unmistakably clear. The vital interests of the nation have been jeopardized. Friends and allies of the United States in all parts of the world need to understand that this country has found the emergence of offensive Communist power in the Caribbean intolerable and has launched the necessary measures to liquidate that threat. . .No rational person can say that this defensive posture on the part of the United States is carrying the world to the brink of war.'

The Gulf of Tonkin incident: 6 August 1964

'President Johnson has earned the gratitude of the free world as well as of the nation for his careful and effective handling of the Vietnam crisis. The paramount need was to show the North Vietnamese aggressors their self-defeating folly in ignoring an unequivocal American warning and again attack the American Navy on the high seas. This Mr Johnson did by means of a severe but measured response deftly fitted to the aggression: retaliation against the boats and bases used in the attack.'

China's nuclear weapon: 17 October 1964

'For the United States, and presumably for the Soviet Union as well, China's baptismal blast vastly complicates the world scene. It renders more difficult their separate efforts to contain and control local military ambitions and conflicts, and it brings closer the day when Peking may feel compelled to prove that it is not the "paper tiger" which it accuses other nuclear powers of being. On the part of Washington, the explosion will require steady nerves and a continuing, quiet display of resolve to uphold American responsiblities in Asia.'

Rhodesia's UDI: 12 November 1965

'The independence proclaimed by Prime Minister Ian Smith and his white supremacists is built upon a false basis, upon a denial of human rights that affronts much of the world. . .Britain has behaved with the highest international responsibility. . .And so Rhodesia begins international existence as a pariah.'

The Russian invasion of Czechoslovakia: 22 August 1968

'There is, thus, in this affair, a grave threat to the mood and temper of a world already quite sufficiently volatile. There is the danger of a new era of calculated hostility on the part of Russia. And there is the possibility that even a Russia eager to make amends for its barbarism by conciliation with the outside world would encounter unbridled hostility from the people of this country. It would be too much to expect outrage to be stifled. But outrage that overrides the stark reality – that the safety and security of the world can best be assured by an ultimate reconciliation between East and West – is as stark and as urgent now as it was before the Russians rolled across Czechoslovakia.'

Israel's occupation of the West Bank: 23 October 1973

'Reports from the region suggest that while Egypt may have acquired in battle the measure of self-confidence whose absence kept it from moving toward a political settlement earlier, Israel may have hardened its conviction that retention of territory is essential in order to prevent the success of another Arab surprise attack. If that is so, the burden will fall on the United States to help Israel obtain settlement terms for its security – terms which offer a viable alternative to retention of Egyptian territory. Such terms could include: demilitarization of evacuated territory, phased withdrawal, rights of patrol or inspection, early normalization of Israel-Egyptian relations, introduction of foreign or international buffer units, guarantees of reliable arms supplies, perhaps even an American-Israeli security treaty. . . Syria's self-isolating stand ensures the Israelis that they will keep their excellent military position on its territory. It in effect releases the Egyptians to cut their own deal with Israel. Jordan, which committed troops in Syria but did not go directly to war with Israel, emerges in a fine position to continue the precarious but real accommodation it was quietly pursuing before the war. . .The Palestinian terrorists will remain a thorn, but no more than a thorn so long as the other parties deal reasonably with the mass of Palestinians who reject terror.'

The OPEC price rise: 26 December 1973

'Perhaps this massive leap upward in world oil prices foreshadows the ultimate resolution of the Great Boycott of 1973. The Arabs are not likely to get Jerusalem, and the industrial nations are not likely to get 20 million barrels a day of Saudi oil. Instead, the industrial nations will pay more, use less, and look much harder for alternative fuels. The Arabs will pump less and make more money. Here at home we shall begin the new year with the prospect of crude oil at $10 a barrel and gasoline at 60 cents a gallon. Given the other possibilities, that would be far from the worst outcome.'

Watergate: 6 November 1973

'It seems to us that an overwhelming case can be made and has been that Mr Nixon's presidency is now freighted with more than enough liabilities of his own making to recommend his removal and replacement.'
But note also:

6 August 1974

'Over the past many months we have argued in this space that a presidential resignation unaccompanied by a body of material demonstrating his guilt beyond serious challenge would invite public suspicion and damaging divisions in this country.'

The fall of Saigon: 30 April 1975

'If much of the actual conduct of Vietnam policy over the years was wrong and misguided – even tragic – it cannot be denied that some part of the purpose of that policy was right and defensible. Specifically, it was right to hope that the people of South Vietnam would be able to decide on their own form of government and social order.'

Sport and politics: 7 July 1976

'Canada is sorely misguided in its eleventh-hour attempt to impose its own one-China policy on the Olympic Games. Many countries over the years have attempted to use sports for political purposes, and these attempts are becoming increasingly dangerous to the whole idea of the Olympic Games. The issue here is a piece of folly totally and strangely uncharacteristic of the Canadians. . .The Canadian government plaintively observes that the Republic of China marched under the designation "Taiwan" in the 1960 Olympics. Why not follow that precedent? The reason is simply that infringing the rule of political neutrality is getting rapidly more expensive. Canadians can point to many occasions in the past when other governments, including the United States, have violated that rule to score one advantage or another. True, but the threat to the Games' integrity is now reaching a point at which it imperils the whole splendid enterprise. . .If Canada persists in trying to force its own foreign policy on the Olympics, it will do damage to the Olympic principle that neither Canadians nor anyone else will easily remedy in the Games to come.'

The space venture: 13 April 1961

'Whether man would have come this far this soon in his conquest of space without the spur of military technology and the Cold War may be questioned. And if conflict has helped to produce this astounding scientific advance, it has tended in some ways to dull the lustre of the accomplishment. The conquest of space thus becomes more the by-product of man's terrestrial divisions and failures than the pure product of his search for knowledge.'

Freedom of information: 11 March 1979

'If the monthly magazine, *The Progressive*, has what the Department of Justice says it has – secret information on how a hydrogen bomb works – it should forget about publishing it. There is not exactly a large public interest to be served – or even a small one – in making available to all information on how to build nuclear weapons. . .As a press-versus-government First Amendment contest, this, as far as we can tell, is John Mitchell's dream case – the one the Nixon administration was never lucky enough to get: a real First Amendment loser. . .While the Supreme Court has never sanctioned a court order barring the publication of anything, there are strong indications that it would do so if confronted with a case of this nature and magnitude.'

11

Toronto Globe and Mail

The *Globe and Mail* is Canada's only national newspaper, printed and distributed around the country, and traditionally committed to reporting foreign and national affairs. The commitment can be traced back to the 1930s, when it was the first Canadian paper to operate its own air service to distribute the paper throughout this most widespread of Western countries. And in 1887, the original *Globe* began its own train service to get the paper into the hinterland of what was then an undeveloped region. In 1980, the *Globe and Mail* began building its own satellite receiving stations in Edmonton and Ottawa, where electronic facsimiles of a new national edition could be beamed, via space satellite from the Toronto main office, and then locally printed. Already selling 15,000 copies a day in Canada's Western states, the *Globe and Mail* hoped to increase this Western circulation to 50,000 within two years.[1]

The *Globe and Mail*'s credentials as a national paper are well established. It is the newspaper the Canadian government chooses to send to its foreign missions; a paper which published, from England, its own international edition. It is Canada's only paper of record, printing in full, for example, the texts of papal encyclicals and the lengthy manifestos of the 'yes' and 'no' groups for the Quebec referendum. In the words of one senior CBC executive: 'The fifteen civil servants who run this country from Ottawa, they read the *Globe and Mail* and that's all they read. If it isn't in the *Globe*, it hasn't happened.'[2] It sells over 3,000 copies a day outside Canada, sixty of them in Moscow, and it has had in Peking the longest-established bureau of any Western newspaper. It is a paper with a sense of responsibility to its own self-image as Canada's Establishment journal – on election nights, it spends $6,000 to charter a plane to fly the last editions up to the national capital.

In its 136-year history, the *Globe* has been the key propaganda vehicle for the creation of a united, confederated Canada; the voice of the Liberal Party, of the Progressive Conservative Party; of an asinine and quasi-fascist group called the Leadership League, and the voice of the country's mining interests. It has employed future Prime Ministers; its publisher has discreetly (and profitably) managed the investment portfolio of another Prime Minister; and there have been attempts to ban it from the press gallery of the national parliament. It has always been privately owned, with a tradition of Trappist secrecy about its income, its profits and its finances.[3] Throughout this century, it has never dominated its home market of Toronto. In 1980, only 45% of its circulation was sold in the city. Its nation-wide ambitions, and financial survival, force it further afield.

The *Globe* began in 1844 as a weekly paper in the frontier settlement of Toronto, in what was then known as Upper Canada. The founder, George Brown, had arrived in Toronto the previous year with his father, to establish a weekly journal devoted to the affairs of the Presbyterian church, *The Banner*. For the five years before settling in Canada, they had lived in New York, publishing the *British Chronicle*, a faltering journal which is remembered mainly for the vehemence of its anti-slavery views. Partly because it made economic sense to print a second journal on the presses of *The Banner* and partly because of his growing involvement in reform politics, George Brown launched the *Globe* to compete with five other weekly newspapers for the tiny Toronto market. His first issue sold 300 copies. The front page was devoted to British and Canadian parliamentary debates, and feature articles reprinted directly from English and American papers. Page two contained editorials, and columns of world news, as brought by the most recently arrived steamship. Page three contained commercial and local news and page four was devoted to advertisements, a striking proportion of them offering whiskey for sale by the barrel.[4]

The *Globe*'s early success rested on the power of Brown's editorials, devoted as they were to the rising fortunes of the Reform cause, later to be organized as Canada's Liberal Party. Brown wrote strong stuff; his rivals accused him of bringing 'literary terrorism' to

Canada. He replied to one such charge in the *British Chronicle* that he had found in its columns 'such a mass of putridity we felt as if we had been cutting up a dead dog'.[5] A man of boundless confidence, Brown was so sure that his venture would succeed that, two months after founding the *Globe*, he bought Canada's first cylinder press, capable of printing 2,500 pages an hour so that his entire weekly circulation could be churned out in two hours. Throughout his career, Brown was always determined to invest in the hardware of newspapers, confident that the sales and ads would follow to justify his risk. Personally convinced that Canada was a land of boundless opportunity, he gambled on growth. By the end of his life, when economic depression had temporarily stifled the growth, Brown and his *Globe* were almost bankrupt. But in his early years, the boldness paid off. In 1847, he publicly committed himself to the policy by spending almost a quarter of the *Globe*'s income on buying the latest news through the new telegraph line to New York. 'The publisher of the *Globe* is determined that, at whatever cost, he shall receive the English news at the earliest possible moment,' he announced on page one.[6] By this time, the *Globe* had expanded into a bi-weekly, and it began to appear three times a week in 1849, with a claimed circulation of 4,000. Many of them were doubtless attracted by Brown's purchase of the rights to serialize the new Charles Dickens novel, *Dombey and Son*.

Brown's own political success grew with the fame of his paper. In 1851, he was elected to parliament on the Reform ticket. His views were straightforward; he wanted responsible government, a firm commitment to the development of Ontario, personal and religious freedom, and close links with Britain. His liberalism did not extend to sympathy with his own workforce. In 1854, he had the leaders of a printing strike arrested for conspiracy, but he later expressed satisfaction that they had each been fined a token one penny. The *Globe* had become a financial success, selling some 4,000 copies by the early 1850s, and solvent enough to send its first foreign correspondent abroad; Gordon Brown, George's younger brother, was sent off to London to furnish reports of the Great Exhibition. On Gordon's return, he took over the day-to-day running of the paper, while his brother concentrated on politics.

In 1853, Brown bought a new rotary printing press and re-launched the *Globe* as a daily. He was running a complex operation, with weekly and bi-weekly editions still being published for Toronto's far-spreading hinterland and a total circulation of about 6,000 copies. His first daily edition was well enough supported to attract seventeen columns of advertisements, and his domination of the Toronto press was underlined by his steady purchases of his former rivals, the *Examiner*, the *North American*, and the *Message*. By 1856, with each of these rivals absorbed, circulation had reached 15,000, spurred on by Brown's own political reputation as a leader of the Liberals and the most effective counterweight to the Conservative Party. Relations between the parties were frosty; it was then the tradition for a newspaper of one allegiance not to report the speeches of the Opposition. But Brown had a wider vision. From the late 1850s, he began printing regular articles and letters from the far west of Canada, to support his proposition that Canada was destined to be one nation. The question was the nature of that nation, given the traditional hostilities between the English and French provinces, and the different economic interests of underdeveloped, under-populated Ontario and the West, and the more settled society of Montreal.

Brown took the initiative of entering into an effective coalition with the rival Conservatives, led by Sir John Macdonald, to bring about the confederation of Canada in 1867. Brown was repaid for his political and journalistic efforts by a Conservative awareness of the powers of the press, and their decision to found a rival Tory paper, the *Mail*, in 1872. But the fledgling *Mail* faced a market that was saturated by the *Globe*. By 1861, Brown was claiming a total circulation of 30,000 for all his various editions – at a time when Toronto's population was perhaps 40,000, and the whole wide-flung continent of Upper Canada numbered no more than 1¼ million. By 1869, his daily paper alone was selling over 16,000 and Brown characteristically boasted in his columns: 'Nowhere else in the world is one journal read by so large a proportion of the public.'[7]

Brown invested in new printing type, and began a face-lift of the paper. He began a sports department, launched new columns for literary and financial affairs, and began a new city column to comment on the local Toronto news that was still exhaustively reported. He opened branch offices in the fast-growing new towns of Ontario, in Hamilton and London, and another office in Montreal. By 1870, he had an office in Britain, in Cheapside in the heart of London. And he was well enough known in the mother country to be fêted when he went there in 1873 to protest against the scandals of government Ministers taking bribes in the railway boom. The senior editors of *The Times* gave him lunch, and supported his arguments in their editorials.

It was the height of his career, as a classically Victorian self-made man, a publisher and statesman who had prospered in an era of apparently endless growth. Expansion was the very essence of the man, but expansion within a canny limit of Scots caution. In 1867, when he incorporated as the Globe Publishing Company, he carefully kept all the voting shares in the family hands. And perhaps the best insight into the man came in 1866, during the pathetic Fenian invasion of Canada by a large mob of Irish nationalists living in the USA and resolved to free Ireland by invading another British possession. The Fenians invaded on a Saturday, and Toronto was in a state of heroic panic, with volunteers and militiamen heading for the border to confront the Irish. Brown was in a state of even worse distress. A story breaking on a Saturday means that the public will want to read about it on the Sunday. Brown's Presbyterianism forbade him from working or printing on the Sabbath, even though crowds of Canadians clustered around the *Globe*'s offices to hear the latest news. But conscience said no Sunday newspaper. In the end, Brown compromised. He would not let the steam printing machines desecrate the Lord's Day, but from the attic he unearthed a hand printing set, and God and readers were both half-satisfied as sheets of news and smudged casualty lists came laboriously from the office.

But in the 1870s, under the growing competition from the Conservative rival, the *Mail*, and with economic recession biting into his revenues from the *Globe* and sending his personal estate at Bow Park into heavy loss, Brown's fortunes began to sink. He carried his commitment to Ontario into his private life, investing heavily in importing prime British livestock to Bow Park in order to improve the Canadian breed. This venture, years ahead of its time, failed miserably, and his efforts to launch lumber mills and small industries at Bow Park were savaged by the recession. In 1878, the election of a Conservative government not only cut into the *Globe*'s official advertising revenue, it also suggested that Brown's politics were becoming old-fashioned. In 1879, the circulation of the *Globe*'s daily edition fell for the first time, from 24,000 to 20,000. Brown had always lived by the principle, when in doubt, expand. He announced that he would transform Canadian journalism by breaking away from the traditional four-page format, and bring out smaller-sized papers of eight or even sixteen pages. The problems of Bow Park meant that he was already mortgaged to the hilt, and in 1880 he announced to shareholders that he would be unable to pay any dividend. However, his idiosyncratic methods of labour relations caught up with him, and he was shot in his office by an employee he had recently dismissed. Wounded in the leg, he died of gangrene.[8]

The *Globe* was near bankruptcy, although it continued to publish, subsidized by a syndicate of Canadian Liberals. But by 1888, the long-suffering bankers asked the *Globe* to withdraw its account, and it was bought by the Jaffray family, Liberals and Presbyterian in the Brown tradition. Their religious scruples were to hamper the paper until they sold it in 1936. They forbade any references to horseracing or gambling – which turned away many potential readers – and refused to print many advertisements on moral grounds. Tobacco, for example, was not to be sold in the God-fearing pages of the *Globe*.[9] But in appointing Sir John Willison as editor in 1890, the Jaffrays put the *Globe* back on the path to solvency and quality. Willison, against all Canadian tradition, resolved that news was non-partisan. He made a point of printing the political speeches and views of Conservatives as well as of Liberals, or indeed of anyone else whom he thought of interest. Circulation began to recover from its long decline, and by 1895 the *Globe* was lusty enough to have fought off the challenge of yet another Conservative rival, the *Empire*, which had staggered on for eight years before the *Mail* absorbed it. By 1899, finances were sturdy enough for the *Globe* to send two of its own correspondents out to South Africa to cover the Boer War and the Canadian volunteers who fought on Britain's side. The *Globe*, launched as a radical voice of reform, had become the newspaper of the carriage trade, the prosperous citizens of Ontario. Its editorials remained a powerful, Liberal voice within the Canadian Establishment, and its political columns were the most thorough, if not the most inspired, in the country. In its layout, its tone and its advertisements, the tradition was Victorian English rather than North American, much given to portraits of fey little girls and small boys in sailor-suits, and the merits of the British Empire. A characteristic full-page example appeared on 24 February 1900, when a patent medicine and news of the battle of Paardeburg in the Boer War was announced. The huge headline announced 'GENERAL CRONJE HAS SURRENDERED', and went on in slightly smaller type 'just as disease has always surrendered to the treatment prescribed by Dr A. W. Chase'. Grateful comments from the troops about their medicine was then interspersed with an account of the battle and engravings of the dead.[10]

The *Globe*'s self-image as part of the Establishment led to some questionable relations with ambitious politicians. Mackenzie King, who as Prime Minister was to dominate Canadian politics for a generation, began submitting articles to the *Globe* in the 1890s. In 1908, when running for parliament and hoping for an immediate ministerial appointment, he came to a curious arrangement with F. A. Acland, the *Globe*'s news editor: Acland would be deputy Minister of Labour in the next government if King were to get an even higher post. This of course depended on massive support for King's election campaign.[11] The *Globe* responded with glowing articles about 'this brilliant young administrator' and went on to eulogize his 'splendid and uniformly successful record'. When he was duly elected, the *Globe* celebrated by publishing a laudatory poem which included the notable line: 'Thrice welcome then, O wise beloved son'. Politics were livelier in those days. When the Tory victory in the 1911 election was announced, the mob celebrated by breaking all the *Globe*'s windows.

The rival *Mail* was no more scrupulous in its relations with politicians, but its Conservative, imperial tones, its assiduous reports of race meetings (banned in the Presbyterian *Globe*) and its liveliness let it steadily overhaul the *Globe*'s static circulation. From 28,000 copies a day in 1899, the *Mail* climbed steadily to 65,000 by 1913, and to 80,000 by 1915, when the desire for news of the First World War boosted newspaper circulations everywhere.[12] The intense censorship of the British High Command in France meant that only five fully accredited war correspondents were permitted to cover the British side of the war; and although Canadians, New Zealand and Australian forces were being used as the British shock troops, journalists from those countries were even further hindered. The *Globe* counted itself fortunate to have the services, through syndication, of the doyen of the British correspondents, Sir Philip Gibbs who, although arrested five times by the British Army, was able to give the least censored, least sanguine and most realistic reports. It was he, for example, who reported the early 1914 battles as the routs which they became, rather than the 'strategic change of front' which the British generals asserted.[13]

But in spite of the desperately depressing news of war, and the endless lists of casualties, there was a constant smugness about the *Globe* throughout and well after the First World War. It was a paper which made no waves, which made undistinguished profits from its worthy but dreary pages. It ran its fourteen or sixteen pages in the week, and twenty-four pages on Saturdays, plump with eleven pages of ads, and the last page was always, as if by divine right, a full-page ad for Eatons, Toronto's up-market department store. The *Globe*'s only self-promotion was to note that 84% of its readers owned their own homes. It was a paper without surprises, and throughout the 1920s it dozed while rivals like the *Mail* and the *Telegram* cut its readership away from under it. The *Mail* had absorbed the old *Empire* in 1895, the *Times* in 1919 and the *World* in 1921. By 1929 it was selling 112,440 copies a day to the *Globe*'s 92,000. Within seven years, the *Globe* had sunk to 78,000.[14]

But in 1936, the minnow turned and swallowed the whale. One of the few Canadian industries which had prospered during the 1930s was mining, and one of the richest mining magnates was William Wright. He financed a self-made young financier, a former advertising salesman on the *Globe* named George McCullagh who had become rich as a stockbroker, to purchase the *Globe* from the disillusioned Jaffray family. 'I didn't even look at the balance sheet. I was buying character and tradition,' the young McCullagh told the National Club just after his purchase. He also had to deny rumours that he was acting on behalf of Mitch Hepburn, the Prime Minister of Ontario, in buying the paper, even though Hepburn had taken part in the negotiations leading to the sale. Ontario governments have always been sensitive to the needs of the mining interests, and the political love-affair which began between McCullagh and Premier Hepburn suggested a series of dubious relationships between government, press and big business which led to endless controversy. The criticism redoubled within weeks when McCullagh, again financed by Wright, bought the *Globe*'s key rival, the *Mail and Empire*, and merged them into something uncomfortably close to a monopoly. The voice of the press, which is used to expressing concern on such occasions, was tame. The *Globe*'s mining editor, in a special column on the purchases, announced of the Wright–McCullagh deals: 'Cleaner money and cleaner intent have never been joined to better purpose.'[15]

Money cemented the press–government relationships. McCullagh bought mining shares, knowing that they would increase in value, for Premier Hepburn, and effectively managed the politician's share portfolio.[16] And McCullagh's new paper, the *Globe and Mail*, backed the Hepburn government to the hilt – particularly against the efforts of the American trade union, the CIO, to organize Ontario workers. The *Globe and Mail*'s reporters were used as an intelligence and communications service on the Premier's behalf in the effort to defeat the CIO.[17]

Ironically, it was the megalomaniac ambitions of McCullagh himself which prevented this dubious alliance from dominating Ontario politics. 'I make and unmake governments,' he announced, when Hepburn balked at some of his proposals.[18] McCullagh went on to use radio broadcasts and the *Globe and Mail* to try and establish a new political party, the short-lived and bizarre Leadership League. It called for a curious blend of national government, business leadership, patriotism and spiritual calisthenics.[19] The veteran Canadian Prime Minister, Mackenzie King, saw very clearly what McCullagh was aiming at and wrote in his diaries of their attempts to form 'a fascist government'.[20] McCullagh's political caprices led him to drop the Leadership League within months of its launch, and then to shift the *Globe and Mail*'s support away from Hepburn's Liberal government (and the *Globe*'s century of Liberal tradition) to the Conservative Party of George Drew.

In spite of his politicking, George McCullagh has retained in Canada the reputation of a shrewd newspaperman, the man who saved the *Globe* and launched the successful combined *Globe and Mail*. Certainly by running the racing results, which the Presbyterian owners had never permitted, and by removing all the restraints from his advertising department he improved circulation revenues – but it was not until the 1950s that the unified *Globe and Mail* circulation reached the sum of the two papers' circulations of 1929. His courage in building an imposing new office and printing plant in central Toronto in the middle of the Depression is often praised – although McCullagh himself boasted that land and labour would never be so cheap again. Certainly McCullagh, a man fascinated by technology, kept the *Globe* at the forefront of innovations, joining the *New York Times* to finance long-distance wire-photo research.[21] Perhaps the most telling fact of his stewardship is that by 1948 his paper was being swamped by a new rival, the *Star*, which was selling 370,000 copies each evening. Against this threat, McCullagh threw his greatest asset – money. He bought the Toronto *Telegram*, another evening paper, and told the staff that their task was 'to knock off the *Star*'. This he never managed to do, and the *Telegram* itself was sold after McCullagh's death, lingering on until its extinction in 1971. McCullagh himself died in 1952, in circumstances which never quite silenced the rumours of suicide, and the *Globe and Mail* remained briefly in his family's hands. But by 1955, the paper was owned again by a Canadian industrialist, Reg Webster of Montreal, whose wealth lay in coal and oil. 'Reg who?' the newsroom asked when the purchase was announced. Britain's Lord Rothermere had tried to buy the paper; the rival Toronto *Star* had offered $10 million, and Webster secured it with a bid of $10.8 million.[22]

Webster's major impact on the paper was to retain as editor the almost visionary Oakley Dalgleish. Famous in Canada for his black eye-patch, Dalgleish had a number of ambitions for the *Globe and Mail* and, in trying to implement them, launched it into a series of financial setbacks. Quite simply, he was ahead of his time. In 1957, he saw that newspapers had to entertain as well as inform, and launched two projects: a magazine-size TV supplement, and a sixteen-page tabloid called 'Youth', both of them inserted in the Saturday *Globe and Mail*. They both lost money for two years, and then closed. The market, and the advertisers, were simply not ready in Canada for this kind of publishing, although it was becoming commonplace and profitable in the USA. In 1958, Dalgleish launched an international edition of the paper, printed in England, with a respectable circulation of some 20,000. It lost money, and in 1963 it was decided to try flying the international edition to Europe from Toronto. This experiment lasted for five years, and cost $1 million before it was ended. He gave the *Globe and Mail* a colour magazine, another venture which lost money and closed. But with one key innovation, Dalgleish gave the *Globe and Mail* an asset which was to sustain it through recessions and crises to come.[23]

He saw that the small but influential and affluent market for publications like the *Wall Street Journal* and London's *Financial Times* could be won for a daily newspaper, particularly one such as the *Globe and Mail* which already dominated the 'quality' market in English-speaking Canada. He launched 'Report on Business', a daily separate section which contained stock market listings, financial news, company news and informed economic comment. It is now the lynch-pin of the paper's profits, contributing 68% of the nation-wide ads in 1979. It contained only 26% of the total ads run in the paper, because the nation-wide advertisers see as their market the business-men who read the financial section. A full-page ad in 'Report on Business' cost $10,000 in 1979, whereas a full-page ad for a Toronto retail company in the rest of the paper cost only $4,300. The 'Report on Business', although an integral part of the parent paper, is also circulated separately throughout Canada and abroad, with a sale of 34,000 in 1979. Without it, the *Globe and Mail* would have run at a loss throughout the 1970s.[24]

For all his gifts as a publisher, Dalgleish had matured in the *Globe and Mail* tradition of intimacy with the Canadian political Establishment. There were times when he overcame his friendships and his prejudices. An old and close friend of the Conservative Prime

Minister John Diefenbaker, in 1963 Dalgleish ran an editorial on the front page to announce: 'Mr Diefenbaker has destroyed the Conservative Party. This great nation is in peril because it has been betrayed by an indolent and indecisive leader who would not lead, by a man who clung, and would still cling, to an office which he does not have the capacity to fill.' There were other occasions when he rose less decisively to the challenge. In 1961, after a three-man team of reporters had spent over a year investigating links between organized crime and leading figures in the Ontario government, Dalgleish suggested that the Ontario Premier, an old friend of his, be shown the evidence, allegedly in an attempt to winkle some sort of official reaction from the Premier or the Attorney-General. One of the journalists, convinced that this was the prelude to a cover-up, passed on the evidence to the leader of the Opposition in parliament, where the story eventually surfaced.[25]

In retrospect, Dalgleish's greatest contribution to the *Globe and Mail* may have been his insistence that it was a national newspaper, but one that operated upon an international stage. It was not only his dedication, at great financial cost, to the international editions; it was also his determination to have the paper's voice heard internationally. During the Quemoy-Matsu crisis, when America seemed to threaten war to stop Red China bombarding off-shore islands which were claimed by Taiwan, Dalgleish bought space in the *New York Times* to reproduce his angry *Globe* editorials attacking US policy.[26] Dalgleish was fascinated by China, campaigned tirelessly for recognition of the Communist regime, visited Peking and arranged for the *Globe and Mail* to station the first correspondent of a Western newspaper there from the late 1950s.

It was an envied, if controversial, privilege. *Time* magazine repeatedly attacked the *Globe and Mail*'s correspondent for being partial to Chinese Communism, even though the reporter, Fred Mossel, was writing such forthright reports as 'the handful of fanatics who rule China have embarked on a crusade to convert the world to Communism, even if it means global war with nuclear weapons'.[27] What Dalgleish had foreseen was that a correspondent in Peking put the *Globe and Mail* firmly on the international media map – even if it cost $100,000 a year to do it. Major newspapers around the world scurried to buy the *Globe*'s syndication service and use the articles with the rare Peking dateline – with suitable acknowledgements to the *Globe and Mail*. The Peking bureau has remained a feature of the *Globe and Mail*'s foreign coverage, even though the cost had risen to something approaching $200,000 a year by 1980, and in spite of suggestions by foreign editors that the money could be better spent elsewhere. Africa and South America were the places most mentioned as new bases for foreign staff, to flesh out the sparse coverage provided by *Globe and Mail* men from Britain, Washington DC and China. But the *Globe* has been wary of foreign correspondents ever since the embarrassing affair of the Nairobi bureau, when a staff correspondent was sent out to open an office in Kenya and cover Africa. He did remarkably well, filling the paper with scoops and even being suggested as a candidate for a National Press award. But then the *Globe*'s editor happened to be Britain on business and met the fabled Nairobi correspondent in Bond Street. The truth emerged: the man had not left England for months and had filed his copy (complete with Kenya dateline) after plagiarizing the BBC World Service and the wire agencies. He was fired and a man was sent out to Nairobi to clear up. He discovered that the *Globe and Mail*'s office had been sold and the office furniture pawned.[28] Not wholly deterred by the experience, the *Globe and Mail* management of 1980 was planning bureaux in South America, Tokyo, Africa and Brussels to lessen the paper's dependence on the wire agencies and the forty 'stringers' who provide the average fifteen columns a day of foreign news.[29] 'I know our foreign coverage is a weakness, but we have to pay that cost. We are selling quality in this newspaper,' Mr Roy McGarry, the current publisher, said in an interview. 'For the same reason, I want to keep the editorial-advertising ratio in our columns at 50–50. We could sell more ads, but we would dilute the very quality that readers are buying.'[30]

Dalgleish died in 1963, to be replaced as publisher and editor-in-chief by James Cooper, a veteran of the London *Daily Express* who had run the *Globe*'s international edition. Almost immediately, Cooper was confronted by a strike of the Typographical Union, which the managements of the *Globe and Mail*, the *Star* and the *Telegram* combined to defeat. The strike centred on the introduction of new technology and foreshadowed the disputes that would hit almost every paper in the world in the course of the next two decades. By dragooning *Globe* executives into unaccustomed printing jobs, Cooper was able to continue publishing, and the strike was eventually broken, leaving Toronto as a non-union city in publishing. The long-term result of that strike, according to the management in 1980, was to ensure that in the 1970s production costs fell in real terms as printers accepted the introduction of cold-type printing, and

reporters moved smoothly from their typewriters to computer key-
boards. The strike had cost money – but it had enormously improved
the potential profitability of the paper. And in 1965, the *Globe*'s
owner Howard Webster accepted a bid from FP Publications, a chain
of newspapers which included the highly respected Winnipeg *Free
Press*. The bid had the merit of reducing Webster's death-duties
liabilities, and a condition of the sale was that the *Globe and Mail*'s
management, editorial and news direction would remain unchanged.[31]

The FP group took over at a time when demographic change was
transforming the nature of the *Globe and Mail*'s home market. Massive immigration into Toronto, combined with the move of the middle
class to the suburbs, began to reduce the *Globe*'s city sales, increase
its distribution costs and dilute its once healthy income from inner-
city retail advertisers. The nature of the change was illustrated by the
success of the down-market tabloid Toronto *Sun*, launched in 1971,
which overtook the *Globe*'s Toronto circulation in 1975. In 1976, the
decision by one department store, Eatons, to cut back its *Globe* ads
cost the paper some $200,000 a year in revenue.[32] The result was a
cost-cutting, penny-pinching style of management which began to
undermine the *Globe*'s reputation as a quality newspaper. Expensive
foreign news, for example, was reduced. The *Globe* had traditionally
bought syndication rights to all the *New York Times* stories, but this
was sharply cut back to the *Times*'s ordinary (and much leaner)
service. The *Globe* was able to fight off attempts to merge its own
foreign bureaux with the bureaux of the parent FP chain.[33] And in the
attempt to win back Toronto readership, the *Globe* began running a
series of investigative reports on Toronto; it focused on cases of police
brutality and on local administrative scandals. One story of the police
gaining illegal access to suspects' health records led to a subpoena for
the reporter concerned – which he was able to avoid, having been
moved to the Washington bureau where he was out of the Canadian
courts' jurisdiction. It was a courageous strategy to win back circulation, although it led to reader complaints of a new shrillness in the
Globe's tone, and between 1975 and 1977, the Toronto circulation
rose from 120,000 to 140,000.[34]

But the *Globe* was running itself into the ground. Its overall circulation grew very little in the 1970s – more Toronto readers were offset
by lost readers elsewhere. And whereas the cost per thousand of
advertising in the rival *Sun* actually fell in the period 1972–8, it rose by
14% at the *Globe*. It was pricing itself out of the advertising market,
and without the steady 4% annual growth in nation-wide ads, contri-

buted by the 'Report on Business', the combination of inflation and over-priced ad space would have brought a crisis of survival.[35]

The parent FP chain was also in trouble. A damaging nine-month strike at its Vancouver paper, and another strike at the Montreal *Star* which led to that paper's closure led the FP chain in 1980 to sell the *Globe and Mail* to the Thomson Organization, the Canadian-based oil and publishing conglomerate which also then owned the London *Times* and *Sunday Times*. The purchase price for the *Globe* was $164 million – seen as high by press observers who had not allowed for the potential of the new, satellite-transmitted national edition.

But the *Globe and Mail* itself was beginning to recover financially, even before the Thomson purchase. A new publisher, Roy McGarry, and a new management team armed with modern administrative tools, such as budget targeting, marketing analysis, long-range planning and readership surveys, increased advertising lineage by 11% in 1979, and by 14% in the first quarter of 1980. All of that new revenue was ploughed back into the paper. The editorial budget was increased by $2.5 million, or 20%, in the course of 1979. Some 2,500 new vending boxes were installed around Toronto when the decision was taken to ignore the mounting rate of unsold papers, but at least to make them available.[36]

The look of the paper was transformed, based on the principle that the *Globe* had to become a daily magazine, as well as a newspaper. On each weekday the *Globe* now comes in four sections. Each day, the first section is the twenty-page basic newspaper, national, local and foreign news and the editorials. And each day the 'Report on Business' is the second section, with twenty pages, three and a half of them giving the Stock Exchange listings, five and a half pages of editorial matter, and the rest the high-priced ads. The third section varies each day. On Mondays, it is a special science section, with a little over one page of science stories, backed up by ads. On Tuesdays, it is a fashion section; on Wednesdays, a colour-printed retail advertising section called 'Shopping Basket'; on Thursdays, it is called simply the Thursday section, which is the traditional woman's page; on Fridays, a tabloid filled with property advertisements and some editorial matter called 'Better Living'. The fourth section each day is for sports news and classified ads. On Saturdays, the *Globe* has seven sections: the basic newspaper, 'Report on Business' and the sports supplement, fleshed out by an entertainments section, a travel section, a tabloid magazine based on leisure and Toronto life called 'Fanfare', and a TV magazine.

A typical weekday will see a sixty-four-page paper, composed of 52% ads, with 250 editorial columns. On average, these are divided into fifteen columns of foreign news, fifteen columns of city news, up to eighteen columns of national news (boosted by the decision to run almost daily columns from *Globe* journalists based in Montreal and Edmonton), two full pages of editorials, letters and columns, and the rest of the editorial space divided among sport, finance, entertainment and so on. It is still a rather messy package, with little logic about the organization of the pages, and a layout that looks lumpy and old-fashioned, although a modular layout is planned for the new national edition. Layout is hampered by the primacy of advertising requirements on some pages which are usually, but not always, scheduled for colour advertisements.

The national coverage is by far the fullest in Canada, with four new regional correspondents to give a total of seventeen staff reporters spread among six bureaux around Canada. The foreign news rests heavily on syndicated stories from the *New York Times*, the London *Economist, Le Monde* and the London *Times*, but their copy and that of wire services is regularly re-written by the seven-man foreign desk. The foreign desk has a budget just short of $1 million a year, which has to service three foreign bureaux, forty stringers and subscriptions to eight wire services. There are glaring gaps in the coverage. The only time the *Globe and Mail* had a staff correspondent in Iran throughout the long crisis of the Shah's fall was when a provincial political reporter travelled with the Ontario Premier on an official visit.[37]

For the future, the paper claims to have little fear of heavy-handed interference by the new owners, Thomsons, so long as the paper stays profitable. And this, like so much else on the *Globe and Mail*, will depend on the success of the new national edition, printed across Canada after satellite transmission. The national edition, which will include 'Report on Business', will be an amended version of the Toronto first section, with many local news stories replaced by a national sports and cultural coverage. 'We have to do it,' publisher Roy McGarry said in 1980. 'There just isn't room for three papers in Toronto any more – and we have to be one of the survivors. We have claimed for a long time to be Canada's only national newspaper, and technology now allows us to do it properly.'[38] The future holds other changes. Like his colleagues in the USA, McGarry sees newspapers losing a growing proportion of their classified ads to the electronic media. His solution is to gamble that *Globe and Mail* readers will be prepared to pay a higher price for the paper, as the proportion of advertising revenue falls. In 1974, sales provided only 19% of the paper's income. McGarry's goal is to raise that proportion to 29% by 1981, and to 45% in the long term: 'We have forgotten that papers once lived without ads. And we will have to live with a lot fewer in the future.'[39] In the two years since his arrival, McGarry raised the paper's price from 15 cents to 25 cents, with further price rises in view, to pay for the ambitious programme of expansion in foreign and national coverage. 'Old George Brown loved technology; he believed in the future,' Richard Doyle, the editor-in-chief, said in 1980. 'I think he would be doing exactly the same – satellites and all.'[40]

But just as satellite printing began to make the *Globe's* dream of becoming a genuinely national paper a reality, Canada's Royal Commission on the daily press reported the findings of its $3.1 million study. Describing the *Globe* as 'a uniquely powerful agent of information and opinion', the Commission judged that its ownership by the Thomson Organization (which owned one-third of all other Canadian newspapers) represented 'an entirely unacceptable concentration of power'.[41] It proposed a new press law to control such newspaper chains which would prevent any group which owned papers in two or more distinct locations in separate Canadian provinces from owning or controlling any other daily newspaper in Canada. In the Royal Commission's words: 'Thomson would thus be required to divest itself within five years of the *Globe and Mail* or of its other papers.'[42] The Royal Commission's report was greeted, not surprisingly, with horrified editorials across Canada. But the Thomson group's determined pursuit of a press monopoly (or at best duopoly with the Southam group) had made such proposals politically inevitable. The Royal Commission's proposals were the less impressive because of their strident tone and occasional exaggeration. To assert: 'Industrial conglomerates produce poor newspapers; it is a law of general application,' was plainly wrong-headed.[43] The *Washington Post, Asahi Shimbun, Die Welt, Al-Ahram,* the *New York Times* and *The Times* are newspapers belonging to conglomerates. But the reaction of the *Globe and Mail* was significant for the priority it chose. 'Editors' contracts, advisory editorial boards, press rights panels and Canadian Newspaper Acts are what we expected would come from the Commission's ivory tower. They are concepts we can and will debate,' its editorial said.[44] But the paper would have no interference with its fundamental objective: 'Anything which interferes with the *Globe's* lifelong dream of serving Canadians from coast to coast is not a subject for debate.'[45]

Notes

1. Interviews with Roy McGarry, publisher, and Richard Doyle, editor-in-chief. All interviews cited took place in Toronto, between 1 and 14 April 1980.
2. Ron Haggart, former press columnist and now with Canadian Broadcasting Commission. Quoted in *Toronto Life* magazine, October 1977, article by D. Fetherling.
3. McGarry interview. Mr McGarry tried to obtain a dispensation from the *Globe and Mail* board to give me full financial statistics, without success.
4. For the George Brown years, I am indebted to *Brown of the Globe*, J. M. S. Careless.
5. Careless, *op. cit.*, p. 77.
6. *Globe*, 3.iv.1847.
7. *Globe*, 25.i.1869.
8. See *George Brown* by J. Lewis.
9. Fetherling, *op. cit.*
10. *Globe*, 24.ii.1900.
11. *The Age of Mackenzie King*, H. S. Ferns and B. Ostry, p. 95.
12. In 1972, the *Toronto Globe and Mail* published a special section on the centenary of the founding of the *Mail*.
13. See *The War Dispatches*, Sir Philip Gibbs (Tandem, 1968) p. 6.
14. Fetherling, *op. cit.*
15. *Mitch Hepburn* by Neil McKenty is the source for the curious relationship between Hepburn and McCullagh.
16. *ibid.*, pp. 92–3.
17. *ibid.*, p. 122.
18. *ibid.*, p. 122.
19. See the *Globe and Mail, passim,* January–May 1939.
20. McKenty, *op. cit.*, pp. 192–3.
21. Interview with Richard Doyle.
22. See *News and the Southams* by Charles Bruce.
23. Doyle interview; and Fetherling, *op. cit.*
24. Interview with Doug Evans, director of operations at the *Globe and Mail* in 1980.
25. Doyle interview; and Fetherling, *op. cit.*
26. Doyle interview.
27. In 1960, the *Globe and Mail* reprinted Mossel's China stories in a special pamphlet, entitled 'China'. See also *Reporter in Red China* by C. Taylor.
28. This anecdote, widespread in Canadian press circles, was confirmed for me by Richard Doyle.
29. Interview with Don Manley, *Globe and Mail* foreign editor in 1980.
30. McGarry interview.
31. Obituary of James Cooper, *Globe and Mail*, 10.iv.1980, p. 15.
32. Fetherling, *op. cit.*
33. Manley interview.
34. Interview with Warren Barton, Metro editor, at the *Globe and Mail* in 1980.
35. Evans interview.
36. McGarry interview.
37. Manley interview.

38. McGarry interview.
39. *ibid.*
40. Doyle interview.
41. The Royal Commission on Newspapers; Commission Royale sur les quotidiens, Information Canada, 1981.
42. *ibid.*
43. *ibid.*
44. *Globe and Mail*, 19.viii.1981.
45. *ibid.*

Note: The Toronto *Globe and Mail* kindly permitted me to interview a number of other staff, including Cameron Smith, executive editor, John King, national editor, and Amanda Valpy, librarian, to whose assistance and files I am indebted.

I was fortunate enough to have the insights of Professor Robert Bothwell, University of Toronto, into Canadian history, and the assistance of Professor Paul Rutherford, also of the University of Toronto, in the specialist field of the history of journalism in Canada.

TORONTO GLOBE AND MAIL: EDITORIALS

The independence of India: 4 June 1947

'It is fitting to salute the British achievement and welcome the Indians to nationhood. As events unroll, many critics of British rule in India must be (if they have any conscience) eating their words and repenting. . ."Divide and Rule" had been the critics' description of British India policy. How clear it is that what the British did was "Unite and Rule". No sooner is British authority lifted than India falls apart.'

The independence of Israel: 4 June 1948

'There are some who argue that the UN has no authority to create nations and that Israel derives whatever sovereignty it may have from its own acts. . .Which was the legitimate way to fill the power vacuum created when Britain's control ended – by a trial of military strength between Jews and Arabs or peacefully in accordance with a verdict given by world opinion?'

The Berlin blockade and airlift: 28 June 1948

'There is assuredly nothing to be gained, in the struggle to establish a free and prosperous Europe, by knuckling down to Moscow's brutal tactics. On the contrary, appeasement of that kind would be merely an encouragement to further coercive actions by the aggressor. . .If the Western powers teach this lesson firmly enough, the present battle of Berlin will be a Soviet defeat.'

The Communists win power in China: 23 May 1949

'This will be a calamitous defeat for the West in the global struggle between democracy and Communism. It is quite possibly true that some of the Chinese Communist leaders are "reformers" rather than Marxists of the Moscow variety and that the Chiang regime has become moribund through corruption. It is also true, however, that the victors in this Chinese war are unfriendly to the Western powers and will look to the Kremlin for their cues in international dealings.'

The Korean war: 29 September 1950

'Korea was a failure from the Russian point of view. What the Western powers have now to do is to ensure that similar aggressive adventures elsewhere will come to grief in the same way – and if possible, in less time.'

The Suez invasion : 2 November 1956

'Britain intervened, and rightly so. She has gone into Egypt not to make war but to make peace. She has gone in, that is to say, to do the job which the United Nations ought to have done, but did not do; ought to be doing, but is not doing. And will not. It can scarcely be doubted that this use of Anglo-French power will restore peace in the Middle East.'

The Russian invasion of Hungary: 6 November 1956

'Hungary's gallant bid for freedom stirred men's hearts. But no country came to her aid, and even the United Nations ignored her appeals. . .The last despairing words of the last free radio station in Hungary will recall, for many, the last despairing words of Polish radio stations in September 1939. There is this difference – the Poles had allies who carried on the fight after they had gone down; the Hungarians had none.'

The Bay of Pigs assault on Cuba: 21 April 1961

'The United States has damaged its moral position in the world as a peaceful, law-abiding nation, by seemingly resorting to undercover methods of warfare normally associated with the Communist bloc.'

The Cuban missile crisis: 24 October 1962

'Any attempt to sit on the fence in this period of crisis, to remain uncommitted, would be interpreted around the world as a rebuke to the United States, and as aid and comfort for her enemies. Such a course is unthinkable.'

The Gulf of Tonkin incident: 6 August 1964

'The USA has moved carefully, trying only to stem the attack, and not to mount counter-aggression. But attacked itself, it has retaliated – with a strength calculated to discourage further attack. It had to do so; a strong giant who will not use his strength as far as it is needed is as ineffectual in defence of peace as one that has no strength.'

China's nuclear weapon: 20 October 1964

'If the public's antipathy is so great that it prevents the pursuit of a rational and realistic policy, including UN membership for China and eventually diplomatic recognition, then the public must be educated. The lesson is simple enough. One out of every four persons on this earth is Chinese. And one of the five nuclear powers is China – the first of the non-white countries to have come so far so fast.'

Rhodesia's UDI: 12 November 1965

'Canada could not justifiably refuse to trade with Rhodesia when it does not draw the trade line with any other country in the world, except in strategic goods. Especially when the people whom the trade embargo was designed to help, the Negro majority, would be the one to suffer most.'

The Russian invasion of Czechoslovakia: 22 August 1968

'Nobody is going to do anything about the Russian invasion, just as nobody is going to do anything about the US invasion of Vietnam. The facts of Big Power politics rule out all but verbal interventions. . .Russian tyranny in Czechoslovakia, it seems only too likely, will increase the tyranny of reaction in the United States.'

Israel's occupation of the West Bank: 23 October 1973

'Peacemaking. . .must give Israel not only secure boundaries, but the knowledge that it is not constantly under the threat of attack. It cannot do this unless it also settles the question of the Arab refugees, and convinces Israel's Arab neighbours that peace spells justice.'

The OPEC price rise: 7 January 1974

'The political dramatics have perhaps obscured the significance of the price increases that went along with the oil squeeze. Sooner or later the oil embargo will be lifted but the cost of oil will not be rolled backward; if anything, it might go higher. The whole range of economic life in the industrial countries will be affected. . .it is a slippery slope and nobody knows where the bottom might be.'

Watergate: 17 August 1973

'President Nixon was undoubtedly right when he told the American people that the US stands in immediate need of strong leadership. What was sad about Mr Nixon's speech was that it disclosed him as a man not equal to the task of leading.'

The fall of Saigon: 1 May 1975

'The Americans have made many tragic errors in Vietnam – the greatest of them in going there. Many wrongs were committed by all parties to this foul war. They have been condemned, as they should be, no matter what mistaken good intentions might have set them in motion. . .We have no reason for confidence that this will be any peaceful festival of liberation. This is not a day to be celebrated, except as an end to the war.'

Sport and politics: 21 July 1976

'Are the Olympic Games, as presently organized, worth holding? We think they are not. The whole concept of open global sports competition is being debased before the world's eyes. In human terms, the most poignant travesty is the patent exploitation of skilled young athletes by their governments. Beyond that, what is happening is an appalling distortion of competition of sport into political expression.'

The space venture: 13 April 1961

'Is there not now a hope that man, confronted with the challenge and the mystery of space, will refuse to squander his resources on paltry, earth-bound conflicts?'

Freedom of information: 3 March 1975

'In Canada, the Government still functions on the premise that everything should be secret unless it can be proven otherwise. . .It still has the mistaken idea that there is no difference between the country's interests and its own interests. The country's interests are the public's business. That is the difference.'

12

The Age, Melbourne

The Melbourne *Age* is one of the most profitable newspapers in the world. In 1977, it made a profit of £1.67 million on sales of 230,000 copies – £7.25 on each issue sold over the year. These figures were achieved in a tough competitive market, in a city with three other morning dailies, two evening and three Sunday papers vying for circulation and advertising.[1]

Perhaps more impressive is the alarm *The Age* causes to Australian politicians. On the eve of the 1972 general election, Prime Minister McMahon received a letter from the federal president of his ruling Liberal Party. It said: 'Whoever the real enemy is on *The Age*, and I think it is probably Perkin, he must be brought into line or circumvented.'[2]

For *Age* editor Graham Perkin, it was an Australian echo of the Nixon White House vendetta against its press critics. It was not as though *The Age* was an anti-Liberal Party paper. Indeed, in its 128 years of history, *The Age* helped, more than any other Australian institution, to bring the Liberal Party into being, to nurture and support it. The Liberal Party's opposition in 1972 was rooted in alarm. Under Perkin, *The Age* was calling for change in Australia, and was cautiously supporting the election of Gough Whitlam's Labour government. 'We offer a Whitlam government nothing, except our advocacy today and our sternest scrutiny for the next three years. It is all we would offer any party we chose to endorse,' were the words of *The Age* editorial on the eve of the election.[3]

The Age's scrutiny of Whitlam's government was a factor in his eventual defeat. Its investigative work on the Whitlam government's attempts to raise over £2,000 million in private loans from Iranian sources succeeded in obtaining (and printing) copies of the cheques of commission payments to mysterious Iranian go-betweens whom the government had denied paying. *The Age* also obtained letters showing that a £100 million commission had been arranged. The scandal played a vital part in discrediting the Whitlam government. After his fall, an *Age* investigation which showed that his government had sent contradictory diplomatic assurances to North and South Vietnam led to further controversy – with *The Age* widely criticized for publishing secret government documents.[4]

It was a remarkable transformation for a newspaper which had seemed, throughout the middle decades of the twentieth century, to be falling into a cosy and permanent sleep in the loyal embrace of the Liberal Party and its conservative Premier, Sir Robert Menzies. It would be fairer to say that *The Age* had rediscovered its own tradition, as the outspoken, radical Thunderer of its early days in the 1850s, when it was kept alive only by being turned into a workers' co-operative.

Newspapers do not, however, survive or recover only on the strength of their journalism. Newspaper morale and the resources to cover and work on the major home and foreign stories of the day depend to an alarming degree upon the health of their revenues. For *The Age*, its growing dominance of the classified ads market in the highly concentrated marketing area of Melbourne has provided the profits. By 1978–9, 68% of *The Age*'s earnings came from classified, with a further 22% from other ads. A bare 8% of income came from *The Age*'s circulation revenues – which leaves it potentially vulnerable to the kind of economic recession which cut profits by almost 25% between 1973–4 and 1975–6 (down from £1,146,000 to £855,000; circulation and display advertising both rose – the profit drop followed a 14% decline in classifieds).[5] But a history of *The Age*'s 128-year career gives an almost classic portrait of a newspaper which prospered in spite of losses and abuse, and which later began to falter because of its own success and complacency.

The Age was founded in Melbourne, in the flourishing and gold-rich Australian colony of Victoria, on 17 October 1854. Its launch was timed to exploit the dramatic growth of the colony's population and prospects. *The Age*'s first edition spelt out the change, that the population of the colony around Melbourne had leapt from 50,000 in

1848 to 230,000 in 1853. The lure was gold. As *The Age* said: 'Every month brings to light some new fields of profitable enterprise, some new mine of undeveloped wealth justifying a confident hope of indefinite prosperity.'[6]

Founded by a company of merchants, Francis Cooke and Co., to be 'a journal of politics, commerce and philanthropy', its political stance was declared to be 'liberal, aiming at a wide extension of the rights of free citizenship and a full development of representative institutions'.[7] These bland phrases represented in the Melbourne of the day a defiant political challenge to the small group of wealthy landowners and established tradesmen who dominated the colony's affairs. The sheer numbers of the new immigrants, gold seekers and their families, had transformed the social composition of the colony. But they did not have the right to vote, for which a property qualification was required. If they wanted to settle on the land, they would have to acquire it from the Crown, or from the established landowners, known to this day in Australia as 'the squattocracy', from the often dubious way their land was first acquired.[8]

The Age, therefore, began as almost a revolutionary organ. Within weeks of its first appearance, its radical character was confirmed by its staunch support of the goldminers at the Eureka stockade, the nearest approach to a rebellion in Australian history. Angered by the government's imposition of a costly licence for the right to mine, a group of miners technically declared a revolt by building a defensive stockade, and by swearing allegiance to a new Australian flag. In fact, their main demands were abolition of the mining licences, universal manhood suffrage, payment of elected MPs and an end to property qualifications for electors and MPs alike. The government ordered British infantry to storm the Eureka stockade. Five soldiers were killed, and twenty-two of the miners. A further 128 of the 'insurgents' were taken prisoner and their leaders charged with rebellion.

The Age had supported the miners' grievances, but counselled them to remain within the law. When the violence broke out, *The Age* condemned the government, accusing it of 'having provoked, by their utter want of sagacity and prudence, and by their petty tyranny of disposition, the late fatal events at Ballarat'.[9]

The result of this outspoken stand was a boycott by advertisers and a financial crisis. On 28 December, three months after *The Age*'s first issue, the owners put the paper up for sale for £3,000. Their initial investment had been £7,000, much of it spent on a new steam-driven printing press. With government and the bulk of the colony's merchants refusing to advertise in the radical *Age*, its finances depended utterly upon its sales. But a copy of *The Age* cost 6d – at a time when a labourer could not expect to earn five shillings a day. The papers of the day were densely printed and densely written, and the ordinary man worked in the daylight hours and read, if he had the energy, by candlelight. And if he read a newspaper on Sunday, his day of rest, it was most often an old English newspaper, which were imported into Australia in the tens of thousands until late in the century. The economics of radical journalism were not promising.[10]

The Age, however, survived and maintained its outspoken political line by becoming perhaps the first workers' co-operative in modern journalism. *The Age*'s printers and compositors, forty of them, each subscribed £25 to make a down-payment of £1,000 and continued uninterrupted printing, and uninterrupted abuse of the government and the local authorities.[11]

The governors of the state were a prime target: 'Sir Charles Fitzroy is gone, with his feebleness, his utter worthlessness both as a man and as a ruler, his immoralities and his hopeful family.' He was followed by Sir Charles Hotham, of whom *The Age* commented: 'The sudden promotion of a poor, ignorant, half-pay captain to a position of so much power, responsibility and wealth would be romantic, were it not so preposterous. . .Ignorance and sheer rascality are now at a premium.'[12]

In its first issue, *The Age* had promised its readers that it would try to bring to Australia the literacy and the political plain-speaking of the great English papers of the day. Indeed, it aped the tone of Delane, the great editor of *The Times* in the days when it became known as The Thunderer. And like Delane, the young journalists of *The Age* felt themselves competent to pontificate on almost every aspect of the young colony's economy and life. They called for the establishment of an Australian wine industry: 'When we become quaffers of the pleasant juice of our native grapes, and no longer bibbers of muddy, stupefying malt or maddening brandy, the inspirations of a sunbright climate will have room to display themselves.'[13] It was one of the first newspapers to campaign for the environment: 'He who cuts down a tree unnecessarily is a criminal.' And it supported the rights of the Aborigines and called for Crown land to be returned to them 'to introduce them to the semi-civilization of a pastoral existence, secluded from the contamination of vicious European contact'.[14]

The steady financial decline of *The Age* in the eighteen brief months that it was owned by its workers was compensated by the printers' decision to appoint young Ebenezer Syme, the political correspondent of the rival newspaper *The Argus*, to the editorship. He had worked on the *Westminster Gazette* in London, and found the political line of his employers at *The Argus* too conservative for his taste. The political causes he promoted were almost precisely those which had been declared by the doomed miners of the Eureka stockade: the right of all men to vote and to stand for public office, irrespective of their wealth or poverty. In the Victoria elections of 1856, Ebenezer Syme and three other writers on the staff of *The Age* were elected to the Legislative Council, on a platform of universal male suffrage, and free secular education for all.

By the time of his election, Ebenezer Syme and his brother David had purchased the bankrupt *Age* at a public auction in June 1856, after the printers' partnership was declared insolvent. For £2,000, they bought the name, the goodwill, the printing machines and stocks of paper. And they bought the whaleboat, vital to newspapers of the day, when a scoop meant getting to the ships arriving with newspapers from England before a rival.[15]

The paper's finances were too feeble to support both Syme brothers, and until Ebenezer's death in 1860, David worked as a building contractor. But Ebenezer set the radical pattern of the paper's future. The farcical and tragic 'rebellion' of the Eureka stockade had been a symptom of the way the colony was changing and growing. The traditional political dominance of the early landowners and the merchants of Melbourne had been challenged by the gold-miners and by the new waves of immigrants who wanted small farms, or to establish local industries and shops. For Victoria's established landowners, land reform implied dispossession. And any suggestion of imposing protective tariffs to foster Victorian industry was opposed by the established merchants. Throughout the 1850s and 1860s, the colony was a textbook example of directly opposing class interests. And while the early *Age* paid the price for opposing the traditional establishment in advertising boycotts, it was on the side of the colony's future.

David Syme put it succinctly in *The Age* on 7 December 1860: 'We cannot remain a race of gold diggers and mere traffickers of commerce, with a small sprinkling of tillers of the soil amongst us and yet become a great nation . . . If we would stave off poverty, barbarism and crime, we must seek to become a nation at all points, agricultural, mining, manufacturing, trading and shipping.'

The Mayor of Melbourne announced that anyone brought before him accused of assaulting *The Age*'s editor would receive only a nominal fine. Ebenezer Syme began to carry a revolver. An organized boycott by advertisers in 1858 drew this response: 'We shall go on as we have begun, calling a spade a spade, exposing imposters, unmasking hypocrites, denouncing falsehoods, gibbeting shams and showing no quarter to men who have been guilty of political infamy and who seem to glory in their shame.' It was very brave, and financially it was almost foolish. In 1860, when David Syme succeeded his dead brother, the circulation of *The Age* was 2,000 copies a day.[16]

David Syme continued his brother's work and politics, attacking them as 'designing knaves and unprincipled schemers. . .mendacious adventurers'. The government responded by proposing a law to muzzle the press in a subtle way, by making each newspaper deposit a £1,500 surety against suits for libel. David Syme responded with a classic statement on press freedom: 'It is essential to the public interest that newspapers, if they are to exist at all, should be placed under no restriction that would tend to diminish their independence.'[17]

Throughout the 1860s, *The Age* suffered from the organized boycotts of advertisers, while rival papers prospered. The rival *Argus* of the 1860s carried, on average, two pages of advertising to each page of editorial matter. The embattled *Age* under David Syme shrank at first to twelve columns of ads in a fifty-six-column paper, and then to six columns of ads in a thirty-six-column issue. David Syme responded to each boycott by cutting the cover price of *The Age*, hoping to make up in circulation revenue from new readers what he lost from the advertisers. In 1868, he claimed a circulation of 5,000 copies a day, selling at 2d each. He cut the price to 1d, and by 1869 his circulation had leapt to 15,000 a day. By 1874, with a circulation of 22,000, he proudly boasted in *The Age* 'more than double the circulation of any other daily journal south of the Equator'.[18] By then, the battle was won. In 1870, David Syme had sailed to Britain to replace the old steam printing presses, capable of turning out only 4,000 copies of a four-page paper each hour, and in 1872 the two new rotary presses were installed. In 1879, with its circulation at 38,000 copies a day, he spent £20,000 on new offices and printing works.[19]

The Age had become a part of the new Australian Establishment. In May 1877, it reprinted without comment this tribute from a rival: 'Without the warm support of *The Age*, no Liberal government can stand. Its enormous circulation, the ability with which it is conducted, the pungency of its leaders and the general delectability of the form in which its pabulum is served up to suit the democratic taste of the people of this colony, render it a most formidable, as it is the most merciless organ of public opinion in the country.'[20]

The explanation for this transformation lies in the quotation above, in the words 'Liberal government' and 'democratic taste'. The original founders of *The Age* and its radicalism had been premature, rather than mistaken, in their sense of what a changing population would seek in a newspaper. The boycotts by advertisers had always coincided with political crises in Victoria, and the crisis of 1868 – when David Syme made *The Age* into a penny paper – revealed the political isolation of the old landowning squattocracy. Their political power rested in the colony's Legislative Council, which was elected by 30,000 property owners. Below the Council was the popularly elected Assembly; above it was the Governor, appointed from England. In 1868, the Governor, Sir Charles Darling, took the side of the Assembly (and *The Age*) against the Council, by supporting the land reforms, the constitutional reforms, and the tariff protection which *The Age* had consistently urged. In the short term the reformers lost. Darling was recalled to England. In the long term, they and the principles of universal suffrage, protection for Victoria's infant industries, and the release of land to new settlers and small farmers, were triumphant. *The Age*'s part in that triumph gave it an influence almost without parallel in modern journalism.

Its owner-editor was known throughout Australia as 'King David' Syme. The first Prime Minister of federal Australia, George Reid, told parliament in 1901 that King David was 'the virtual dictator of Victoria'. The 10,000th issue of *The Age*, on 10 March 1887, boasted of the successful campaigns it had fought; universal manhood suffrage; the secret ballot; free, secular and compulsory education; state ownership of the railways; and tariff protection. When *The Age* was not making policy, it was making politicians. Alfred Deakin, three times Prime Minister, began as an *Age* leader-writer.[21]

But a rumbustious, colonial newspaper was one thing – gaining an international reputation was another. The question hardly arose until 1872, when the first electric telegraph linked London and Melbourne, bringing international news as close to *The Age* as it was to the London *Times*. At first, there were problems. In 1877, *The Age* reported that the ships *Margaret Galbraith*, *Czarewitch*, *Rhibilarious*, *Macaroon* and *Phoebe* had arrived safely in London from Australia. The following day, after bewilderment in shipping offices, it issued a correction: the Cesarewitch handicap at Newmarket racecourse had been won by Hibarious, with Macaroon second and Belphoebe third.[22]

It was in direct emulation of the great London papers, whose *Daily Telegraph* had sent H. M. Stanley into central Africa in the 1870s, that David Syme sent George Morrison to explore the wilds of New Guinea in 1883. It took seven weeks for Morrison's reports (including the news that he had been speared) to reach Australia and appear in print. Morrison, after considerable arguments with *The Age* about his expenses, went on to China, to become 'Chinese Morrison' and write his celebrated account of the siege of the Peking legation for the London *Times*. King David never forgave him.[23]

The Age was so much the premier paper of Australia that Syme saw it increasingly in an imperial role, fit to take its place with the celebrated papers of Fleet Street. In 1883, with circulation at 52,000 he proudly announced that the Saturday edition of sixteen pages made *The Age* the largest penny paper, in terms of sheer size, in the whole British Empire. By the year of Syme's death in 1908, the Saturday edition was twenty-four pages, with twelve-page papers on weekdays, and the circulation was 130,000.[24]

The horizons of Syme's thinking broadened with commercial success. He began to campaign for an Australian view of Empire defence, arguing passionately that Australia should no longer depend on the Royal Navy, but should acquire a fleet of its own. And in 1907 at the Imperial Conference in London, Alfred Deakin, the former leader-writer on *The Age*, successfully negotiated Australia's right to an independent navy. It is never easy to decide how far a newspaper influences events and how far it simply records them. But Deakin, in one of his three terms as Prime Minister, claimed of *The Age*: 'The *Times* in its palmiest days was not more omnipotent in London, nor the *Tribune* of Horace Greeley in New York.'[25]

The power and, perhaps, the political insight of King David were clearly on the wane by the end of the century. He had never quite become reconciled to the rise of the Labour Party in Australia, even though under Deakin's influence *The Age* campaigned for the legalization of trade unions, for the forty-eight-hour week and the prohibition of child labour. And the decision to create a single federal government of Australia from the various states was one over which Syme long hesitated, largely because it seemed to diminish the role of his beloved state of Victoria and city of Melbourne. Nor did Syme ever quite come to grips with the nature of modern political parties; he always felt that the labels of Liberal or Labour were of much less importance than whether a man was a free trader or whether he, like Syme, believed in tariff protection as Australia's economic panacea.

But Syme's importance to Australian journalism does not rest on his political power, nor even on the astonishing commercial success of *The Age*. It rests much more on the tradition of free and independent journalism which he, more than any other man, established in his country. His determination to defy established authority, to publish and be damned, to fight libel cases when their cost threatened to bankrupt his paper, and to educate his readers in the importance to them as citizens of a press freedom, underpinned his entire career.

During *The Age*'s first financial crisis, just before the printers' partnership took over, its first editor, David Blair, had complained: 'People, it is clear, do not care for newspapers, otherwise than as mere vehicles for trade advertisements.'[26] David Syme never took that view – Syme's vision of the role of the press was at once confident and rather humble: 'A newspaper is something more than an organ of public opinion; it may represent public opinion, but it also helps to form it . . .It presents [the man in the street] with the facts, shows him what those facts imply and how they affect him as a member of the community . . . Public criticism of public news is now a recognized function of the press. As long as this criticism is exercised in the public interest the press is unassailable . . . And the press claims to be free only on this condition, and in this respect it claims no more than the humblest individual possesses.'[27]

Syme's view of his work was always enormously serious, and *The Age*'s columns reflected this. They were closely printed, often ponderously written, never brightened by social gossip or fashions or puzzles. Bankruptcies and debts and court cases and funerals were fully reported; an elaborate coffin might be described, but not a bride's dress. Weather forecasts had no place, but yesterday's climate was fully recorded. *The Age* was a dour newspaper, obsessed with politics. And so strong was the legacy of David Syme that this style continued long after his death. In the 1920s, the paper went into a relative decline, losing readers and advertisers to the brash new tabloid, the *Sun News-Pictorial*. *The Age* reserved its front page for advertisements until the Second World War, shunning bold headlines and brisk reporting. The appearance of the paper changed little from David Syme's death in 1908 to the 1940s.

The force of Syme's personality, even from the grave, seems to have inhibited change. *The Age* became, in the generation after his death, something of a mausoleum to the man. Its senior executives had been trained by him, and they were able men. J. S. Stephens, universally known as 'The Sub', became an almost legendary figure in his own right. Appalled to read in a correspondent's cable that a group of Australian Ministers at a Geneva conference had 'lunched sparingly on cheese sandwiches and tea', Stephens changed the menu to inform *The Age*'s readers that the Ministers had enjoyed turkey, ham and champagne.[28] Ray Austin, the chief reporter and political correspondent, was desperate for a scoop during the constitutional crisis of 1913, when nobody was certain whether the Prime Minister, Jo Cook, would dissolve one or both – or neither – houses of parliament. Pleading with Cook for some sort of statement, Austin was told enigmatically, 'take your courage in both hands, young man', and he gambled – correctly – on a prediction that both houses would be dissolved. There was nothing wrong with the ability of the men Syme had appointed, but they and the newspaper had become locked into the classically Victorian Syme style. More than that, Syme's intimacy and influence with the political Establishment locked the paper into a closeness with government, into a sense of loyalty to the 'national interest', which seems to have left it out of step with public opinion.

Twice during the First World War Australia held a national referendum on whether or not conscription should be introduced. On each occasion, *The Age* campaigned for conscription – and each time the public voted, albeit narrowly, against it. The greater interest in news during the war (and in the casualty lists) helped to push *The Age*'s circulation to its highest point – 152,000 copies in 1916. But the readers were getting a tamed newspaper. Throughout the belligerent world, war censorship, military control of news, became a fact of publishing life. In Australia, the War Precautions Act said, in plain language, that anything the government described as an offence was an offence. *The Age* had begun by sending its own correspondent with the first Australian troops, but the British High Command quickly established a control system under which all war news was to come through one official, and a handful of accredited (and approved) war correspondents. The arguments for military censorship were clear enough on the battlefield. In Australia, the Hughes government used the War Precautions Act to control political news. *The Age* chose not to lead, not hardly even to join, the opposition to Hughes's dictatorial use of his powers. Indeed, when in 1918 an advisory board system of editors and censors was established to consult over what might and might not be printed, they met in *The Age* offices in Melbourne each week. In the rooms where David Syme had spelt out the principles of press freedom, *The Age* co-operated in its own muzzling, arguing only about how tight the straps should be.[29]

The rising prices of wartime forced *The Age* to increase the price of its Saturday paper from 1d to 2d. In 1921, the weekday *Age* also went up to 2d. The price was cut back to 1½d in 1923, in response to the competition from the *Sun*. In 1925, the competition increased with the publication of another rival, the *Morning Post*. Circulation of *The Age* declined steadily from its 1916 peak until, in 1936, it was selling fewer than 100,000 copies a day – its worst performance since the 1890s. Its advertising revenue took longer to suffer, with an average sixty-five columns daily in 1927, compared to an average of sixty even in the highly successful year of 1907. But the Depression of the 1930s cut deeply, with classified columns falling below forty a day by 1931.[30] Falling revenues meant that it was difficult to buy modern printing equipment; until 1938, *The Age* was still using the machines which David Syme had installed. Its managers were also labouring under the terms of the Trust which his will had established. It was not until 1948 that an application to the Supreme Court enabled his descendants to break its terms and use the locked capital to invest in new plant and machinery. The Trust was dissolved and a public company, David Syme and Co. Ltd., established.[31]

The war had stimulated sales, which had risen to 120,000 by 1945, and to 140,000 in 1952. But costs had risen, newsprint rising from an average £12 a ton in the 1930s to £100 a ton in 1943, and £170 a ton in 1947. Wartime controls on labour had almost abolished classified advertising for jobs. In 1943, *The Age* carried an average twenty-six columns of advertising a day, the lowest proportion since the 1870s.[32]

Even with news, rather than advertisements, on the front page, *The Age* was still a staid and antiquated newspaper in the late 1940s. Its political line loyally followed the postures of the Liberal Party which had now become the dominant conservative force in Australian politics. When in 1950 the Liberal government introduced a bill to dissolve and then to ban the Communist Party, *The Age*'s editorials rallied behind it, 'because of the proofs of a world pattern of Communist conspiracy'.[33] Loyalty to conservative principles and loyalty to Great Britain were the hallmarks of *The Age*.

Slowly, the paper brightened, with pictures on the front page, striking headlines, full and enthusiastic sports coverage. But it was a jumbled paper. Its editorials, its features, and its exhaustive coverage of local politics still bore the Victorian imprint of David Syme. It remained a fundamentally serious paper, the first in Australia to post a resident correspondent in Washington (1954) and South-East Asia (1959). It was also the first paper to defy convention by printing Prime Ministers' press conferences verbatim. Beyond those pages, there was a breeziness, an almost desperate hunt for the human angle in news stories, pictures of cuddly animals and chatty captions that seemed to come from a different newspaper altogether. The effect was almost schizophrenic, like the *Church Times* mated with the *Daily Mirror*. Circulation declined slowly year by year until 1957, when a major rival, the *Argus*, ceased publication, and *The Age* began selling 170,000 copies a day. But its sales figures were puny by comparison with the *Sun* – 562,000 – and the Melbourne evening paper, the *Herald*, with 464,000. Nor was it a great financial success. Annual profits were £95,000 in 1951, down to £59,500 the following year, £90,000 in 1957.[34] There were occasional good years when economic booms brought in the classified ads on which *The Age*'s profits had long depended. But the performance should have been better. Melbourne was a large and prosperous city, and *The Age* had the advantage of all essentially local or metropolitan papers: a well-defined marketing area and low distribution costs. The English national newspapers, by comparison, face the problems of delivering their copies to breakfast tables all over Great Britain, while not being able to draw on the London advertising market. The British press depends on advertisements of nationally sold products. *The Age* of Melbourne, like the *New York Times*, is a natural vehicle for local retail stores to advertise, and for the kind of classified ads which only a tightly defined area can generate.

The Age began the process of modernization in 1960 when for the first time it began its own aggressive advertising campaign. One reason for the new approach was a new member of the Syme family on the board, Randall Macdonald, fresh from a course in journalism and business studies at Columbia University in New York.[35]

More important was the new generation of journalists, most of them cadets from *The Age*'s own training scheme, who began to sharpen the paper's content and layout. In Australian journalism as a whole, and particularly in Canberra, the end of the Menzies era and an increasing sense of frustration with the smugness of Australian society led to a new sharpness in reporting. Allen Barnes, *The Age* bureau chief in Canberra, and Max Walsh of the *Financial Review* and Laurie Oakes of the Melbourne *Sun* (and later *The Age*) and Alan Ramsey of *The Australian* were not content with the deference and long quotations from speeches that had characterized Australian political journalism. One of their colleagues later recalled their work: 'Energetic, iconoclastic, self-confident and eloquent, they transformed political reporting in Australia.'[36] The Vietnam war had sharpened journalists' perceptions in America, and Australia's part in the war had a similar if less widespread effect on its journalists. And Australian journalists (and their readers) were becoming better educated. The Age's cadet scheme involved a three-year part-time course at Melbourne University, leading to a Diploma in Journalism. One of its graduates was Graham Perkin, who had joined The Age in 1949, and never worked for any other paper. In 1966, at a time of fundamental change for The Age, he was appointed editor, a post in which he was to rival the original David Syme for influence and determination to mould the paper into his own shape and form.

In the mid-1960s, The Age management faced the dilemma of stagnant revenues and sharply rising costs. The Age's share of Australian major metropolitan newspaper advertising had remained unchanged at 14% since 1951.[37] In spite of costly promotion campaigns, circulation was stagnant at about 180,000, and in 1965 it began to fall below that. A major competitor was looming in the form of Rupert Murdoch's new national daily, The Australian. And an extensive new wage agreement increased the annual payroll by some 14% in 1965, while profit on turnover was a gloomy 4%.[38] It was, in short, a classic candidate for a takeover bid. The Syme family decided, after examining the alternatives, to merge with the Fairfax company, which owned the Sydney Morning Herald. 'The independent traditions, character and reputation of The Age, and its future commercial operations, might be impaired if the company came under control of rival newspapers at present in direct competition with The Age.'[39] Under the first phase of the deal, in 1967, Fairfax bought a 35.7% interest, increased to 57% by 1979. Complex safeguards were written into the terms of the partnership, which gave Syme nominees equal voting rights on the board with Fairfax nominees, and a guarantee of editorial independence. The new company's increased financial confidence was quickly seen; the number of editorial staff rose sharply from 154 in 1965 to 216, five years later.[40] The paper thickened, the layout was transformed, and a progressive merging of the foreign correspondent facilities of The Age and the Sydney Morning Herald meant more overseas news and commentaries.

Much of the credit for the improvement must go to Graham Perkin. The Age's own obituary on this most dynamic of its twentieth-century editors put it plainly: 'Because of the gruff, tough, pertinacious

Perkin, *The Age* abandoned its conservative, pussy-footing style of journalism to become a crusader.' Normally there are few more disgusting sounds than a newspaper slapping itself clammily on the back. Perkin himself loathed the process, warning a conference of journalists discussing press freedom in the future that 'the principal risk is the unshatterable smugness of newspaper publishers and editors – myself included'.[41] Perkin launched a process of endless self-criticism and self-analysis on the paper. He doubled the space for readers' letters, began a regular feature which explained and apologized for *The Age*'s mistakes. *The Age* began to campaign against the disparities and harshness of the various state libel laws across Australia, attacking in particular the use of 'the gagging writ', which was designed not to lead to a court hearing, but to frighten reporters away from a subject. Between 1952 and 1967, there were 831 defamation actions begun in Australia, of which only twenty-one reached court.[42] *The Age* began to fill with new special supplements, fat with advertising, that covered everything from how to care for household pets to an everyman's guide to nuclear physics. (The least successful was a supplement on how to play football – to *The Age*'s surprise.)[43] There were failures; an evening edition, 'Newsday', was launched and cancelled after three disastrous months.

Newspapers exist in a marketplace and, by those commercial standards, Graham Perkin was the best editor since David Syme. Under his editorship, circulation rose from 180,000 to 220,000. Average daily columns of advertising (display and classified) rose from 233 to 324. Profits rose from $818,000 to $2,868,000.[44] Perkin had his critics. He could be an abrasive boss and for a man of liberal views he had an old-fashioned idea about the role of women. He clung to the tradition of specific women's pages, and would not promote or encourage women journalists.[45] His main contribution to *The Age*, apart from its profits and its new hunger for scoops and campaigns and exclusives, was to stress that a richer and better-informed audience was demanding that the press improve its own standards, while the press fought off another kind of commercial threat from the electronic media. 'We in the media are at an all-time low in credibility. I don't think newspapers are any worse than they were . . . but the audience is a lot better, more critical,' was the message he insisted *The Age* should learn.[46] Superficially, it looked as if Perkin had shifted *The Age* from its automatic anti-Communism and pro-government approach of the 1950s to a trendy radicalism. But it was more fundamental. Macdonald and Perkin had jointly agreed that

The Age should never give automatic support to any institution, be it government, ideology or corporation, ever again. 'It is the approach of honest pragmatism, and if we are wrong we will say so and correct it,' Randall Macdonald says.[47] Perkin's new broom did not always succeed. He had talked of bringing *The Age* home to its own state of Victoria, and focusing much more on state politics and rather less on the federal capital of Canberra. This he failed to do. When he died in 1975, there were still eight *Age* staff in Canberra, and one man on Victoria state politics; a proportion perhaps explained more by the new controversies and dynamics of national government in the Whitlam era than by Perkin's design.[48]

After Perkin's death, *The Age* was to run through three editors in six years, finishing with Michael Davie, an Englishman who had won the Columnist of the Year Award for his 'Notebook' in the London *Observer*. Davie took the view that Australian newspapers, at least in terms of marketing and advertising, had more to learn from the US than from the traditional Fleet Street mentors.[49] Davie and Macdonald drafted a plan to double the number of foreign correspondents by 1983, from its 1980 base of two correspondents in London, one in Amman, Singapore, San Francisco and Washington, and (shared with the Sydney *Morning Herald*) correspondents in Tokyo and Peking. *The Age* was also planning a consortium with the *Washington Post* to publish a regular feature of articles on the Third World, mainly by Third World writers. 'We want to have a news hole 20–30% larger than it is now – we can always cut back on the midweek racing tables,' Macdonald says.[50]

The plans for *The Age* in the 1980s received a sudden setback in November 1979, when Rupert Murdoch suddenly bid $126 million for Australia's biggest media group, the Melbourne-based Herald and Weekly Times Ltd – which would have given Murdoch a near-monopoly of the Australian media. In a spectacular $70 million shopping spree on the floor of Melbourne's Stock Exchange in one afternoon, the John Fairfax group bought 15% of the *Herald*'s shares – enough to block the Murdoch bid. But the *Herald* company's 14% holding in the David Syme Company, combined with the Fairfax group's 57% share of the Syme company, gave the new Herald–Fairfax alliance a 71% share of *The Age* – the paper which was the *Herald*'s main competitor in Melbourne. Randall Macdonald announced that the deal 'threatens the coverage of news and the presentation of diverse opinion in the Victorian press', and formally asked Fairfax to sell back its holdings in David Syme to the Syme family.[51] Behind this request was a decade in which *The Age* had consistently done better than the Sydney *Morning Herald*, Fairfax's flagship. In that decade, after-tax profits on *The Age* had grown by 249%, while the *Morning Herald* profits had grown by only 173%. In the same ten years, return on shareholders' funds had grown by 69% on *The Age*, but by only 3% on the *Herald*. The readership of the *Herald* was much older (42% over fifty years of age, compared to only 29% of *Age* readers) which made the *Herald* steadily less attractive to advertisers.[52] Financial logic suggested that *The Age* would do better on its own; it equally suggested to the Fairfax group that *The Age* had better be retained. In spite of appeals to the Trades Practices Commission, *The Age*'s attempt to recover its full independence stalled, with the Fairfax group repeating their determination to allow *The Age* full editorial freedom. But the campaign has barely begun.

While the boardroom battle was under way, the differences between *The Age* and the Sydney *Morning Herald* were underlined by the bitter industrial disputes which shook the *Herald* over the introduction of computer typesetting, while *The Age* had relatively little difficulty in negotiating the use of computers, and eventual computerized page make-up and editing. It would lead to a theoretical saving of 250 jobs on *The Age*, which the company undertook to try to make up by going for growth in pages and circulation. *The Age* has never been stopped by a strike in its 128-year history.

No portrait of *The Age* would be complete without reference to one of its greatest traditional strengths, the cartoonists. It is an oddity of British journalism that its finest cartoonists have been bred and trained overseas: Will Dyson was an Australian, David Low an Australian-trained New Zealander, and the immortal Vicky was a Hungarian. Some of Fleet Street's finest cartoonists of the 1970s continued the tradition: Les Gibbard from New Zealand, and Keith Waite from Australia. And back in Melbourne, *The Age* maintains a team of five cartoonists, the highest proportion on any major newspaper in the world. 'It is the last bastion of the simplistic statement in modern journalism,' says their publisher. And sometimes cartoons can be more than that. When ex-Premier Gough Whitlam was touring China during the disastrous earthquake of 1978, *The Age* ran a cartoon which showed the Whitlams in bed in a Chinese hotel, having just made love. Through the window, Great Walls and Forbidden Palaces could be seen toppling. Gough asks: 'Did the earth move for you too, darling?' *The Age* ran it front-page, and was deluged with complaints – and a telegram from Whitlam asking for the original.[53]

Notes

1. David Syme & Co. Ltd, annual report 1978.
2. Sir Robert Southey to Premier McMahon, March 1972 letter. Quoted in *The Whitlam Venture*, Alan Reid.
3. *The Age*, 1.xii.1972.
4. *The Age*, September 1975, *passim*.
5. Author's interview and letter, Bruce Welch, circulation manager, *The Age*.
6. *The Age*, 17.x.1854.
7. *ibid.*
8. *The Age*, 17.x.1954, 100th anniversary supplement.
9. *ibid.*
10. *125 Years of Age*, eds G. Hutton and L. Tanner. See introduction by Professor M. Blainey.
11. *The Australian Thunderer*, M. Cannon.
12. *ibid.*
13. *The Age*, 7.xii.1860.
14. *The Age*, 12.xi.1857 and 9.ix.1858.
15. Blainey, *op. cit.*
16. Anniversary supplement, *op. cit.*
17. *ibid.*
18. *ibid.* See also Blainey, *op. cit.*
19. *The Age*, 23.viii.1879. Also anniversary supplement, *op. cit.*
20. *The Age*, 19.v.1877.
21. Anniversary supplement, *op. cit.*
22. *ibid.*
23. *ibid.* See also *The First Casualty*, P. Knightley.
24. Anniversary supplement, *op. cit.*
25. Quoted, *ibid.*
26. Quoted in Blainey, *op. cit.*
27. *125 Years of Age, op. cit.* See foreword, Randall Macdonald.
28. Anniversary supplement, *op. cit.*
29. *ibid.* See also Knightley, *op. cit.*
30. Anniversary supplement, *op. cit.* Also communication from B. Welch, circulation manager.
31. David Syme & Co. Ltd, annual report 1949.
32. Communication to author from B. Welch, *op. cit.* Further communications to author from Sally A. White, executive assistant to managing director, *The Age*.
33. *The Age*, 18.ix.1950.
34. Communications from B. Welch, S. White, *op. cit.* See also annual reports, relevant years.
35. Author's interview, Randall Macdonald.
36. *The Age*, 13.vi.1977.
37. Communications from B. Welch and S. White, *op. cit.*
38. *ibid.*
39. John Fairfax Ltd, annual report, 1967. 'The Age partnership'.
40. Communications to author from S. White, *op. cit.*
41. *The Age*, 12.vi.1977. Peter Smark series on the Press in Australia.

42. *The Age*, 12.vi.1977; *ibid*.
43. *The Age*, 15.vi.1977; *ibid*.
44. Communications to author, B. Welch and S. White, *op. cit.*
45. Interview, S. White.
46. Interview in *Quadrant*, Melbourne, October 1975.
47. Author's interview, Macdonald.
48. *The Age*, 15.vi.1977. Peter Smark series, *op. cit.*
49. Three months after taking over in Melbourne, Davie undertook an extensive tour of US suburban newspapers. Author's interview, Macdonald.
50. Author's interview, Macdonald.
51. *The Age*, 29.xi.1979. See also the *Sun*, 30.xi.1979.
52. Communications from S. White and B. Welch, *op. cit.*
53. Author's interview, Macdonald.

THE MELBOURNE AGE: EDITORIALS

The independence of India: 21 July 1947

'Britain is carrying out a pledge, and giving to the Asian peoples the chance to show that they are capable of directing their own affairs, without tutelage.'

The independence of Israel: 14 May 1948

'Whatever happens after British authority ceases, Britain will leave Palestine with an honourable record and only one regret: that Jews and Arabs have never found the road to compromise and mutual tolerance. . .Britain certainly has no cause for self-reproach at any omission and no reason to apologize for any aspect of its regime.'

The Berlin blockade and airlift: 25 June 1948

'The Western powers cannot be expected to yield to the dictates and demands of Soviet Russia. . .A firm line towards Russia would almost certainly create temporary difficulties but it is the only policy which can promise lasting and satisfactory results for the Western democracies.'

The Communists win power in China: 4 October 1949

'Things have gone so badly for Chiang Kai-shek and the Communists have established such a mastery that it is only possible to lament what might have been.'

The Korean war: 18 September 1950

'Because of the proofs of a world pattern of Communist conspiracy against all non-Communist regimes, ranging from internal subversion to open aggression, as in Korea, Australia and other countries must set about strengthening their defences. World events have strengthened the case for the Bill [to dissolve and ban Australia's Communist Party] and underlined the need for stringent precautions against Communist sabotage and treachery.'

The Suez invasion: 1 November 1956

'It would be bad faith as well as bad politics for Britain to forget about a treaty she signed two years ago [to maintain the status quo in the Middle East and freedom of passage in the Canal] for fear of upsetting her allies.'

The Russian invasion of Hungary: 5 November 1956

'Russia's swift and brutal assault upon rebellious Hungary has shocked the civilized world and made a mockery of the sanctimonious statements of the Soviet government. It is the act of a whole nation determined to gain its freedom.'

The Bay of Pigs assault on Cuba: 17 April 1961

'Nobody in his senses would seriously imagine that President Kennedy would paint obsolete wartime bombers with Cuban colours and send them on a bombing and strafing mission against Cuba's military bases. This is a frivolous charge against the US. . .there is a comic opera touch about these thunderous denunciations.'

The Cuban missile crisis: 24 October 1962

'President Kennedy has played one of his strongest cards, it is too late to ask him to think again. We can only support him, and hope that events justify his brinkmanship, undertaken without prior consultation with his allies.'

The Gulf of Tonkin incident: 6 August 1964

'The United States whose role has been to support and guide South Vietnam in its struggle against Communist infiltration and subversion, now finds herself a victim of aggression on the high seas.'

China's nuclear weapon: 30 December 1966

'This week's proof that China is fast catching up in the nuclear race underlines the importance of bringing it into the UN. . .It is possible to ignore the existence of a country which can be contained, but not one which may soon be able to leap out and menace the world.'

Rhodesia's UDI: 12 November 1965

'The danger does not lie in immediate warlike acts. . .the final tragedy of British de-colonization in Africa is that it may have created a running sore, which will not heal in a generation.'

The Russian invasion of Czechoslovakia: 22 August 1968

'The Kremlin's savage answer to the Prague challenge was not only morally indefensible but tactically foolish. At one blow, it has destroyed the position of moral authority it had painstakingly built up in the Afro-Asian world by its comparatively moderate foreign and domestic policies since the Cuban missile affair.'

Israel's occupation of the West Bank: 22 October 1973

'Perhaps the best we can hope for is, when the fighting stops, an uneasy co-existence as before, some measure of justice for the dispossessed Palestinians, a continued flow of oil to the Western world, and a tacit agreement between the superpowers to keep the Middle East under control.'

The OPEC price rise: 26 December 1973

'The decision of the six Persian Gulf oil-producing states to double their prices is based on economic, rather than political motives. . .To some extent, the major industrial nations have themselves to blame for the steep price rises. . .The producer countries were exchanging valuable commodities for devalued bank balances and highly-priced imports.'

Watergate: 15 October 1973

'Richard M. Nixon should no longer be President. . .the sooner America dispatches him, the sooner it can be believed, and believe in itself.'

The fall of Saigon: 1 May 1975

'What began for the US as an experiment in counter-insurgency and for Australia as an insurance premium for American protection, deteriorated into a brutal war of attrition and the destruction of all it hoped to achieve.'

Sport and politics: The boycott of the Olympics over New Zealand's decision to play rugby with South Africa: 8 July 1976

'The protest over New Zealand is mischievous politicking. The questionable wisdom of the All-Blacks' tour of South Africa should not be pervertedly seized upon by black nations who see it as a support for white racism and carried into a totally different arena.'

The space venture: 25 May 1962

'No reason is immediately obvious why the Federal Government [of Australia] should not allow both Russia and America to set up satellite-tracking stations in Australia and her territories.'

Freedom of information: 5 June 1978

'The public's right to know what a government does in its name, and why, should be overriden only when secrecy is a necessity. . .Secrecy is now practised for its own sake, and for the convenience of politicians and bureaucrats. This is both absurd and dangerous.'

13

The Rand Daily Mail

The *Rand Daily Mail* (*RDM*) was born almost as a whim in the rowdy atmosphere of Johannesburg just as the Boer War ended. It was a gold-rush boom town, full of soldiers and brothels and brand-new millionaires and taverns and, fittingly, the paper began in the crowded bar-room of Heath's Hotel. Emmanuel Mendelssohn was complaining to his companions that he had been saddled with a warehouse full of linotype machines and printing presses, all that was left of *The Standard and Diggers' News* which had made the mistake of being backed by the losing Kruger government while the war was on. Freeman Cohen, a merchant and gold dealer, offered to buy the printing equipment, musing that the Rand goldfields needed a newspaper. Shortly afterwards, an imperious young man strode into the bar. Edgar Wallace, to become famous as a writer of thrillers, was then a hot-shot young journalist for Harmsworth's *Daily Mail*. Cohen made inquiries around the bar, heard that Wallace was hated by Kitchener for getting the scoop of the peace treaty from under the censors' noses, and offered him a job as editor. They shook hands, had a drink to seal it, and the *Rand Daily Mail* was under way.[1]

It almost foundered in its first year. Wallace was accustomed to the lavish expenditure of Harmsworth's papers. He also thought Cohen was a gold millionaire. Wallace hired the best journalists he could buy with the highest salaries then being paid anywhere outside Fleet Street and New York. He was determined to make the new paper dominant in the political capital, Pretoria, and hired a special nightly train, the '699 Down', to get his edition on to the streets. There was a fleet of delivery vans and, in the major cities around the world, special correspondents were wiring dispatches to Johannesburg, spurred on by Wallace's orders that money was no object and that the *RDM* was determined to become a major international paper overnight. Johannesburg was plastered with the slogan of Wallace's advertising campaign: 'Money, Brains and Energy are employed without stint in making the *RDM*'. Ten months later, when the cable bills finally came in, at 10s 3d a word from Tokyo, and 6s 2d a word from Buenos Aires, Freeman Cohen had to clean out his bank accounts to pay the bills.[2]

Cohen borrowed more money to buy off Edgar Wallace who sailed back to England; Cohen cancelled the train, sold off the delivery vans, fired the foreign correspondents and began producing a modest local paper for the goldfields. But he died within months, and his executors put the paper up for sale. A group of Boer nationalists, still critical of British rule, made the first offer, a prospect which so alarmed the British pro-consul, Lord Milner, that he persuaded Abe Bailey, a real goldfield millionaire this time and later to become Sir Abraham, that the British Empire had need of his money.[3] Bailey bought the paper by taking over its overdraft, and immediately leased it out to a syndicate of three able young men. George Kingswell, an Australian journalist, was general manager; Ralph Ward-Jackson, a former cavalry officer and member of the Stock Exchange, became editor; and the third, and key commercial figure, was A. V. Lindbergh, chairman and founder of the Central News Agency, which dominated newspaper distribution in South Africa into the 1970s.

Their prime objective was to make money in the booming town of 70,000 white people that had grown in the space of a generation from a shanty town of tents and saloons into an imposing small city. But the years before the First World War saw economic recession, exacerbated by labour disputes. The *RDM*'s ancillary businesses, particularly its printing plant and the successful *Sunday Times* started in 1906, made up the profits which the paper itself lost and paid for a new building in 1911.[4] It was very much a businessman's paper, devoted to the mining interests and to the white mineworkers. This was very nearly a contradictory position, and the *RDM*'s editorial position was to try and keep a balance between the two: 'Our duty is to encourage capital within reasonable limits, and to support the cause of labour whenever the interests of the latter are unfairly attacked.'[5] The bulk of its pre-war readers were the white mine employees and, from the beginning, the *RDM* adhered firmly to the view that the white man's interests were best served by excluding non-whites from jobs: 'One need not fear for the kaffirs. There is ample work for them on the mines if they want it; and it is certainly a reproach to see natives in employment whilst white men walk the streets unable to secure a job.'[6] The blacks were to be restricted to the crudest of labouring jobs and white supremacy ensured by employment policies.

This was very far from an extreme position in the South Africa of the day. Editorials were constantly referring to 'the indolent native, the parasite of our civilization', and the *RDM* once even toyed with the idea of supporting one reader's scheme to deport all non-whites north of the Zambezi. Were it not for the fact that the mines needed the labour, the *RDM* would have bitterly opposed the importing of Chinese workers to the mines. Indeed, its first editorial reaction was: 'Don't give a Chinkie a footing, we have colours enough as it is.' The *RDM* campaigned against the granting of shop or trading licences to Indians, and backed a campaign to revive a law of 1899 which banned non-whites from city pavements. It had no time for the more liberal ideas that occasionally seeped through from Europe, calling upon South African churchmen to 'discard all the sickly sentimentality of the shrieking sisterhood for equality of privilege with the "black brothers"'.[7] Being an English-language paper in a predominantly English-speaking town in the aftermath of a war against the Boers, the *RDM*'s innate racism could also be turned on the Afrikaners. Official government policy was that peace had brought a new Anglo-Boer partnership, and certainly the *RDM* maintained friendly relations with the Transvaal government of Louis Botha and Jan Smuts in Pretoria. But the anti-Boer attitudes died hard: 'The more the Boers get, the more, apparently, they will ask for.'[8] And the funeral of Paul Kruger was reported almost as if it were an occasion at a zoo, an anthropological exhibit where the loyal old Boers who had voted and fought for Kruger were exposed to the city slickers of the *RDM*. But in the last resort, the Boers were white men too: 'We have the deepest sympathy with the preservation of the purity of the race, with the high ideals that inspire the wish to make this purely a white man's country.'[9]

Certain of its racial position, the *RDM* was in constant internal difficulty about its stand for or against the mine owners. In 1907, when Smuts sternly put down a white miners' strike with imperial troops, the *RDM* was piously to regret the need for the troops and the Boer politicians to be involved, to sympathize with the miners' objectives and the economic hardships they faced, without ever quite saying that the mine owners were a singularly selfish and uncompromising breed of men who were determined to cling to their profits even if they provoked class war. In 1913, the grumbling discontent in the mines reached a new pitch; riots erupted, the police were unable to keep order, the Colonial Office was unwilling for British troops to be used once more, and the South African Defence Force was still in the process of being formed. Botha and Smuts were forced to drive to Johannesburg and surrender to the miners' demands while implacable miners stood armed guard around them. By January of 1914, Smuts was ready for revenge. There was a plan for a general strike, but Smuts declared martial law, put his Defence Force on the streets, and arrested and deported without trial all the miners' leaders. They were on the high seas before a court order could be obtained to free them from detention. The *RDM* was happy to condemn the tactics of the government and of the miners' leaders. And when miners' representatives won a handful of seats in local government elections shortly after the failed strike, the *RDM* was able to declare, in tones of some relief: 'The recent successes of Labour at the polls have done more to rid South Africa of the strike madness than all the repressive legislature [*sic*] the Government could devise in five years.'[10]

That general strike also showed that the *RDM* was run by enterprising men. The compositors and linotypers voted to join the strike, so the journalists conscripted women typists from around the city and had them type out the cables and the news stories, and the typed pages were then photographed and made into blocks, just as if they had been pictures. The paper was then printed in the usual way. Disheartened at the paper's refusal to be stopped, the printers returned to work the next day.[11]

The paper they normally produced was a lively and fundamentally a local daily that ran between eight and twelve pages. It had a women's page, with drawings of the latest London and Paris fashions, and a strong features section that had begun with Edgar Wallace writing his own short stories. It ran extracts, invariably the romantic scenes, from popular novels of the day, and usually devoted two pages to the theatre and music-halls and concerts which filled the growing town. It paid as much attention to local sports, reporting boxing, racing, walking races and the new motor-car events with equal, gushing enthusiasm. Its most celebrated journalist was Wallace Duncan, better known as 'True Blue' for the remarkable accuracy of his racing tips. Its social page was filled with the names of passengers on the trains reaching Johannesburg, the new guests at the hotels and the big winners at the races.[12]

It remained an amateurish product. Letters to the editor were slotted in around the paper, wherever there was a space to fill. There was one exception; serious letters, by which was meant letters to the mining editor, had a showcase of their own. The front page was reserved for advertising, with an occasional cartoon; for special events, like the Grasfontein diamond rush, the front page would be filled with photographs – a pattern that was to last until the Second World War. Like the community it served, the paper cultivated a spirit of energetic informality. L. E. Neame, to become editor in the 1920s, joined the new *RDM* in 1904 after serving his press apprentice-ship in India, and he later recalled: 'Journalistically, the town made a pleasant change for me after the stiffness and formality of Victorian England and Curzon's India, where newspapermen found it difficult to get past a doorkeeper or a third secretary. Lord Milner was readily accessible, and one could go to Pretoria, fairly certain of a chat with Louis Botha or Jan Smuts.'[13]

The *RDM* did not have the Johannesburg market to itself. The *Star*, an evening paper, had been founded in 1887, and its major shareholders were also mine owners. The *Transvaal Leader* was the morning competition, although the *RDM* easily won a brief circula-tion war. The South African press tradition is one of combines and monopolies, rather than of individual papers, and the *RDM*'s direct-ing triumvirate followed that pattern. The most acute historian of the press in South Africa, Miss Elaine Potter, has observed that 'the English press in South Africa was not born of a struggle for freedom, nor to meet the needs of immigrant masses. Rather, it asserted itself on the grounds of a right to run a business for profit.'[14] In dramatic contrast, the Afrikaans press was born of a cultural, political and even tribal reaction against the dominant English culture. The Afrikaans press was and remains governed by the imperatives of cultural survival. Until the second half of the twentieth century, the English press knew no such absolutes. There had been a half-struggle in 1827 when the *Commercial Advertiser* had been banned by an imperious colonial governor, Lord Charles Somerset, merely for reprinting an article from *The Times* of London on Somerset's vindictive ways. The matter was quickly appealed to the government in London, Somerset was recalled, and the political tradition of the right to criticize governments was born. It was to remain unchallenged for over a century.[15]

As a result, the main challenges the young *RDM* had to face were the almost banal problems of circulation and competition. Having founded the highly successful *Sunday Times* in 1906, the triumvirate moved to safeguard their position, and in 1910, the *Rand Daily Mail*, the *Cape Times* and the dominant Argus paper group made a joint arrangement with Reuters to deliver news from South Africa to the British news agency, and receive the Reuters international wire in return. In short, a cartel was formed. And then the joint managements of the *RDM* and *Sunday Times* moved to consolidate their position in the Transvaal. In 1915, they bought out the *RDM*'s only rival, the *Transvaal Leader*, and the *Sunday Times*'s competitor, the *Sunday Post*. In 1920, the cartel was developed, when the Argus group and the *RDM* formally agreed not to publish newspapers in direct competition with each other – an agreement that remains in force. In 1929 the *RDM* and Argus jointly bought the *Pretoria News*. The Argus group, which included the *Cape Argus* and the Johannesburg evening *Star*, remained the dominant press group, and in 1932, the *RDM* management took the initiative to form South African Morning Newspapers (SAMN) from the *RDM*, the *Cape Times* and *Natal Mercury*. The first real competition the *RDM* ever had to face came in 1934, when I. W. Schlesinger, the wealthy owner of the South African Broadcasting Company, set up the *Sunday Express*, followed by the *Daily Express* in 1937. The time was significant; with Hitler's anti-semitism becoming blatant, and pro-Nazi Afrikaners bringing the foul doctrine to South Africa, the Jewish community of the Rand prevailed upon Schlesinger, himself a Jew, to pull back from antagonizing an English-language press which had traditionally been sympathetic. Again, the cartel was mobilized, and the Argus group, the *RDM* and the *Sunday Times* jointly bought out Schlesinger, closed the *Daily Express*, and then Argus sold its shares in the *Sunday Express* to the other two papers, who ran it as a down-market publication, in no position to challenge the dominant *Sunday Times*, but a useful repository for its spare advertising.[16]

The Afrikaans threat had to be taken seriously. In 1937, the nationalist Prime Minister Hertzog had called in all South Africa's editors to threaten a tough new press law if they did not stop attacking the Nazi and fascist governments in Europe. While the black population remained cowed, the most visible group tension in South Africa was that between the English-speakers and the Afrikaners, with the former dominating commercial, professional and intellectual life, and the Afrikaners remaining rooted in the rural areas. But in the 1930s, an Afrikaans cultural revival was under way, determined to win full political power. In 1938, Dr Malan, later to be Prime Minister, raised £100,000 to found *Die Transvaler*, an uncompromisingly Afrikaans and nationalist daily. Its first editor was the intellectual father of apartheid, Dr Hendrik Verwoerd. His rivalry as a newspaper editor in the 1930s became something very much more serious when Verwoerd became the Prime Minister of a government which was to declare legal war upon the *Rand Daily Mail* in the 1960s.[17]

The Afrikaans revival was to have the salutary effect of shocking the *RDM*, and the English-speaking community as a whole, out of their traditional and cosy illusion that they remained somehow a part of the British homeland. The *RDM* reacted to Britain's successive crises with an instinctive Anglophile patriotism. In 1914, when large sections of the Afrikaans community were honestly troubled by the prospect of a new war on behalf of the very British Empire that they had fought barely a decade ago, the *RDM* called instantly and stridently for war at Britain's side.[18] More strikingly, the *RDM*'s usual sensitivity to the problems of the mining corporations turned into venomous scorn when the De Beers Corporation began to close down their operations within two days of war being declared, on the brisk commercial principle that war would do the diamond market little good. 'The people of South Africa have a striking object lesson of the folly of placing great national enterprises at the mercy of cosmo-politan financiers. . .diamond patriotism is revealed today as the cheapest cut glass,' its editorial sneered.[19] In 1926, during the British general strike, the *RDM*'s pages were dominated by the affairs of the mother-nation a hemisphere away, and its editorial comment stressed that, Britain being Britain, such industrial convulsions should not be taken too seriously: 'Almost anything may happen, except we believe the revolution of which some of the firebrands, who have regrettably allied themselves in later years with the admirable trade-union movement, are wont to talk so glibly.'[20] During Britain's 1931 crisis, when the Labour government split and a coalition National Govern-ment was formed, the *RDM* gave it exhaustive coverage and, when the crisis was over, the paper concluded that all observers 'must have been struck by the significance of the part played in it by the King'.[21] While the King was on his throne, all was well with England, particu-larly since the *RDM* was confident that His Majesty's new government 'will certainly have the support of that great body of middle-class opinion which, whatever government is in office, actually governs England'.[22] The *RDM*'s editors were fascinated by British statesmen, sometimes against their own better judgement. Having commented with growing alarm and perception on the dangers of Hitler's rise throughout the 1930s, the *RDM* found itself during the Munich crisis praising to the skies Sir Neville Chamberlain, the British Premier whose appeasement policies made Hitler's job all the easier. Of Sir Neville, the *RDM* judged that 'he possesses the complete confidence of the entire nation in one of the most magnificent fights that has ever been waged by a single individual in the whole history of British statesmanship'.[23]

This kind of Anglo-centrism made the bitterness of Afrikaans reaction all the more understandable. While moderate Afrikanerdom was tearing itself apart in 1939, trying to decide whether to support Hitler or Britain when war came, with the Cabinet splitting by seven votes to six on the issue and Prime Minister Hertzog resigning, the *RDM* called bluntly for war and announced: 'With the British Commonwealth of nations, South Africa's deepest aspirations have found the fullest possible expression.'[24]

While certain of its international loyalties, the *RDM* continued to vacillate between the sides of labour and capital within South Africa. If it had a consistent policy, it was to believe in trade unions, except when they went on strike, and to believe in profits and capitalism, except (as in the case of De Beers) when they seemed to flout their public responsibilities. The *RDM* was a unionized newspaper from the beginning and, when threatened by the 1914 strike, its editorial gritted its teeth and said the paper would remain a union shop: 'The fault is not that of the system, in which we still believe, but of the madmen who rule the Federation today.'[25] During the 1922 general strike, when the government declared martial law and nineteen people were shot dead on the streets of Johannesburg, the *RDM* began moderately: 'Once more we advise the men to drop the double-edged weapon of the general strike, re-start the industry and go frankly to the government and to parliament and ask them to do their best for them and for the white man ideal in South Africa.'[26] Once martial law was declared, the *RDM* detected a Bolshevik menace among the strikers: 'men who, if they had their way, would repeat in South Africa the horrors of Soviet Russia'.[27] As a result, the *RDM* called upon all of its able-bodied readers to volunteer for the government militia.

Perhaps one reason for the *RDM*'s increasing hostility to the mineworkers, as opposed to the mine owners, lay in the steady growth of its circulation in the rural hinterland of the Rand. During the First World War, special arrangements had been made with the Central News Agency to win subscribers in the farming districts, and a regular page on local agriculture began to appear. But the *RDM* was owned by a mine owner and, in the last resort, that was the side the paper would back. On the very eve of war in 1939, with a sudden boom in gold shares tripling dividends, the government decided to impose a windfall profits tax. 'The confiscation of gold profits is bad ethics, bad politics and bad finance,' the *RDM* thundered.[28] Sir Abraham Bailey, one of the biggest gold shareholders of all, found it a suitable year to assume the chairmanship of the newspaper that he had owned, and largely ignored, for the previous thirty-five years.

The victory of the predominantly Afrikaans Nationalist Party in the 1948 elections saw the declaration of the long war of attrition between government and the English newspapers. At the beginning, as later, the *Rand Daily Mail* was in the front line. In December 1950, the *RDM* reported on the medical condition of Prime Minister Malan, on the grounds that his state of health was a topic of national concern. Dr Malan, who had wished his serious operations to remain a private matter, instantly ordered all government press officials and spokesmen to sever relations with the paper, to refuse them briefings and press releases.[29] In the new year, Dr Malan announced the formation of a Press Commission, to make recommendations for possible changes in the press law. One of the Commission's first concerns was to increase the presence of the Afrikaans press in SAPA, the South African Press Association, which was then dominated by the English press, who controlled 87.4% of the votes on the SAPA council.[30] The Commission was also worried by South Africa's image overseas, particularly in Britain, and its eventual report charged that reports to the London press concealed 'the barbarity or semi-civilized nature of the native' and focused on 'the supposedly unjust, harsh and oppressive treatment meted out to the natives by the whites'.[31] Since the bulk of foreign press reports were initiated by the English press in South Africa, the Commission was clearly aiming its criticisms at them. The Commission's report led to the 1963 Publications and Entertainments Act, which allowed for pre-publication censorship of any newspaper which did not agree to sign up for a self-policing, and self-censoring code of conduct.

This was the kind of attack that the *RDM* was not really equipped, either ideologically or practically, to handle. There was no militant tradition of press freedom. The *RDM* was seen by its managers and editors as a daily newspaper for the businessmen and the white middle classes of the Rand, not as a crusading sheet. It was in this spirit that Laurence Gandar was appointed to the editorship in 1957. If anybody symbolized the link between the *RDM* and the predominantly English commercial world, it was Gandar. Before joining the *RDM*, he had been the public relations adviser to Harry Oppenheimer of the giant Anglo American gold and diamonds group.[32]

Gandar was a man of the Establishment, a former Intelligence Officer in the South African army. But he found himself radicalized by the growing government pressure on his paper and by the fundamental changes under way within the English-speaking community. Its hardliners were increasingly supporting the Nationalist Party, its Liberals were becoming angrily impatient with the United Party, which looked more and more like a pale shadow of the Nationalists, and were moving towards the 1959 schism to form the Progressive Party which opposed the apartheid system and looked forward to a non-racial and democratic South Africa. Gandar's first changes were cosmetic. He banned the word 'native' from the *RDM*'s pages and replaced it with 'African', and insisted that black people be referred to as 'Mister' in print. Then he published a series of exposés on the treatment of black labourers and their difficulties under the now notorious Pass Laws. Gandar's management reacted to the government threats in their traditional way, by looking for mergers and press concentrations to build up comfortable monopolies. In 1955, the *RDM* and the *Sunday Times* were formally joined together in SAAN (South African Associated Newspapers), which firmly linked the ailing finances of the *RDM* to the healthy and profitable *Sunday Times*. In 1963, SAAN bought 20% of the *Cape Times*, and ten years later it bought the rest, at last building a conglomerate with something approaching the market spread and resources of the Argus group. At a time of severe government pressure in 1968, SAAN suggested to Argus a cross between a merger and a sale, offering 66% of SAAN shares. This would have given Argus over 60% of all daily newspaper sales in the country, and some 77% of English-language paper sales. The government, perhaps understandably, vetoed the scheme. But in 1971, Argus was allowed to buy 33% of SAAN.[33]

But these moves towards financial security did not begin to meet the political challenge that was now under way. Gandar, like his former employer at Anglo American, had come out in support of the Progressive faction in the 1959 split. The next year saw the symbol of the implacable determination of the Nationalist government to maintain white supremacy, the massacre of an unarmed crowd of black demonstrators at Sharpeville. The government continued to clamp down hard on the sporadic outbreaks of unrest and sabotage that followed. A flurry of new laws to permit detention without trial, house arrests and banning orders, to suppress Communism and terrorism, were quickly enacted. The United Party, which still represented the great bulk of English-speaking voters, supported them in parliament. The solitary Progressive MP, Mrs Helen Suzman, voted against. Gandar backed her, and found himself increasingly and dangerously exposed in the South African press. Gandar had the support of his journalists and steadily turned the *RDM* into a bastion of opposition, based upon the classic doctrines of liberalism and non-racism. The *RDM*'s editorial criticism of the feeble United Party was put in bluntly moral terms: 'The fact of the matter is that the choice is not so much between the Government's Bantustan policy and the United Party's race federation, but between policies of race domination and the policies of complete non-discrimination in race and colour. This is the only choice that matters and it is the one demanded of us by the rest of mankind.'[34] Gandar fought his campaign not only in the editorial pages, but among his own workforce, writing some of his most impassioned articles in '174', the SAAN house journal. 'We have a clear and unambiguous political policy which is liberal in content and contemporary in spirit. . .we are a paper of vigorous dissent and social protest,' he told his staff.[35] When the tough Minister of Justice, Mr Vorster, announced that liberalism was already halfway down the slippery slope to Communism, Gandar retorted in an editorial: 'We are not disconcerted by Mr Vorster. He can make note of the fact that the *RDM* is a liberal newspaper and is not proposing to change.'[36] Gandar did not see his fight as a defensive, rearguard action, but as a positive, even an inspiring approach to his country's future. In 'Viewpoint', his personal column in the *RDM*, he would argue that full racial integration, including mixed marriage, was in the end inevitable. This was extremist stuff in the South Africa of 1964. 'There could scarcely be a greater challenge, a more stimulating mission than this,' he enthused.[37]

A cynic could argue that there was method in this apparent madness. As the government-controlled South African Broadcasting Corporation ran an anti-Gandar propaganda campaign, and as the non-liberal readers began to turn away from the *RDM* circulation fell from 125,000 in 1961 to 110,000 in 1968.[38] There was only one other market to attract. In the course of the 1960s, the paper increased its black readership by just over 50%. Blacks bought few copies, but each copy would be read by twelve or more people.[39] In the long-term economic marketplace of South Africa, Gandar's decision to look towards a growing black readership was a rational investment. In the short term, it meant mounting losses for the *RDM* and financial uncertainty just as government pressure was reaching its peak.

Gandar was encouraged in this by the staff whom he trained and inspired, a new generation of South African journalists: Allister Sparks, later editor of the *RDA*; Rex Gibson, later editor of the *Sunday Express*; Harry O'Connor, later editor of the *Eastern Province Herald*; and his own successor, Raymond Louw. This team of politically liberal (if not all Progressive) journalists was exhilarated by the changes that Gandar introduced to the South African press. Hitherto, there had been no combative editorials, no philosophizing in the leaders, no firm statement that the press had a right and a duty to lead South African political thinking, rather than just comment on the thoughts of the politicians. 'It had a galvanizing effect on those of us who worked for him. It seemed the first injection of intellectual content into the political debate. Newspapers suddenly seemed to stand for a lot more than just the news,' Allister Sparks said in an interview.[40]

In July 1965, the *RDM* published a three-part series, based upon the affidavits of a former prisoner, about bad conditions and systematic ill-treatment inside the gaols. On the second day, the police raided the *RDM* newsroom and confiscated all the papers they could. Strachan, the *RDM*'s source, was banned – a legal measure which meant that no South African publication could quote or mention him again. Undeterred, the *RDM* promised in an editorial that 'unless speedy and effective action is taken to deal with the utterly deplorable situation which has been shown to exist in certain spheres of our prison system we shall be obliged to publish further evidence'.[41] It did so on the last day of July, this time using a prison officer as a source for allegations that black prisoners were being tortured with electric shocks. The police raided the newspaper again, and Gandar's passport was confiscated, along with the passport of the reporter, Ben Pogrund. The next year, the two journalists were formally charged with publishing false information, and Joel Mervis, editor of the *Sunday Times*, and SAAN managing director Leycester Walton were charged with them. The trial was marked by the prosecution taking the jury to a prison, and standing them where the *RDM*'s source had said that he had seen some men being tortured in a small yard. Any sight of the yard was blocked by a wall. Only after the trial was over and Gandar had been fined an almost token £100, did the prison authorities admit that the wall had been erected just before the jury's visit. But the government had not wanted to court international outrage by imprisoning Gandar. The £150,000 legal bill which the *RDM* faced was effective enough as a warning to newspaper managements. The government's strategy was subtle. Why bother with a controversial sledgehammer of a press law, when shareholders and managements could be persuaded to police their editors in the interest of profits? The immediate reaction of SAAN's directors was to instruct all editors to get board clearance before publishing any future articles which might involve a confrontation with the government.[42]

In the month after the prison articles first appeared, there was an ill-planned and minority attempt by some directors to force Gandar to take immediate and indefinite leave. The move was defeated, largely because the *RDM* journalists mobilized on Gandar's behalf. But in 1966, Laurance Gandar was effectively kicked upstairs as editor-in-chief and replaced by his deputy, Raymond Louw.[43] The Board had hoped to appoint Johnny Johnstone, later to become editor of the government-backed and controversial daily *The Citizen*. But suspicious of Johnstone's political stance, the *RDM* journalists, led by Allister Sparks, protested against his appointment. Gandar himself insisted that Johnstone was not acceptable to the *RDM* staff.

Raymond Louw, the news editor, and seen as a nuts and bolts newspaperman, was appointed instead. He began by insisting that 'If the *Rand Daily Mail* is going to run an unpopular political policy, we have to have the best damn newsgathering team in the country. We have to win on news.'[44] Louw delegated the editorials, and effectively the paper's political policy, to Harry O'Connor and later to Allister Sparks, while backing them and improving the news service. Although he had been something of a compromise appointment, he grew in the job.

Louw was a courageous man, in the same mould as Gandar, but he found himself working under severe constraints. Such was the power of the Defence Acts, for example, that he was forced to make it 'a common practice' to consult the Minister when reporting on defence matters. When a reader on a golf course saw a South African Air Force plane take off and then eject a pair of trousers and a fluttering tie, official government permission had to be sought before the story could be published. The *RDM*'s exposés continued, but at a burdensome economic cost. To report on the ill-treatment of 2,000 evicted blacks in the Morgsat area in 1969, the *RDM* had to send a team of white and black reporters into the area, equipped with a questionnaire drawn up by lawyers, spend three months on the investigations, then submit the questionnaires to government officials, and finally submit a formal list of sixty-four questions to the government. After sixteen days, and five formal requests for answers, the *RDM* was able to publish its critical articles. But few newspapers can afford to conduct business in this way, particularly when the reporters in Morgsat had been arrested by the Special Branch, and they and the Morgsat Africans followed and harassed.[46]

The *RDM* was publishing under the constant threat of a tough press law being passed, and as each new Bill was drafted the *RDM* had to assess what its effect might be. In May of 1965, its editorial said of the Ministry of Justice's latest effort: 'When this Bill is passed the Minister will be free to run a real Gestapo, with his security men operating in the dark and the newspapers trying to guess how much they can report. The onus of guessing right will be on the press, and the onus for guessing wrong will be heavy.' Nor was there much need for a press law as such, when over a hundred other laws contained measures to regulate the profession. The Official Secrets Act was as tough as its British parent; the Sabotage, Terrorism and Defence Acts made it illegal to publish some stories; the Suppression of Communism Act made it illegal to publish or even write about some people; the Key Points Act made it illegal to visit some places; the Criminal Procedures Act made it illegal to protect a journalist's sources; the BOSS Act made it effectively illegal to criticize anything done in the name of State security; while the Prisons and Police Amendment Acts made it illegal to publish 'untrue statements' about those two services. The Atomic Energy Act forbids publication of details of uranium production and contracts, or of atomic research, even if performed outside South Africa. The National Supplies Procurement Act gives a Minister the right to declare whole swathes of the economy to be officially secret, and the Petroleum Products Amendment Act bans publications of details of oil purchase, supplies, storage or distribution. There is also a weekly list of banned publications, which has included that famous Victorian children's book about a horse, with the subversive title *Black Beauty*.[47]

In spite of these constraints, Raymond Louw continued Gandar's tradition, and began to see increasing signs of success in attracting a new readership among black people. The *RDM* was not alone in this. Another liberal paper, the *East London Daily Despatch* (whose editor, Donald Woods, was to become a friend of Steve Biko of the Black Consciousness Movement, to become a regular columnist for the *RDM*, and who was later forced to flee into exile) found in a 1967 survey that it had saturation coverage of the white market, and it too began to look for black readers. At the *RDM*, the obvious place to start was in Soweto, the huge black township outside Johannesburg. In the 1960s, Gandar and Louw had produced a special edition, titled 'Township' for the Soweto market. At first, filled with sport and black beauty competitions and social notes, it seemed an almost patronizing act of tokenism; but as the *RDM* began to hire steadily more black journalists and photographers, and as the *RDM*'s editors realized that the standards of black education had improved sharply and that Soweto was an increasingly sophisticated political and cultural market, the *RDM* moved towards becoming a genuinely multiracial paper. By 1977, although whites bought 72% of all copies sold, more than 60% of the *RDM*'s readers were non-white. Circulation began to rise steadily in the 1970s, to 151,000 in the last quarter of 1973, a 38% increase on the last year of Gandar's editorship.[48] Hopeful as this was, the *RDM* continued to lose money and to be dependent on the success of its partner, the *Sunday Times*. Its penetration of the black market was severely limited by the success of the all-black newspaper *The World* whose slogan, 'Our own, our very own', had taken it to twenty-four-hour printing, three editions a day, by 1975. The financial situation was not helped by the economic structure of the South African press which has traditionally depended on advertising revenues for the bulk of its income. The SAAN group, for example, had an advertising revenue of Rands (R)18.15 million (£11.32 million at the then exchange rate) compared to a circulation revenue of only R3.024 (£1.890 million). The cost of newsprint alone, at R4.79 million for the year, exceeded the income from sales.[49] This was a costs structure which worked in favour of the advertisement-rich *Sunday Times* and against the *RDM*. It helped to explain that of the nine newspapers against which the *RDM* competed in the Rand market, only two of them were profitable. Moreover, the joint production facilities which the *RDM* shared with the *Sunday Times* makes it difficult to allocate a real share of production costs, beyond saying that the *RDM* employs 124 editorial staff, and its 370 printing and technical staff and 380 administrative employees are shared with its Sunday stablemate.[50]

Throughout the 1970s, the *Rand Daily Mail* usually ran between twenty-four and thirty-two pages, and a contents analysis conducted in 1979 assessed its editorial structure as follows:[51]

	%		%
Foreign news	5	Business	6
National news	7	Home	3
Local news	5	TV, radio schedules and	
Features, cultural	7	syndicated copy	3
Editorials	2	Advertisements	55
Sport	7		

Throughout the 1970s, it ran a Thursday colour supplement, titled 'Eve' and aimed at women readers (black and white) and including TV news and a guide after the introduction of television to South Africa in 1975. The paper ran two to three pages on local entertainment and cultural events every day, and throughout 1975–7 a progressive face-lift sharpened the layout and tightly re-organized the paper into a Metropolitan page, an Africa page, a World page, a Politics page and so on.

But the real changes of the mid-1970s were political, with the explosion of black unrest in Soweto in 1976 and a new sophistication in the government's determination to break or cow the standard-bearer of opposition, the English press. Far from ignoring the Nationalist and Afrikaans positions, the *RDM* made deliberate efforts to present it, in June of 1975 hiring Dirk Rezelman, the former press officer of the Nationalist Party, as a regular columnist. It did little good. In October 1975, a pro-Nationalist millionaire, Louis Luyt, tried to mount a conventional takeover of SAAN by offering R4.50 for the outstanding shares, which were being traded at R1.90. The total offer amounted to £7.5 million. Announcing its formal opposition, the *RDM* editorial of 31 October said that the purchase 'would realise Nationalist Afrikanerdom's last dream of controlling its own English-language newspapers to spread propaganda'.[52] The *Sunday Times* of London was able to discover Luyt's backers in the venture. They included Axel Springer, owner of the German publishing empire of *Bild*, *Hör Zu* and *Die Welt* (he pulled out early); John McGoff, a right-wing millionaire publisher with newspapers in the US Midwest, a friend of President Ford and co-owner of a South African ranch with Dr Connie Mulder, South Africa's Minister of Information; Sir de Villiers Graaf, former leader of South Africa's United

Party; and the backers of *To The Point* magazine, a Netherlands-based news weekly that was backed and financed by Dr Eschel Rhoodie and Dr Muller, and by the Department of Information.[53] Luyt's offer was rejected, but it was only the opening salvo of a concerted campaign.

The seriousness of Luyt's challenge was reflected in quite unprecedented steps which the English-speaking commercial leaders of South Africa had to take to surmount it. Effectively, Harry Oppenheimer had to become something very like the owner of the *Rand Daily Mail*. Two of Oppenheimer's close friends, stockbroker Max Borkum and financier Gordon Waddell put together an 'Advowson Trust' which bought up 20% of the *RDM* shares, while the Argus group, which was dominated by Oppenheimer group interests, bought up another 39%. The entire deal was stitched together within a week, organized through Waddell's company, Johannesburg Consolidated Investments. The English Establishment had been mobilized to fight off the Afrikaner takeover.[54]

The government's determination to crush its press opposition was stiffened by the Soweto riots of the following year. After the banning, imprisonment or exile of the leaders of the ANC and PAC (the traditional black opposition groups) in the 1960s, two new trends of black opposition had emerged within South Africa. The first was represented by Chief Buthelezi, leader of the Bantustan of Zululand. Buthelezi denounced the autonomy of the Bantustans as a fiction, but was prepared to work within the system, clawing whatever concessions he could from the Pretoria government. Raymond Louw had given Buthelezi a regular column in the *RDM* and saw him and the emergent black trade-union movement as the keys to the peaceful change the *RDM* still hoped could come. The second opposition force was rather different, the Black Consciousness Movement that had found its inspiration in the young black Steve Biko, and its expression in the schoolchildren's riots of Soweto. Because of its black reporters and its Soweto readership, the *RDM*'s coverage of the riots and the forces behind them not only dominated South Africa's perception of the events, but became the key source for the foreign press coverage of this long-prophesied revolution in South Africa. The government's reaction was merciless. Fourteen black journalists were arrested, including five from the *RDM*. Nat Serache, the gifted *RDM* journalist who infiltrated the mining compounds to get the story that the South African police were recruiting and hiring black mineworkers to beat up student militants, was one of the first on the list. Peter Magubane,

Willie Nkosi, Jan Tugwana, all found themselves under indefinite arrest by September.[55] And in that same month, the government fired the second barrel. Ostensibly owned by Louis Luyt, a new English daily, the *Citizen*, was launched – conveniently timed to rally support for the government in the general election of the following year. The *Citizen* quickly claimed a circulation of 90,000 a day, but *RDM* reporters mounted a complex surveillance scheme with binoculars, a team of radio-cars and infra-red cameras, and were able to prove that at least 30,000 of those copies were being driven directly from the printing presses to Louis Luyt's farm, and later pulped.[56]

Some £7 million of government money was channelled through the Department of Information, to Louis Luyt's Triomf fertilizer company to finance the *Citizen*, and the South African taxpayer eventually and unwittingly put a grand total of £16 million into the pro-government paper. This was just a part of the £40 million propaganda package that Eschel Rhoodie and Connie Mulder put together to sell apartheid to their own voters and to the Western world as a whole. The scheme was grandiose enough to be without parallel in the history of international publishing. They tried to buy *Paris-Match*, the *Washington Star*, the Morgan-Grampian magazine group in Britain, Hutchinsons the publishers and UPITN, the international TV news agency. Louis Luyt's attempt to buy SAAN had been part of the operation, with the code-name of Annemarie, after Rhoodie's daughter. The grand design involved intelligence work as well as propaganda, dreamed up as much by BOSS, the Bureau of State Security, as by the Department of Information.[57]

The scandal that became known as Muldergate, echoing the American Watergate affair, saw the *RDM* play a very similar role to that pioneered by the *Washington Post*. The paper's new editor, Allister Sparks, had to restrain his reporters and embolden his managers in much the same way as the *Washington Post*'s Ben Bradlee. Mervyn Rees and Chris Day of the *RDM* were the Woodward—Bernstein of the South African story. They had begun with their exposure of the *Citizen*, gone on to prove that government money was behind the shadowy Club of Ten, who were presented as a group of rich overseas businessmen, friendly to South Africa, who were financing a series of sophisticated advertising campaigns in the Western media. Partly because of Rees and Day, partly because of internal rivalries within the Afrikaans and Nationalist political elite, and partly because of the integrity of key officials in the South African civil service and the judiciary, a judicial commission of inquiry was established under Judge Mostert. His remarkable decision to make public all the evidence that had been presented saw the *RDM* use its expensive new computer-editing system to clear features, sport and business from its pages and publish the evidence in full. The editorial read proudly: 'Yesterday's disclosures came as a massive vindication of all this newspaper has published.'[58] But more was to come. The scandal eventually saw the resignation of Vorster from the State presidency, the breaking of General van den Bergh, the all-powerful head of BOSS, the breaking of the power of the Transvaal Afrikaners in the Nationalist Party and the success of the Cape Province Nationalists, and the wretched Eschel Rhoodie hounded through hiding holes from Ecuador to the French Riviera. At the end, both Rhoodie and van den Bergh turned for help, and for publication of their version of events, to the newspaper which they had tried to throttle, the *Rand Daily Mail*.

It had been a desperately difficult time for the newspaper. Convinced that at least one colleague was a BOSS agent and that their offices were bugged, the *RDM* journalists had to hold important meetings and make key phone-calls in hotel rooms and conduct interviews in the open air or in moving cars. Their final editorial judgement was the more impressive for its very sobriety: 'When you cast aside the tried and tested mechanism of democratic control in the name of "state security" you invite abuses far worse than anything that might be threatening the state.'[59]

South Africa being the country it is, the vindication of the *RDM* did it little good. It was legally charged with 'contempt of the Commission' for drawing obvious inferences from the evidence released by Judge Mostert and was convicted, until the paper won on appeal in 1980. More was to come. The Ministry of Justice announced a new inquiry into the press. Wearily, the *RDM* took up the challenge once more: 'The Nationalist Party wants a press totally subservient and totally harassed, a press that supports its policies,' said the editorial for 29 June 1980. It faced further charges for reporting, with quotations, what the British press was saying about the riots in South Africa. But something had changed. The Afrikaans press, horrified out of its usual partisan stand by the Muldergate revelations, came to the *RDM*'s support. More than that, the Afrikaans press began to campaign against the government's proposed press laws and for wider press freedoms. The new keenness of the Afrikaans press did not necessarily help the *RDM*; when *Die Transvaaler* sought official permission to publish an interview with a banned person, a leader of the ANC liberation movement, it was given clearance. The *RDM*'s identical application was turned down.[60]

Allister Sparks was a very different kind of editor from Laurence Gandar, who had come from the world of military intelligence and multinational corporations. Gandar had been a traditional figure, a believer in justice, in equality for all before the law, in the classical tenets of Victorian liberalism. In Western Europe, Gandar could easily have voted Conservative. But just as Sharpeville was different from Soweto, so Sparks differed from Gandar. Gandar had believed in the law to let him and to help him print articles. Allister Sparks spent his editorship with a legal tome on his desk, trying to pick his way between laws that had been passed to stop him. He had to outwit the law, rather than rely on it. Allister Sparks was not a revolutionary, although he gave editorial support to Robert Mugabe in Zimbabwe, to the Black Consciousness Movement and to militant black trade-unionists. But when the South African armed forces briefly invaded Angola and Mozambique, to attack the guerrilla bases of SWAPO and the ANC, the *RDM* gave the assaults grudging approval in its editorials – probably the more grudging because of the little they were allowed to print by military censorship. In 1975, the paper had appeared with white spaces in its columns, where the stories banned by the censor would have been published.

For all its courage, and for all its public service in rooting out the Muldergate corruption, the *RDM* remained a financial failure. In the course of 1980, it lost some £2 million. Ostensibly this was the reason for the dismissal of Allister Sparks as editor in June 1981. But in the overseas press it was widely seen as a management decision to sacrifice Sparks to the government's threat of yet another press law.[61] Just as the *RDM*'s prison revelations had led to a new law to close that loophole of press disclosure, and as the press criticisms of the police and inquest procedures had led to a Police Amendment Act which closed another stable door, the government was determined that the press would not be capable of exposing any more Muldergates.

It is not easy to understand why any further controls might conceivably be needed. Raymond Louw had observed, during his time as editor, that the South African State had erected such a hedge of press restrictions that every newspaperman in the country had become his own censor, working under the threat of legal punishments, fines and even closure. The black newspaper *The World* had been closed down in 1977. Allister Sparks had defined the process precisely: 'The temptation is always there to hold back and censor yourself because otherwise you will be blamed for bringing press freedom to an end. The job for us in South African newspapers has been to try to use what limited freedom we have.'[62]

The future of the *RDM* was placed in the hands of Tertius Myburgh, a liberal Afrikaner who also maintained his editorship of the *RDM*'s stablemate, the *Sunday Times*. Myburgh won his spurs as an editor by making a financial and newsgathering success of the *Pretoria News*. His first editorial in the *RDM* promised: 'This newspaper will continue to forage beyond the front lines in the cause of civil liberties, racial justice and full participation for all.'[63] But his task was to stop the continuing financial erosion of the *RDM*'s losses, running at almost £3 million for 1981. Successive price rises made the *RDM* at 25 cents the most expensive paper to buy in its saturated market. Advertisers and ad agencies took the opportunity to stress publicly that the *RDM* was losing too many white readers, while the black market was not yet economically viable for their purposes.[64] Laurence Gandar's reaction was gloomy. 'SAAN has always been uneasy about the image of the *Mail* as a forthright, thrusting, crusading paper and has tended too readily to blame this image for any disappointments in its trading position. Now, I feel, it has decided once and for all to tone down the paper and make it like other opposition papers, quieter and less willing to get involved in controversial matters.'[65] But this same fear had been voiced when Gandar himself had been unseated from the editor's chair, when Raymond Louw had gone, and indeed back in 1953, when George Rainer Ellis was removed. Each time, the *RDM* found itself reacting to governmental and economic pressure with courage and liberal determination.

And in February 1982, that tradition was maintained when another of Gandar's press disciples, Rex Gibson, was made editor of the *RDM*. He took over the editor's chair on the very eve of publication of the government's latest assault on the press, the report of the Steyn Commission. This proposed that journalists in South Africa be licensed by a national press council and expelled from the profession if they were deemed to have breached a tough, government-approved code of conduct. The council itself would be set up in such a way as to ensure that the liberal, English-speaking press would be in a minority. Rex Gibson's instant editorial reaction in the *RDM* was to condemn the scheme and dedicate the paper again to its liberal and brave traditions. But with a circulation that had dwindled to a bare 106,000, mounting financial losses, the renewed government pressure has put his editorship on to the defensive from the very first day. The struggle continues.[66]

Notes

1. *Rand Daily Mail*, 75th Anniversary Supplement, 22.ix.1977.
2. *ibid*. See also *The Press as Opposition*, Elaine Potter, pp. 40–2.
3. *ibid*. See also *The Times*, London, 21.ix.1977.
4. *RDM* supplement, *op. cit.*
5. *RDM*, 1.x.1902.
6. *RDM*, 26.xi.1906. See also 17.xii.1906.
7. Quoted in *RDM* supplement, *op. cit.*
8. *RDM*, 31.xii.1902.
9. *RDM*, 3.iv.1903.
10. *RDM*, 31.iii.1914.
11. Memoir of L. E. Neame, *RDM*, 22.ix.1952.
12. *RDM* supplement, *op. cit.*
13. L. E. Neame memoir, *op. cit.*
14. Potter, *op. cit.*, p. 31.
15. See *English-speaking South Africa Today*, proceedings of the national conference, *1974*, De Villiers.
16. Potter, *op. cit.*, p. 44.
17. *The Press in Africa*, R. Ainslie, pp. 46–7.
18. *RDM*, 5.viii.1914.
19. *RDM*, 7.viii.1914.
20. *RDM*, 4.v.1926.
21. *RDM*, 26.viii.1931.
22. *ibid*.
23. *RDM*, 29.ix.1938.
24. *RDM*, 4.ix.1939.
25. *RDM*, 14.i.1914.
26. *RDM*, 7.iii.1922.
27. *RDM*, 10.iii.1922.
28. *RDM*, 1.ix.1939.
29. *The Times*, London, 4.xii.1950.
30. Potter, *op. cit.*, p. 106.
31. *ibid*., pp. 106–7.
32. *Daily Telegraph*, London, 17.vii.1969. Also author's interviews.
33. *The Press of Africa*, Frank Burton, p. 206.
34. *RDM*, 19.ii.1962.
35. '174', SAAN house journal, summer 1962. Also quoted in 'South African Journalist', October–November 1962.
36. *RDM*, 12.x.1962.
37. *RDM*, 4.iv.1964.

38. Author's interviews. See also Merrill & Fisher, *The World's Great Dailies* (chapter on *RDM*).
39. Potter, *op. cit.*, p. 93.
40. Author's interview with Allister Sparks.
41. *RDM*, 21.vii.1965.
42. Potter, *op. cit.*, pp. 62–4.
43. *ibid*.
44. Author's interview, Sparks.
45. Potter, *op. cit.*, pp. 122–3.
46. *ibid.*, p. 156.
47. International Press Institute Report: on *The Press in South Africa*, B. Rubin, IPI, Zurich, January–April 1981. See also *Financial Times*, London, 26.vi.1979.
48. *The Times*, London, 21.ix.1977.
49. *RDM*, 26.iii.1974. See also SAAN annual report, 1974.
50. Merrill & Fisher, *op. cit.*, p. 260.
51. *ibid.*, p. 262.
52. *RDM*, 31.x.1975.
53. *Sunday Times*, London, 9.xi.1975.
54. Author's interview, Sparks.
55. Merrill & Fisher, *op. cit.* See also the *Observer*, London, 7.vi.1981.
56. *Race, Propaganda and South Africa*, John C. Laurence, p. 11.
57. *Muldergate*, Mervyn Rees and Chris Day, p. 133 and pp. 186ff.
58. *RDM*, 3.xi.1978.
59. *RDM*, 6.xii.1978.
60. IPI report, *op. cit.*
61. See, for example, *The Times*, London, 2.vi.1981, and the *Guardian*, London, 3.vi.1981.
62. *Guardian*, London, 24.iii.1979.
63. *RDM*, 6.vi.1981.
64. *Financial Mail* (Johannesburg), p. 1285, 12.vi.1981.
65. *Sunday Times* (Johannesburg), 7.vi.1981.
66. *RDM*, 2.ii.82. Also author's interview, Rex Gibson. See also the *Observer*, London, 7.ii.1982.

RAND DAILY MAIL: EDITORIALS

The independence of India: 6 June 1947

'Britain's offer, of full sovereignty of India, is the most astonishing thing in the entire history of Imperial rule. . .Whether united or divided, the people of India will have to stand on their own legs.'

The independence of Israel: 15 May 1948

'Their [the Jews'] colonization effort has few parallels in this century and provides a most striking contrast to the apathy and indolence of the Arabs. Everywhere the Arabs have lived they have reduced the land to desert and desolation. (North Africa, peopled by the Arabs for centuries, was once the granary of Rome.) In contradistinction, the Jews have in thirty years made the desert bloom like a rose. It is right and just that they should have this land and we are glad indeed that Britain has given up her onerous mandate.'

The Berlin blockade and airlift: 25 June 1948

'As we remarked when the Four-Power Kommandatura was set up, nothing could be more likely to cause trouble between the Allies than the attempt to create occupational islands for all in a single city. This has only made it more difficult for the Powers to live together in Berlin – or to leave without losing face.'

The Communists win power in China: 30 November 1949

'Since the end of the last war, in its somewhat vacillating attempts to help Nationalist China, the United States spent 2 billion dollars. Now America has introduced a resolution in the United Nations, calling on members of the UN to respect the "open door" policy in China and insisting on the right of the Chinese people to choose and maintain a government independent of foreign control. It is a fair and honour-

able proposal. But in all the circumstances it is not without an element
of humour.'

The Korean war: 11 October 1950

'What the course of the Korean war has shown decisively (apart from
the fact that air power can do anything) is that the Russians don't want
a world war. If they did, they would have sent Russian troops to
support the North Koreans and the fat would then have been in the
fire. Their real policy is to gain as much as possible without a world
war and they undoubtedly hoped that they could seize South Korea
without any serious opposition from the Western Powers. . .Just as
the Russians cannot beat America, so it is impossible for the
Americans to obliterate a creed which now dominates about one third
of the world.'

The Suez invasion: 1 November 1956

'Britain and France are firm in their declarations that this is an
'intervention' not a war. Unfortunately interventions that begin with
bombing tend to look like wars. . . There will be criticism throughout
the world. But there is also a hardening of opinion against the growing
tendency of some states to play ducks and drakes with the rules of
international behaviour.'

The Russian invasion of Hungary: 6 November 1956

'Russian action in Hungary, and the desperate appeals of a dying
nation, overshadow even the situation in the Middle East. There is
really no parallel between the two crises. Not even the extremists
have charged Britain and France with anything approaching the crime
that Russia has clearly committed against Hungary. While the UN
accepted the Soviet delegation's assurances that Hungary would be
allowed a form of independence, the whole might of Russia, with
tanks and artillery behind it, was descending on a virtually defenceless
people.'

The Bay of Pigs assault on Cuba: 20 April 1961

'However obnoxious the Castro regime (whose brutalities do not
seem to worry the Communists) America's attitude is vulnerable. Her

encouragement of the rebels can easily be represented as 'the wicked hand of imperialism', and there are signs that the Latin-American and the Afro-Asian groups of countries are reacting adversely. This is a great pity for it may mean the loss of much of the ground Mr Kennedy has gained in those great regions since taking office.'

The Cuban missile crisis: 24 October 1962

'It is not being forgotten around the Western world that if it comes to counting missile bases, America has established a more effective ring round Russia than anything that Cuba can represent.'

The Gulf of Tonkin incident: 24 August 1964

'The two crises (the other being Cyprus) can only have the effect of raising the prestige and hence the political status of President Johnson. There is no doubt that his firm action and refusal to be panicked over Vietnam were the chief factors in restoring the situation there. He reacted to Chinese aggression promptly, but only used enough force to contain the threat.'

China's nuclear weapon: 7 January 1967

'It is the behaviour of China that is causing some hard re-thinking in countries in her immediate neighbourood – the desperate internal struggle for power, the wild activity of the Red Guards, the development of the Chinese atom bomb and the mounting hostility between the two Eastern giants, China and Russia. China is beginning to look anything but the wise, helpful and reliable ally who can best ensure the peace and progress of South-East Asia. Indeed, she often gives the impression of being hell-bent on confrontations that could eventually send the whole region up in mushroom-shaped clouds.'

Rhodesia's UDI: 12 November 1965

'For our part, we see the gravest trouble coming to South Africa out of this hot-headed and ill-considered action by Mr Ian Smith. We are almost certainly going to be involved to our disadvantage and may well come to look on yesterday as a black day in our history as well as that of Rhodesia – whether Mr Smith gets away with his UDI or not. Either way, the implications are alarming.'

The Russian invasion of Czechoslovakia: 22 August 1968

'There are shrewd observers who see other signs, too, in the ruthless Soviet action against Czech liberalism. These are that the Russian leaders are deeply aware of stirrings in Russian minds – particularly among the intelligentsia, the scientists and other pioneers of the revolutionary industrial age that the whole world is entering. There is evidence that among such people the rigid Communist doctrine is coming to be regarded as out-moded and that a search may be on for a more flexible doctrine. So it is possible that the Soviet leaders believed they simply dared not allow the development of Czech liberalism for fear of its rippling through the Communist world. The effects in Russia especially might be incalculable.'

Israel's occupation of the West Bank: 23 October 1973

'On the Israeli side one must hope for some readiness to be magnanimous from their present position of military superiority. The Israelis have every reason to feel aggrieved but as General Smuts understood so well at Versailles, a peace bargain driven too hard against a vanquished foe can only ensure that there will be war again another day.'

The OPEC price rise: 19 December 1973

'The short-sightedness was evident from the first moment the Arabs decided to employ their embargo against the West. The move, as a long-term tactic, was foolish simply because it would inevitably drive the major consuming nations to find alternatives to Gulf oil. . . Whether the Arabs will succeed in applying enough pressure on the West to realise the concessions they are seeking in the Middle East – essentially the withdrawal of all Israeli forces from all occupied Arab territory – remains to be seen. But in the long-term view, the Gulf oil producers can only be spiting their face. And the tragedy is that, like lemmings, they are unlikely to alter their course.'

Watergate: 19 April 1974

'Mr Nixon may at last be on the way out, and not before time. The situation has now become so critical that international relations stand to suffer with every passing week he continues to remain in office.

What started as a domestic squabble has assumed far greater proportions. . .Hopefully they [the American people] will now be forced
to decide that Mr Nixon's downfall is not only inevitable but
imperative.'

The fall of Saigon: 2 May 1975

'The fact that American fire power, immense as it was, proved insufficient is surely because it was based on the wrong premises. The first
of these was that, for much of the war, it was used to prop up a
patently undemocratic and increasingly corrupt government. Whatever idealism may have existed in the initial American intervention
became debased. Secondly, and deriving from this, was that so much
of the war was fought without the involvement and support of the
ordinary people in whose cause it was supposed to have been all
about; to them, the conclusion of the war can only be an enormous
relief, and so what if it is a Communist government which now
takes over?'

Sport and politics: 19 July 1976

'If it is admirable to keep politics out of sport, then it should happen
here. We cannot point a finger at any country as long as South Africa
has a Government-created "sports policy", a Ministry of Sport
designed to dictate to sportsmen and a political prohibition on who
may play with whom. End these, and South African sportsmen could
be standing proudly in an Olympic stadium next time round.'

The space venture: 13 April 1961

'A man has been sent into space and lives to tell the tale – What next?
Scientists already seem to be thinking of a journey to the moon.
Perhaps a more appropriate question would be – What good? That
also is difficult to answer. Space is being conquered because of the
knowledge it yields. We can but hope that young Yuri Gagarin will
turn out to be a herald of greater happiness for civilisation and not
greater strife.'

Freedom of information: 7 February 1966

'We have seen the steady accumulation of a mass of legislation

hedging the press about with one restriction after another and sub-
jecting journalists to the threat of severe penalties for transgression.
The effect is often to make newspapers hesitant about publishing, and
sometimes even investigating, matters of clear public concern.'

14

Each newspaper's coverage of Iran from 1971 to the fall of the Shah

Newspapers are so much the product of their own cultures that any attempt to compare the quality and depth of their coverage becomes an exercise in comparative nationalism. Simply to count up the number of column-inches devoted to national politics or to international affairs leaves the researcher begging several questions. How many column-inches are devoted to news rather than advertising, and how many columns are there in a paper? Comparisons between a twenty-four-page *Asahi Shimbun* and a 116-page *New York Times* are almost meaningless. Comparisons between particular newspapers on a given day can be bizarre. Stanford University once launched an ambitious project to attempt such a comparison. Three years of research and translation were devoted to an analysis of the contents of leading newspapers around the world on 2 November 1956. The date is significant: the height of the twin crises of the Anglo-French-Israeli attack on the Suez Canal, and the Soviet invasion of rebellious Hungary. The analysis of editorial content went like this:

	Stories from parent country	Stories from parent region	Stories from rest of world
	%	%	%
Pravda	55	67	33
Le Monde	34	50	50
Al-Ahram	59	69	31

Asahi Shimbun	60	62	38
The Times	64	70	30
New York Times	74	75	25

The figure that stands out, given the drama and impact of the Suez and Hungary stories, is the continuing concern of the *New York Times* with American affairs. But we are looking at a distortion. Even *Le Monde*'s celebrated obsession with international affairs rarely stretches to half the newspaper. Any serious analysis of the comparative interest and skill and performance of the world's press ought to be more sophisticated than this. So, for the purpose of this comparison, it seems logical to take one long-running story, of international significance, and examine the record of each newspaper over a period of years.

The choice has not been arbitrary. As a test of each paper's concern for international news, it makes sense to choose a story which was not domestic news for any of the twelve papers under consideration, but which impinged dramatically upon the parent country of each newspaper; a story with economic, strategic, social and even moral implications for each newspaper; a story which nobody could ignore. The chosen topic is the coverage of Iran by each paper over the decade up to the fall of the Shah. It should be borne in mind that the Shah maintained a sophisticated international propaganda apparatus, through embassies, free trips for journalists (and potentially corrupting gifts), and a well-funded and ruthless intelligence machine throughout this period.

Adolph Ochs, founder of the modern *New York Times*, once said: 'No reader of my newspaper should ever be surprised.' A great newspaper should be so analysing the economic and social forces at work in a particular country, so in touch with its political movements and the mood of its citizens, that readers should be in a general sense prepared for tomorrow's headlines. Let us see how well our twelve great papers performed.

THE BACKGROUND

There is no such thing as an objective account of modern Iran, but readers should have in mind at least a sketchy knowledge of its recent history. During the Second World War, Iran was occupied by Russian, British and US troops, to ensure that Iranian oil supplies, the Persian Gulf and the land transport route up into the Soviet Union were secured for the Allies. After the war, overt military occupation ended, but the influence of the great powers continued and became a factor in the rise of Iranian nationalism. The nationalist leader, Dr Mossadegh, became head of government and announced the nationalization of oil in 1953. The young Shah fled. The CIA financed and organized the coup which toppled Mossadegh and restored the Shah; it also helped to reduce British influence in the region and replace it with American. The Shah embarked on a policy of economic development and land reform, backed by US loans and aid, and a ruthless system of political repression to ensure that no new Mossadegh would arise and that the Left in Iran, particularly the Tudeh Communist Party, would be so crushed that his reign would be secure. This repression and his insistence on institutional reforms led to open hostility with key sectors of Iranian society, including the fundamentalist Muslim clergy and the faithful. The Shah survived a desperate wave of riots in 1963, and oil-based prosperity made many observers in the West believe that his authoritarian regime was succeeding in its goals of modernization and that it was also becoming popularly accepted. True or not – and there is still wide disagreement as to whether the land reforms were effective – there were two major social effects: first, large numbers of peasants flocked to the cities, overcrowding them and providing a pool of underemployed poor; and second, the food production of the country began to stagnate and then decline, forcing the country to earn more from oil to pay for food imports. The steady withdrawal of British influence from the Gulf area persuaded the Shah to take over the British role as guardian of the Gulf, and the OPEC price rises of 1973–4 gave him the money to pay for his strategic and industrial ambitions. In 1975, the Shah saw himself as an emergent superpower. By 1977, it was becoming clear that the flood of money was dislocating the social and economic fabric of the country.

Massive expenditure on advanced weaponry and grandiose investments in new industrial plant formed a glossily impressive superstructure which rested on a flimsy, barely-educated and discontented social base. Continued left-wing opposition to the Shah and spasmodic urban guerrilla movements persuaded the regime to expand its security force, SAVAK, which by 1977 had become internationally notorious for its torture and repression. The Muslim

opposition had never died and, with the social strains of industrialization, inflation and economic crisis, new sources of opposition began
to emerge. The Shah's anti-inflation drive, which tried to freeze prices
by decree, lost him whatever support he had enjoyed among the small
business classes. His drive against corruption – and there was much
corruption within his own royal family – eroded at least some of his
support among these super-rich who owed most to him. And
increasing international concern for the excesses of his repression
meant that he faced mounting international pressure to liberalize his
regime, just at the very time when it was about to face a wave of
hostility and public unrest unparalleled since 1953. During the course
of 1978, the wave of strikes, riots, demonstrations and street battles
steadily escalated as the opposition grew in confidence. At the
beginning of 1979, the Shah left his country 'for a holiday'. He was
never to return.

THE TIMES

In October of 1971, the Shah announced a lavish celebration of the
2500th anniversary of the Persian Empire (his own dynasty was only
into its second generation) at the ancient capital of Persepolis. The
interest of *The Times* in the Shah and his country was symbolized by
the presence, as an official guest, of the newspaper's owner Lord
Thomson at the Shah's Persepolis festivities. 'This country needs to
be better known in the world,' the publisher announced to his correspondent on arrival in Tehran. 'And this of course will do it,'
(11 October 1971). Within the previous two weeks, *The Times* had published two highly lucrative special advertising supplements on Iran
and its economy. Much of them had been written by *The Times*'s able
correspondent, David Housego, who was experienced enough to
look past the social glitter of Persepolis and inform his readers: 'One
of the great sadnesses of the whole festivities is that the necessity for
such heavy security precautions has robbed them of much of their
popular appeal.' (13 October 1971). He reported regularly on Iran's
internal security and the endless war between SAVAK and the anti-
Shah guerrillas. When the government imposed security restrictions
on news of trials, Housego was still able to report in March that 'at
least nineteen executions' had taken place since January. 'The poli-

tical trials which the Iranian government formerly declared were open, are now proceeding in secret,' he began one lengthy account (14 March 1972).

During 1972, *The Times* published 129 stories on Iran, nineteen of them on oil, twenty-three on the economy, and eighteen on the royal family itself. There were twelve articles on SAVAK and internal security, four on the army, five on the government, eight on earthquakes, and four on the arts and culture. It was an all-round coverage, although somewhat distorted by the arrival of the Shah on a state visit to Britain in June. On the Shah's arrival, the diplomatic correspondent observed: 'He still inspires a mystic veneration among the Iranian peasantry. . .and the bitterest execration among the thousands of students who study in Europe. The press in Iran is muzzled and compliant, and opposition violently repressed by means of torture and the execution squads.' (20 June 1972). *The Times*'s editorials, in what was to be a recurrent pattern, stayed safely on the topic of oil prices.

The Times had naturally paid particular attention to the withdrawal of British forces from the Persian Gulf, and to the Shah's determination to step into the consequent vacuum. In a shrewd series entitled 'The Midas with the military touch', it noted the Shah's ambitions, his ruthlessness and the long-term political problem that the Shah's reforms would bring: 'The people have a rich culture, independence of mind, sophistication and a pride, if not arrogance, born of these qualities. They will ask more and more questions as they become better off.' (13 December 1972).

In 1973, with 107 stories, *The Times* published forty-four articles on oil, twenty on economic development, ten on Iraqi and Kurdish relations, and eleven on the royal family. Only seven articles on SAVAK were printed, and none on the Shah's external critics. The well-rounded reporting of 1972 was giving way to an oil-fuelled economic story. There were more of the financially profitable special reports, and *The Times* provided the traditional arena of its letters columns for a public debate between the BBC and the Iranian Ambassador over Iran's decision to deport the BBC's man in Tehran, in objection to a marginally critical TV programme. *The Times* itself took no editorial view on the expulsion.

In 1974, there was a special advertising supplement on banking in Iran on 24 February and further advertising supplements on 21 May and 25 October. There was a highly respectful interview with the Shah on 27 June, in which he was asked no questions about internal security, SAVAK or political prisoners. *The Times* published 155 stories during the year, fifty-two on oil, forty-two on economic development and ten on international relations. There were fourteen stories on the royal family, eight on Iraqi and Kurdish relations and four on Gulf strategy. There were seven articles on SAVAK, and three on the Shah's external critics. The balance of reporting continued to shift towards economic opportunities.

During this period, *The Times* began to win an impressive reputation for its able and concerned coverage of the fate of the Kurdish minority in their guerrilla war against Iraq. It was a war which lasted for as long as the Shah supported the Kurds, and collapsed, with appalling consequences for the Kurds, as soon as the Shah abandoned them in return for frontier concessions from Iraq in the Gulf. Although *The Times* wrote a powerful editorial on 'Leaving the Kurds in the lurch', it did not mention that it was the Shah who left them there, in the interest of *Realpolitik*.

During 1975, of *The Times*'s 198 articles on Iran, eighteen were primarily concerned with the Kurdish question. There were thirty stories on oil, fifty-nine on economic development, twelve on arms deals and twenty-one on the royal family. There were nine stories on SAVAK and thirteen on the Shah's critics abroad. In March, *The Times* published one of its rare editorials on the Shah and his system of rule: 'The Shah has been careful to keep all real power in Iran in his own hands, ruling not only through the party system and Cabinet, but also through the Army, the court, and the ubiquitous intelligence and security organisation SAVAK. . .His government has in many ways been an extraordinarily successful one. He has raised the standard of living of his people, put through land reform and other reforms of the White Revolution and used the oil revenues to strengthen and expand the economy. . .Nevertheless, in the absence of freedom, there is no check on the abuse of power.' (4 March 1975).

This was measured and cautious. But in 1975, *The Times* also began to publish the regular articles of Lord Chalfont, the paper's defence correspondent before he had become a junior Minister for disarmament in Harold Wilson's Labour government of 1964. Chalfont became the leading British apologist for the Shah, and his defence of the Shah, and his vicious attacks on the Shah's critics, were to become increasingly controversial and distort the image of *The Times*'s reporting. Chalfont's first major piece set the tone: 'If the Western press, having discharged its statutory duty as the conscience of humanity, would occasionally turn its attention from the secret police, the evils of single-party government and the colour of the Shah's necktie, and place on record some of the remarkable progress which is taking place in Iran, Europeans might begin to understand its profound significance for the rest of the world. . .His stature in the eyes of the great majority of the Iranian people. . .springs from a burning conviction that the Shah, and only the Shah, can take the country into the first rank as a world power. There is an almost mystical bond between the throne and the people.' (24 March 1975).

In giving space to Chalfont's combative enthusiasm, *The Times* felt that its duty was to hold the ring, printing both passionate defenders and infuriated critics, while keeping its own editorial tone almost neutral. It printed a report by two members of the British Parliamentary Committee for the defence of Iranian political prisoners which concluded: 'Iran remains perhaps the worst country in the world in which to fall foul of the regime.' (12 February 1976). During that year *The Times* ran 141 articles, twenty-two on oil, twenty-nine on the economy, sixteen on arms deals and fifteen on the royal family. On the critical side, there were fourteen stories on SAVAK, six on corruption and six on the Shah's external critics. This was the year in which the Iranian economy began visibly to overheat, and Lord Chalfont was quick to leap to the Shah's defence: 'Anyone who really believes that the bubble has burst is in for some very considerable surprises.' (1 March 1976). In the same article, he put his defence of the Shah in almost apocalyptic terms: 'The survival of Western industrial society is a matter in which Iran, like Brazil and South Africa, may yet have an important part to play. If we alienate such countries by the application of double standards and irrelevant criteria to their internal political systems, we shall have only ourselves and our own feeble-minded hypocrisy to blame.'

The Times continued, in its regular series on political prisoners around the world, to focus on the Iranian victims of the state which won Lord Chalfont's fervent admiration. In a long interview with the Shah's sister, Princess Ashraf, *The Times* reporter questioned her firmly on the use of torture. The Princess denied that physical torture was used: 'There are more sophisticated ways of getting at the truth – injections,' her Royal Highness said (7 June 1976). *The Times*'s own questioning of the increasing sums Iran was spending on arms (more than the British defence budget) brought Lord Chalfont back to the defence: 'The Iranian Army does not seem a disproportionately large force for the defence of a country of vital strategic importance,' (11 October 1976).

In 1977, *The Times*'s coverage of the country fell to 116 articles, six on oil, thirty on the troubled economy, fifteen on arms deals and fifteen on the royal family. There were four articles about SAVAK, and sixteen on the Shah's external critics, largely because of the international interest in the anti-Shah demonstrations during his visit to the US. Early in the year, *The Times* editorial for the first time took a firm and principled stance upon the Shah's methods of rule, and drew the obvious conclusion: 'Could any threat justify the systematic torture, executions and other violations of human rights?. . . Economic growth is certainly desirable, but it should be accompanied by progress towards a more humane and tolerant society. Otherwise the tensions it generates must sooner or later erupt in violent form and carry away the regime that has presided over it.' (5 January 1977).

Nonetheless, the paper gave space to other views. A film-maker, Alan Hart, was given almost a full page to defend the Shah: 'The Shah, at considerable risk to his throne and to his life, is actually trying to create the institutions for a democratic style of government. . .The record proves that the Shah is putting into practice some of the policies which many who call themselves revolutionaries only shout about,' (9 June 1977). The next month Fred Halliday, one of the Shah's leading academic critics, was given space to reply. And the Shah's economic policies continued to founder. As one editorial put it: 'Iran has found that there is a limit to the amount of investment which an underdeveloped society can productively absorb in a short time.' (8 August 1977).

During the year of revolution, *The Times* was closed for the whole month of December by an industrial dispute, but in the first eleven months of 1978, it published 372 articles on Iran. This time, the balance was dramatically reversed. With twenty-seven stories on oil and only thirteen on the economy, the coverage was swamped by the eighty-five stories about riots, by thirty-four articles on religion and the role of Islam in the opposition, forty articles on SAVAK and forty-seven on the threatened royal family. While maintaining a devoted rearguard action, Lord Chalfont was moved to admit: 'I do not deny that there is suppression of political dissent and ruthlessly draconian police action against subversion.' (6 February 1978).

But the real merits of *The Times*'s reporting staff began to show. The Tehran correspondent rejected the Shah's own description of the opposition: 'The term Islamic Marxists is something of a contradiction and at present such an organised coalition of opposition to the Shah's rule is purely notional.' (11 May 1978). Later in the month,

David Watts in Tehran published a long assessment of the disparate groups who were threatening the regime: 'Both the left-wing elements and the fundamentalist religious groups have a community of interest in their opposition, but there is no underlying, long-term ideological basis for the union. But the Shah is in danger of welding together just such a unified opposition through his crack-down on the latest protests.' (26 May 1978).

Lord Chalfont's breezy confidence was deployed again: 'The police and the armed forces are totally loyal to the monarchy and certainly powerful enough to deal with the sort of internal security threat posed by the fragmented and unorganised opposition.' (21 August 1978). *The Times* was still unclear about the roots and impact of the Islamic opposition, and slow to appreciate the importance of the Bazaar trading community in financing and organizing the revolts. But its editorial staff could recognize a coalition when they saw one: 'The religious leaders have become progressively more liberal and constitutional in their demands, while the nationalists have shown more sympathy for religious grievances against certain symptoms of Western "corruption" such as cinemas or casinos.' (8 September 1978). This analysis suffered from the fact that the Ayatollah Khomeini was not calling for 'liberal and constitutional' reforms, but *The Times* had at least begun to accept that: 'It is now clear that dislike, even hatred for the regime go very much wider than. . .a left-wing intellectual fringe,' (8 September 1978). Lord Chalfont returned to insist that the riots were not 'a spontaneous uprising of a suppressed people against a brutal and corrupt dictatorship' (18 September 1978), which is exactly what they were, as a series of angry rebuttals in *The Times* letter columns was quick to point out.

In the end, with its own industrial dispute about to close the paper for almost a year, *The Times* editorials confessed that the paper did not really know what was going on in Iran: 'All that has emerged so far is that the Shah is far more unpopular with his own people than most Western observers had realised.' (2 November 1978). (That, of course, depended on which Western observers *The Times* meant.) Finally, on the eve of its own dissolution, *The Times* realized that the Shah's time was up: 'The Shah has nothing to be ashamed of in his ambitions. . .(but). . .he should be helped now to start preparing for the moment of departure, for the good of himself and of Iran.' (29 November 1978).

LE MONDE

Le Monde's coverage of Iran was never sketchy. Long before the oil price rises catapulted the Shah on to the world's news pages, *Le Monde* readers had been well informed. In April 1970 its pages were a forum for debate between the Committee for Iranian political prisoners and General Pakravan, the Ambassador to Paris, on the work of SAVAK and the systematic use of torture (8 and 16 April 1970). Lengthy articles on Iran's importance in the Gulf after the British withdrawal accompanied a long series on Iranian archaeology and a comprehensive review of Iran's annual theatre festival. Djaval Alamir, *Le Monde*'s Tehran correspondent (who was later to be accused of SAVAK links) gave a regular and efficient service on the news, but little comment. Articles of opinion were left to 'special envoys', and they were very good indeed. Alain Murcier predicted the OPEC price rise and the Shah's role in it, a good three years in advance: 'The Shah is not going to compromise his position as political leader of the Persian Gulf countries by showing himself too conciliatory to the oil companies,' (1 February 1971). A long survey of the political unrest, including accounts of strikes, torture, an analysis of the failure of land reform, the role of religion and the importance of Khomeini, was simply years ahead of its time (26 May 1971). Eric Rouleau's interview with the Shah at the time of the Persepolis festivities concentrated upon torture, the role of the opposition, and Khomeini (8 October 1971). And *Le Monde* retained a sense of balance, printing full-page debates between the Shah's supporters and detractors (24 November 1971).

In the course of 1972, *Le Monde* printed 163 articles on Iran, of which twenty-nine were about oil, six about the economy, eleven about Iraq-Kurdish affairs and twenty-five on other international relations. There were thirty-nine articles on SAVAK and internal security (more than the *New York Times* published in any year), and a further thirteen on the Shah's external critics. With twelve articles on Iranian arts and culture, six on natural disasters, and four on the role of drugs in Iranian life, *Le Monde* was providing an unparalleled coverage.

Le Monde's editorials of 1972 were prescient: 'The strikes of workers, the endemic agitation in the universities, the development of urban guerrillas, show that Iran has not succeeded in resolving its most acute political and social problems. The suppression of all the political opposition parties, followed by a pitiless repression, the absence of fundamental liberties, while depriving Iranians of an indispensable safety valve, contribute to aggravate an evil, when more liberal methods would doubtless work more easily.' (8 February 1972). This was not simply rhetoric. It was rooted in a deeply sophisticated understanding of the social forces at work, and then expressed in *Le Monde*'s sternest moral tones: 'There is a climate of mobilized public opinion in Iran which evokes the most dreadful memories of the inter-war years of Stalinism. . .The rapid growth of the economy, the success of the battle against illiteracy, have provoked the appearance of a middle class and an intelligentsia, open to the outside world, who cannot but be shocked by the vast social disparities in the country, and by the survival of a despotic system which, however enlightened it claims to be, is too distant from the spirit of the twentieth century.' (3 March 1972). On 16 May, *Le Monde*'s Tehran office was badly damaged by a bomb.

In 1973, *Le Monde* ran 181 stories (more than the *Washington Post* did in 1978, the year of the revolution). There were fifty-three stories on oil, twenty on the economy, ten on arms deals, eleven on Iraq, six on Gulf strategy and eleven on Iranian culture. And there were twenty-six articles on SAVAK, and four on the Shah's external critics. *Le Monde* was still enough of France's official newspaper to publish dutiful editorials on the occasion of state visits. For M. Pompidou's visit to Tehran, *Le Monde*'s bulletin was diplomatically polite: 'In paying his respects to the person of the Shah, to his "independent policy" and the "genuine peaceful revolution" which the Shah has accomplished in the development field, M. Pompidou has sought to seal the new-found friendship.' (19 September 1973).

But the following month, in a four-part series by Eric Rouleau, *Le Monde*'s traditionally sharp eye was focused on that 'development': 'A cruel paradox means that in spite of a remarkable development designed to free Iran from the control of foreign hands, Iran's dependence has continued to increase, as much through borrowing as through production. Never has foreign capital, above all American, played such a major part in the economy.' And what growth there had been was causing social strains, with the new middle class as 'little islands of prosperity in a sea of indigence. The south of Tehran and the countryside must be seen to measure the gap between the summit and the base of the social pyramid.' Rouleau probed into the vaunted land reform, and judged that the planned revolution in agriculture had failed, run by 'state bureaucrats too often incompetent or corrupt'. He examined the role of the opposition and the nature of the Shah's controls: 'the system of repression is designed to discourage all forms of dissent, violent or not. . .the extreme brutality of the repression surprises one. . .The suppression of organized political groups bestows on the army an ascendancy too exclusive not to become dangerous.' (7, 8, 9 and 10 October 1973).

In 1974, *Le Monde* ran 212 articles, forty-three on oil, forty-seven on economic development and fifteen on arms deals. There were eighteen pieces on Iraqi relations and the Kurdish minority, eight on Gulf strategy and eight on the royal family itself. There were eleven articles on the Shah's external critics, but the number of stories on SAVAK and internal security showed a marked fall to twelve. It is difficult not to deduce that the dramatic economic opportunities that oil-rich Iran presented were obscuring *Le Monde*'s hitherto critical vision. For the Shah's official visit to Paris, *Le Monde*'s official bulletin was couched in almost purely business terms: 'The place Iran has today, and will occupy tomorrow in its supplies of gas and oil to France, the horizons it opens to our exporters, for the development of our industry (notably the nuclear industry), the interest Iran shows in Concorde, in the eventual construction of a metro in Tehran, and yet further industrial projects, builds an obvious complementary relationship between our two countries. . .For the harmony to be complete, the Shah should open to his people the way to political liberty, as well as to power.' (25 June 1974).

This is a marked change of tone, but *Le Monde* had not gone soft. In a two-page interview with the Shah during his Paris visit, one in four of André Fontaine's questions covered torture, repression and social inequalities. And while the rest of the world's press was focusing on the potential damage (and opportunities) the OPEC price rise might bring to the Western economies, *Le Monde* put the matter in a broader perspective. Noting that the Shah had imposed an 84% price rise on the amount Moscow paid for Iran's gas, the paper commented: 'A great power, in spite of the means of pressure at its disposal, has thus been placed in check by a small neighbour, because of its precious resource of gas.' (20 August 1974).

In 1975, *Le Monde* continued the pattern of paying much less attention to the Shah's repression, and very much more to his economy. The paper ran 219 stories, of which thirty-seven were about oil, fifty-two on economic development, ten on arms deals and thirty-one on international relations. There were only four articles on culture, ten on SAVAK and eleven on the Shah's external critics.

There were seventeen articles on the Shah's role in the Persian Gulf, twenty-seven on Iraq and the Kurds and seven on the royal family. The pattern of *Le Monde*'s coverage was now almost identical with that of the *New York Times* and *Washington Post*. During the year, *Le Monde* twice ran respectful interviews with the Prime Minister, Mr Hoveida, which covered purely economic and energy affairs, without questions on the political or security situation. Although some 300 people had been executed in the years 1973–5, *Le Monde*'s criticisms were markedly more tame than they had been before the OPEC price rise. What had been a uniquely well-informed and determined coverage had become a rather average performance.

In 1976, *Le Monde* ran 195 stories, and as the pace of Iran's economic performance began to falter and social discontent to mount, the reporting sharpened. There were thirty-one stories on SAVAK, and thirty-five on the Shah's external critics. There were thirty articles on Iran's oil, thirty-seven on its economy, four on arms deals, but the pre-OPEC balance of *Le Monde*'s coverage had been restored.

Le Monde signalled its renewed sharpness with an editorial: 'The recourse to violence is logical against a regime which treats its adversaries, no matter what the roots of their dissatisfaction or the form of their opposition, as partisans who are attacking the rear of an army on active service.' (4 February 1976). In March, an interview with the Shah was limited to financial questions only, but in May, an interview with Premier Hoveida led to sharp questions about political opponents. Hoveida gave the usual answer: 'We have two oppositions, one I call Red and Communist, the other fanatic and religious. But neither one has deep roots. No more than groups of terrorists.' (28 May 1976).

President Giscard d'Estaing paid a formal state visit to Iran in October, and *Le Monde*'s formal bulletin was waspish: 'The perfume of milliards of francs is most agreeable in this diplomacy of merchandise, which is unembarrassed by any moral questions,' (6 October 1976). But in the same week, Eric Rouleau published a three-part series which had all the traditional *Le Monde* virtues of analysis and understanding but which still contrived to miss a number of important points. He covered the work of SAVAK, its victims and pervasiveness in Iranian society, and examined the new soft line that the Shah was taking to at least some of his opponents: 'The Shah has chosen to respond to the social tensions engendered by his policy of super-growth by successive measures of appeasement to some, while maintaining the repression against others. . .There are no more than 300 Islam-Marxist guerrillas, and the Shah is not wrong when he says his throne is not threatened by a handful of terrorists. He has nothing to fear from the Tudeh Communist Party, nor the defiant National Front of Dr Mossadegh, both pulverized by SAVAK.' So why the repression, Rouleau asked. He wrote of growing social strains, of impoverished peasants, ruined by agricultural 'reforms', and of down-trodden workers, and of the costs of arms purchases dislocating the economy, and middle-class anger at the Shah's attacks on inflation and his reforms to give the workers a share in profits. What Rouleau missed was the religious factor, the importance of Islam, and its capacity to mobilize all these disparate strands of opposition into one force. It was this perspective which *Le Monde* had comprehended, uniquely, in 1970 and 1971.

In 1977, *Le Monde* ran 138 articles on Iran, fewer than in any year since 1971. There were twenty-two on oil, twenty-six on the economy, five on corruption and five on the arms trade. There were five articles on politics, five on riots, thirteen on SAVAK and twenty-two on the Shah's critics abroad. For the best reporting on Iran, readers had to turn to *Le Monde Diplomatique* which ran a major piece on Iran-Saudi rivalries in July, and a prescient and profound article on Islam and politics in August. These religious perspectives did not extend to *Le Monde* itself, although Eric Rouleau noted that the rioters had taken to shouting 'Mossadegh and Khomeini', which suggested some kind of association between the National Front and Islam. Rouleau focused on the international roots of the unrest: 'Persuaded that the regime, already weakened by severe economic and social crisis, will not dare in the Carter era to strike back at them, individuals and organizations are beginning to demand respect for basic liberties.' It was significant that one loyal reader chose *Le Monde* to place an advertisement, thanking people for the condolences that had been sent on the murder of his son. The ad was placed by the Ayatollah Khomeini, who went on to appeal to the army to liberate Iran, and to the intellectuals and all good Muslims to continue their criticism of the Shah, and not to collaborate. The year 1977 had seen the development of a new kind of opposition within the country, of organized poetry readings of traditional Persian writers. Organized by intellectual dissidents, the meetings became a kind of cultural protest movement, attracting middle-class Iranians and students. *Le Monde* appeared hardly to notice them, although other papers, principally the *Guardian*, gave them considerable attention.

In 1978, *Le Monde*'s reporting recovered its excellence. With 257 stories in the eleven months to the end of November, only fourteen covered oil, and only twelve the economy. There were twenty-three pieces on SAVAK, and seventeen on the external critics, thirty-two on the army, forty on religion, twenty-five on politics and sixty-seven on riots. And the articles were good. By April, Jean-Claude Guillebaud had identified Khomeini's MLI (Iran Liberation Movement) as the most significant force in the opposition, and stressed: 'These riots have been neither blind nor disordered,' (6 April 1978).

Guillebaud did not make the American press mistake of dismissing the religious movement as a feudal anachronism: 'The apparently "reactionary" character of the religious opposition is not as clear as one might think. Certainly, the mullahs fear being robbed of their traditional authority by modernization, but Shi'ite Islam joins the reformist or progressive critics of the Shah on the same ground.' (6 April 1978). He stressed that the return to religion was a symbol of hostility to the Shah and that a new coalition of disaffected businessmen, liberals and reformers had joined deliberately with the religious leaders. On 6 May *Le Monde* became the first major Western paper to run a lengthy interview with the Ayatollah Khomeini, then in exile in Iraq. 'We would not collaborate with Marxists, even to overthrow the Shah,' Khomeini said. During May and June, *Le Monde*'s Jean de la Guerivière interviewed the political opposition inside Iran, printing articles on the National Front, on Bakhtiar, on the Association of Writers which had helped to organize the poetry meetings, and talking to the businessmen and the Bazaar merchants. 'All these groups are suffering from another form of violence than political repression and police aggression – that of a society in the vanguard of raw capitalism.' (9 June 1978).

In August, as the Shah tried to bolster his regime with belated attempts at liberalization, Jean-Claud Guillebaud stressed the essential issue: 'The hostility to the Shah himself and his family is so strong and widespread throughout the country that it overwhelms any political or religious divisions that would otherwise be fundamental.' (18 August 1978). *Le Monde* drew on a broad panel of contributors to explain the nature of the Iranian revolution. On 23 August, Moussa El-Sadr, the president of the Shi'ite council in Lebanon, explained 'The appeal of the Prophets'. Karim Sandjabi was given a page to explain the policies of his National Front (1 November). Jean Gueyras was sent to Tehran to assess Khomeini's appeal, Paul Balta to analyse the morale of the Iranian army. *Le Monde*'s editorials hammered home the lessons that the US press seemed unable to learn: 'Menaced by popular unrest, the Shah gets more support from the great powers than he does from his own people.' (26 August). 'No longer is there any political force worthy of the name on which the Shah can lean – only SAVAK, the army and the American alliance. Any hope of a peaceful transition to democracy through an enlightened monarchy has collapsed under the army's bullets.' (11 September). It was *Le Monde* which appreciated the parallels to the French Revolution, of a popular uprising against a repressive monarch: 'We are living through a 1789,' (31 October). And it was *Le Monde* which coined the perfect phrase to define the high-technology police state, with its computerized surveillance, that SAVAK had built: 'A people is moving, and the technological net which was supposed to hold them down is breaking everywhere.' (9 November).

DIE WELT

Die Welt's coverage of Iran was spasmodic, with insufficient articles each year to justify the kind of statistical tables one can prepare for *The Times, Le Monde*, the *New York Times* and the *Washington Post*. Moreover, *Die Welt* saw Iran in such politically committed terms, as a Manichean struggle between the good, reforming Shah and the evil, feudal-Communist opposition, that the German paper hardly seems to be writing about the same country. For the Shah's Persepolis festivities of 1971, Hermann Schaeffer set *Die Welt*'s tone: 'The ruin of Persepolis is not just a historical memory, but also a political reminder, a warning of expanding Communist revolution. . .This greatest year for Iran is also the hardest – the battlefield lies between the ancient Persian religion of the fire temples and the mosques of Islam.' (16 August 1971). Schaeffer went on to report 'the alarm of Iran's security service over the work of exiled Iranian academics, working with Amnesty International on the political fate of the opposition'. Schaeffer's SAVAK contacts gave him something of a scoop on an alleged international conspiracy to overthrow the Shah: 'A long-planned scheme for subversion, with foreign arms and agents, with Communist backing and Soviet machine pistols on one side, and the vast Soviet economic help to Iraq on the other, was planned to reach its critical point in December. . .but the defection of an Iraqi secret service officer warned the Iranians to tighten their security.' (17 August 1971).

For *Die Welt*, Iran was a security story, a cautionary example from which Germany could learn of subversive threats at home. Peter Meyer-Ranke wrote approvingly that: 'the Iran government will fight back hard. It will not let its inner security be endangered by Communist or anarchist groups.' (4 March 1972). He went on to interview SAVAK's director and quote the names, addresses and phone numbers of anti-Shah saboteurs, based in Iraq, subsidized by the Iraqi secret police, who had been students in West Germany. He took the opportunity to criticize 'a manipulated Western "open society" in which terrorists are seen as freedom fighters for democracy,' (4 March 1972). In a signed editorial, Lothar Ruehl sounded a more cautious note: 'It is not likely that the social goals of forced industrialization can be controlled by the one man in the palace. But his attempt deserves respect and support.' (10 March 1972). *Die Welt* saw little to criticize in Iran, and much for the West to learn. In another signed editorial (they outnumber the news reports), Peter Meyer-Ranke commented on 'the chagrin of the radical Left in the West, who can neither forgive nor forget that a Third World country has worked its way up to relative prosperity without their revolution and without their ideology,' (29 January 1973). *Die Welt* did not ignore the Shah's repression but accepted it as a reasonable price to pay: 'The repression, which during the evolution of Iran is acting as a controlling curb, will presumably be loosened when the economic democracy actually gets under way.' (1 February 1973).

The OPEC price rise, and the consequent enriching of the Shah's Iran, attracted little editorial attention at *Die Welt*, for all the economic implications they caused for Germany. The editor of *Die Welt*'s op-ed page, Enno von Loewenstern, focused on the Shah's merits and the evils of his opponents: 'Do we really need instruction, in a world such as this, in which chaos and dictatorship live side by side, on the merits of an enlightened monarch such as Shah Reza Pahlevi, with his great services to the development of his ancient land, on whose solitary shoulders rest all these cares? How right he is, every thinking man in Germany knows.' (31 December 1974).

Die Welt's reporters were able men, aware of the economic and social disruptions implicit in the Shah's drive to industrialization. But they drew very different conclusions from their colleagues at *Le Monde*: 'The Shah and the handful of men in his governing team chase after their ambitious economic targets with such speed that their people cannot keep up the pace. . .But the foreseeable future, the popularity of the monarchy will be a stabilizing factor.' (Heinz Barth, 27 November 1975). But *Die Welt* clearly saw that the Shah's peaceful revolution was in trouble: 'The mentality of the people has the effect not only of working against his good objectives, but it is also acting as a brake on the vigorous drive of the Shah. . .The White Revolution has become grey.' (Peter Brinkman, 3 January 1976).

Six days later, the occupation of the Iran Embassy in Germany by anti-Shah demonstrators showed that *Die Welt* reporters knew their job. 'They accused the Persian royal family and government of "fascist methods" in the struggle against the opposition, swung blood-red scarves and sang the battle hymn of the Persian poet Golesorchi, who was put to death last year for his activities against the State. . . They were political refugees from the Mohammedan-Marxist splinter-groups of Persia.' (Eberhard Nitschke, 29 January 1976). Peter Meyer-Ranke returned to Iran to take a cool look at the Shah's economic progress: 'The Shah is watching his life's dream, to turn Iran into an economic and military power, endangered for the first time. The Shah built on oil, but he now stands on sand.' (19 January 1977).

Die Welt paid little attention to the rising tide of riots and opposition in early 1978 until April, when President Scheel of West Germany paid a state visit to Tehran. *Die Welt*'s editorial indirectly pointed to repression as a cause of the Shah's difficulties: 'For the entire German Left, Iran is a quite indispensable Aunt Sally [literally *Schiessscheibe* – shooting target]. But whatever one may think of the Shah's methods of internal politics, there can be no doubt but that the majority of the internal opposition to him comes from those who have to surrender their privileges.' Bernt Conrad, one of *Die Welt*'s most experienced political reporters, accompanied Scheel and broke away from the official party to interview ordinary people, opposition figures and Cabinet Ministers. The result was a straightforward, balanced article on the long legacy of bitterness which burdened the regime, and the difficulties of organizing against it. The following month, Peter Meyer-Ranke returned to Iran. He began with an article justifying the Shah's vast appetite for arms: 'the Shah arms himself to meet the threats of agents, terror and narcotics,' (9 May 1978), adding that the 1977 coup in Afghanistan justified the Shah's fears of subversion. But he went on to write some able articles on the troubles, an excellent description of a bazaar riot, explaining the views of the religious opposition, of the Shah, and describing the main religious leaders (13 May 1978).

Die Welt's editorial writers stuck to the theme of Communist subversion, although accepting that the riots might have other roots as well: 'The youth unrest in Tehran and other Persian cities is in the widest sense orchestrated. The Communist agitators can operate the generational conflict, striking back from the remaining cadres of the old Tudeh Communist Party, with religious protest groups and a social discontent which is not in all ways unjustified.' (17 May 1978). As the riots intensified, *Die Welt*'s Peter Meyer-Ranke assured his readers that the Shah's main strength was still secure: 'The officer corps is the strongest support of the Peacock Throne. It is well trained, and it will equally well fulfil its duty.' (17 August 1978).

By September, *Die Welt*'s editorials felt able to draw a lasting social lesson from the Shah's problems: 'Economic revolution and social transformation should only be joined together in a harmonious combination, where the unshakeable decision has been taken to prevent Soviet infiltration. These decisive prerequisites were lacking in Iran' (20 September 1978). The verdict of the Iranians themselves upon the Shah and his government became plain to *Die Welt* by November: 'For his people, the Shah is too modern and too foreign. The mullahs hate him. The state administration is corrupt.' (7 November 1978).

Die Welt's clippings library has a file marked 'Iran death sentences'. It consists of a handful of single-paragraph reports. At no time did the paper examine the nature of the Shah's repression, the unpopularity of SAVAK or the stability of a regime that clearly depended upon state terror. By 1979, under a new editor, Peter Boenisch, *Die Welt* acknowledged that the Shah had been repressive. And it then lost no time in looking at the excesses of the new regime: 'The Shah's regime was unjust, it is said. And so it was. The secret police were cruel, it is said. And so they were. . .But now, [the new government] wields the sword of revenge, no less awful and no less cruel. What is happening now, and looks to happen further, is a barbarity.' (Peter Boenisch editorial, 21 February 1979).

CORRIERE DELLA SERA

Corriere's coverage of Iran was brief and politically bland until 1978. In spite of the tradition of highly personalized and subjective journalism which distinguishes the Italian press, the reporting of Iran was remarkable for its laconic plainness. The tone was set by a lengthy account, during the time of the Persepolis festivities, of the Shah's press conference with the world's press. The questions by German reporters on why 'only boy scouts' seemed to represent the Iranian public at formal occasions were quoted, and the Shah's reply set down verbatim. The comment of Silvano Villani, *Corriere*'s special correspondent, was limited to the Shah's tone, to his moments of irritation, and to quoting the Shah's critical attitude to the Western press. This was one of eight significant stories on Iran printed during 1971. Five of them related to the royal family, one to oil policy, and two were concerned mainly with SAVAK and the problems of internal security.

In the following year, without the Persepolis anniversary to report, *Corriere*'s coverage was almost non-existent, with but one major story, on oil and the economy in December: 'No other country in the world has made such rapid progress in so little time, passing without transition from a nomadic and pastoral feudalism into a typical Western capitalism; from being the vassal of two imperial nations, Russia and Britain, who cared only to exploit its natural resources. . .to a country pledged to place itself alongside the most advanced European nations.'

In 1973, the oil crisis which followed the Yom Kippur war persuaded *Corriere* to publish eight major articles on Iran, four of them on oil, one on arms deals, and two on SAVAK. *Corriere*'s reports on the repression were factual accounts of arrests and shootings, without any degree of perspective about the roots of opposition to the Shah, or the possible political impact of SAVAK's methods.

In 1974, Iran's growing importance as a market for Western goods and as a source of oil led to thirty-one *Corriere* articles, eight concerning energy supplies, seven on Iran's economy, and twelve on its international relations. There was one story of significance on SAVAK and, early in the year, the Shah granted *Corriere*'s Ettore Petta a lengthy interview. It dealt almost exclusively with oil, economic development and the strategic implications of the Persian Gulf and Iran's new armament programme. If questions on repression and internal politics were asked, they were not printed (4 January 1974). Later in the month Giorgio Amadei published an assessment on Iran's declining food production, the population explosion and the flood of the rural population into the cities. The land reform programme was described as 'grandiose but effective. . . leading to a massive problem of unemployment and under-employment. . .Development capital must come from oil, the only weapon Iran possesses.' (28 January 1974).

In 1975, *Corriere* published twenty-one articles, five on oil, four on the economy, six on international relations, two on arms deals and one on SAVAK. In 1976, there were only eight major articles, two on SAVAK, three on economic development, and two on the role of Islam in society, although they did not explore Islam's political potential. In 1977, there were only four articles of substance, three of them on SAVAK and one on the Shah.

In 1978, *Corriere della Sera* published 100 articles, forty-one on riots, twelve on the role of Islam, six on the military, seventeen on politics, six on oil and only one story on the economy. Having effectively ignored the story for years, *Corriere* began to swamp Iran with its special correspondents, and they performed well enough. Dino Frescobaldi, in a long article on 'The Islamic Rightists', made the usual mistake of assuming that the Shah had confiscated religious lands (15 August 1978). Renato Ferraro made the same error later in the month in an otherwise excellent full-page story which went back to academic surveys of 1975 to show that the genesis of the Iranian revolution had been apparent then, in economic overheating and rural distress. Late as his reporting was, Ferraro covered the main elements in the troubles: 'The mosques have become the tribunals of the opposition. . .while upstairs students talk of a synthesis between Marxism and the traditional culture, on the ground floor are the young, progressive Mullahs, who are becoming the spokesmen of protest.' (29 August 1978). This was an improvement on the usual facile articles on 'reactionary feudal Islam'.

Throughout September, Ferraro sent back dispatches saying that the Shah's attempts at liberalism were doomed to failure: 'His power base is now reduced to the army and US support,' (4 September 1978). And later in the month, the Shah granted an interview to *Corriere*'s Dino Frescobaldi, during the martial law period, and confessed 'I have committed some errors.' Under sharp questioning, the Shah said 'SAVAK? That belongs to the past.' Over the interview, *Corriere* printed: 'This does not mean that we approve of his ideas, nor of his political line,' (21 September 1978). But of the five 'special envoys' that *Corriere* sent to Iran in those last weeks of 1978, it was Ferraro again who wrote the hard assessments of Bakhtiar as a possible successor, who described the collapsing morale of the army, and who hammered home the Shah's 'essential illusion of building a modern and eventually democratic country through corruption, terror and despotism,' (8 November 1978).

As the collapse became inevitable, the *Corriere* editorial turned to the possibility of foreign intervention: 'Even the self-interest of the great powers – justifiably apprehensive – loses its validity when faced with the courage and convictions of the Iranian people. . .At this point, the illegitimacy of the regime, arising from its own fundamental illiberalism and its wholly unrepresentative character, is wholly irreversible. Not even the most cynical *Realpolitik* can change that.' (11 December 1978).

PRAVDA

Pravda did not give its readers a regular or informative account of events in Iran until the very last months of the Shah's regime and, even then, it was put very firmly within the context of Soviet-American relations. It took the Western newspapers long enough to realize that a revolutionary process was under way in Iran; *Pravda*'s readers were served considerably worse. As a neighbouring State, with significant trade in Iranian natural gas, and joint responsibilities for the Caspian Sea, the Soviet Union cultivated good relations with the Shah's regime until his fall. Even the prohibition and persecution of the Tudeh (Communist Party) inside Iran, and the Shah's ambitious and pro-Western foreign policy did not lead to criticism in the Soviet press. The Soviet Union's support for the Dhofar rebels in the sultanate of Oman in the mid-1970s meant that *Pravda* regularly condemned the 'British mercenaries' who fought for the Sultan, but the Shah's helicopter battalions which hunted down the rebels received only passing mention in *Pravda*'s columns.

Pravda's main themes in covering Iran were the need for good Iran-Soviet relations; the admirable determination of the Shah to modernize and reform his country; the legacy of British imperialism and Anglo-American greed in exploiting Iran's oil; and the way in which American arms sales were endangering peace and Iranian prosperity. But for weeks at a time, Iran disappeared from *Pravda*'s pages. On the eve of the 1971 Persepolis festivities, with President Podgorny scheduled to attend, *Pravda* began a spate of articles. The first, on 3 October, was a prominent review of a Russian book *Iran – the friendly country* which focused on Britain's imperial presence there. 'Iran was assigned a major anti-Soviet role in Britain's designs,'

Pravda commented. The following day there was a report on a Soviet aid project, helping to build Iran's new Caspian ports at Bandar e Pahlavi and Bandar Nowshahr. This was followed by a report on EEC–Iranian trade, which claimed that Iran was 'being bled white' by buying $600 million of EEC exports, while selling only $42 million in return. *Pravda* did not add that this excluded oil exports. During Podgorny's week at Persepolis, there were dry statistical accounts of Iranian economic development, a bland description of Podgorny's 'long, friendly talks with the Shah' and, on the 17th, *Pravda* commented that the week had seen 'a new step towards all-embracing co-operation between the two countries'. On the 19th, *Pravda* ran extracts from the Shah's press conference, emphasizing the Shah's statement that 'relations between Iran and the USSR have never been so good and these relations are improving every year'.

On 23 October, Aleksey Vasilyev, a *Pravda* economics commentator, wrote a lengthy study of Iran's oil policy and OPEC's future which was shrewd and prophetic. He wrote about the Tehran OPEC meeting and the falling value of the US dollar, explaining that 'the oil monopolies pay royalties to oil-rich countries in dollars, and sell this oil in Western Europe and Japan for local, more sound currency'. He argued that OPEC's frustration would increase, and prophesied 'conflict between OPEC and the oil tycoons. . .the OPEC people demand that an end be put gradually to the impudent plunder of their wealth'. On the following day, *Pravda* noted that Iran had been a member of the US-dominated CENTO alliance for ten years, and that treaty commitments had so far cost the country $600 million 'which could have been spent on the establishment of many factories'. Apart from brief accounts of official delegations, economic projects and Iran's voice in OPEC, the country then virtually disappears from *Pravda*'s pages, returning in some prominence in late 1973 and early 1974, when OPEC's price rise was dominating the Western press. Coverage of Iran was sympathetic: on 23 January 1974, an article on Iranian culture quoted Tehran newspapers to say that it was under threat from 'the trashy and harmful culture of the West'. In the following week, there were several stories on Soviet-Iranian agreements on joint anti-pollution measures in the Caspian Sea, and on the export of Soviet steel technology. 'Relations between the two countries have reached their highest point,' *Pravda* said on 9 February. The pattern was to continue until June, when the OPEC weapon was turned upon the Soviet Union, and the Shah demanded a 400% increase in the price of Iran's natural gas. This went 'against all principles of international agreements'. On 25 September, announcing the arrival of Prince Golam Pahlavi on a formal visit, *Pravda* made it plain that relations were back to normal.

The spate of shootings of Iranian 'terrorists' received no mention in *Pravda*, even when they were condemned as Communists by the Iranians. But as the Iranian economy began to show signs of overheating, *Pravda* began a series of articles which laid the blame for Iran's troubles on the West. Commenting on the rising inflation in Tehran, *Pravda* said: 'These symptoms of the sickness of the capitalist economic system know no boundaries. . .and, like a chain reaction, affect all countries whose economies are one-sidedly oriented towards the West.' But there was at this stage no mention of the role of arms purchases in distorting the Iranian economy. And in January 1976, in a series on the need for détente in the Persian Gulf, which included a general condemnation of Western arms sales in the region, there was no specific analysis or criticism of Iran. Its role as a major arms buyer, and its part in quelling the Dhofar rebellion, were simply mentioned without comment.

Pravda's comments on Iran were usually inspired not by events inside Iran but by the comments and stories that predominated in the Western press. The summer of 1976 saw some concern in the *New York Times* and *Le Monde* about the level of arms sales, and it was in response to these that *Pravda* commented, on 26 August, that 'the intensive US arming of Iran should not be viewed separately from the general imperial policy pursued by Washington in the Persian Gulf', adding that the US arms were the more alarming as they were 'stockpiled close to the gunpowder barrel of the Middle East'. Similarly, the Kissinger visit to the Gulf earlier in August had led to almost daily articles on the dangers of a regional arms race in the Gulf, and to a condemnation of US policy generally: 'US arms sales to Iran and the other Persian Gulf states are aimed at gaining control over the area and the security of US oil interests.' *Pravda* was cautious never to criticize Iran's policy as such, but to sympathize with Iran for the economic difficulties that *Pravda* saw as caused by the West. In the same way, *Pravda* would attack Britain or the US for their Gulf policy, which certainly involved an indirect criticism of Iran, but nothing specific enough to provoke official Iranian displeasure. When a delegation from the Iran Workers' Association arrived in Moscow for the 1977 May Day celebration, *Pravda* swallowed the fiction of describing them as an entirely legitimate trade-union body, (but then similar criticisms of 'trade unions' in authoritarian states could be made of such bodies throughout the Soviet empire). This determination not to criticize the Shah and his policies, but to lay all blame on the USA, led to serious distortions of the facts early in 1978, when the US press began to discuss the Shah's proposal that the Americans maintain a naval presence in the Persian Gulf. The Shah had made it publicly and repeatedly clear that his arms purchases were designed to make Iran into a regional superpower immediately, and a power of global significance in the long term. On 14 February, Yuriy Glukhov, one of *Pravda*'s foreign affairs columnists, put it this way: 'All statements of Washington betray the smell of oil, trade in arms, and cunning contrivances with whose help it is sought to turn Iran into a shield for ensuring American interests in the Gulf.'

The wave of anti-Shah riots which began early in 1978 went unreported by *Pravda* until the Iranian press began to blame 'Red Marxists'. On 8 April, *Pravda* retorted: 'It is clear that the wave of demonstrations and violence engulfing Iran is directed against the existing situation in the country. . .one is amazed at what nonsense individuals concoct to level accusations against Marxism. . .these actions are indubitably manifestations from pro-Maoist quarters.' When Iran's Ambassador to the USA, Ardeshir Zahedi, suggested that Moscow was behind the unrest, *Pravda* and *Izvestia* and Moscow's Radio Peace and Progress combined to condemn him: 'He has selected as the main target of his angry attacks the Soviet Union, a country with which Iran maintains traditionally good-neighbourly relations. The peoples of the two countries have been entertaining feelings of sympathy and friendship for each other.'

Pravda was slow to examine the roots of the unrest but, on 24 August, an analysis which rested heavily on Iranian press reports said: 'Everyone knows that for a long time now there have been clashes and friction between secular and religious powers in Iran. But the present incidents are of a different nature – in the sharp and serious economic and social problems besetting Iran.' It went on to quote the Iranian press on rising rents, the lack of municipal services, bad transport and the exodus of the rural population to the cities. 'These without doubt are the reasons for the explosion of the people's anger and wrath.'

In the weekly round-up of world affairs, there came a further analysis on 16 September: 'The social character of the events in Iran is obvious. The thousands of millions that Iran has been reaping in recent years from oil exports have in no way improved the lot of the working people. All they have done is widen the abyss between rich and poor. The open-door policy towards foreign capital and the massive arms purchases in the USA have had the result that these thousands of millions of petro-dollars are ending up in the vaults of the West, chiefly American monopolies. Foreigners are taking up to $3,000 million out of Iran each year. Another $1,000 million goes to pay for the tens of thousands of American advisers at various levels of the State machinery, and especially in the army. . .These events have thrown a bright light on the truly hypocritical attitude of imperialist forces to the Iranian people. Their problems and aspirations are not of the slightest interest to the Western monopolies. Indeed, the USA views Iran only from the standpoint of its strategic role and value as a supplier of raw materials.'

As the anti-Shah movement gathered momentum, *Pravda* began to give more coverage of a simple descriptive kind, but great care was still taken not to offend the Shah himself. On 4 November, *Pravda* published an article praising the Shah for his reforms: 'Agrarian reforms practically eliminated feudalism in the countryside. Women received equal rights with men, which for a Muslim country is very important. A struggle began against illiteracy and disease. Water sources were nationalized.' But *Pravda*'s real concern was with the impact of the Iranian crisis on the US. On 18 November, *Pravda* ran a lengthy interview with Leonid Brezhnev, which amounted to a public warning to the Americans not to intervene: 'The events taking place are of a purely internal nature and the issues they raise should be dealt with by the Iranian people themselves. . .Any interference, let alone military intervention, in Iran, a state with a common frontier with the Soviet Union, will be regarded by the USSR as a matter affecting its security interests,' Brezhnev said.

Articles on the riots were used as pegs on which *Pravda* hung warnings to the USA. On 26 November, without exploring the nature of the revolts or of the means used to suppress them, it announced: 'Anti-government actions are continuing, suppressed by force of arms. . .certain forces in the US fear a turn of affairs which could influence their military-strategic positions in the Persian Gulf and in the Middle East as a whole. It is not fortuitous that the Pentagon and the CIA are being named as the main initiators of the plans for a US military interference in Iran's affairs.'

Pravda's articles were blunt, factual and didactic. Its writers were not given the kind of latitude to convey something of Iran's mood which allowed *Izvestia*'s Ashraf Akhmadzhanov to write scene-setting accounts of the darkened streets, the marches of the strikers, the bustle of the Grand Bazaar – the atmospheric pieces that were filling the Western press at this time. *Pravda*'s Vitaly Korionov stuck to the main concern in a 1 January article which looked back at Iran's turbulent year: 'The Americans are seeking some way of justifying military intervention in Iran's internal affairs. Blatantly provocative means, spear-headed against the USSR, are being employed.' Turning to the roots of the crisis, Korionov went on: 'When the US speaks of defending human rights in Iran, it means specifically those Iranians who buy American-made Cadillacs. . .the thousand families who have amassed fabulous riches thanks to the corruption and bribery which have engulfed the upper echelons of society.'

But by the end of the first week in January, *Pravda* seems to have reckoned that the Shah's reign was effectively over. For the first time, it began to print the anti-Shah slogans which had been the backbone of the riots all year. On 11 January, in an article by the rector of Tashkent University, *Pravda* began to give formal recognition to the anti-Shah forces: 'We are deeply aware of the just character of the Iranian people's struggle for democratic transformations.' But not until the Shah finally left the country did *Pravda* begin to attack him personally, in an article on 17 January that was itself a TASS dispatch. Throughout the week, *Pravda*'s main concern had been whether the US General Huyser would succeed in mounting a military coup.

ASHAI SHIMBUN

Asahi's coverage of Iran during the 1970s was focused overwhelmingly upon economic affairs. Almost until the end of the Shah's rule, *Asahi* editors in Tokyo discouraged their prize-winning Tehran correspondent from writing about politics. Hata Kaigo was sent to Tehran in August 1976. At the height of the 1978 riots, he employed four Iranian assistants. 'By late 1977, it was clear that something was deeply wrong with the regime,' Kaigo said in an interview. 'From late April 1978, I was personally convinced that he was doomed, but I did not put this into my articles until June or July. I was never consulted by my paper on the editorials about Iran, but my first critical articles were read by the Japanese Embassy in Tehran and they warned me that I was being too strong and I should be cautious. I took no notice.

Mainly, I was asked to send economic reports and news stories. I only wrote two or three background or feature articles, until I wrote a long series after the Shah fell.' During the early 1970s, *Asahi* ran brief news pieces about accusations of repression in Iran, if the accusations came from respected bodies like Amnesty or the International Commission of Jurists. But there were no denunciations of the Shah. Iran was presented as a land of economic opportunity, of oil wealth and cultural exotica, and hardly as a political entity at all.

Kaigo's critical article which excited the Japanese Embassy was tame enough by Western standards: 'Although the Shah has clearly stated his policy to sustain his politics of liberalization, and keeps open the possibility of abdicating in his son's favour at some future date, in reality he faces anti-government riots, and increasing popular fear that he will revert to a tough repression. Faced with pressure on human rights from the Carter administration, Iran will respond by placing even more emphasis on the need to eliminate Russian influence in the Persian Gulf.' (21 May 1978).

In August, under the headlines 'Shah system shaken, dignity severely shaken', Kaigo reported on the assault on a crowded cinema: 'The dignity of the Shah's regime has been badly shaken because the terrorist activity took place in spite of martial law. Iran's government is now swaying uncertainly between offering the carrot of further freedoms, or waving the stick of firm government.' (22 August 1978). In a news-feature on the same day, he analysed the religious forces at work, describing the riots in the holy city of Qom, the Ayatollah Khomeini, the Shi'ite tradition, and concluded: 'Such a complex series of developments is not the simple Islamic Marxism which the Shah defines.'

Asahi's first editorial on the troubles came late, and said little that was new: 'Exposed in the present confusion in Iran are the distortions that come from the forced reforms of the last fifteen years. Because of the policy giving priority to modernization based on wealth, the voices of the masses have been suppressed. Despite the shift from a sham civilian government to an open military regime, power politics is sure to give rise to distortions of a different kind.' (9 November 1978).

Kaigo's next news analysis went into the roots of the crisis, but still made no reference to SAVAK or to torture: 'It would be unfair to the Shah not to give him some credit for considerable success in the White Revolution, and substantial progress in the modernization of Iran. But the White Revolution failed to establish a politically mature or free middle class, and in fact created a large gap which made the differences between poor and rich that much more obvious. Political decisions in today's complex society are all made by a highly suspicious Shah, so the bureaucrats lost their sense of responsibility, efficiency declined and the whole structure became corrupt.' (12 November 1978).

Asahi's next editorial finally accepted Kaigo's view that the Shah was doomed: 'If the Shah fails to solve the situation with his own power, the only alternative will be not just abdication, but collapse of the Pahlavi dynasty. . .Since it is taught that the cause of the poverty of the masses is the wealth of the rich, it can be said that Khomeini is the one and only spokesman for the poor people.' (23 November 1978). Once the Shah left Iran for his enforced holiday, *Asahi*'s editorials became sharper in tone: 'The policy of attaining a super-high rate of economic growth to enable Iran, a developing country, to join the advanced nations at a single stroke, was akin to making the legs of a giant with mud.' (19 January 1979).

From 12–19 February, *Asahi* paid Kaigo the remarkable compliment of running a nine-part series on the Shah's collapse, beginning with half the front page, and totalling some 20,000 words overall. It was a highly competent piece of work although, by Western press standards, it came very late. Still, the key issues were identified and assessed: 'What does Islamic democracy mean? Not the kind of ideology they had in the seventh century, but a clear distinction, based on the Koran, between moral right and wrong in running a modern society,' (16 February 1979). He analysed in considerable detail the way in which the Shah's price-control decrees offended the Bazaar merchants, and described how the merchants then subsidized poor workers who went on strike and helped to finance the opposition movement with the moral and, in some cases, financial backing of the mosques. He explained the nature of SAVAK, and showed how the mullahs, by claiming that Israeli Intelligence had helped to train SAVAK, were able to explain that it was an affront to Islam. Kaigo, like the vast bulk of Western journalists, took at face value many of the Shah's claims that his White Revolution had genuinely distributed the land, and that women had in fact been emancipated – claims that seem in retrospect highly dubious. But overall, Kaigo's reporting was of a high order, the more so in view of the lukewarm encouragement he initially received in Tokyo.

NEW YORK TIMES

Traditionally, the *New York Times* had seen Iran as an arena in which the Cold War was being fought. In 1956, its correspondent, Sam Pope Brewer (a former US Intelligence officer who maintained intimate CIA connections), wrote of the Shah's success against Communism, and of 'a highly successful campaign against subversive elements. . . the pro-Soviet party is now considered to have been completely liquidated,' (2 December 1956). Five years later, Harrison Salisbury maintained the tone with a long article headlined 'A Showplace in Fight on Reds' (5 November 1971).

In October 1971, the *New York Times*'s editorial took the opportunity to comment on the Shah's record, following the announcement of the Persepolis celebration. It hailed his 'modest liberalism' and added: 'Most Iranians have reason to celebrate the nation's accomplishments under the White Revolution.' (12 October 1971). Charlotte Curtis, the *New York Times* reporter who covered the Persepolis festivities, was struck by the intense security arrangements, and wrote sardonically about the social life, but added: 'The Iranians, nearly 85% of whom are illiterate peasants, are delighted. They see themselves as having arrived.' (19 October 1971).

In 1972, Cy Sulzberger, the *New York Times*'s veteran roving foreign correspondent (and a member of the family who owned the *New York Times*), interviewed the Shah and wrote a thoughtful series on the new Iran. He sounded a cautionary note, judging that Iran had: 'a long, long way to go before the façade of democracy, vitality and countrywide progress is replaced by reality,' (9–11 February 1972). The country was still of only marginal interest to the paper. In the whole of 1972, there were only fifty articles on Iran, twenty-nine of them about its international relations – mainly brief paragraphs on official visits by the Shah. There were no stories on oil and Iran at all, only four about SAVAK or internal repression. There were two stories on protests against repression mounted outside Iran, and one story on Iranian purchase of foreign arms, but little real interest in the country as a source of news.

In 1973, the Yom Kippur war and the consequent oil shortage and OPEC price rise combined to make Iran into a new kind of power. *New York Times* news coverage almost tripled, with 131 stories in the year, seventy-two about international relations, seventeen about arms deals, ten about Iran's oil, and five about the royal family itself.

Shortly before the Yom Kippur war, the Shah visited Washington, and the *New York Times* took the opportunity to write a warm editorial: 'Given the tradition from which he springs, and the climate in which he operates, the Shah has been in many ways an admirable ruler.' (24 July 1973). The only note of caution it chose to sound was on the possibility of arms deals and too close a friendship 'ensnaring' the US into backing the Shah's own adventures. It was the time of the bitter aftermath of the Vietnam war; the *New York Times* was against being 'ensnared' into foreign lands.

In 1974, the *New York Times* ran 212 stories on Iran, of which forty-one were about oil, sixty-two about international relations, another forty about the country's plans for economic development, fifteen on Iran's arms purchases and three on the work of SAVAK or the existence of opposition inside the country. There were six stories about non-Iranian criticisms of the Shah and SAVAK's use of torture. The *New York Times* magazine, however, ran a long and excellently-informed article by a British journalist, David Holden, which looked at the darker side of the Shah's rule. 'The trials, executions and secret disappearances seem to continue,' it said, and although there was no mention of the role of religion or of opposition among the Muslims, he concluded: 'While the Shah's ambitions are spectacular, it is hard not to feel they outreach the dreams and perhaps even the capacities of his people,' (26 May 1974). In general, however, the *New York Times*'s image of Iran in this year was the very image the Shah was trying to present: an oil-rich friend of the West, attractive to American business and arms dealers, a country that was on course to be a great power by the year 2000.

In 1975, that image was almost wholly maintained. There were 290 stories (an average of almost one a day) of which ninety-four were on international relations, twenty-one on oil, forty-three on Iran's economic development, twenty-three on arms deals, nine on Iran's strategic role in the Gulf, thirteen on the royal family, and seven stories on corruption. Some of the methods used to win arms deals were coming home to roost. And some of the targets of the Shah's militant opponents were now US servicemen, gunned down by 'terrorists'. These killings increased the number of stories about Iranian internal security to fourteen. There were six stories about Iranian dissenters outside the country. One of them made it clear that the *New York Times* was not blind to the manner in which the Shah's rule was upheld. Ahmad Faroughy wrote a powerful, analytical study of the way in which the Shah's police state went hand in hand with a new cultural invasion. The country was in danger of losing its psychic roots, he argued, with the combination of 'ferocious and pitiless repression and the onslaught of Western cultural propaganda' (6 March 1975). It was an article which explained why, three years later, the Tehran rioters first attacked the cinemas. But the rest of the *New York Times*'s coverage was less imaginative. In June, a brief wave of religious riots inspired Eric Pace to report: 'In general, however, the power of the Islamic clergy and its influence has dwindled in this century.' (11 June 1975). Cy Sulzberger also returned for more interviews with the Shah, and wrote a series of articles on the politics of oil, arms deals, Iran's new geo-political role, and the Shah's political 'reforms' – the introduction of the formal one-party state. This, Sulzberger reported, amounted to 'a far from libertarian political apparatus', which seemed of less importance than the fact that the Shah was 'resolutely determined to force rapid economic, social and educational progress' (19, 22, 23 March 1975). Sulzberger concluded with a cautionary note about the benefits of democracy, perhaps inspired by the report of the International Commission of Jurists which, with Amnesty International, was beginning to force upon the world's attention the role of SAVAK and the widespread use of torture in the Shah's prisons.

In 1976, the tone of the coverage sharpened noticeably. Of the 250 stories on Iran published by the *New York Times*, there were eighteen reports of non-Iranian criticism of the repression, and twenty-four stories on SAVAK and internal security. The bulk of the reports, however, were in the classic pattern: forty stories on international relations, twenty-three on oil, twenty-nine on economic develop- ment, thirty-eight on arms deals – and thirty-four on corruption, mainly concerning bribery among US arms dealers. There were nine stories on the royal family, seven on strategy and the Persian Gulf. The Shah himself was of enough interest for the *New York Times* to print a transcript of a CBS-TV interview with him (22 October 1976), which included some probing questions on torture. The *New York Times*'s own Eric Pace, in a long report on the US military technicians based in Iran (written the day after three of them were assassinated), noted: 'Some quiet but fervent opposition exists in this police state to the Shah's militarist and dictatorial rule.' (30 August 1976).

In 1977, the shape of the *New York Times*'s reporting changed quite dramatically. The number of stories fell by almost half to 146, and the former pattern of stories about international relations, oil and economic development dominating the news pages came to an end.

Only four stories on oil, seventeen on international relations and nineteen on the economy were overwhelmed by twenty-nine stories on non-Iranian opposition to the Shah. This figure was dictated by the Shah's official visit to Washington, and the consequent anti-Shah riots. Newspapers around the world ran pictures of President Carter and the Shah wiping their eyes against the tear gas. There were eight stories on SAVAK and internal security within Iran, thirty-six on arms deals, and seven on corruption. As the steadily growing number of *New York Times* reports on the Shah's critics suggests, Iran's reputation for torture (and President Carter's policy on human rights) were having their own political effect on the Shah. Torture was officially banned, and the police were ordered to abide by judicial procedures. The *New York Times* took note in an editorial: 'There has been progress in human rights. . .the Shah's autocracy is more tolerable for some Iranians,' (17 November 1977). At one point, it seemed almost as if the *New York Times* were apologizing for its own excessive criticism when it invited the Shah's Ambassador to the UN, Fareydoun Hoveyda, to announce Iran's support for the UN Declaration on Human Rights on the *New York Times*'s main op-ed page, and then to explain: 'It is not reasonable to expect a complete realization of all the rights, economic and social, political and civil, immediately and everywhere.' (18 May 1977).

By the end of 1977, the readers of the *New York Times* were aware of the ruthless autocracy of the Shah's rule. They were also aware of the economic strains that the waves of oil wealth were beginning to impose on his country. But Iran's importance as a market for arms sales (many of which the *New York Times* opposed) and the corruption of so many of its business dealings, loomed very much larger in the reader's mind than any sense of how much opposition there was to the Shah, and what sort of social groups and forces were combining against him. *New York Times* readers knew little of the role of religion in Iran, nor of the influence of the mullahs, nor of the social impact of the Shah's White Revolution.

In the course of 1978, the *New York Times* printed 362 stories on Iran. Only five of them were about oil, nineteen on arms deals and eleven about economic development. Almost one story in three was about the growing crisis. There were eighty-six stories on riots, seventeen on strikes, twenty-seven on religion (between 1972 and 1977, there had only been one *New York Times* story on the Muslim religion) and a further twenty stories on 'politics', most of them about the abortive attempt to bring the Majlis (parliament) into the system of government. There were twenty-one stories about SAVAK, twenty-five about external dissent to the Shah, and twenty-two about corruption. There were seventeen stories on drugs and fifty-one on international relations. By *New York Times* standards, Iran was being given blanket coverage during 1978, even though the figures are distorted in part by a strike.

How good was it? The *Columbia Journalism Review* published a highly critical assessment of the American media's comprehension of the crisis in March 1980, suggesting that too often the journalists followed the Shah's own definition of the mullahs as a reactionary force. Paul Hofmann, the *New York Times* man in Tehran, reported: 'The demonstrations were apparently started by religious militants who oppose greater freedom for women and other Shah-sponsored reforms, such as a land reform programme.' *Review* commented: 'Opposition to the Shah's land reform is not an issue for the Iranian resistance movement – religious or secular – and it never has been, largely because no significant amount of land has been redistributed. What the religious leaders have objected to is the *administration* of endowed lands by religious foundations. The foundations have always been controlled by government. With the beginning of modernization, however, *de facto* administration passed from the hands of bureaucrats to SAVAK, which began to use the foundations' resources for political purposes.' In the academic world, books and articles on the failure of the Shah's land reform programme, and the way in which it was being abused by SAVAK, were commonplace. Other newspapers, such as *Le Monde* and the London *Guardian* were aware of the academic studies and used them as source material. The *New York Times* was not. On 18 May, a new *New York Times* man in Iran, Nicholas Gage, repeated the claim: 'Khomeini, the Shi'ite spiritual leader, has been in exile in Iraq since 1963, when he launched a nation-wide drive against the Shah following the introduction of land reforms and other modernization measures that he opposed.' In fact the 'land reforms' had not reduced religious landholdings at all, although they had caused so much chaos on the land that Iran was importing almost exactly 50% of its food by 1978. Gage's conclusion was unfortunate: 'While the Shah looks secure in his nearly absolute power, he might meditate about the popular disaffection that keeps erupting.' (18 May 1978).

But Gage learned his job quickly. By July, he was commenting on the failure of the US diplomats in Iran to keep in touch with the opposition to the Shah, and noted that this round of unrest had become something rather different: 'People are not afraid any more,' (9 July 1978). As the crisis deepened and military rule was imposed, Gage published an intelligent survey of the loose coalition that was about to topple the Shah: 'These varied groups have been brought together by what they feel characterized Iran's ruling class – oppression, corruption and disdain for Islamic traditions.' (7 November 1978).

Back in New York, the op-ed page hired Islamic and Iranian scholars to explain the new mood in Iran, and they canvassed a broad spectrum of opinion. Fouad Ajami put the cautionary view: 'The dream of turning Iran into an Islamic republic is as elusive as the Shah's dream of a great industrial future.' (15 November 1978). And the future President of Iran, Abol-Hassan Bani-Sadr, warned *New York Times* readers not to swallow rumours of a regency or a benign military coup: 'The crisis cannot be resolved by a compromise.' (11 December 1978). Three days later, a *New York Times* editorial summed up the Shah's collapse: 'He teeters on the throne because the rapid economic and social changes that he brought about created political tensions that had no outlet, and could no longer be contained by repression.' (14 December 1978). The next day, the *New York Times* published a column by James Reston which reported the bitter arguments within the White House as to whether American policy should still throw all its weight behind the Shah or whether it should look to reform and a new government. Given that the *New York Times* had reported on the failure of US diplomacy to contact, let alone comprehend, the opposition to the Shah, there was a heavy burden on the US media to enlighten its government, as well as the rest of its readership, about the roots and growth of crisis in Iran. The US government was confused, America surprised, and journalists were confounded by the toppling of the Shah – in large part because of the way the *New York Times* had defined the story throughout the 1970s. As the leading American paper, the *New York Times* had set the tone for American perception, and it had not done it well.

WASHINGTON POST

Over the period 1972 to 1979, the *Washington Post* published about half as many articles on Iran as the *New York Times*, largely because the *Post* did not give the detailed and even minute coverage of international relations which the *Times*, as a paper of record, felt obliged to publish. Nor did it offer anything like the *New York Times*'s intense coverage of Iran's economic development and its opportunities for US businessmen – largely because the *Post* did not have the Wall Street and business community readers of the New York paper. This aside, the general pattern of coverage between the two papers is comparable.

The *Washington Post* sent two reporters to the Persepolis festivities of 1971. Sally Quinn reported waspishly on the social event, commenting on crowds of kings 'peering over each other's crowns'. More seriously, Jonathan Randal wrote a perceptive study of Iran's opportunities and problems, under the headline 'Arms debts and repression are the price of progress' (10 October 1971). He noted the existence of armed opposition to the Shah – 'The guerrillas had remained an isolated island of extreme discontent in Iran's otherwise go-go success story' – and quoted an anonymous (but prescient) economist as saying: 'The real problem will be the social and political strains which are growing all the time. If the Shah is right and the guerrillas are wrong, he has a decade before danger point.'

This shrewdness did not last. In 1972 the *Post* ran thirty-five stories on Iran, ten of them dealing with the Shah's relations with Iraq and the Kurdish minority, and five of them on earthquakes and floods. Of the remainder, there were no stories on oil, on international relations or on economic development, but six on SAVAK and internal security, three on official trips to the US and two on Persian Gulf strategy.

In 1973, there were eighty-two stories, twenty-two of them about oil, seven about arms deals, three on SAVAK and four on external criticism of repression. There were nine stories on US trips, including Kissinger's visit to Iran, five on Iraq and eight on international relations. The greater interest in Iran in 1973 was clearly related to the Shah's increased influence through oil, but in 1974, the year when the Shah's oil power was really deployed, the *Washington Post*'s coverage of Iran declined to only seventy-two stories. Of these, sixteen were about oil, fourteen about arms deals, five on economic development and eight on Iraq. There were no stories on SAVAK and none on the Shah's external critics. What the *Post* did publish was perceptive, witness an article on the Shah's grandiose promise to make Iran a great power by the year 2000: 'Western specialists consider the Shah's goals unattainable. . .They predict mounting public discontent as promises are not kept.' (26 May 1974).

In 1975, the *Washington Post* published 102 articles, sixteen about oil, twenty on arms deals, thirteen on the economy and twelve on relations with Iraq. The activities of SAVAK began to be covered more thoroughly, with ten articles, and another two on the Shah's critics abroad. The *Post* clearly understood the nature of the Shah's rule, and ran an editorial which provoked a formal royal complaint: 'He rules his country in a tight, sometimes brutal, military way that at once provokes a certain amount of internal opposition and prevents that opposition from being expressed by means other than terror.' (23 May 1975). In June, the *Post* happened to have an occasional correspondent, Andrew Boroviec, in the country during the religious riots at Qom and during the wave of attacks on US servicemen. His analysis of the Shah's opponents, under the headline 'Moslem traditionalists fight Shah's reforms', was simplistic: 'A wild anti-government demonstration organized by professional agitators who easily exploited the religious fervour of Iranians.' (24 June 1975).

In 1976, the *Washington Post* ran ninety-seven stories on Iran, twenty-one on oil, three on economic development, including the Shah's real and proposed investments in the West, eleven on arms deals, nine on corruption and eight on international relations. But the twenty-two separate stories on SAVAK and internal security suggested a growing concern for the human-rights question which the formal complaint from the Shah had done nothing to dispel. The *Post*'s editorials on Iran focused overwhelmingly on the dangers involved in the sale of advanced US arms: 'The US is making a profoundly serious mistake in selling this kind of weaponry.' (13 February 1976). But a significant proportion of the *Post*'s articles on Iran were not generated internally; rather, they came from syndicated columnists. Jack Anderson, for example, had five strongly critical articles on SAVAK, torture and the Shah's repression, during 1976 alone. The counter-view was put by another independent columnist, Joseph Kraft, who interviewed the Shah, mainly about oil prices, and concluded warmly that 'the Shah's sense of his international responsibilities . . . limited the oil price increase,' (30 November 1976). The *Post*'s own reporting was not impressive. One of the key stories on the world's changing perception, the International Commission of Jurists' report on torture in Iran, came through the wire services (29 August 1976). On 3 September, a *Post* correspondent in Iran, H.D.S. Greenaway, secured a rare interview with a senior SAVAK man, the deputy director. The *Washington Post* ran a bare half-column of the story, and it began in a curiously light, even jocular way: 'SAVAK is worried about its image.' Perhaps the shrewdest piece in the *Post* that year came from the syndication service of the London *Guardian*: 'The very survival of the Shah's government depends on the success of his economic revolution, and the difficulties he has encountered in recent months are ominous portents for the future.' (26 December 1976).

1977 showed the *Washington Post* at its best and at its worst. In May it ran an excellent six-part series, amounting to some 30,000 words, by a freelance journalist, Richard T. Sale, whose marriage to the daughter of an Iranian Cabinet Minister gave him unparalleled access to Iranian society. He secured an interview with SAVAK, visited SAVAK prisons and army bases, reported on the work of SAVAK agents within American universities, upon the difficulties that US servicemen and technicians were finding when they confronted traditional Iranian culture, upon corruption and arms deals. If the series had a weakness, it lay in a cursory sketch of the importance and role of Islam. Overall, it was the best single study in the US daily press. But in the same year, the *Washington Post* published a total of seventeen stories about SAVAK. Ten of them were on the riots during the Shah's visit to Washington; two were by Jack Anderson, the columnist, one from Paris about a murder plot against the future Iran Foreign Minister, Sadegh Ghotbzadeh, one from Norway upon the exiled Iranian writer Reza Baraheni, and two of the five remaining from Iran were from the *Guardian*'s syndication service. The *Post*'s own resources were simply not deployed on the matter. The paper's editorials took the perspective of US interests: 'The violent demonstrations sparked by the Shah of Iran's visit have dumped on President Carter's doorstep a vivid reminder of the contradictions that his advocacy of human rights has imposed on US foreign policy.' (16 November 1977).

The *Washington Post*'s overall coverage of Iran in 1977 amounted to 134 stories, of which seventeen referred to SAVAK and twenty-three to the Shah's external critics. There were nine stories on oil, three on international relations, three on economic development, twenty-six on arms deals, twenty-five on the royal family, and five on Iranian politics.

In 1978, the *Washington Post* ran 161 stories, of which twenty were about oil, seven about the economy, twelve about arms deals, nine about corruption, and forty-four on politics. There were seventeen articles on SAVAK, eleven on external dissent, and nineteen on religion. But the stark figures conceal a dramatic policy debate on whether or not to back the Shah, matching the debate which was taking place in the White House at the same time. In the first half of the year, with Jack Anderson hammering away at the grim record of repression, and the shrewd Jonathan C. Randal back in Tehran to write an early and intelligent piece on the nature of the Islamic opposition and the role of Khomeini, the *Washington Post* was giving a more sensitive picture of events than the *New York Times*. Randal stressed that the Islamic leaders were not mindless reactionaries, but cautious men affronted by the Shah's personal rule and his rough-riding through the constitution (4 March 1978). Better still was a study of the impact of cassette tape-recordings of sermons and riots being distributed throughout Iran through the bazaars, by Liz Thurgood, syndicated from the *Guardian* (12 May 1978).

But from August, the *Post*'s tone hardened. Joseph Kraft was uncompromising: 'The opposition in Iran cannot take over. It is incapable of managing the modernization process that has now gone too far to be reversed.' (29 August 1978). The editorial writers seem not to have been reading the stories from their own reporters, commenting on the 'frenzied opposition to the erosion of feudal ways, and such basic policy planks as land redistribution and the granting of rights to women. . .throw in the dimension of Communist subversion and you have a poisonous brew.' (12 September 1978). The *Post*'s misunderstanding of Iran became almost surreal three days later, when William Claiborne assessed the army: 'One thing is certain: the opposition by itself cannot take over the government, and the only force capable of removing the Shah is his highly trained and superbly equipped army. . .It is under the firm control of its officers, who are unflinchingly loyal to the Shah. At a recent reception at the royal palace, this loyalty was vividly displayed as streams of bemedalled generals approached the Shah – and their eyes brimming with pride – sharply clicked their heels, bowed low and kissed his hand reverently.' (15 September 1978).

The *Washington Post*'s editorial line continued: 'For as long as the Shah takes the gamble of political liberalism, the US has no good choice but to help him see it through.' (31 October 1978). The columnists Evans and Novak reiterated the need to forget human rights and back America's ally, the Shah (15 November 1978), and on 11 December the *Post*'s op-ed page was almost entirely devoted to a bizarre, indeed paranoid, piece by a right-wing British journalist which said that Moscow was behind it all.

The *Washington Post* (and its readers) were certainly ill-equipped for any understanding of the complexities that were about to unfold in Iran. But the *Post* rose to the challenge, and fell back on the human-rights issue that its columnists had said should be forgotten. In the first two months of the revolutionary government, the *Post* ran articles on human rights being in danger once a week. In the previous two years of the Shah's rule, they had managed one human-rights article a month. The *Post*'s final judgement on the Shah's years came in an editorial: 'There were good reasons, economic and geopolitical, for the American policy over the years that put an extraordinarily high value on Iranian oil and influence. That policy has been not so much discredited, in our view, as overtaken by internal Iranian events that were very largely beyond effective American control.' (1 January 1979). The *Post*'s own editorials on the folly of US arms sales, and Jack Anderson's articles on the way the CIA trained and helped SAVAK, might never have been written.

TORONTO GLOBE AND MAIL

The *Globe and Mail* has three foreign correspondents, in Peking, London and Washington. As a result, it depends heavily for its foreign reports on the wire services Reuters and AP, and on the *New York Times* and *The Times* of London's syndication service. As a result, it ran no articles on Iran by its own journalists (exept for editorials) until October 1978. It was thus very much at the mercy of the stories syndicated to it. Apart from anodyne articles reprinted from the London *Times*, the first story of substance in the *Globe and Mail* was an interview which was published in the German magazine *Der Spiegel* in January 1974. This article was printed around the world, thanks to the *New York Times* syndication service. It ran in full in the *Globe and Mail*, the *Washington Post, Asahi Shimbun*, and a host of other publications. In a sense, it set the tone for Iran coverage. It focused overwhelmingly on oil and development. There was almost no reference to internal security or internal politics. It was a platform for the Shah to preach to the profligate West: 'Because of the exploit-ation of cheap oil, you had an affluent society and then a permissive society when almost everything was free, and an abuse of liberty followed.' (*Globe and Mail*, 16 January 1974).

But the first editorial on the matter in the *Globe and Mail* pulled no punches: 'The secret police, the real wielders of power in Iran, are responsible to the Shah. . .Iran's political prisons are crowded. Allegations of obscene torture are common. The growing terrorist violence in Iran is the inevitable result of attempting to move a feudal society into the modern age, while blocking all opportunities for peaceful dissent and maintaining a feudal authoritarianism intact.' (19 June 1975). Later in the year, the *Globe and Mail* printed the transcript of a Canadian TV interview with the Shah, which included some probing questions on torture (29 October 1975). The following year saw a thoughtful editorial on 'The hazards of staking the West's strategic interests on the survival of a repressive police state' (10 August 1976). And the *Globe and Mail*'s Washington correspondent reported in considerable detail on the anti-Shah demonstrations in the USA. He wrote further articles on Iran's gargantuan arms purchases, the inability of its armed forces to absorb or operate them, and the sinister role of SAVAK in the US among Iranian students (4 December 1976).

In October of 1978, with Iran ablaze, the Prime Minister of the Canadian province of Ontario made an official visit to the country. He took in his entourage David Lancashire, a *Globe and Mail* political reporter, who sent back the first piece from the *Globe and Mail*'s own correspondent: 'The silent majority stays quietly at home. . . Many Iranians are now prepared to believe that the Communists were indeed behind the unrest. . .and that the Shah remains the best bet for Iran, the only force capable of holding the nation of 34 million together.' (21 October 1978). The editorials took a more measured view: 'Until liberalization began, some twenty months ago, the rule of the Shah was an absolute monarchy, or in effect a dictatorship. It was in many respects a benevolent, or at least a well-intentioned one. . . Under the authoritarian rule of the Shah's officials, and the eye of his secret police, the pressures created by radical economic and social change were bottled up and deprived of political expression.' (7 November 1978).

The wire agency reports, and the *New York Times* syndicated articles which dominated the news pages took a very immediate view of the crisis, and it was left to the *Globe and Mail* editorials to provide some essential background information on the nature of the Shi'ite sect of Islam: 'From its beginnings in the seventh century, Islam in Iran has been anti-establishment, populist and egalitarian.' The same editorial looked gloomily at Iran's prospects for the future, but placed the blame for future instability firmly in the right place: 'A police state is hardly an ideal cradle for democratic institutions.' (13 December 1978).

THE AGE, MELBOURNE

The Age of Melbourne paid only cursory attention to Iran until the year of revolution, 1978, was almost run. What articles did appear were taken on the whole from the *New York Times, Newsweek,* Reuter and the Australian press agency. Apart from occasional articles by senior journalists passing through Iran, *The Age* did not base a correspondent there until March 1979, after the Shah had fallen.

The first major article appeared in *The Age* on 20 September 1974, on the eve of the Shah's state visit to Australia. Creighton Burns, the assistant editor, interviewed the Shah and reported: 'His place and power seem remarkably secure. His rule is apparently accepted with enthusiasm and sometimes with adoration by the great majority of his people.' Burns was aware of the methods by which the Shah under-pinned his rule, and described them almost coyly: 'The Shahanshah is certainly not a squeamish man when it comes to dealing with traitors. . .his definition [of traitors] seems to include on occasion those who reject the implied doctrine of monarchical infallibility.'

In its editorials, *The Age* greeted the Shah's arrival in Australia with enthusiasm: 'A modern, go-ahead ruler who is modernising Iran like a human dynamo. . .He may also realise that the day of the most intelligent despot may be drawing to its close, and that the spread of education in his own county may produce demands for more popular rule.' (23 September 1974). The news columns gave a rather different picture, reporting the angry demonstrations against the Shah, and its letters columns ran highly critical accounts of SAVAK from members of the Australian branch of Amnesty International.

In 1976, the foreign editor, Cameron Forbes, visited Iran and published a two-part series on the country, its economic ambitions and the social strains they produced: 'But there is this problem called people. Iran's social and cultural infrastructure creaks under the strain of sudden progress.' (20 December 1976). For the second article, Forbes interviewed Manoucher Kalanatani, the exiled Iranian student leader in London, and quoted from Amnesty and International Commission of Jurists' reports on 'the darker side of the Shah of Iran's White Revolution, the internal security force SAVAK, the charges of repression, torture and death' (21 December 1976).

Until August 1978, *The Age* relied on the wire services and features reprinted from other newspapers for its reports. The burning of a cinema in Abadan by unknown terrorists then inspired an angry leader on 'the no-holds-barred terror brigades' who had caused 377 deaths. 'Not that the Iranian monarch is without his pluses. Reforms introduced over the past fifteen years, notably the land redistribution of the "White Revolution" and female emancipation, have provided positive and promising relief from the Shah's expansionist vision of reviving ancient Persia. . .It would be a tragedy for more than Iran if opposition to change on the one hand, or perhaps a precipitate demand for too much change on the other, were to lead to the Shah reasserting his iron authoritarianism just at the point he has committed himself to major reform.' (22 August 1978).

In November, *The Age* commissioned a 1,500-word article from Amin Saikal, an academic at the Australian National University. It gave a thorough background review of the Shah's years, including the political effect of his repression, and concluded: 'The future of the Shah's rule seems to be bleak. Time does not seem to be on his side and the Iranian people's mood is that he has had his chance.' (2 November 1978). Later in the week, a second editorial gave a simplistic analysis: 'The present disorders were largely triggered by Islamic zealots seeking to undermine the Shah's liberalisation. . . There is no guarantee that the situation will not now be increasingly exploited by Marxist students and others who look to Moscow to inspiration. . .The irony is that the Shah, for all his warts when measured against the human-rights values of Western democracies, finds himself under siege largely as a result of his efforts to press constitutional, social and economic reforms.' (7 November 1978). Understandably, this article provoked a series of highly critical letters to the editor. In response, another editorial was published: 'The Shah is now paying the price for the way in which he concentrated power in his own hands and the way he used it. . .the regime has been oppressive, stifling debate, silencing criticism and using, according to this week's Amnesty International report, torture and cruel treatment.' (13 December 1978).

Again *The Age* turned to an Australian academic, Dr Coral Bell, for what it clearly thought was a deeper analysis: 'Both the Left and the Right opposition are likely to be anti-Western, the Right because Western values have been identified as supplanting Islamic values; the Left because of an ideological rejection of capitalism. And the centre has not enough strength to be a real alternative. So the Shah and the generals, whatever their shortcomings from the point of view of democracy, look like the only useful friends, as far as Western policy-makers are concerned.' (28 December 1978). The following day, *The Age* editorial column continued with its simplistic explanation of the crisis: 'In part, the Shah is paying the price for oppression in the name of progress; in part he is the victim of the social trauma modernisation has caused among the bulk of the population. Many of his reforms either ran into entrenched opposition or became mired in corruption or waste.' (29 December 1978).

The Age's final view was cautious: 'Any rejoicing among those who see him merely as an insensitive autocrat and human-rights violator would be utterly premature. The alternative rule Iran may yet end up with from among its rioting students, extremists, religious and political factions, and powerful military leaders could well prove far worse for Iranians and disastrous for the West.' (11 January 1979).

RAND DAILY MAIL

The *Rand Daily Mail*'s coverage of events in Iran during the 1970s was too spasmodic and too dependent upon the wire services of UPI and SAPA-Reuter to permit any meaningful analysis of the frequency or content of articles to be made. During the first quarter of 1974, for example, when the impact of the OPEC oil price rise upon the world's economy and the acceleration of the Shah's grandiose development schemes saw a dramatic rise in international media interest, the *Rand Daily Mail* ran a total of six stories on Iran, all of them from the wire services. Three related to oil and OPEC, and in two of them Iran's role was of minor interest in the story. One referred to the Shah's industrial development plan, one to regional security in the Indian Ocean, and one to the Shah's act of clemency in commuting the death sentences of four terrorists.

On the face of it, this seemed a curious oversight by the *Rand Daily Mail*. Generally, its interest in foreign affairs and its determination to invest in their coverage was higher than that of any other South African paper. Moreover, South Africa had a special relationship with the Iranian dynasty; the Shah's father, Reza Khan, had died in exile in South Africa in 1944, and the house where he had lived was bought by the Shah twenty years later, and turned into a museum. The *Rand Daily Mail*'s coverage of the Persepolis festivities in October 1971 saw it predominantly as a social event. On 12 October, the society page saw a feature on the former Shah and his house, and an account of the presence of South Africa's President Fouche at the Persepolis party. On the main feature page, a special correspondent wrote of the intense security precautions being taken, but suggested that they were justified more by the illustrious international targets of heads of state than by any animosity towards the Shah's regime. 'It is unquestionably the year of the Shah,' the article went on. 'Shah Reza Pahlavi. . .by the sweeping social and economic reforms of the White [i.e. bloodless] Revolution has helped to make his country among the wealthiest and healthiest in the Middle East.'

The main disturbances which suggested the presence of opposition to the Shah in the 1970s received little or no coverage in the *Rand Daily Mail*. The riots of June 1975 went unreported, and the killing of three US technicians in August 1976 was mentioned cursorily in wire service reports. The visit of the Shah to Washington in November 1977, when anti-Shah demonstrations provoked the use of tear gas, was the lead story on the foreign page for 16 November, with a photograph of the Shah wiping tears from his eye. The story was given in eleven short paragraphs, filed from UPI and Reuter, one of which read: 'The Shah, denying that torture exists in Iran, had described his vociferous opponents in the US as "Marxists".' Perhaps the coverage might have been greater had that day not also seen the inquest on the death of Steve Biko, one of the biggest South African domestic stories of the decade. The foreign page for that day also contained a single-paragraph note on student riots in Tehran.

Perhaps the main reason for this reticence was the way the South African government used laws relating to non-press matters to impose an effective censorship on the topics that newspapers could cover. The Petroleum Products Amendment Act meant that through-out the 1970s newspapers were forbidden from writing about the details of oil procurement, storage, supplies or distribution. Iran provided some 90% of South Africa's oil, under a convention of secrecy which was agreed by both governments. And that other main source of stories on Iran, the reports from Amnesty International, were on occasion banned from being distributed in South Africa by government *fiat*.

During 1978, the swelling wave of riots was reported, again through the wire services and, by December, the story of the Shah's collapse and its implications for South Africa had become too big to ignore, even though the Muldergate scandal was reaching its peak. On 3 December, for example, the foreign news page was dominated by a UPI report on Tehran street-battles and an account of a UPI correspondent being beaten up by troops, but the issue of 6 December, which should have reported a heavier outbreak of street clashes, devoted eleven pages of the paper to the findings of the Erasmus Commission in the Muldergate affair. On 15 December, the *Rand Daily Mail*'s senior foreign correspondent, Stanley Uys, wrote an op-ed page column from London saying that 'the Peacock Throne is tottering, and South Africa's future oil supplies have become uncertain'. Uys courted legal retaliation by writing that 'Iran supplies South Africa with 90% of its oil,' and went on to give a cogent analysis of the Shah's crisis and its implications for the *Rand Daily Mail*'s readers: 'The major myth of the present Iran situation is that the Shah is a kind of modern-day Ataturk, who has provoked the fanaticism of the Mullahs and religious masses by a well-intentioned programme of modernisation and westernisation. This is only part of the picture. There are other equally important factors. For example, three out of five rural families are either landless or nearly landless, millions of agricultural workers have been forced off the land and into the cities, where rents have tripled, in search of work, 60% of the adult population remains illiterate, the inequalities of wealth are among the worst in the world, and inflation is rampant. There is also widespread corruption, involving not only generals taking their 10% on arms contracts, but also the royal family, and Iran's record on human rights is among the worst in the world. The two major opposition groups in Iran, the Moslem authorities and the National Front (led by Western-educated democrats) have both been misrepresented. They are not as inchoate as their street appearances make them out to be; they want specific constitutional, political, economic and cultural changes.' Although this was a delayed analysis, it was clearly worth waiting for. Uys went on to analyse what he called 'the minimum scenario' for South Africa: 'While Iran, whether under the Shah or under a religious leader, might not actively seek to withdraw South Africa's oil supplies, it would no longer provide the specific protection that has existed for the Republic's supplies so far.'

The cat was now well out of the bag and, on 16 December, the *Rand Daily Mail* splashed its front page with the Iranian Premier's appeal to the oilfield strikers to return to work. The story, which again came from UPI in Tehran and Paris, also included quotes from Ayatollah Khomeini, and an inside-page story featured the capture of some tanks by anti-Shah demonstrators in Tabriz.

On 19 December, the *Rand Daily Mail* devoted its op-ed page 'Inside Mail' to the Iranian crisis. Colin Smith of the *Observer*'s London-based foreign news service wrote from Tehran a perceptive story on the opposition groups which predicted that once their uniting factor – the Shah – had gone, they would become rival and even warring factions. Iran would become 'a new Lebanon'. Alongside, Robert Manning wrote a lengthy analysis from Washington on the cancellation of the Shah's industrial development schemes, and the imminent economic collapse of the country. There were daily wire service reports throughout December, but no editorials, as the *Rand Daily Mail*'s attention remained fixed on the domestic scandal which toppled South Africa's Department of Information, the head of BOSS and the country's President. But on 29 December, the main front-page story was headlined 'Threat to SA as Shah's rule totters', again based on wire service reports. On the op-ed page, the *Observer*'s Colin Smith assessed the Shah's dwindling support in the armed forces, and judged that the Shah was now beyond rescue.

CONCLUSION

Perhaps the kindest word that can be used to describe the performance of these leading newspapers in covering the Iran story is 'disappointing'. In some cases, their reports were wholly misleading; in all cases except that of *Le Monde*, they proved less than adequate at the fundamental task of explaining to their readers what was taking place in Iran. It must be remembered that we are talking about a generalized failure of the world's press at doing the job which is their very reason for existence. Readers buy newspapers for a complex blend of motives, but they are entitled to expect that the prestige newspapers examined here will report the major news events around the world, put them into coherent context, and assess the major social and political trends that are under way in the world's regions, and in its key states. By any standards, the Iran of the 1970s was an important news story. Although none of the parent countries of these newspapers (except *Pravda*) bordered Iran, the country's strategic importance on the Persian Gulf, and its oil resources and the Shah's repeatedly published ambitions for great power status, meant that no significant newspaper could afford to ignore the story. South Africa depended on Iran for almost all of its oil imports. Japan, Russia, Britain, France, Germany, Italy, Egypt and the US each took at least 10% of its energy imports from Iran for at least one year in the 1970s. For Australia, Iran was a major market for agricultural exports and, for each of the parent countries of the other newspapers assessed here, Iran was a major customer. The Shah's role in bringing about the OPEC price rise, and the continuing fascination with royalty and the glamour of the Peacock Throne made him an integral part of the story. Moreover, he deliberately cultivated his own starring role.

In terms of quantity of coverage of Iran, we can divide our twelve papers into three distinct groups. *Le Monde*, the *New York Times*, the *Washington Post* and *The Times* all gave the Iran story a great deal of editorial space, each paper averaging over 100 stories a year. *Asahi Shimbun, Corriere, Die Welt* and *Al-Ahram* each gave Iran a moderate amount of coverage, averaging something approaching a story a week. There were significant differences in the style of their coverage. *Asahi* was concerned with economic news, *Die Welt* with the security and terrorist aspects, *Corriere* with the royal family itself, and *Al-Ahram* with regional issues. The final group of *Pravda, The Age*, the Toronto *Globe and Mail*, and the *Rand Daily Mail* gave Iran only cursory coverage until the final year of riots. The differences in terms of stories and column inches put *Le Monde*, the *New York Times* and *The Times* in a class of their own, with the *Washington Post* a not particularly distinguished fourth.

Comparisons of the quality of coverage offered by each newspaper are bound to be subjective. But the advantage of hindsight would suggest that *Le Monde* was distinguished for the depth, prescience and sensitivity of its reporting. The *New York Times* would be second, and *The Times* would be dragged down by the bizarre lack of comprehension that Lord Chalfont showed for the Shah's critics. But their sheer volume of coverage meant that, for all their failures of interpretation and almost total ignorance of the Muslim opposition, *The Times* and the *Washington Post* would come third and fourth in the quality stakes. *Asahi Shimbun, The Age* of Melbourne and *Corriere della Sera* make up the next grouping, of getting the story moderately right, noting that opposition did exist, although paying it very little attention. And finally, *Pravda*, the Toronto *Globe and*

Mail, Die Welt, the *Rand Daily Mail* and *Al-Ahram* showed very little
sign of caring whether they informed their readers accurately or not.
The political constraints upon *Pravda* make it almost unfair to judge
the paper by Western standards. But given that Iran was building up
to one of the most sweeping and significant revolutions the world has
seen since 1917, *Pravda*'s determination *not* to see what was going on
is quite breathtaking. The *Rand Daily Mail* was also under some
political restraint, and the South African laws that forbade the press
to write about the country's smuggled oil supplies meant that reporting Iran was a delicate matter. Criticism of the Shah could have had
calamitous consequences for the nation's energy supply. At *Die Welt*,
the political prejudices of the most autocratic press proprietor in the
West presented stiff obstacles to the journalists which they made little
effort to overcome. *Al-Ahram* was, for the bulk of the 1970s, under
discreet censorship by a regime that grew steadily closer to the Shah
and, indeed, gave him sanctuary in his exile. But in spite of a common
(or partly common) faith in Allah, *Al-Ahram*'s reports on Iran largely
failed to comprehend the force of Islam, or the depth of the opposition. The failures of the Toronto *Globe and Mail* have no such excuse.
The lack of coverage, and its broadly miserable quality, very nearly
disqualify the newspaper from serious consideration. For all its status
as one of the four leading papers of the Western hemisphere, its
performance in covering Iran was simply appalling.

Once again, it must be stressed, these newspapers represent about
the best information and analytical packages at the disposal of their
various nations and cultures. Not only did the world's leading newspapers fail to do their job well, their failings meant that the majority
of the world's literate and interested citizens were quite seriously
misinformed. As a participant in the world's political process as it
unfolds from day to day, from year to year, the press acted as a
distorting mirror. With the exeption of *Le Monde*, it failed in the job
that it is designed to do.

This failure is not confined to the Iran story. One has seen echoes of
this process elsewhere, and in particular in covering Islamic countries.
The long and vicious guerrilla war in Oman in the 1970s was signally
under-reported. And where coverage is full, it can be seriously unbalanced. Libya's Colonel Gadafy is almost universally reported as a
terrorist-backing, trouble-making, ruthless and aggressive megalomaniac. While this may be true, the fact remains that he has probably
done more to spread the benefits of oil wealth among his citizens than
any other oil-rich leader; his extremism has caught the imaginations

of large numbers of poor and nationalist Arabs throughout the Islamic world. And yet a cursory examination of the files of these twelve newspapers suggests that there has been more coverage of Colonel Gadafy than of the internal affairs of the rest of the North African Arab states put together.

There is a simple reason for this. The mechanics of *news* means that the press is very much better at responding to a single event, to an announcement, to a shock or surprise, than to comprehending or analysing a long, slow, social process that unfolds without news 'peaks' to spur instant coverage. The events of the Shah's final year, the riots and the street battles and demonstrations and attacks on cinemas, were reported with professional competence. The fact that they were almost incomprehensible without serious assessment of the political forces and social developments which had provoked them meant that most newspaper readers were left in a vacuum of understanding.

The press requires simplicity. A riot is a simple fact and provides a good press photograph. An erratic and outspoken leader such as Gadafy provides simple headlines: threats to the West, terror to his opponents, oil wealth at the disposal of a madman. And yet when closely analysed, the policies of a Gadafy do not differ dramatically from those of under-reported Algeria. Idi Amin was probably not a great deal more corrupt or murderous than Zaire's Mobutu. But Amin and Gadafy have a kind of media charisma that gives them an undue media prominence. Their very irrationality, their taste and talent for the unpredictable, means that they provide news 'peaks' which virtually guarantee them a media fame.

The way these news 'peaks' affect newspapers played a key role in the coverage of Iran in the 1970s. Reports of the dark side of the Shah's rule, the systematic torture and repression of SAVAK, were almost always provoked by the press conferences, or publications of groups like Amnesty International and the International Jurists. The press did not go and look for itself or, when it did so, it was at Amnesty's inspiration.

Other sources were available. Academics in the West who knew Iranian society and its history were not hard to find. Some of them, such as Hamid Algar and Ervand Abrahamian, were writing in English, about forces of religious and political opposition, yet remained untapped by the quality press. On occasion, when the news 'peaks' of a Shah's visit or the first riots inspired some instant analysis, the academics were commissioned to write feature articles – in almost all of the papers assessed here. But most of them wrote from a Western perspective and provided little counterbalance to the main thrust of Western reporting – which was usually the only source material on recent events that was available. This is not a political point; some of the best of the radical or 'leftist' academic studies of Iran, such as those of Fred Halliday or Maxime Rodinson, also largely failed to take into account the nature and force of the Muslim opposition. But *Le Monde* was aware of it, and Britain's *Guardian* was writing about it, when the rest of the Western press was still presenting the Shah as the modernizing autocrat, the benevolent dictator, the tough-minded, oil-rich friend of the West. These very clichés point to the rather dangerous and simplistic way in which the press tends to write and think.

This kind of failure by the world's press has some very serious implications. At its most strident, this view is expressed by Professor Edward Said of Columbia University, whose angry attack upon the West's media (and the bulk of its academics) was published in 1981 under the title *Covering Islam*. Crudely condensed, Said's arguments are these: 'It is only a slight overstatement to say that Muslims and Arabs are essentially covered, discussed, apprehended as either oil suppliers or as potential terrorists. . .What is most serious about the media's failure and what does not augur well for the future, is that so far as urgent international issues during a period of acute crisis are concerned, the media do not securely and easily see themselves as performing an independent, truly informational task.'

One does not have to share Said's perspective to admit that if the West's media fails in its fundamental job of describing and analysing world events, then the West's voters will be taking this planet's fragile life in their ignorant hands every time they lift a ballot paper. This is not a happy prospect. Nor is it to suggest that there is any conscious conspiracy, or any sinister manipulation of the news on behalf of Western interests. There is doubtless some degree of subjective and even unconscious bias in this direction and, as I explained in the introduction to this book, most Western journalists carry with them a mental briefcase of values, preconceptions and perspectives – and many of us endeavour quite conscientiously to allow for them. But there is already a mounting pressure from non-Western governments, and even from non-Western colleagues, for the West's media to be forced to change its ways. The evidence from this survey of Iran coverage makes a most powerful case for the need for improvement. But improvement, and giving non-Western governments some kind of control over the press, are two very different matters. However, unless that improvement takes place, the pressure through bodies like UNESCO could become overwhelming, simply because more and more Western journalists acknowledge the failures and inadequacies of our press. It would not be an easy task to defend the Western tradition of press freedom when we examine the performance of that free press in covering Iran. The fact that *Pravda* and *Al-Ahram* did no better – and indeed rather worse – is of little comfort. If this entire book can be condensed to a single conclusion, it is that our newspapers and our journalists have traditionally served their own freedoms and constitutional rights (and thus, by extension, the rights that Western society holds dear) rather better than we have served our readers' perceptions of the world around them. And plainly, as the twentieth century draws to a close, this will no longer suffice. The tasks are too fundamental and too important for us to fail at either one.

Bibliography

1. General

Studies on the press, Boyd-Barrett *et al*. HMSO, 1977
One week's news, J. Kayser. UNESCO, Paris, 1953.
Whose News? R. Righter. Deutsch, London, 1978.
The International News Agencies, O. Boyd-Barrett. Sage-Constable, London, 1980.
Newspapers and democracy, ed. A. Smith. MIT Publications, Cambridge, Mass., 1980.
The Elite Press, John C. Merrill. Pitman, New York, 1968.
The World's Great Dailies, J.C. Merrill and H.A. Fraser. Communications Arts Books, New York, 1980.
A history of communications, M. Fabre. Hawthorn Books, New York, 1963.
The press and foreign policy, B.C. Cohen. Princeton Univ. Press, 1963.
The Opinionmakers, W.L. Rivers. Beacon Press, Boston, 1965.
One day in the world's press, W. Schramm. Stanford Univ. Press, 1959.
Communications, R. Williams. Chatto & Windus, London, 1966.
Communications and Political Power, Lord Windlesham. Cape, London, 1966.
Twentieth Century Reporting at its best, ed. B.W. Rucker. Iowa State Univ. Press, 1964.
Pressures on the Press, C. Wintour. Deutsch, London, 1972.
The Press, H. Wickham-Steed. Penguin, London, 1938.
The British Press since the War, A. Smith. David & Charles, 1974.
The Press, Politics and the Public, C. Seymour-Ure. Methuen, 1968.
Newspapers; the money and the power, S. Jenkins. Faber, 1979.
The British Press: a Manifesto, ed. J. Tunstall. Macmillan, London, 1978.

The Press we deserve, R. Boston. Routledge & Kegan Paul, 1970.

The Press and the Organisation of Society, A. Angell. Labour Publishing Co., London, 1922.

History of the taxes on knowledge, C.D. Collet. Fisher Unwin, London, 1899.

The First Casualty, P. Knightley, Deutsch, London, 1975; Quartet, 1982.

The Newspaper: an international history, A. Smith. Thames & Hudson, 1979.

Four theories of the press, F. Siebert, T. Peterson, W. Schramm. Univ. of Illinois Press, 1956.

Newspaper history, eds. G. Boyce, J. Curran and P. Wingate. Constable, 1978.

Processes of mass communications, D. Chaney. Macmillan, London, 1972.

Mass Communications and society, eds. J. Curran, M. Gurevitch and J. Woolacott. Open University and Edward Arnold, 1977.

'Royal Commission on the Press, Interim Report, 1976' (Cmnd 6553).

'Royal Commission on the Press, 1974–7 Final Report, 1977' (Cmnd 6810).

'Royal Commission on the Press, Final Report Appendices, 1977' (Cmnd 6810-1-6).

The Press and Society, G.A. Cranfield. Longman, London, 1978.

2. *The Times*

History of The Times, vols I–IV, Times Publishing Co. London, 1935 and onwards.

The Rise and Fall of the British Political Press. S. Koss. Hamish Hamilton, London, 1981.

'The Times', Report of the Monopolies Commission. HMSO, 1966.

Report of the Royal Commission of the Press, Working paper 3. HMSO, 1977.

'The Times and the Bolshevik Revolution'. *Journalism Quarterly*, vol. 56, 1979.

Stop Press, E. Jacobs. Deutsch, London, 1980.

The Pearl of Days, H. Hobson *et al.* Hamish Hamilton, 1972.

In the chair, D. McLachlan. Weidenfeld & Nicolson, 1971.

'The sociology of journalism and the press', ed. H. Christian. *Sociology Review Monographs 29*, University of Keele, 1980.

High Pressure, Col. Lionel James. John Murray, 1929.

Delane of The Times, Sir Edward Cook. Constable, 1915.

Memoirs, Henri de Blowitz. Arnold, 1903.

Moberley Bell and The Times, F.H. Kitchin. Allan & Co., 1925.

Geoffrey Dawson and our Times, J.E. Wrench. Hutchinson, 1955.

A man of The Times, I. MacDonald. Hamish Hamilton, 1976.

Growing up on The Times, L. Heren. Hamish Hamilton, 1978.

3. *Le Monde*

Supplement aux dossiers et documents du Monde, December 1977. Le Monde, Paris.
Le Monde de Beuve-Méry, Jean-Noel Jeanneney and Jacques Julliard. Editors. Seuil, Paris, 1979.
Reflexions politiques, H. Beuve-Méry. Le Monde & Seuil, Paris, 1951.
Le Suicide de la IVe Republique, Sirius (Beuve-Méry). Editions du Cerf, Paris, 1958.
Le Monde et ses lecteurs sous la IVe Republique, Colin. Collection Kiosque, Paris, 1962.
Le presse, le pouvoir et l'argent, J. Schwoebel. Seuil, Paris, 1968.
Histoire générale de la Presse française, Bellanger *et al.*, vol. 4, 1940–58; vol. 5, 1958 à nos jours. PUF, Paris, 1975 and 1976.
Le Journal Le Monde et le Marxisme, G. Hostert. La Pensée Universelle, Paris, 1973.
Le Monde tel qu'il est, M. Legris. Plon, Paris, 1976.
Le Monde et le pouvoir, P. Simmonot. Les Presses d'aujourd'hui, Paris, 1977.
Le Monde – humanisme, objectivité et politique, A. Guedj and J. Girault. Editions Sociales, Paris, 1970.
Questionnaire pour demain, Servan-Schreiber. Ramsay, Paris, 1977.
Le Monde, Jacques Thibou. Editions Simoen, Paris, 1979.

4. *Die Welt*

Beitrage für Zeitgeschichte, Axel Springer Verlag. Berlin, April–May 1976.
Press power, H. Dieter Muller. Macdonald, London, 1969.
'*Die Welt 1946–53: ein deutsche oder eine bristischer Zeitung?*', Karl-Heinz Harenberg. Ph.D. thesis, Hamburg University, 1976.
Die Welt, K.-H. Harenberg. *EDIT, Magazin für Pressmanagement*, vol. 2. Hamburger Fachverlag, Hamburg, 1979.
20 Millionen taglich, G. Boddeker, Gerhard Stalling Verlag, Hamburg 1967.
Die grossen Zeitungen, H.-D. Fischer. Deutsche Taschenbuch Verlag, Munich 1966.
Jeder vierte zahlt an Axel Springer, F. Knipping. Rutten & Lohning, Berlin 1963.
Deutsche Presse seit 1945, ed H. Pross. Scherz Verlag, Munich 1965.

5. *Corriere della Sera*

'*Cento anni del Corriere della Sera*', Corriere della Sera, Milan, 13.x.1976.
Storia di cento anni di vita Italiana, visti attraverso il Corriere della Sera, D. Mack Smith. Rizzoli, Milan, 1978.

Storia del Corriere della Sera, G. Licata. Rizzoli, Milan, 1976.
Vita di Luigi Albertini, A. Albertini. Milan, 1945.
Luigi Albertini, C. Alvaro. Rome, 1925.
Luigi Albertini, O. Barie. Turin, 1972.
La stampa in camicia nera 1932–43, A. Signoretti. Rome, 1968.
100 anni di quotidiani milanesi, F. Nasi. Milan, 1948.
La stampa italiana del dopoguerra 1943–72, P. Murialdi. Bari, 1973.
Mussolini, C. Hibbert. Penguin, London, 1962.
The Italian anti-fascist press, F. Rosengarten. Case Western Reserve Univ. Press, Cleveland, 1968.

6. *Pravda*

Lenin and the Press. International Organization of Journalists, Prague, 1972.
How the Communist Press Works, Antony Buzek. Pall Mall, London, 1964.
Public Opinion in the Soviet Union, Alex Inkeles. Harvard Univ. Press, 1967.
Voices of the Red Giants, J.W. Markham. Iowa State Univ. Press, 1967.
Soviet Political Indoctrination, G.D. Hollander. Praeger, New York, 1972.
Mass Media in the Soviet Union, Mark Hopkins. Pegasus, New York, 1970.
'Pre-Revolutionary Pravda and Tsarist Censorship', Whitman Bassow. *American Slavic and East European Review*, vol. XIII, 1954.
Brezhnev, John Dornberg. Deutsch, London, 1974.
Stalin, A.B. Ulam. Allen Lane, London, 1974.
Khrushchev Remembers, N. Khrushchev. Little Brown, Boston, 1970.
Lenin and the Bolsheviks, A.B. Ulam. Fontana, London, 1968.
The Communist Party of the Soviet Union, L. Schapiro, Vintage, New York, 1960.
Lenin, D. Shub. Pelican, London, 1966.
The Press in Authoritarian Countries, International Press Institute, Zurich, 1959.
History of the All-Union Communist Party, Rothstein *et al.* Moscow, 1960.
Russia, R.G. Kaiser. Pelican, London, 1977.
The Bureaucracy of Truth, P. Lendvai. Deutsch, London, 1981.

7. *Al-Ahram*

'International Affairs in the Arab Press', Abu Lughod. *Public Opinion Quarterly*, vol. 26, 1962, pp. 600–12.
'Foreign News in the Arab Press', Dajoni and Donahoe. *Gazette*, vol. XIX, No. 3, pp. 155–65.
'News agencies and propaganda in 5 Arab states', Tom J. McFadden. *Journalism Quarterly*, vol. 30, No. 3, Fall, 1953, pp. 482–91.

The Arab Press, W.A. Rugh. Croom Helm, London, 1979.

Nasser and his generation, P. Vakitiotis. Croom Helm, London, 1978.

Egypt: Imperialism and Revolution, Jacques Berque. Faber & Faber, London, 1972.

'*Al-Ahram, The Times* of the Arab World', Helen Kitchen. *Middle East Journal*, vol. 4 (2), April 1950.

'The Egyptian Press and its current problems', H.L. Smith. *Journalism Quarterly*, vol. 31 (2), Summer 1954.

'The rise and fall of Heykal', Desmond Stewart. *Encounter*, June 1974.

Cairo Documents, M. Hassanein Heykal. Doubleday, New York, 1973.

'Government control of the press in the United Arab Republic', Adnam Almaney. *Journalism Quarterly*, vol. 49, 1972.

Nasser, Robert Stephens. Allen Lane, London, 1971.

Press, politics and power, Munir K. Nasser. Iowa State Univ. Press, 1979.

Mass media and ideological change in Egypt 1950–73, Ibrahim Elsheik. Univ. of Amsterdam, 1977.

'The cartoon in Egypt', Afal Marsot. *Comparative Studies in Society and History*, 13.i.1971.

8. *Asahi Shimbun*

'The Meiji Roots and contemporary practices in the Japanese press', J. Huffman. *Japan Interpreter*, vol. II, No. 4, Spring 1977.

The Japanese Press 1976. Nihon Shimbun Kyokai, Tokyo, 1977.

'A National newspaper in Japan', Hisashi Maeda. *Nieman Reports*, April 1956.

Japan: images and realities, R. Halloran. Knopf, New York, 1969.

Japan, the fragile superpower, F. Gibney. Tuttle Books, Tokyo, 1975.

The Asahi Story. Asahi Shimbun Publishing Co., Tokyo, 1965.

A history of modern Japan, R. Storry. Pelican, 1976.

Western Influence in Modern Japan, ed. Nihobe, Univ. of Chicago Press, 1931.

Japanese Press, Past and Present. Nihon Shimbun Kyokai, Tokyo, 1949.

Conquered Press, W.J. Coughlin. Pacific Books, 1952.

The press in Japan today, E.P. Whittemore. Columbia Univ. of South Carolina Press, 1961.

'Japan's big dailies', the *Economist*, London, 22 May 1965.

'Tanaka's resignation and the Japanese press', S. Sato. *Japan Echo*, vol. II, No. 1, 1975

Characteristics of the Japanese press, S. Ejiri. *Nihon Shimbun Kyokai*, Tokyo, 1972.

'Comparative contents analysis of two Japanese papers', S. Hoshino, MA thesis, School of Journalism, Indiana University, April 1976.

NELSON – a new editing and layout system for newspapers. Asahi Shimbun Publications, May 1977.

The new main Tokyo office: computerised newspaper production system, Asahi Shimbun Publications, November 1980.

Asahi Shimbun facts and figures. Asahi Shimbun Publishing Co., 1977.

9. *New York Times*

The New York Times, its making and its meaning, ed. New York Times. Scribners, New York, 1945.

Miscellany of facts and data, ed. Research Dept., New York Times, New York, 1958.

New York Times, 100 years of famous pages, ed. H.S. Commagher. Simon & Schuster, New York, 1951.

New York Times, update 1979. Arno, New York, 1979.

The Depression Years, as reported in the New York Times, ed. A. Keylin. Arno, New York, 1976.

European Socialism since World War One, articles from the New York Times, ed. N. Green. Quadrangle Books, New York, 1971.

Page One, 1920–76, as presented in the New York Times, Arno, New York, 1976.

Times Talk, ed. R. Adler. Putnam, New York, 1976.

A day in the life of the New York Times, R. Adler. Lippincott, New York, 1971.

The story of the New York Times, Meyer Burger. Simon & Schuster, New York, 1951.

My life and The Times, Turner Catledge. Harper & Row, New York, 1971.

History of the New York Times, E.H. Davis, *New York Times*, 1921.

All the news that fits, H.H. Dinsmore. Arlington House, New York, 1969.

The Kingdom and the Power, Gay Talese. World Publishing Co., New York, 1969.

Henry J. Raymond and the New York press, A. Maverick. A.S. Hale, Hartford, 1870.

Behind the front page, C. Agyris. San Francisco, 1974.

Without fear or favour, H.E. Salisbury. Times Books, New York, 1980.

10. *Washington Post*

Update, facts about the Washington Post Company, Washington Post Publications, April 1979.

Keeping Posted, ed. L.L. Babb. Washington Post Publications, 1977.

Centennial, anniversary issue of the Washington Post magazine, 18.xii.1977.

The Powers That Be, D. Halberstam. Knopf, New York, 1979.

The Washington Journalism Review, April–May 1979. Interview with Donald Graham.

Pillars of the Post, H. Bray. Norton, New York, 1980.

Lords of the Press, G. Seldes. Messner, New York, 1938.

The Washington Post, the first 100 years, C.M. Roberts. Houghton Mifflin, Boston, 1977.

Eugene Meyer, M.J. Pusey. Knopf, New York, 1974.

Editorials from the Washington Post, 1917–20, ed. I.E. Bennett. Washington Post Publications, 1921.

All the President's Men, Bernstein & Woodward. Simon & Schuster, New York, 1974.

Conversations with Kennedy, B.C. Bradlee, Norton, New York, 1975.

The Presidents and the Press, J.E. Pollard. vol. 1, Macmillan, New York, 1947; vol. II, Public Affairs Press, Washington, DC, 1964.

First Rough Draft, C.M. Roberts. Praeger, New York, 1973.

The Washington Correspondents, Leo C. Rosten. Harcourt, Brace, New York, 1937.

With Kennedy, P. Salinger. Doubleday, New York, 1966.

A Thousand Days, A. Schlesinger. Houghton Mifflin, Boston, 1965.

The Papers and the Papers, S.J. Ungar. Dutton, New York, 1972.

'Katherine Graham: the power that didn't corrupt', J. Howard. *Ms* Magazine, October 1974.

'Big Ben', J. Fallowes. *Esquire* magazine, April 1976.

'The Rise of the Washington Post', *Fortune* magazine, December 1944.

'Of the Press, by the Press, for the Press (and others too)', ed. L.L. Babb. Washington Press Writers' Group, Washington, DC, 1974.

11. Toronto *Globe and Mail*

Brown of The Globe, J.M.S. Careless. Macmillan, Toronto, vol. I, 1963, vol. II, 1967.

Historic Headlines, ed. Barton. McClelland & Stewart, Toronto, 1967.

History of Journalism in Canada, W.H. Kesterton. McClelland & Stewart, Toronto, 1967.

Reporter in Red China, C. Taylor. Random House, New York, 1966.

The Age of Mackenzie King, H.S. Ferns & B. Ostry. Heinemann, Toronto, 1955.

George Brown, J. Lewis, Morang & Co., Toronto, 1906.

The Mackenzie King Record, ed. Pickersgill. Univ. of Toronto Press, vol. I, 1960.

Life and speeches of George Brown, Alex Mackenzie. Globe Printing Co., Toronto, 1887.

Mitch Hepburn, Neil McKenty. McClelland & Stewart, Toronto, 1967.

News and the Southams, C. Bruce. Macmillan, Toronto, 1968.

Mass Media, Report of the Select Committee of the Senate of Canada. Information Canada, 3 vols, 1970.

Canada since 1945, Bothwell *et al.* Univ. of Toronto Press, 1981.

The Royal Commission on Newspapers; Commission Royale sur les quotidiens, Information Canada, 1981.

12. *The Age*, Melbourne

'The Paper Game', series in *The Age* by Peter Smark, 11–17 June 1977.
Aims and Practices, The Australian Press Council, Booklet No 1, Sydney, 1977.
125 years of Age, G. Hutton & L. Tanner, Melbourne, 1979.
The Australian Thunderer, M. Cannon, Heritage Publications, Melbourne, 1968.
The Whitlam Venture, A. Reid. Sydney, 1976.
The Age supplement, 100th anniversary, 17 October 1954.
The Press in Australia, H. Mayer. Melbourne Univ. Press, 1964.
Australia goes to press, W.S. Holden. Wayne State Univ. Press, Detroit, 1961.
A study of the Australian press, F.C. Banner. Pennsylvania State College, 1950.
Politics and the media, H. Rosenbloom. Scribe publications, Sydney, 1976.
The mass media in Australia; use and evalaution, J.S. Western & C.A. Hughes. Univ. of Queensland Press, 1971.

13. *Rand Daily Mail*

A newspaper history of South Africa, V. Alhadeff. Nelson, Capetown, 1936.
South Africa and the Press and the politics of Liberation, C.C. Chimutengwende. Barbican Press, London, 1978.
Race, propaganda and South Africa, J.C. Laurence. Gollancz, London, 1979.
History of the Press in South Africa, Theo Cutten. Central News Agency, London, 1936.
The birth of a great newspaper, Rand Daily Mail 75th anniversary supplement, 22.ix.1977.
The Press in Africa, R. Ainslie. Gollancz, London, 1966.
The Press in Authoritarian Countries, International Press Institute Report, Zurich, 1959.
IPI report, vol. 29, Nos 7–9. Zurich, January–March 1981.
Muldergate, M. Rees and C. Day. Macmillan, Johannesburg, 1980.
The Press of Africa, F. Barton, Macmillan, London, 1979.
The Press as Opposition, E. Potter. Chatto & Windus, London, 1975.
English-speaking South Africa today, Proceedings of the National Conference 1974, Oxford Univ. Press, Capetown, 1976.
Asking for Trouble, D. Woods. Gollancz, London, 1980.